CW01215485

Planning Armageddon

Studies in the History of Science, Technology and Medicine
Edited by John Krige, CRHST, Paris, France

Studies in the History of Science, Technology and Medicine aims to stimulate research in the field, concentrating on the twentieth century. It seeks to contribute to our understanding of science, technology and medicine as they are embedded in society, exploring the links between the subjects on the one hand and the cultural, economic, political and institutional contexts of their genesis and development on the other. Within this framework, and while not favouring any particular methodological approach, the series welcomes studies which examine relations between science, technology, medicine and society in new ways e.g. the social construction of technologies, large technical systems.

Other Titles in the Series

Volume 1
Technological Change: Methods and Themes in the History of Technology
Edited by Robert Fox

Volume 2
Technology Transfer out of Germany after 1945
Edited by Matthias Judt and Burghard Ciesla

Volume 3
Entomology, Ecology and Agriculture: The Making of Scientific Careers in North America, 1885–1985
Paolo Palladino

Volume 4
The Historiography of Contemporary Science and Technology
Edited by Thomas Söderqvist

Volume 5
Science and Spectacle: The Work of Jodrell Bank in Post-war British Culture
Jon Agar

Volume 6
Molecularizing Biology and Medicine: New Practices and Alliances, 1910s–1970s
Edited by Soraya de Chadarevian and Harmke Kamminga

Volume 7
Cold War, Hot Science: Applied Research in Britain's Defence Laboratories 1945–1990
Edited by Robert Bud and Philip Gummett

Volume 8
Planning Armageddon: Britain, the United States and the Command of Western Nuclear Forces 1945–1964
Stephen Twigge and Len Scott

This book is part of a series. The publisher will accept continuation orders which may be cancelled at any time and which provide for automatic billing and shipping of each title in the series upon publication. Please write for details.

Planning Armageddon

BRITAIN, THE UNITED STATES AND THE COMMAND OF WESTERN NUCLEAR FORCES
1945–1964

Stephen Twigge
European Studies Research Institute
University of Salford, England

and

Len Scott
University of Wales, Aberystwyth, Wales

harwood academic publishers
Australia • Canada • France • Germany • India • Japan
Luxembourg • Malaysia • The Netherlands • Russia
Singapore • Switzerland

Copyright © 2000 OPA (Overseas Publishers Association) N.V. Published by license under the Harwood Academic Publishers imprint, part of The Gordon and Breach Publishing Group.

All rights reserved.

No part of this book may be reproduced or utilized in any form or by any means, electronic or mechanical, including photocopying and recording, or by any information storage or retrieval system, without permission in writing from the publisher. Printed in Singapore.

Amsteldijk 166
1st Floor
1079 LH Amsterdam
The Netherlands

British Library Cataloguing in Publication Data

A catalogue record for this book is available from the British Library.

ISBN: 90-5823-006-6
ISSN: 1024-8048

Contents

	Acknowledgements	vii
	Glossary	ix
1.	Introduction	1
2.	The Atomic Bomb and the Command and Control of Western Nuclear Forces 1945–1953	17
3.	National Control 1953–1964	47
4.	Bilateral Control 1953–1964	99
5.	Alliance Control 1953–1964	147
6.	Defence Communications 1945–1964	201
7.	Atomic Intelligence: Operations and Estimates 1945–1964	231
8.	Tactical Early Warning Intelligence 1945–1964	265
9.	Conclusion	293
Appendix 1	Explanation of Key Terms	319
Appendix 2	Supplementary Directive to Air Marshal Cross	321
Appendix 3	Terms of Reference for Measures to Furnish the RAF with US Atomic Weapons in Event of General War and to Co-ordinate the Atomic Strike Plan of USAF with the RAF	323
Appendix 4	The Murphy-Dean Agreement	326
Appendix 5	Eisenhower Assurance concerning Polaris	334
Appendix 6	Memorandum by the Prime Minister concerning Polaris	335

Appendix 7	Control of Nuclear Weapons in ACE — Release Procedures	336
Appendix 8	United Kingdom Air Defence Network	344
Appendix 9	Prime Minister's Communications	345
	Bibliography	347
	Index	359

Acknowledgements

No book is an island. And this one could not have been completed without the support of many individuals and institutions. In particular, we would like to express our thanks to the Nuclear History Program and the Higher Education Funding Council for Wales for their generous financial assistance, and to the Department of International Politics at Aberystwyth which provided invaluable research support and academic encouragement. We are particularly indebted to the following who read and commented upon various drafts, including the 180,000-word NHP report *Fail Deadly? Britain and the Command and Control of Nuclear Forces 1945–1964*, on which this book is based: Dr Richard Aldrich, Professor John Baylis, Professor Ian Clark, Sir Frank Cooper, Professor Peter Hennessy, Group Captain Ian Madelin and Air Marshal Sir Frederick Sowrey. John Baylis and Peter Hennessy provided much needed support and encouragement. We are also grateful to Professor Bob O'Neill for his help in relation to the NHP. Guy Finch produced the index and some helpful comments.

Numerous individuals provided us with written or oral evidence: Dr Richard Aldrich; Lorna Arnold; R.G. Bowerman; Squadron Leader Colin Burch; Dr William Burr; Air Vice-Marshal Ian Campbell; Sir Frank Cooper; Air Vice-Marshal Arthur Griffiths; Michael Herman; Group Captain K. G. Hubbard; Peter Jones; T. H. Kerr; Squadron Leader Frank Leatherdale; Group Captain Ian Madelin; Air Vice-Marshal Paul Mallorie; Dr Roger Miller; Flight Lieutenant Dennis Moore; Frank Mottershead; Air Chief Marshal Sir Thomas Prickett; Group Captain Kenneth Pugh; Professor Jeffrey Richelson, Air Vice-Marshal Michael Robinson; Air Marshal Sir Frederick Sowrey; Flight Lieutenant George Stalker; Norman Tindal; Air Chief Marshal Sir Ruthven Wade; Sam Wein; we thank them all. The conclusions and inferences are entirely our own.

Finally, on a personal note the authors would like to thank the following for their help and forbearance in the preparation of this book, Rob Ramwell, Susi Schrafstetter and Frances Gerrard.

Glossary
(for explanation of key terms, see Appendix 1)

ABM	Anti-Ballistic Missile
ACE	Allied Command Europe
ADUK	Air Defence of the United Kingdom
BMEWS	Ballistic Missile Early Warning System
BNDSG	British Nuclear Defence Study Group
C3i	Command, Control, Communications and Intelligence
CAS	Chief of the Air Staff
CDS	Chief of the Defence Staff
CIA	Central Intelligence Agency
CINCEUR	Commander-in-Chief, Europe
CINCLANT	Commander-in-Chief Atlantic Command
CND	Campaign for Nuclear Disarmament
DEFCON	Defense Condition
ECM	Electronic Counter Measures
ELINT	Electronic Intelligence
GRU	Chief Intelligence Directorate of the Soviet General Staff
HF	High Frequency
HMG	His/Her Majesty's Government
ICBM	Intercontinental Ballistic Missile
IRBM	Intermediate Range Ballistic Missile
JIB	Joint Intelligence Bureau
JIC	Joint Intelligence Committee
MCC	Main Control Centre
Mi5	British Security Service
MIDAS	Missile Defense Alarm System
MLF	Multilateral Force
MOD	Ministry of Defence
MRBM	Medium Range Ballistic Missile
NAC	North Atlantic Council
NADGE	NATO Air Defence Ground Environment
NATO	North Atlantic Treaty Organisation

GLOSSARY

NCA	National Command Authority
NHP	Nuclear History Program
NIE	National Intelligence Estimate
NORAD	North American Air Defense
NSC	National Security Council
NSCC	Nuclear Strike Co-ordinating Committee
PAL	Permissive Action Links
QRA	Quick Reaction Alert
RAF	Royal Air Force
RATO	Rocket Assisted Take-off
ROC	Royal Observer Corps
SAC	Strategic Air Command
SACEUR	Supreme Allied Commander Europe
SIS	Secret Intelligence Service
SLBM	Submarine Launched Ballistic Missile
SSBN	Nuclear-powered Ballistic Missile Submarine
UHF	Ultra High Frequency
UKWMO	United Kingdom Warning and Monitoring Organisation
USAF	United States Air Force
VHF	Very High Frequency

CHAPTER 1

Introduction

'Today, war is too important to be left to politicians. They have neither the time, the training nor the inclination for strategic thought.' (General Jack D. Ripper, Commander, Burpelson Air Force Base[1])

Writing in the July 1989 edition of *Survival*, François Heisbourg, the then Director of the International Institute for Strategic Studies, lamented 'the dearth of open literature' on British command and control.[2] Without such information, he argued, a precise comparison of British defence policy with that of other nuclear weapons states was almost impossible. The lack of information on British command and control was all the more apparent when viewed against the growth of the subject in the United States.[3] Indeed, in the years since Heisbourg made his remark (with a few exceptions) little has changed.[4] Moreover, with the collapse of the Soviet Union various academic studies and previously classified government reports on the development of US command and control have emerged which provide a very different portrayal of American command and control, and which detail various failures of US nuclear Command, Control, Communications and Intelligence (C³I).[5] This book is designed to fill a gap in British nuclear history. Various studies have dealt with aspects of command and control.[6] This book provides the first systematic historical analysis of Britain's C³I infrastructure, based on recently released government documents.

The issue of command and control has been termed the second great debate of nuclear strategy. The first began in the mid-1950s and was concerned with vulnerability of strategic nuclear forces to a disarming first-strike. Represented by the work of Wohlstetter and Snyder, debate focused on measures to increase the survivability of the US nuclear arsenal and reduce the incentive for a Soviet first-strike.[7] The second debate, on command and control, emerged in the 1970s and addressed an aspect

INTRODUCTION

inadequately covered in the previous debate: command and control vulnerability was as essential to securing a second-strike capability as were survivable forces. In short, as Blair later explained, 'if command and control fails almost nothing else matters'.[8] The third and ongoing debate, focuses on 'the political *process* by which decisions were made in addition to the *substance* or final outcome of nuclear operations'.[9] Represented by the work of Blair, Sagan and Feaver, the major focus is with emerging nuclear states, the collapse of the Soviet Union and unauthorized or accidental use of nuclear weapons.[10] This study attempts to build on the main themes generated within each debate, in the context of British command and control. It is also an examination of large technological systems, and the difficulties inherent in reconciling political, bureaucratic and technical requirements.[11]

SURPRISE ATTACK AND COMMAND VULNERABILITY

By the late 1940s, nuclear weapons programmes were underway in the USA, the USSR and the UK. With the intensification of the Cold War these programmes were accelerated. For the Americans, atomic weapons were believed to perform two key functions: at the diplomatic level, to deter further Soviet expansion, and second, should deterrence fail, to destroy the Soviet capability to wage war. To achieve these aims with credibility required a bomber force capable of striking enemy territory. To perform this task, the Strategic Air Command (SAC) was created. The ability of SAC to undertake such a mission, however, depended both on its ability to reach the target and to avoid being destroyed on the ground. While the first of these was considered possible (especially with forward bases in the UK), the second was more problematic. The threat of surprise attack was a constant fear, reinforced by memories of Pearl Harbor.

To guard against this, President Eisenhower established the Technological Capabilities Panel—commonly known, after its chairman, as the Killian Committee. Its 1955 report, *Meeting the Threat of Surprise Attack* has been described as 'one of the most influential in American nuclear policy.'[12] Among its recommendations was an acceleration of the US ballistic missile programme, new procedures for collection of strategic intelligence and development of advanced early warning systems capable of detecting both bombers and ballistic missiles. In short, Killian laid out the fundamental requirements of a secure second-strike capability. In the following years, these procedures were expanded to include aircraft dispersal and airborne alert. The report also had important ramifications for Britain. A primary concern was that to re-establish nuclear collaboration with America (broken off after the war), Britain needed a viable nuclear force. This not only demanded a stock of nuclear weapons but a bomber force capable of avoiding destruction on the ground. For SAC, this was a cardinal requirement for meaningful cooperation between the two countries. Consequently, operational readiness became an obsession for Britain's newly developed V-force.[13]

To maintain control of nuclear forces under the threat of surprise attack required development of sophisticated command systems. Moreover, to function effectively these systems were required to satisfy two fundamental objectives: to maintain positive and negative control. Positive control relates to the authorization of nuclear operations. A fundamental requirement is that such authorization can only be given by authorized decision-makers. The procedures by which this is granted depends on a state's constitution and political culture. Whatever the mechanism, a cardinal principle of positive control is that correctly authorized instructions are carried out. In contrast, negative control ensures that bogus or unauthorized instructions are ignored. The essential requirement of negative control is to prevent accidental or unauthorized use of nuclear weapons including possible theft by sub-state actors. A paramount threat to positive control is the inability of the National Command Authority (NCA) to communicate with its military forces. This can occur in two ways. First an enemy attack on vital command centres can destroy a state's entire political and military leadership. Destruction of the NCA is known as 'decapitation' attack and renders nuclear forces incapable of receiving an authenticated executive order.[14] The second challenge to positive control is failure in communications. A result of either sabotage or malfunction, a communication blackout severs the connection linking nuclear forces to the NCA. In both cases the attack so disrupts command and control that retaliation becomes infeasible. In short, failure of positive control places severe constraints on a state's ability to mount a nuclear retaliatory strike.[15]

To maintain a secure second-strike capability, an essential pre-requisite of deterrence, a number of options are available: to harden communications and command centres; to adopt a launch-on-warning strategy; or delegate nuclear use authority to the military.[16] All three have disadvantages. Hardened facilities are expensive and can be defeated by increasing the yield of weapon selected for attack. To launch-on-warning runs the risk of inadvertent nuclear use and raises the nightmare of accidental nuclear war triggered by false warning or miscalculation.[17] Delegation of control to the military removes all civilian constraints and makes war termination more problematic. A balance has therefore to be found between command vulnerability and the risk of nuclear inadvertence. Moreover, there is an implicit trade-off between these positions. Measures that address the threat of nuclear decapitation increase the probability of catastrophic nuclear failure.[18] The way a state approaches this dilemma is ultimately dependent on political judgement.

To buttress the credibility of the retaliatory threat, nuclear forces are required to operate at high levels of alert. To monitor the alert status of nuclear forces and effect transition from one alert state to another is a major function of C^{3}I. The compression of reaction time, however, places heavy reliance on early warning. Moreover, to remain effective and provide a rapid military response, early warning sensors have to be integrated into the C^{3}I system. The monitoring of an adversary's alert state introduces further complications. In time of crisis, both systems can interact, with an increase in one alert state matched by a corresponding rise in the other. The result can be a 'security dilemma' in which measures intended to deter aggression by assured retaliation are interpreted as preparations for a nuclear first-strike.[19] The outcome is a mutually reinforcing action-reaction spiral that produces destabilising effects on the system, increasing the likelihood of inadvertent nuclear use.[20]

A command and control system that displays a tendency towards positive control is described as 'delegative'.[21] A significant feature of a delegative system is that while overall command is retained under civilian authority there are few if any physical restraints to stop unauthorized use of nuclear weapons. The operation of nuclear codes reflects this position. In a delegative system, the use of nuclear codes is to signify that the order originates from the NCA but is not required to arm the weapon. Consequently, in the conduct of nuclear operations, the military possess a considerable degree of autonomy. Indeed, the primary measure to achieve compliance is usually the military's oath of allegiance. Under this system, weapons are retained in military custody and deployed in operational configuration often collocated with their delivery systems. In contrast, a command and control system that favours negative control is termed 'assertive'. The system is distinguished by measures that restrain military freedom of action. Weapons are often stored under civilian supervision and fitted with physical restraints such as Permissive Action Links (PALs), installed in the US in the early-1960s and which blocked unauthorized detonation to ensure central control over all operations.[22] In an assertive system, nuclear codes serve a dual function: they indicate that the order originated from the NCA and contain information required by the military to disable the PALs and arm the weapon.

To function effectively, a C^3I system requires an agreed set of rules and operating procedures to enable the NCA to maintain continuity of operations in peacetime and during a period of tension or warfare. These include organisational aspects such as code management procedures, the operation of a 'two-person' rule and personnel monitoring programmes and technical measures such as PALs and positive arming procedures. The function of a C^3I system, however, is largely dependent on strategic objectives. A war fighting strategy, for example, requires the system to operate both during and after a nuclear exchange. In contrast, a system designed for retaliation only is not required to survive. Its primary purpose is to transmit the executive order prior to the system's destruction. Despite their different requirements, each type of system comprises three fundamental elements: command authority, warning and connectivity.

COMMAND AUTHORITY

The organisational structure of a C^3I system is hierarchical. At the apex of the system is the NCA. Composed of the President or Prime Minister and senior civilian and military figures, the NCA has authority to order nuclear forces into action. In the United States authority to make war is vested in the President, who is Commander-in-Chief of US armed forces. This authority is constrained by the powers of Congress as laid down by the constitution and clarified by subsequent constitutional amendments. The advent of nuclear weapons, and of delivery systems that meant decisions might have to be taken in minutes, have seen the development of procedures that have been subject to public and academic scrutiny.[23] The constitutional position in the UK is much less clear, and indeed potentially ambiguous, reflecting the absence of a formal constitution and the peculiar nature of British constitutional practice. Quite how the British constitution would operate under the circumstances of nuclear war can only be a matter for speculation, and on which official records provide only fragmentary glimpses of official thinking and likely practice. British constitutional development has rested on incremental change. This has reflected consensus among those involved, concerned with continuity and the long-term interests of the constitution, in which the respective powers and limitations of Parliament, Monarch, Cabinet and Prime Minister have been calibrated. Essential to this approach has been the idea of convention—practices accepted by those involved.[24] In the circumstances in which weapons of mass destruction were to be used by the government it is difficult to envisage how such concerns would weigh against the calculations of decision-makers.

Exploring constitutional authority for the use of nuclear weapons in Britain is nevertheless necessary in evaluating political authority for their use and how decisions might have been taken. In the absence of definitive documentation, however, this exercise must perforce remain speculative. Crucial constitutional questions about the role of the monarchy in the event of a hung Parliament in 1963/4, for example, were undertaken in an *ad hoc* manner.[25] It is clear that in the circumstances of imminent or actual nuclear attack, authority to use nuclear weapons would reside with the Prime Minister. This is discussed in Chapter 3. This authority appears to have derived from the existing basis for the declaration of war and the use of British armed forces. Although members of the Army and the RAF (though not the navy) individually swear allegiance to the monarch, the constitutional authority of the Prime Minister to declare war is clear, and has been exercised by the Royal Prerogative, executed through Orders in Council.[26] The Prime Minister can also send British forces into war without formal declaration of war using these powers.[27] The procedures detailing these powers are contained in the government War Book that sets out actions to be taken by government departments in the event of hostilities or civil emergency.[28]

While the Prime Minister possesses authority to initiate British nuclear strikes, there are potential limits on his/her power. The first is that military commanders might refuse to order such an attack. While this would violate the principle of military subordination to political authority, senior military commanders would be likely to have sufficient knowledge to assess the Prime Minister's decision. *Prima facie*, international law, and the precedent of the Nuremberg War Trials, provide potential legal circumstances in which military commanders might refuse to order the use of nuclear weapons. Moral or political conviction could be crucial. In 1956, for example, the First Sea Lord and acting Chairman of the Chiefs of Staff Committee, Earl Mountbatten submitted (but later withdrew) his resignation as British troops were preparing to attack Egypt.[29] The use of weapons of mass destruction in a manner that invited retaliatory attack on UK cities, or which violated accepted norms, such as attacking non-nuclear states, might well pose strains on the 'loyalty' of senior officers. Air Marshal Ralph Cochrane apparently once shocked a group of Americans, when asked whether he thought a British pilot would think twice about dropping an atomic bomb on Moscow, he replied: 'I hope so'.[30] For most Bomber Command officers involved however, 'conscience' was obviated by 'duty': 'we believed firmly that if we were really efficient in all that we did, we could play a crucial role in deterring nuclear war… in the meantime we were in every respect ready (although not eager!) to go if we were ordered to.'[31]

A second potential challenge concerns the monarch. The constitutional convention is that Prime Ministers consult with the monarch, and Macmillan for example took time to appraise the Queen of events during the week of the Cuban missile crisis.[32] The Prime Minister might well consult about the possible use of nuclear weapons in a crisis, assuming there was time and opportunity. Although the monarch could not veto the use of nuclear weapons, he or she could, conceivably, dismiss the Prime Minister or dissolve Parliament. In the circumstances of a government with a small majority (as obtained with the 1950–1 Attlee and 1964–6 Wilson administrations), and more intriguingly with a hung Parliament, such issues would assume a greater saliency and complexity.

During the Cold War, British involvement in nuclear combat would almost certainly have involved attacks on British cities, and quite probably the destruction of Parliament. Whether any Prime Minister would have retained the support of surviving members of their party is a matter for speculation. Whether any Prime Minister who had lost their majority (to internal revolt or external attack) might also risk losing the constitutional authority to initiate or continue nuclear operations is an intriguing and largely unanswerable question. Should the Prime Minister be killed or incapacitated such conjecture is less arcane though no less speculative, when the possible powers of a deputy or successor individual are considered. Available documents do make clear that a designated deputy would be granted authority to use nuclear weapons, the implications of which are discussed in Chapter 3.

In such circumstances the constitutional position of the person delegated authority might depend, *inter alia*, on how the monarch viewed their position, and whether she or he was prepared to accept the person designated by the (possibly now deceased) Prime Minister. How a monarch might behave in such extraordinary and constitutionally complex circumstances is again a matter of conjecture. The constitutional powers of the monarch are nowhere set down, and operate on a mixture of received wisdoms and accepted practices. It seems, nevertheless, reasonably clear that the monarch is not automatically bound by the advice of the Prime Minister either concerning his/her successor (or the holding of a general election). Whether a monarch might chose to disregard such advice in wartime or with nuclear war imminent remains a matter for speculation. A final conjecture is whether the monarch could appeal direct to the military in the event of a disagreement between the monarch and Prime Minister. Such disagreement, moreover, would involve the initiation of nuclear war and the probable destruction of the Sovereign's realm, the protection of which is a requirement of the Royal oath of office.

WARNING

To retain a second-strike capability, early warning of enemy attack is vital. In the absence of such information (and assuming a vulnerable force structure), a state's nuclear forces can be disarmed in a pre-emptive attack. To guard against this possibility, an early warning system is required that provides the NCA with timely information concerning enemy preparations and the disposition of forces both before and during attack. Warning intelligence comprises two distinct categories: 'Strategic warning is warning of impending attack prior to its actual execution. Tactical warning, in contrast, refers to warning of an executed attack.'[33] The term strategic intelligence, often associated with early American writing on the subject, covers 'high-level foreign policy intelligence', and involves intentions (including political intentions) and capabilities.[34] Warning intelligence (both tactical and strategic) may be considered one aspect of strategic intelligence. Strategic warning intelligence may cover both political and military warning indicators, which can be obtained through various means: signals intelligence, including communications intelligence and the monitoring of electronic emissions, photo-reconnaissance and image-intelligence, and espionage and other forms of human intelligence.[35] These are discussed in Chapter 7. The provision of tactical intelligence, supplied by various early warning sensors, is examined in Chapter 8.

In common with other aspects of C^{3}I, warning intelligence is subject

INTRODUCTION

to error and disruption. First, the system is capable of technical malfunction. A number of such cases have been well documented. In June 1980, for example, a component in the North American Air Defense system (NORAD) malfunctioned and indicated that two Soviet submarine-launched missiles had been fired at the US. In response, SAC B-52 bombers were scrambled.[36] Occurring in a period of relative calm, the error was eventually rectified. In time of crisis, however, a similar malfunction could have disastrous consequences. During the Cuban missile crisis, on 28 October 1962, a simulation tape was inadvertently inserted into the equipment at Moorestown radar site in New Jersey, resulting in warning, immediately communicated to NORAD, that a missile had been fired from Cuba and would shortly impact in Florida.[37] Six days earlier President Kennedy had stated that any missile fired from Cuba would result in 'a full retaliatory response' against the Soviet Union.[38] To guard against malfunction, the concept of dual phenomenology was introduced into US systems in the early-1980s in which positive confirmation of enemy attack was required from two separate sources.

Second, in a period of alert, the volume of intelligence supplied to the NCA increases dramatically. The need to process the additional information can cause the system to overload, resulting in erroneous assessment or the oversight of vital information. Moreover, individuals are often more responsive to information that supports pre-existing beliefs than to information which contradicts it, and consequently there is a tendency to discount warnings that do not correspond to expectations.[39] Finally, the management of real-time warning intelligence can result in political problems, especially if consultation with allies is required in the evaluation of ambiguous data.[40]

CONNECTIVITY

To function effectively a C^{3}I system must be able to monitor the status of opposing forces and pass commands to its own forces in the field. This ability is usually expressed by the term *connectivity*, which describes the integrated network of early warning, communications and command centres used to alert the NCA of imminent attack and relay orders from the NCA to strategic nuclear forces.[41] The priority functions of connectivity are to:

– enable the NCA to communicate with allies, adversaries, and civilian populations during the pre-, trans- and post-attack phases;

- maintain and monitor the readiness of nuclear forces at various levels of alert without accidents or unauthorized use of weapons, and without contributing to increased tensions;
- assess the status of opposing forces in order to direct operations that might require alterations in peacetime deployments;
- direct the exercising and alerting of forces in a manner consistent with operational doctrine, alliance commitments, and the requirements of strict political control;
- provide reliable warning of an imminent attack (strategic warning) and to detect the actual launch of opposing forces (tactical warning).[42]

The task of maintaining strategic connectivity during attack is the most critical and problematic aspect of C³I operations and is discussed in Chapter 6. A major problem in this is presented by electromagnetic pulse (EMP) and transient radiation effects on electronic systems.[43] In most systems, communication is mediated via high frequency (HF) radio signals which are 'bounced' back to earth using the refracting properties of the upper ionosphere. A high-atmospheric nuclear explosion would disrupt this pathway and effectively blackout HF signals for several days. Altering the frequency of communication is no answer, as UHF and VHF signals would be affected in a similar manner. EMP is generated when gamma rays from a high-atmospheric nuclear explosion disrupt the earth's ionosphere. The pulse of radiation will also enter electronic equipment and travel along power lines and conductors causing a surge in voltage and interruptions in transmission. To protect communications from EMP, two options are available: to construct hardened facilities or provide redundancy. In the latter, many different communications systems are employed on the basis that at least one will survive to retain connectivity between the NCA and the strategic nuclear forces.[44]

SCOPE OF THE BOOK

The primary purpose of this study is to provide an account of the development of Britain's system of nuclear command and control from 1945 to 1964. A comprehensive account would require access to much classified information that is not in the public domain. Significant material has recently been released enabling us to write our account. Nevertheless the study is inevitably circumscribed and cannot be considered as definitive. The methodology relies predominately on documentary evidence gathered in Britain and the US, supplemented by correspondence and interviews—an approach adopted in other studies of British nuclear history.

The aim is to provide both a corpus of knowledge and a framework for future inquiry. The study should also assist theoretical discussion of command and control issues. Paul Bracken, one of the pioneers of the study of command and control in the United States, has argued that, 'the absence of even a rudimentary theory creates barriers to our understanding of command and control'.[45] Peter Feaver, who has made a significant contribution to recent theoretical discussions, has suggested that within the field of security studies 'nuclear policy issues are perhaps the least accessible of all to normal social-scientific modes of analysis'.[46]

There are indeed various challenges in developing models of command and control, not least what is termed the structure-agency problem and the issue of assessing the role of the individual in the system. As Chris Bellamy has argued: 'C³I is closely intertwined with... the vast and unquantifiable area of human intellect, instinct and judgement. The evolution and future of C³I cannot be separated from personal command, generalship and the art of war itself.'[47] Nor, it should be noted, can it be separated from ethical considerations. Command and control involves consideration of what happens when deterrence breaks down and nuclear war becomes a reality not a means of preventing conflict. During the period 1945–1964, whatever interest in counterforce targeting doctrines and strategies, nuclear war would have meant attacks on cities with weapons of mass destruction. The moral problem of attacking centres of civilian population confronted all those involved in taking or implementing the decision to use nuclear weapons. Whatever their training and prior preparation the use of weapons of mass destruction would have presented individual military and political figures with momentous moral choices. Any theory of command and control would need to encompass the moral reality of nuclear warfare, not least because of the potential for political or military officials to refuse to give or obey orders to use nuclear weapons. Moreover, as any such moral choices would need to be set in broader organisational and cultural contexts, the scope for any theoretical endeavour extends far beyond formal structures into the realms of psychology, organisational theory and, of course, ethics.

Such a study is beyond the scope of this book, which focuses primarily on structures, policies and procedures. In explaining their development we do cast some light on the various aspects discussed above, and moreover

INTRODUCTION

attempt to contribute to examining and refining theoretical approaches. In particular Peter Feaver's work provides a valuable basis for examining C^{3}I that we apply to our 'case study'. Feaver outlines a model for understanding civilian control over nuclear operations which takes the pattern of civilian control as the dependent variable and argues that this pattern shifts between 'assertive and delegative control in response to changes in four independent variables: arsenal characteristics, vulnerability, doctrine, and presidential style'.[48] Applying a model developed in the American context to the British experience is not unproblematic, and as will be shown is further complicated by the fact that British attitudes developed in the context of not simply national but bilateral (US) and multilateral (NATO) contexts.

ORGANISATION OF THE BOOK

The analysis begins in World War II with an examination of Britain's role in the decision to attack Hiroshima and Nagasaki. The post-war British-American nuclear relationship is examined with particular emphasis on the control of US nuclear forces based in the UK and the informal understandings reached between the two airforces. The chapter also explores initial proposals for the custodial system adopted in Britain and examines reasons for the lack of debate on civilian control of nuclear weapons.

The book's central section comprises three chapters, which examine British attitudes to command and control between 1953–64 under three separate categories: *national control*, *bilateral control* and *alliance control*. National control is explored in Chapter 3, which outlines the main factors in the development of command and control arrangements for British nuclear forces. Emphasis is placed on the growth of the British nuclear arsenal, the vulnerability of nuclear forces, target policy and the political culture of the British state. Consideration is given to the dispersal of nuclear weapons overseas and the subsequent requirement to establish a national co-ordinated strike plan. The constitutional position occupied by the Prime Minister and the succession of nuclear authority is explored in some detail. Attention is also given to the decision to establish an alternate seat of government away from London to authorize nuclear retaliation, and the significance of delegating nuclear use authority to the military.

Chapter 4 examines bilateral control and explores the various political initiatives undertaken by HMG to restore nuclear collaboration with

Washington. Attention focuses on the transfer of US nuclear weapons to the RAF, with particular emphasis on the 1956 decision to establish a fully co-ordinated nuclear strike plan between the RAF and USAF. Subsequent analysis centres on deployment of US ballistic missiles in the UK and the problem of reconciling British demands for bilateral control with the American desire to establish wider NATO participation. Discussion concentrates on custodial arrangements for the supply of US nuclear weapons and examines the selection of targets contained in the co-ordinated strike plan. Particular attention is given to the Murphy-Dean agreement that established procedures for the use of nuclear weapons by US forces stationed in Britain, and the Holy Loch agreement which allowed US Polaris submarines to operate in British territorial waters. The significance of these agreements is examined against the background of the Cuban missile crisis of October 1962. Finally, a detailed analysis is provided of the Nassau agreement, negotiated between Macmillan and Kennedy in December 1962, and its consequences for the future command and control of the British nuclear deterrent.

Alliance control is explored in Chapter 5. The main focus is on Britain's relationship with NATO. Analysis centres on proposals to increase collective control over the use of nuclear weapons within Europe. Two approaches are discussed in detail. The first is the hardware solution, which resulted in the creation of the NATO atomic stockpile and proposals to establish the NATO Multilateral Force. The second concentrates on procedural arrangements, which came to partial fruition with the Athens guidelines on nuclear use in 1962, culminating in the creation of the Nuclear Planning Group in 1966. The position of HMG in both these debates is discussed in detail with consideration given to Britain's proposal for a NATO strategy based on discriminate use of tactical nuclear weapons. Particular attention is paid to the authority invested in the Supreme Allied Commander Europe (SACEUR) and the implications of his dual role as US Commander in Chief, Europe (CINCEUR), including the predelegated authority to employ nuclear weapons.

The final three chapters of the book concentrate on communications and intelligence. Chapter 6 analyses the development of Britain's defence communications infrastructure. Chapter 7 examines assessments of Soviet intentions and capabilities and discusses various aspects of British strategic intelligence on the Soviet Union. The provision of tactical early warning intelligence is discussed in Chapter 8 which concentrates on the development of British radar and air defence, and subsequent linkages with NATO and US early warning systems. The final chapter draws these various strands together and offers an assessment of the performance of Britain's C^{3}I system.

As historians we are conscious that archival records provide for often only partial understanding of events. Equally these particular archival records are often incomplete, and frequently inaccessible. Furthermore, we inevitably seek to bring coherence and clarity to our study. Yet as Sir Frank Cooper reminds us:

> ... C3I was not the way decision makers at the time viewed their problems. We looked at what equipment we had, what was the forecast threat, what equipment was needed, what plan was required, what would it cost, was it affordable, how would the forces required and their facilities be recruited, trained, built, maintained and how all should be organised in terms of command and control. All this was a continuing, evolutionary process taking place in the midst of many other major events—not least the withdrawal from Empire and financial difficulties of most kinds.[49]

1. General Ripper is the insane base commander who begins a nuclear war in the celebrated 1963 black comedy, *Dr Strangelove or How I Learned to Stop Worrying and Love the Bomb*. The film illustrates and illuminates many key issues in the command and control of nuclear weapons.
2. François Heisbourg, 'The British and French Nuclear Forces', *Survival*, Vol.31, No.4 (July/August 1989), p. 305.
3. See Congressional Budget Office, *Strategic Command, Control and Communications: Alternative Approaches for Modernization* (Washington: USGPO, 1981); Desmond Ball, *Can Nuclear War be Controlled?* Adelphi Paper No.169 (IISS, 1981); Paul Bracken, *The Command and Control of Nuclear Forces* (Yale University Press, 1983); Bruce Blair, *Strategic Command and Control* (Washington: Brookings, 1985); Ashton Carter, John Steinbruner and Charles Zracket (Eds.), *Managing Nuclear Operations* (Washington: Brookings, 1987); Kurt Gottfried and Bruce Blair (Eds.), *Crisis Stability and Nuclear War* (OUP, 1988); Scott Sagan, *Moving Targets: Nuclear Strategy and National Security* (Princeton, New Jersey: Princeton University Press, 1989).
4. The literature on Britain is limited, see Shaun Gregory, *The Command and Control of British Nuclear Weapons* (University of Bradford School of Peace Studies, Peace Research Report No. 13, December 1986) & *Nuclear Command and Control in NATO: Nuclear Weapons Operations and the Strategy of Flexible Response* (Macmillan, 1996), Chapter 4; Lawrence Freedman, 'British Nuclear Targeting', in Desmond Ball and Jeffrey Richelson (Eds.), *Strategic Nuclear Targeting* (Cornell University Press, 1986); Marco Carnovale, *The Control of NATO Nuclear Forces in Europe* (Oxford: Westview Press, 1993), Chapter 5; see also Scilla McLean, *How Nuclear Weapons Decisions Are Made* (Macmillan, 1986) and Hugh Miall, *Nuclear Weapons: Who's in Charge?* (Macmillan, 1987).
5. Peter Feaver, *Guarding the Guardians: Civilian Control of Nuclear Weapons in the United States* (Cornell University Press, 1992); Bruce Blair, *The Logic of Accidental Nuclear War* (Washington: Brookings, 1993); Scott Sagan, *The Limits of Safety: Organisations, Accidents and Nuclear Weapons* (Princeton University Press, 1993); L. Wainstein, et. al., *The Evolution of US Strategic Command*

and Control and Warning, 1945–1972, Study S-467 (Arlington, VA: Institute for Defense Analysis, June 1975).
6. John Simpson, *The Independent Nuclear State: The United States, Britain and the Military Atom* (Macmillan, 1986), Ian Clark and Nicholas Wheeler, *The British Origins of Nuclear Strategy 1945–1955* (OUP, 1989); Martin Navias, *Nuclear Weapons and British Strategic Planning, 1955–1958* (OUP, 1991); Jan Melissen, *The Struggle for Nuclear Partnership: Britain, the United States and the Making of an Ambiguous Alliance 1952–1959* (Groningen: Styx, 1993); Ian Clark, *Nuclear Diplomacy and the Special Relationship: Britain's Deterrent and America, 1957–1962* (OUP, 1994); Christoph Bluth, *Britain, Germany and Western Nuclear Strategy* (OUP, 1995); John Baylis, *Ambiguity and Deterrence: British Nuclear Strategy 1945–1964* (OUP, 1995).
7. Albert Wohlstetter, 'The Delicate Balance of Terror', *Foreign Affairs,* Vol.37, No.2 (January 1959); Glen Snyder, *Deterrence and Defense: Towards a Theory of National Security* (Princeton University Press, 1961).
8. Blair, *Strategic,* p. 4.
9. Peter Feaver, 'The Politics of Inadvertence', *Security Studies,* Vol.3, No.3 (Spring 1994), p. 501. Emphasis in original.
10. For discussion of these three debates, see Bradley Thayer, 'The Risk of Nuclear Inadvertence: A Review Essay', *Security Studies,* Vol.3, No.3 (Spring 1994); see also, James Blight and David Welch, 'Risking "The Destruction of Nations": Lessons of the Cuban Missile Crisis for New and Aspiring Nuclear States', *Security Studies,* Vol.4, No.4 (Summer 1995) and Jordan Seng, 'Less is More: Command and Control Advantages of Minor Nuclear States', *Security Studies,* Vol.6, No.4 (Summer 1997).
11. For further details, see Wiebe Bijker, Thomas Hughes and Trevor Pinch (Eds.), *The Social Construction of Technological Systems: New Directions in the Sociology and History of Technology* (MIT Press, 1987) and Thomas Hughes, *Networks of Power: Electrification in Western Society, 1880–1930* (John Hopkins University Press, 1983).
12. McGeorge Bundy, *Danger and Survival: Choices About the Bomb in the First Fifty Years* (New York: Random House, 1988), p. 325.
13. Baylis, *Ambiguity,* p. 349.
14. John Steinbruner, 'Nuclear Decapitation' *Foreign Policy,* No.45 (Winter 1981–82).
15. Ashton Carter, 'Assessing Command System Vulnerability', in Carter, Steinbruner and Zracket, *Managing.*
16. Jonathan Tucker, 'Strategic Command-and-Control Vulnerabilities: Dangers and Remedies', *Orbis,* Vol.26, No.4 (Winter 1983).
17. See John Steinbruner, 'Launch Under Attack', *Scientific American,* Vol.250, No.1 (January 1984); Blair *Logic,* Chapter 6.
18. John Steinbruner, 'Choices and Tradeoffs', in Carter, Steinbruner and Zracket, *Managing,* p. 540.
19. For discussion, see Robert Jervis, *Perceptions and Misperceptions in International Politics* (Princeton University Press, 1976), pp. 58–113.
20. Sagan, *Moving,* pp. 143–4. This is developed further in *Limits,* pp. 225–37.
21. For discussion of this typology, see Peter Feaver, 'Command and Control in Emerging Nuclear Nations', *International Security,* Vol.17, No.3 (Winter 1992/93).
22. Dan Caldwell, 'Permissive Action Links: A Description and Proposal' *Survival,* Vol.29, No.3 (May/June 1987).
23. For detailed examination of Presidential powers, see Frank Klotz, *The US President and the Control of Strategic Nuclear Weapons,* (DPhil, Oxford University, 1980).
24. For general discussions of the monarch's role and powers, see Peter Hennessy, *The Hidden Wiring: Unearthing the British Constitution* (Victor Gollancz, 1995), pp. 47–72 and Vernon Bogdanor, *The Monarchy and the Constitution* (OUP, 1995).
25. Hennessy, *Hidden,* pp. 63–4.
26. The Royal Prerogative remains an opaque though crucial aspect of the constitution, whereby the

Prime Minister is vested with powers to declare war, make treaties, and dissolve Parliament. It is the 'gradually diminishing residuum of customary authority, privilege and immunity, recognised at common law as belonging to the Crown, and the Crown alone.' Quoted in Philip Norton, *The Constitution in Flux* (Martin Robertson, 1982), p. 6.

27. British forces have seen combat in major conventional conflicts without formal declarations of war in Korea (1950–3), Suez (1956), the Falklands (1982), the Gulf (1991) and Yugoslavia (1999).
28. For details of War Book planning, see Chapter 3.
29. Philip Ziegler, *Mountbatten* (Collins, 1985), pp. 537–47.
30. Denis Healey, *The Time of My Life* (Michael Joseph, 1989), p. 247.
31. Correspondence, Air Vice-Marshal Arthur Griffiths, July 1993.
32. PREM 11/1369, Adeane to Macmillan, 31 October 1962.
33. Bracken, *Command*, p. 5.
34. Sherman Kent, *Strategic Intelligence for American World Policy* (OUP, 1953) p. 3.
35. For discussion of types of intelligence, see Michael Herman, *Intelligence Power in Peace and War* (RIIA/CUP, 1996), pp. 61–81.
36. Daniel Ford, *The Button* (Simon & Schuster, 1985), p. 78.
37. Sagan, *Limits* pp. 130–1.
38. Laurence Chang and Peter Kornbluh (Eds.), *The Cuban Missile Crisis, 1962: A National Security Archives Documents Reader* (New York: New York Press, 1992), p. 153.
39. Jervis, *Perception*, pp. 143–54.
40. For discussion of these problems, see Paul Bracken, 'Accidental Nuclear War', in Graham Allison, Albert Carnesale and Joseph Nye (Eds.), *Hawks, Doves and Owls: An Agenda for Avoiding Nuclear War* (New York: Norton, 1985).
41. See, Richard Ellis, 'Strategic Connectivity', in *Seminar on Command, Control, Communications and Intelligence*, Incidental Paper (Harvard University Center for Information Policy Research, Program on Information Resources Policy, Spring 1982).
42. Lori Esposito and James Schear, *The Command and Control of Nuclear Weapons* (Aspen Institute for Humanistic Studies, Workshop Report, 1985), p. 3.
43. For further details, see Michael King and Paul Flemming, 'An Overview of the Effects of Nuclear Weapons on Communications Capabilities', *Signal* (January 1980); A.J. Culligan, 'An Overview of EMP Effects and their Control', *Journal of the Society of Environmental Engineers* (September 1985); Blair, *Strategic*, Appendix C, 'Electromagnetic Pulse', pp. 321–6.
44. Hans Van Gelder, 'Improving the Survivability of NATO Communications', *Signal* (May 1983).
45. Paul Bracken, 'The Political Command and Control of Nuclear Forces', *Defense Analysis*, Vol.2, No.1 (January 1986), p. 11. For further discussion on the lack of a coherent theory for command and control, see G.D Foster, 'Contemporary Command and Control Theory and Research: The Failed Quest for a Philosophy of Command', *Defense Analysis*, Vol.4, No.3 (September 1988).
46. Feaver, *Guarding*, p. 67.
47. Chris Bellamy, *The Future of Land Warfare* (Croom Helm, 1987), p. 243.
48. Feaver, *Guarding*, pp. 70–80.
49. Correspondence, September 1997.

CHAPTER 2

The Atomic Bomb and the Command and Control of Western Nuclear Forces, 1945–1953

'I was under the impression that I was the only one in authority to order the use of nuclear weapons.' (President Merkin Muffley)

The dawn of the nuclear age posed new and momentous choices for humankind. The twentieth century had already witnessed the phenomenon of total war. Now, unprecedented destructive power could be harnessed to military and political goals. Ideas of international control quickly succumbed to Cold War imperatives and ideological, political and military conflicts that pervaded and configured world politics. In this situation, some states abjured weapons of mass destruction, while others looked to nuclear weapons for military security and political power. The United Kingdom was firmly among the latter.

When a state decides to become a nuclear power, the development of weapons is only one part of a larger process. The appropriate strategy, production of delivery systems, secure and reliable custodial procedures, and a system of control, are all crucial. In the absence of these measures, command authority is either liable to fail or result in accidental or unauthorized use. In the early stages of a nuclear weapons programme, these consequences are often overlooked, or result in compromise between political, economic and technical aspirations. Britain was no exception. This chapter explores the factors that helped shape the first tentative arrangements for nuclear control within the UK. The analysis concentrates on three main themes: the development of British nuclear strategy; the influence of the US; and the transfer of nuclear weapons to the RAF.

THE ATOMIC BOMB AND THE COMMAND AND CONTROL

THE ATOMIC BOMB AND THE DECISION TO ATTACK JAPAN

The possibility of producing an atomic bomb was suggested in 1940 by two refugee scientists, Otto Frisch and Rudolf Peierls, then working at the University of Birmingham. To investigate this, the government established the Maud Committee. Completed in July 1941, the Maud report concluded that a uranium bomb was feasible and that every effort should be made to develop the weapon. The findings of the Maud report were shared with the Americans and helped facilitate the Manhattan Project. In August 1943, Churchill and Roosevelt signed the Quebec agreement, which governed British-American atomic relations until the end of the war. The agreement also established a Combined Policy Committee to manage the joint programme and oversee production of the atomic bomb.[1]

Under the terms of the Quebec agreement, the British and American governments were committed, *inter alia*, not to use the bomb against 'third parties without each other's consent'.[2] In short, the agreement granted HMG a veto over the use of the atomic bomb in whose development their scientists had played a limited though significant part. By the end of 1944 it was apparent that the original fear of a Nazi atom bomb (which had motivated many allied scientists) would not be realized, and that the defeat of Germany was only a matter of time. When Roosevelt met Churchill in September 1944 they agreed that, 'when a "bomb" is finally available, it might perhaps, after mature consideration, be used against the Japanese, who should be warned that this bombardment will be repeated until they surrender.'[3]

Operational planning for the use of atomic weapons against Japan began in October 1944 and according to the official British history: 'the British knew a good deal of the preparations for the event'.[4] This was in part because Dr W. G. Penney, a British scientist at Los Alamos, was also a member of the Target Committee of the Manhattan Project, tasked with identifying suitable targets in Japan for atomic attack. Penney's 'inside' knowledge was relayed to Sir James Chadwick, Nobel physicist and head of the British team at Los Alamos. British interests were further served by Field-Marshal Maitland Wilson, the British military representative on the Combined Policy Committee, who was appraised of developments by General Groves, Director of the Manhattan Project. Wilson subsequently reported to Sir John Anderson, the Minister responsible for 'Tube Alloys', who in turn briefed Churchill.[5] Using these channels, HMG became aware by April 1945 that an atomic bomb was to be used against Japan by the end of August.

In May, Wilson was told by General Marshall in informal discussion, 'some information about US intentions in regard to the operational use of atomic weapons' and a month later given further details 'confidentially and unofficially of the outline plan for the first use of the weapon'.[6] The knowledge that the US was now in the final stage of preparation prompted Anderson and Churchill to consider how British consent to the operation should be given. Both men agreed that the best course would be for Wilson 'in a tactful and friendly way' to draw Marshall's attention to the second provision of the Quebec agreement and to keep Churchill informed.[7] This Wilson did, receiving the indication that the Americans would prefer to record the decision in a minute of the Combined Chiefs of Staff who would then report it to the Combined Policy Committee. On 25 June, Wilson met Secretary of War Stimson and concluded 'that the most secure and satisfactory procedure would, after all, be to record the decision to use the weapon against Japan, in a minute of the Combined Policy Committee rather than the Combined Chiefs of Staff.' These details were conveyed to Anderson by the British Ambassador, Lord Halifax. On 1 July, the Prime Minister gave his consent, with Halifax and Wilson informed of the decision the following day. Britain's formal assent to drop the atomic bomb was presented to the Combined Policy Committee on 4 July 1945, and recorded in the following terms:

> The Committee took note that the Governments of the United Kingdom and the United States had agreed that T.A. weapons should be used against Japan, the agreement of the British Government having been communicated by Field Marshal Sir Henry Maitland Wilson.[8]

In short, the British government gave consent for the use of the bomb without either consulting the Chiefs of Staff or hearing the arguments for its use. The rationale for this 'blank cheque' partly reflected the division of responsibility within the Pacific where the Americans had the dominant role. Churchill's position also reflected his concern with post-war British-American collaboration, and the desire to 'avoid having to insist, at this stage, on any legalistic interpretation' of the clause covering joint decision on the use of the bomb.[9] That Churchill agreed with the decision, however, is not in doubt. As he later recalled: 'there was never a moment's discussion as to whether the atomic bomb should be used or not.'[10] Whether Churchill would have acted differently had the targets been German cities is a matter for speculation.

Defeated in the General Election of July 1945, Churchill was replaced as Prime Minister by Clement Attlee. Although deputy Prime Minister in the wartime coalition, Attlee knew virtually nothing of Tube Alloys. What Attlee learned about US operational planning from the Americans or from his advisors is not clear. However, on 1 August, the day before the Potsdam conference ended, Truman wrote to Attlee informing him that the US was ready to drop the bomb. In reply, Attlee thanked the President for informing him 'about the new weapon to be used on Japan' and requested 'a few minutes' to discuss the matter further.[11] Whether such a meeting took place or what was discussed is unclear. However, fourteen years later, Attlee recalled that 'Agreement for the dropping of the bomb by the United States had already been given by Sir Winston Churchill on behalf of Britain. I was, therefore, not called upon to make a decision, but if I had been I should have agreed with President Truman. His was the decision and courageously he took it.'[12] Churchill remarked to his secretary as they drove through crowds excited by the prospect of victory in the wake of the bomb: 'You know not a single decision has been taken since we left office to bring this about.'[13]

In hindsight, Attlee's view of his responsibilities is remarkable. No consideration appears to have been given by the Labour government as to whether or how the bombs should be used. Indeed, it seems clear that Attlee had no objection to dropping the bomb on the Japanese and there is no indication that senior ministerial colleagues dissented. However, there were reservations within Whitehall. The Head of the Far Eastern Department of the Foreign Office J.C. Sterndale Bennett, speaking for his whole department, believed that:

> The present tactics in the employment of the bomb seem likely to do the maximum damage to our own cause... A more intelligent way of proceeding would surely have been to have given publicity to the discovery and its possible effects, to have given an ultimatum with a time limit to the Japanese before using it, and to have declared the intention of the Allies to drop the bomb on a given city after a given date by way of demonstration, the date being fixed so as to give time for the evacuation of the city.[14]

The issue of an ultimatum had been considered by Lord Halifax who was reluctant to see the bomb used without a clear warning. Discussing the issue with Stimson, he suggested 'that before the bomb was used forty-eight hours warning should be given to the Japanese who should be offered the alternative of unconditional surrender.'[15] There is no evidence that any such misgivings were considered by Churchill or Attlee.

The decision to use atomic weapons did not reflect the 'mature consideration' promised in the Hyde Park *aide mémoire*. Indeed, the stated aim of the strategy was designed 'to make a profound psychological impression on as many inhabitants as possible'.[16] Further, the strategy did not afford the Japanese government any opportunity to surrender after the first bomb. This is evident from the directive sent to General Spaatz of the US Strategic Air Force in the Pacific authorizing the use of atomic weapons, which stated that after the first bomb had been dropped, 'additional bombs will be delivered on the above targets [Hiroshima, Kokura, Niigata and Nagasaki] as soon as made ready by the project staff.'[17]

Authority for the use of the second and subsequent bombs was delegated to General Spaatz. In the event, the choice of target for the plutonium weapon was determined by meteorological and tactical considerations. When Kokura Arsenal was obscured by cloud, the pilot proceeded to the secondary target, Nagasaki. What Attlee knew of the operational aspects is not clear, and although there is no indication that he raised any objection, it is of interest that when he heard of Hiroshima he immediately telegrammed Truman without waiting for news of the second bomb or the Japanese surrender.[18] It is unclear whether Attlee knew of the imminent use of the second bomb. Indeed it has been suggested that Truman himself 'did not know about the attack on Nagasaki until after it happened'.[19] After the destruction of Nagasaki, work on the third bomb was accelerated, and the military prepared to use the weapon by 17–18 August. However, by 10 August, Truman evidently had second thoughts about delegating authority to his military commanders, and he informed Spaatz that any further operations should first be cleared with him.[20] The decision was not required. On 14 August Japan surrendered. Although HMG played no active role in the atomic bombing, a British observer team was nevertheless sent to Tinian Island to monitor the operation and give the UK some representation in the final stages. Composed of Penney and Group Captain Leonard Cheshire, the team was allocated places in the second mission and witnessed first-hand the destruction of Nagasaki. Penney later described his feelings: 'All of us were in a state of emotional shock. We realized that a new age had begun and that possibly we had all made some contribution to raising a monster that would consume us all. None of us could sleep.'[21]

On 10 August, the day after the destruction of Nagasaki, Attlee convened a meeting of senior ministers. Known as Gen 75, the committee became a 'forum for decision-making on atomic energy policy'.[22] On 29 August, Attlee circulated a memorandum that stated a policy decision 'with regard to the atomic bomb is imperative'.[23] Before taking a formal decision, the committee consulted the Chiefs of Staff. They were unequivocal: 'British production of atomic weapons should start as soon as possible. To delay... might well prove fatal to the security of the British Commonwealth.'[24] In January 1947, meeting with a small group of ministers, Attlee sought authorisation to begin production of nuclear weapons. The meeting concluded, 'that research and development work on atomic weapons should be undertaken', and that 'special arrangements conducive to the utmost secrecy' should be adopted.[25] The decision formalised an implicit assumption of British nuclear policy, dating from the 1941 Maud report, that Britain's status as a world power required possession of atomic weapons.

STRATEGY AND THE ATOMIC BOMB

Atomic weapons significantly increased the vulnerability of the United Kingdom. A small, densely populated island, Britain presented the ideal target for atomic attack. Indeed, as the defence correspondent of *The Times* explained, 'few uses are likely to be more effective than of dropping them on this country.'[26] The exposed position of the UK led many to conclude that for Britain, nuclear weapons should be used for 'punishment' rather than 'denial'. A firm proponent of this was Clement Attlee who (in the aftermath of Hiroshima) embraced an early conception of nuclear deterrence in which 'the answer to an atomic bomb on London is an atomic bomb on another great city.'[27] To formulate an effective nuclear strategy, however, Britain needed access to American war plans. The request was repeatedly denied in the late-1940s and early-1950s. As a consequence, British nuclear planning was 'derived from distinctly British conceptions and strategic priorities'.[28]

In assessing the use of nuclear weapons, two options were available: to continue the area offensive undertaken in the Second World War and attack centres of population, or to concentrate attacks on specific military targets such as enemy airfields and naval dockyards. To judge between these, the Chiefs of Staff established the Joint Technical Warfare Committee. In a comprehensive report, the committee reached a mixed conclusion. On one hand: 'the most profitable objects of attack by the new weapon will normally be concentrations of population, centres of distribution and communication.'[29] Against this, however, it was argued that the atomic bomb was an ideal weapon for 'opportunity attacks on main fleets and bases, on convoys and on military concentrations.' Noted by the Chiefs of Staff, the report was approved by the Defence Committee in July 1946.[30]

The report also examined the consequences of atomic attack on British cities. The conclusion was less than encouraging. While several hundred bombs would be required to knock the Soviet Union out of a future war, only '30-120 atomic bombs accurately delivered by the USSR might cause the collapse of the United Kingdom.' These findings were later incorporated into the Chiefs of Staff 1947 review of global strategy (the first comprehensive analysis of the post-war strategic environment). In discussing the implications of the atomic bomb, the Chiefs came to the following conclusion: 'It is essential that before such destruction—from which we might never recover—could be achieved, we ourselves should assume the initiative and destroy the enemy's means of making war... It is only by early offensive action that the weight of attack on the United Kingdom can be materially decreased.'[31]

In contrast, majority opinion within the Air Staff favoured destruction of cities. It was argued that despite the increase in destructive power offered by atomic weapons, lack of navigational aids and accurate maps of the USSR made precision bombing virtually impossible. Intelligence assessments supported this view: by 1949, the Soviets would be able to deploy nearly 2,000 heavy, medium and light bombers in Europe. Of these, approximately 300 Tu-4s (the Soviet version of the US B-29) would be based at a small number of airfields in Eastern Germany, with the remainder deployed throughout central Europe.[32] The Air Staff contended that due to the small number of airfields concerned, the Tu-4 with a conventional payload did not represent a worthwhile target.[33] Given this assessment, the Joint Intelligence Committee (JIC) concluded that in any future conflict with the Soviets, attacks should aim at the destruction of the administration system 'by the bombing of a large number of cities with atomic bombs.'[34]

In August 1949, the USSR conducted her first nuclear test—a development that forced the Air Staff to re-appraise the value of counter-military targeting. Equipped with the atomic bomb, the Tu-4 significantly increased the vulnerability of the UK to atomic attack. To counter this threat, the

THE ATOMIC BOMB AND THE COMMAND AND CONTROL

Air Staff argued that increased emphasis (and resources) should be given to the modern bomber within British strategy. This analysis was supported by the Chiefs of Staff, who concluded that to defend Britain against Soviet atomic attack, Bomber Command would need to target 'the atomic plants and bases of the enemy, as this is the only way of ensuring that this country remains sufficiently undamaged to continue prosecution of the war.'[35] Adoption of a counter-military strategy, however, placed significant demands on the supply of intelligence concerning the scale and deployment of Soviet military forces.

INTELLIGENCE ORGANISATION

During the war of 1939–45 the British achieved some of the greatest recorded triumphs in the history of intelligence. The decryption and exploitation of German signals communication, and the employment of strategic deception were outstanding (and now well documented) achievements.[36] The successes of *Ultra* and the 'Double-Cross' system reflected not only the professional expertise of code-breakers and counter-intelligence staffs but also Whitehall's system for managing and exploiting intelligence and counter-intelligence assets. In 1945 there was an opportunity to learn from wartime success (as well as failure), and from the period before 1939 when the organisation and performance of the intelligence services was recognised as unsatisfactory. As the JIC observed in September 1945:

> Intelligence, before the war, was starved of resources, especially in trained personnel. It was not then fully realized that the less money we have to spend on preparations for war, the more important it is to have a first-class intelligence system in peacetime. An equally important shortcoming was the lack of an adequate machine, on an inter-Service basis, for collating and appreciating intelligence for defence purpose and of a sufficiently authoritative means of putting forward considered views based upon the results of the intelligence produced.[37]

The failure to maintain an adequate intelligence organisation in peacetime had led to 'rapid and largely improvised' expansion in war, which had helped create a 'complicated and uneconomical organisation.'[38] The JIC declared: 'we now have an opportunity to set our house in order'.

Re-organisation of post-war intelligence took place within the reconstruction of the post-war defence machinery as a whole. The Attlee government's reforms of post-war defence organisation included the creation of a new Ministry of Defence (MOD), though with limited responsibilities and resources. A major issue in defence reform was whether to co-ordinate or to integrate. Greater integration meant reducing the power of the service ministries, and this inhibited the government's willingness to undertake more radical action. In the intelligence field, the measures adopted, in particular the creation of the Joint Intelligence Bureau (JIB), similarly fell short of integration, though they marked a step toward greater centralization.

Wartime experience and recognition of the changing nature (and demands) of intelligence work provided the background to reform. Various reviews of the intelligence services and their organisation took place, beginning, toward the end of the war, with a review of intelligence organisation by Brigadier Sir Findlater Stewart.[39] Professor P.M.S. Blackett was tasked by the JIC with an appraisal of the structure of scientific intelligence.[40] The resulting reforms were criticized for their lack of effectiveness and coherence.[41] The Attlee government also undertook a review of the Whitehall intelligence machinery under Sir Douglas Evill, which reported in 1947, and from which it appears no significant changes took place.[42]

At the apex of the British system of intelligence machinery was the Joint Intelligence Committee, refined and developed during the war, which was to remain, 'in its present role and with its present composition' as a sub-committee of the Chiefs of Staff Committee.[43] The JIC was supported by the Joint Intelligence Staff, responsible for drafting strategic intelligence appreciations, and comprising two teams, each composed of representatives from the Foreign Office, the three service departments, the JIB, and other departments on the JIC as appropriate.[44] The Director of the JIB served on the JIC on the same basis as the head of the Secret Intelligence Service (SIS) and the Security Service (MI5). The JIC was at the heart of a web of sub-committees, whose composition and role reflected historical experience and an understanding of emerging challenges.

The major institutional change after 1945 was the creation of the Joint Intelligence Bureau under the JIC 'to fill the need for the adequate collection of overt intelligence, particularly economic and topographical intelligence, and by concentrating the collation of such intelligence on an inter-service basis'.[45] The wartime Chairman of the JIC, Victor ("Bill") Cavendish-Bentinck, was an advocate in the creation of the JIB (as well as an early supporter of a central intelligence organisation in the US), in part reflecting his experience of the wartime use of economic intelligence (and the Ministry of Economic Warfare) by the JIC. The JIB was staffed principally by civil servants, with serving officers attached, and from its creation until its replacement in 1963 its Director was the experienced and highly respected figure of Major-General Sir Kenneth Strong who had served as Eisenhower's chief intelligence officer during the war. His warm relations with senior American officials meant that his appointment had significant implications for intelligence collaboration, and for the role of the JIB.

Wartime experience had underlined the need for acquisition and effective use of scientific, economic, and topographical information and intelligence. The strategic bombing offensive against Germany, for example, had suffered from a paucity of information, failures of analysis, and a breakdown in relations between the head of Bomber Command, Air Marshal Harris, and the intelligence staffs.[46] Modern warfare had also demonstrated the crucial importance of industrial raw materials. The advent of nuclear weapons meant both competition for scarce resources, most importantly uranium, and the need to gauge how much material was available to the Soviets (and other states). Once weapons had been successfully tested, the supply of uranium ore was the limiting factor in the Soviet stockpile. When the uranium ore was available in sufficient quantity reactors could be built to supply the necessary plutonium.[47] Monitoring, or rather estimating, the supply of uranium (and thorium) became a principal method of calculating the Soviet stockpile.[48] Within the MOD, such information was collated by the Technical Research Unit, which reported directly to the Atomic Energy Intelligence Committee, chaired by Sir Frederick Brundrett, the Chief Scientific Advisor to MOD.[49]

In this work Brundrett's committee was assisted by the JIB. The remit of the JIB was limited and as Strong recounts, there was opposition within Whitehall to creation of an organisation that might weaken service intelligence.[50] Consequently, the service departments continued to deal principally with those subjects of main interest to their departments. The advantage of this system, as Strong explained to the Minister of Defence, Emmanuel Shinwell, in 1950, was that it

> ... permits each Service Chief of Staff to have at his hand an intelligence organisation to meet his immediate needs, both for appreciations and factual information regarding that aspect of foreign countries which most concerns him, while the existence of the JIB and other centralized agencies obviate what would become a very large field of duplication between the three Services.[51]

Compared with the newly developed American system the British intelligence organisation was working well, so Strong told Shinwell:

> The US Authorities in 1946 set up a Central Intelligence Organisation (CIA) so that, inter alia, "foreign intelligence activities be planned, developed and co-ordinated to assure the most effective accomplishment of the intelligence mission related to national security", while leaving the existing intelligence agencies, i.e. the three services, to continue to collect, correlate and disseminate departmental intelligence.
>
> CIA has very largely failed to achieve effective centralization far less integration even within the limitations imposed on it and the US Services have relinquished few of their former intelligence responsibilities to the central authority, as they feel it is too remote from service requirements: this is in spite of the fact that the staff of the CIA contain serving officers. We in the UK are thus far ahead of the US in the concept of central intelligence.[52]

British arrangements nevertheless fell short of a central integrated organisation of a kind advocated by Strong, who believed that the system had 'serious weaknesses'. Although he told Shinwell in 1950 that, 'so far as it goes, this measure of centralization has proved satisfactory,' Strong warned that, 'separation of staffs brings separation of minds'. There were too many scattered staffs studying aspects of the same problem.

Centralization had been considered and discounted by the 1947 Evill report, which concluded that 'a system whereby the various departments of intelligence are more closely centralized under a single authority, on the American model, offers important advantages to co-ordination but is likely to introduce new difficulties particularly to the proper performance by the military staffs of their defence responsibilities'.[53] Strong himself recognised that 'so long as the Admiralty, War Office and Air Ministry exist in their present form. i.e. with a CNS, CIGS and CAS, each having their own staffs and overseas Commands and responsibilities, the intelligence organisation, must in general conform'.[54] It was believed that it was 'impracticable to carry the centralization of intelligence further and faster than the centralization of defence as a whole'.[55] Reform of the central machinery for intelligence thus depended on radical recasting of the higher machinery for defence, which did not come until 1964, when the JIB was replaced by the Defence Intelligence Staff, still under Strong.

The role and structure of the component organisations of British intelligence were also reviewed at the end of the war.[56] From 1944 the SIS was increasingly concerned with the Soviet target, though it is not yet clear when espionage operations began. SIS also absorbed the wartime functions of the Special Operations Executive, and engaged in various covert or special operations, as distinct from its intelligence-gathering mission, and often in co-operation with the CIA. Historically, the most significant element of British intelligence, the Government Code and Cypher School was reorganized, retitled and relocated. Government Communications Headquarters (GCHQ) as it became in 1946, moved from Bletchley Park to Cheltenham.[57] It also moved from under the auspices of SIS to the Foreign Office, and in 1950, GCHQ acquired responsibility for electronic intelligence, though according to R.V. Jones it initially failed to appreciate the potential importance of this source of intelligence.[58]

BRITISH-AMERICAN INTELLIGENCE CO-OPERATION:

Probably the most significant developments in British intelligence after 1945 came in the field of co-operation and collaboration with the intelligence services of the United States. The relationship between British and American intelligence after 1945 developed against a background of wartime collaboration, and in the immediate period after the war, amidst organisational restructuring and reorientation.[59] The first collaborative arrangements in the field of signals intelligence predated American entry into the war.[60] During the war British-American co-operation was extended to Canada, Australia and New Zealand, each of which played important roles in signals intelligence-gathering and ocean surveillance. In the period 1946-8 there were early disagreements between the British and the Americans over whether the British would 'represent' these countries or whether they should participate directly with the Americans, with whom they had developed strong wartime relationships. The Americans were particularly anxious for close relations with the Canadians whose geographical position would be of great importance as Soviet strategic capabilities developed.

The nature and scope of the agreements reached after 1945 remains shrouded in official secrecy, though it is clear that a network of agreements developed. Agreements between the individual services in the UK and their American counterparts emerged quickly in 1945–6. Co-operation and collaboration in signals intelligence was complicated, however, by reform of the US intelligence machinery, and a degree of organisational confusion in the period up to (and indeed following) the creation of the CIA in 1947 and the National Security Agency (NSA) in 1952. British attempts to persuade the Americans to continue with a Combined Chiefs of Staff developed during the war, including the wartime Combined Intelligence Committee, came to nought in early 1946.[61]

Agreement was reached on a global division of responsibility on collection of signals intelligence in the 1947 UKUSA Agreement, described by Richelson and Ball as, 'the most secret and in many ways the most consequential of the myriad of ties which link the five UKUSA countries'.[62] Richelson and Ball contend that with minor adjustments for post-war conditions the wartime agreements provided the foundation for those post-war.[63] While this may hold true, the changing organisational context also needs to be borne in mind. CIA occupied a different bureaucratic position compared to its wartime precursor, the Office of Strategic Services (OSS), reflecting in part its different role. The CIA also had a different structure and role to SIS. The CIA's analytical responsibilities, in particular in economic and scientific intelligence, meant that in terms of British-American co-operation, its relations with the JIB were probably as significant as relations with SIS. This relationship also extended into the military field beyond the formal remit of the CIA. When, for example, in November 1953, the Chief of the Air Staff met the Chairman of the US Joint Chiefs, Admiral Radford, he was advised to 'avoid revealing the full extent of our intelligence co-operation with the CIA'.[64]

In the early-1950s three categories of atomic information were distinguished: 'technical know-how', 'plans and operations' and tactics. Technical know-how involved 'such things as the fissile materials used and how produced, the detailed design of the several American atomic weapons, and the various techniques that are employed in all stages of the production of the weapons.'[65] This kind of information was of 'immense value' to the British but a very closely guarded American secret. Indeed, Lord Cherwell, Churchill's scientific adviser, argued against further pursuit of the 'will-o-the wisp' of American collaboration and instead advocated strengthening the Commonwealth relationship.[66]

Notwithstanding the importance of new formal arrangements, the persistence of wartime institutional and personal ties is apparent.[67] The relationship between SIS and CIA, for example, does not appear to have been governed by any specific agreements. Habits of collaboration, bonds of trust, and early American respect for their more experienced, and seemingly successful, British counterparts played a crucial role across the array of organisations involved.[68] The strength of these relationships was evidenced by their survival in the face of various British debacles at the hands of Soviet intelligence. The espionage of Nunn May, Fuchs, Burgess, Maclean and Philby had potentially enormous significance for British-American relations in the field of secret intelligence. Yet the main effects on British-American relations were confined to atomic intelligence. In 1945 the British had wanted to continue collaboration in the field of atomic energy. One consequence of this desire was the structure chosen for handling atomic energy intelligence. A separate committee was established outside the ambit of JIB and its Directorate of Scientific Research.[69] The priority was to do nothing that might be seen to deviate from wartime agreements with the Americans. Yet in 1946 Congress passed the McMahon Act, abruptly terminating American atomic collaboration with her wartime allies. Thereafter, and for the next decade or more, successive British governments strove to reconstruct collaboration while confronting the consequences for British planning.

THE CONTROL OF US ATOMIC FORCES IN THE UNITED KINGDOM

The passage of the McMahon Act occurred as US forces were withdrawing from Europe, including American bomber forces stationed in Britain during the war, and as political relations with the Soviets continued to worsen. Despite post-war withdrawal of US military forces from Britain, informal contacts between the services continued. In the case of the RAF and USAF, the relationship was particularly strong and reflected concerted attempts by both airforces to establish an independent role for airpower within their respective service structures. In 1946, General Carl Spaatz, Commanding General, US Army Air Forces, paid a visit to his British counterpart, Sir Arthur Tedder. In discussing the military situation in Europe, the two airmen informally agreed that in the event of Soviet hostility in Europe, several air bases in East Anglia would be prepared for use by B-29s.[70] These developments were kept from the Attlee government. The omission leaves 'little doubt' that the arrangements for American bombers to return to Britain 'were agreed informally, and perhaps a little more than that, between Spaatz and Tedder in 1946.'[71]

These contacts continued. In May 1948, a delegation of senior USAF officers (including Generals Spaatz and Le May) visited London.[72] In a series of informal meetings with their RAF colleagues, joint policy on the use of the atomic bomb was agreed. In a future war with the Soviets, 'all planning was to be based on the use of atomic bombs from the outset, including the use of the UK as a base for USAF carrying such bombs.'[73] Due to fear of retaliation and 'the humanitarian principles involved', it was agreed HMG would first need to be persuaded to adopt such a strategy. To achieve this, both airforces agreed to combine their intelligence 'to make a strong and convincing case to be put to the politicians to convince them of the need for working on the assumption that atomic bombs would be used from the outset.'[74] The possibility of preventive war with the Soviets was also discussed. The strategy was rejected. No matter how convincing the case, 'the idea of deliberately starting a war' was expected to provoke 'public revulsion' and was considered no more than of academic value.

These informal agreements soon acquired a greater significance. In June, the Soviets blockaded Berlin. To maintain supplies to the Western zones of the city, Britain and America initiated an airlift. To further demonstrate allied resolve, Ernest Bevin, the British Foreign Secretary, suggested to Secretary of State Marshall that the Americans station B-29s in the UK.[75] Taken aback by the implications of the British proposal the US Ambassador, Lewis Douglas, asked Bevin 'whether he had fully explored and considered the effect of the arrival of these two [bomber] groups in Britain upon British public opinion.'[76] When Douglas later relayed Marshall's formal request for B-29s to be deployed in the UK, Bevin obtained the agreement of the Cabinet's Berlin Committee and replied within the day.[77] On 18 July 1948, the first two squadrons of B-29s arrived in Britain. The agreement was confirmed in a brief exchange of letters that granted the USAF the use of four airfields in Britain 'as long as it was in the interests of both countries.'[78] The details were later confirmed by the Defence Committee on 13 September.[79] Later commenting on the arrangements, General Leon Johnson, Commander of the US Third Air Division, reflected: 'Never before in history has one first class power gone into another first class power's country without an agreement. We were just told to come over and "We shall be pleased to have you".'[80]

The arrival of the B-29s underlined the inadequacy of Bomber Command's front-line forces. Equipped with ageing Lancasters and Lincolns, it was incapable of attacking strategic targets in the USSR. Although plans were underway to provide the RAF with the next generation of bombers, these were not expected to enter service until the mid-1950s. To make up the shortfall, the possible acquisition of US B-29s was explored. Again, the first approaches were made through informal airforce contacts. In May

1948, the Air Staff explained to their American colleagues the need to obtain '40 aircraft to give Bomber Command some experience of long range high altitude work'.[81] In response, the USAF suggested the possibility of 'taking B-29s from storage, either to meet this requirement, or to provide for re-equipment and replacement in war'.[82] The issue was discussed further in correspondence between Tedder and Spaatz. In a revealing message to Air Chief Marshal Sir Charles Medhurst, the senior RAF representative at the British Joint Services Mission in Washington, Tedder revealed Air Staff thinking:

> What I should like you to do is to sound out Vandenberg or Norstad quite unofficially and see if there would be any prospects of our obtaining some B-29s from the Americans to put into our Bomber Command which, incidentally, will come under the Strategic Air Command immediately a war breaks out.[83]

Tedder's admission that Bomber Command would be placed under SAC in the event of war is highly significant, not least as the decision appears to have been taken without political approval. Whether the Attlee government would have consented to such an arrangement is open to speculation. Nevertheless, the fact that these 'covert' command structures were in place implies that the working relationship between the two airforces was far closer than previously assumed and 'continued both within and without the laws and policies of both countries.'[84]

The first B-29 was delivered to the RAF in March 1950 and by June 1952, 87 'Washingtons', as the planes became known, formed an integral part of Bomber Command front-line strength.[85] Incorporation of the Washingtons into the RAF raised a number of command issues. HMG came under American pressure to place the force under alliance control. The Chiefs of Staff were strongly opposed and argued that, 'it would be quite unacceptable to place these B-29 aircraft under the operational control of the C-in-C Western European Airforces'. The Chiefs maintained that independent control of the B-29s was essential, both to integrate Bomber Command with SAC and to deploy the full resources of Bomber Command in the defence of the UK. Despite their objections, the Chiefs of Staff conceded that some form of target co-ordination was required. To meet this commitment, the Chiefs agreed that although the B-29s would not be placed under the direct control of NATO 'their primary commitment would be to support the Western Union Forces in resisting attack'.[86]

The 1950 command directive issued to C-in-C of Bomber Command, Air Marshal Sir Hugh Lloyd, reflected this dual responsibility:

> ... your command will be called upon in war to direct its effort against those targets whose destruction will do most to reduce the scale of attack by land and air on Western Europe including the UK... [and] to co-operate with the Air C-in-C Western Europe in organizing and exercising a system of liaison, intercommunication and target selection so that on the occasions when targets are notified by his Headquarters they can be engaged by your squadrons with the minimum of delay. [87]

For HMG, the directive highlighted the problem of attempting to balance national priorities with wider alliance commitments - a conflict which was to become increasingly apparent in the proceeding years. The ambiguity of the command structure surrounding the British Washingtons applied with equal measure to the American B-29s stationed in the UK. In normal conditions, control of these forces was exercised by the newly created Third Air Division which was assigned to United States Air Force Europe (USAFE). At the outbreak of hostilities, however, all US strategic bombers located in Europe came under operational control of SAC. In this capacity, the primary mission of the force was to mount a strategic nuclear attack against the Soviet Union.[88] For General Eisenhower, the Supreme Allied Commander Europe (SACEUR) this procedure was unsatisfactory. He required control of the bomber force for retardation missions against Soviet ground forces. In short, NATO was preparing to fight two separate and uncoordinated campaigns: a strategic nuclear offensive commanded by SAC and a tactical land battle under control of SACEUR. In 1951, to deal with this problem, NATO's command structure was reorganized. The Third Air Division ceased operation, and was replaced by two separate organisations: the 7th Air Division under SAC, responsible for strategic bombing, and the Third Air Force under control of USAFE, responsible for all tactical operations in support of SACEUR.[89]

Coordination of SAC's mission with NATO plans remained unaddressed: a division of responsibility that became more acute with the creation of Supreme Headquarters Allied Powers Europe (SHAPE) in April 1951. In October, General Eisenhower received a briefing on the US nuclear strike plan and projected capabilities up to 1954. To incorporate these projections into future war plans and requirements, Eisenhower requested that key allied officers at SHAPE be given a sanitized version of the briefing paper. Initially, the US Joint Chiefs of Staff (JCS) refused. They later relented and allowed certain restricted information to be released to selected allied personnel on a need-to-know basis.[90]

Eisenhower also initiated discussions with SAC to determine operational planning and command authority within the NATO area. In December 1951, a set of principles was established to co-ordinate SAC operations in Europe with SACEUR's plans: SACEUR was responsible for target selection while SAC would determine operational requirements and selection of weapons. To facilitate the arrangement, the Commander-in-Chief of SAC (CINCSAC), General Curtis LeMay established a command post adjacent to SHAPE to maintain command and control of SAC units that were temporarily assigned to SACEUR. Eisenhower also established SACEUR as the sole command authority within NATO Europe for the planning and use of atomic weapons. In January 1952, he was given authorization (in his capacity as SACEUR), to prepare nuclear strike plans for US Air Force and Naval units located in Europe. In March, fearing that US atomic intelligence would be shared with NATO allies in violation of the McMahon Act, the JCS rescinded this authority: they now directed that nuclear strike plans should be prepared by the three US unified commanders within the European theatre with SACEUR retaining a solely advisory function.[91]

Eisenhower challenged this directive. He demanded that unless SACEUR was granted full control of the forces under his command, he would offer his resignation to President Truman.[92] After 'considerable deliberation' the JCS modified the directive to read: 'SACEUR should be invited to prepare, on a NOFORN [no foreign nationals] basis, appropriate plans for the employment of atomic weapons within his area, effecting mutual coordination with SACLANT [Supreme Allied Commander Atlantic] on a NOFORN basis, and with the Commanding General, Strategic Air Command'.[93] In May 1952, SACEUR instructed major US commanders in Europe to prepare an atomic weapons annex to accompany SACEUR's emergency war plan. Eisenhower made General Norstad responsible for co-ordinating atomic planning with SAC and other forces, such as Bomber Command, which were not directly under SACEUR's command.[94] To facilitate these arrangements, a Joint Coordination Center (JCC) was established at Ruislip in the UK with a European Field representative appointed in October 1952 to co-ordinate the atomic operations of SACEUR, SACLANT, CINCSAC, CINCEUR and CINCNELM.[95]

Despite the impression deliberately conveyed in 1948, the first US nuclear weapons were not deployed to Britain until July 1950. Informing the Prime Minister of the deployment, General Johnson received confirmation from Attlee that 'he fully understood all the various ramifications of bringing these units into the United Kingdom.'[96] The British decision was tempered by the understanding that only the bomb casing was to be stored in Britain, the fissile core remaining in the US. In all 89 sets of non-nuclear components were transferred to Britain and stored at three SAC bases at Marham, Sculthorpe and Lakenheath.[97] Planning was also initiated for the transfer of 60 'nuclear capsules' to be airlifted to Britain on declaration of an emergency alert.[98] The importance of the UK to American war plans is illustrated in a recently declassified 1951 report:

> The current emergency war plans of the Strategic Air Command require that three groups of medium bombers mount strikes against the Soviet Union from bases in the United Kingdom. The role of these three groups in the emergency plan is a vital one. SAC Emergency War Plan 2-50 assigns 54% of the bombs on the first strike to the groups flying from United Kingdom bases... Under these plans the SAC groups occupying bases in the UK would wait a minimum of 3 to 5 days before mounting their first strike against the Soviet Union, this strike being timed to coincide with the strikes by all the other SAC units taking part in the initial strike.[99]

The extent of British knowledge of these plans remains uncertain. Indeed, in the absence of formal agreement covering use of bases in Britain, the USAF was under no requirement to inform the British authorities of its operational intentions. Britain's inability to control US nuclear forces was further underlined by the 1948 decision to revoke the Quebec agreement which removed Britain's nominal veto on the use of American nuclear weapons.[100] Commenting on these developments, the Defence Committee expressed concern that deployment of US bombers in the UK would antagonize the Soviets and encourage aggression. This anxiety was compounded by the fear that America could make a small strike from Britain 'then pull everything back to the States and leave them out on a limb.'[101] Aware of the government's growing disquiet, CAS, Sir John Slessor, revealed details of informal assurances from the USAF that, as soon as hostilities started, 'American aircraft would begin pouring into this island... and that within thirty to sixty days there would be approximately as many American aircraft here as there were British.'[102] Slessor later provided details of the meeting to General Johnson who immediately informed Hoyt Vandenberg,

USAF Chief of Staff, that 'upon this revelation all members of the [Defence] Committee were enthusiastic and all in favour of our aircraft being there.'[103] Discussing the matter further with his fellow Chiefs, Slessor argued that to avoid any misunderstanding in the use of the atomic bomb, Britain was entitled to be consulted and 'a clear cut policy agreed with the Americans in advance of any crisis.'[104] For the government, the outbreak of the Korean War in 1950, coupled with President Truman's remarks on the possible use of nuclear weapons, demonstrated the ambiguity of the agreements covering US nuclear forces stationed in Britain.

In December 1950, to allay public disquiet, Attlee flew to Washington and received Truman's assurance that America would not use the atomic bomb 'without consulting the United Kingdom and Canada, and that the understanding between us on this point was clear even though it depended upon no written agreement.'[105] Despite this assurance misgivings remained. British concern over American intentions was later conveyed to Dean Acheson, the US Secretary of State. In September 1951, Herbert Morrison (Bevin's successor as Foreign Secretary) told Acheson that the present situation was intolerable and that HMG was no longer prepared to risk annihilation 'because of a US atomic strike from the UK over which British ministers had no control.'[106] In response, Acheson concluded that high-level discussions on the use of atomic weapons should be resumed with the British, otherwise 'the United States might find itself in a war with the USSR without allies or of the United States being denied the use of British bases in war.'[107] The US JCS strongly opposed any concessions. They believed that when 'the other Western Powers realize that neutrality in a war between the United States and the USSR is a futile hope, the question of the use of the bases of our allies will require no further resolution.'[108] Under pressure from the State Department, the Joint Chiefs finally relented but with the proviso that the talks did not involve 'any commitment, expressed or implied, on the part of the United States regarding when or under what circumstances United States atomic weapons will be employed.'[109] The outcome was the first formal agreement on the use of American bases in the UK. The National Security Council approved the text (agreed between Acheson and Oliver Franks, the British Ambassador) on 18 October 1951:

> His Majesty's Government originally made available to the US Air Force certain bases and facilities in the United Kingdom at the time of the Berlin airlift. Subsequently, it was decided that the US Air Forces should continue to have

the use of bases and facilities in the United Kingdom in the interests of the common defence of the United Kingdom and the other parties to the North Atlantic Treaty. The arrangements whereby these bases and facilities are made available to the United States depends upon no formal agreement but is being continued as a mutually satisfactory agreement. The question of their use in an emergency naturally remains a matter for joint decision in the light of the circumstances at the time.[110]

The election of Winston Churchill as Prime Minister in October 1951 coincided with a more liberal attitude in US nuclear policy. In January, Churchill visited Washington and was reportedly given a detailed briefing on the US strategic air plan.[111] Churchill also used the opportunity to reaffirm the Truman-Attlee understanding, an amended version of which was made public in a joint communiqué on 9 January 1952.[112] In short, despite private assurances, Britain still did not possess a formal guarantee that American nuclear weapons would not be used from British bases without prior approval of the government.

Throughout this early period, Britain's experiences regarding the command and control of nuclear weapons were not developed internally nor related to control of any indigenously produced nuclear stockpile. Indeed, it could be argued that the sole determinant in shaping British policy in the field of command and control was linkage with the United States. This notion of causality raises two interesting questions. First, is there evidence to suggest that HMG's desire to re-establish the British-American nuclear relationship influenced the command and control arrangements adopted by British nuclear forces? Second, as the UK and the US were in close contact throughout this period are there grounds to support conjecture that later British developments were vicariously modeled on earlier American experiences?[113] To answer these questions, it is necessary to examine the procedural arrangements for the command and control of Britain's strategic nuclear forces.

THE CUSTODY AND TRANSFER OF NUCLEAR WEAPONS

The development of Britain's first nuclear weapon began in early 1947. Known as Blue Danube, the weapon was 290 inches long, 60 inches in diameter and based on the design of the American Mk III weapon detonated over Nagasaki. Using plutonium for its nuclear core, the weapon was expected to produce a variable yield of between 5–30 kilotons. Due to scarcity of fissile material, however, the RAF later agreed that the first 100 bombs off production should be limited to 10 kilotons.[114] Overall responsibility for production of nuclear weapons was given to the Ministry of Supply. The design of the nuclear core was undertaken at HER (High Explosive Research) at Fort Halstead under the direction of William Penney with work on the ballistic casing allocated to the Royal Aircraft Establishment, Farnborough.[115] With production underway, attention focused on procedural arrangements for the storage and custody of British nuclear weapons.

In 1948 the Chiefs of Staff established the Herod Committee, chaired by the Vice-Chief of the Air Staff (VCAS), Air Vice-Marshal Sir Ralph Cochrane.[116] Composed of senior officers responsible for the use and handling of nuclear weapons, the Herod Committee was responsible for 'introducing the atomic bomb into the service and examining all associated training, personnel, equipment, storage and works problems.'[117] The committee examined two proposals. First, due to the special nature of the atomic weapon, delivery to the RAF would only occur in an emergency and responsibility for storage and inspection under secure conditions would be placed with the Ministry of Supply. Second, the atomic bomb was to be regarded as comparable to other modern weapons and that delivery from the site of production to RAF units should proceed in a similar manner to other high security items. In examining both proposals, the Air Ministry conceded that 'maintenance and assembly of the bomb, its potency, complexity, limited numbers and relative cost, make it a special weapon perhaps requiring unorthodox measures'.[118] However, as production of the bomb was not expected until the early-1950s, a final decision on custodial arrangements was deferred.

Information from the US nuclear programme also influenced Britain's custodial system. Although operational details of American nuclear weapons were supposedly forbidden to the British, it is apparent that the RAF had information that showed US nuclear weapons were not finally armed until they became airborne.[119] In comparison, the first prototype British atomic weapon designed in 1950 required an assembly team of 14 men and took 7 hours to assemble.[120] A further design feature entailed insertion of the nuclear core during the third hour of assembly. This meant that for four hours there was a 'risk of fission, or of partial fission... in the event of accident or of enemy attack.'[121] In January 1951, in light of information about the American system, the Herod Committee (with support from the Air Ministry) strongly recommended re-designing the weapon to allow the core to be inserted by using a mechanical system integrated with the bomb.

A particular advantage offered by the 'insertion method' was that the fissile material could now be stored separately from the weapon casing and inserted via a tube or aperture into the fully assembled weapon at the last moment.[122] Consequently, the custodial arrangements for the bomb casing and core could be treated separately. In June 1951, the Herod Committee recommended adoption of such a system for British atomic weapons. In the US, a similar system of dual responsibilities was already in existence. A primary criterion of the American system was that although nuclear bomb components were stored under military supervision, the cores were under the civilian control of the Atomic Energy Commission. Only after receiving Presidential authority could the two elements of the weapon be brought together. In Britain, the possibility of storing the cores under civilian supervision of the Ministry of Supply was examined but rejected. The Ministry of Supply considered that once completed, custody of the weapon was a RAF concern and 'resisted any attempt to transfer part of the responsibility for storage back to them.'[123] It was nevertheless noted that:

> The US Atomic Energy Commission holds the cores for USAF weapons. If our system of holding appeared to the Americans to be less secure politically than their own, this might make it more difficult for us to procure American atom bombs for our use. This is a hypothetical disadvantage which could probably be circumvented.[124]

Given that the storage of nuclear weapons under military control was not a major concern within Britain, why was it still thought advisable to separate the nuclear core from the weapon? To understand the reason, it is necessary to examine the weapon's arming mechanism, especially in relation to the RAF's requirement for 'in-flight' insertion. When viewed in this context, the need for a separate core assembly becomes apparent: the procedure increased both safety and operational flexibility. First, it enabled fissile material to be returned to the UK in the event of an abortive mission when operational circumstances demanded jettisoning the bomb casing. Second, it eliminated the risk of a fissile explosion during take-off. Third, the possibility of an accidental nuclear explosion over friendly territory was eliminated.[125]

In July 1951, custodial arrangements were agreed whereby the RAF became solely responsible for the custody and storage of all atomic bombs which came off production, including responsibility for the cores and all component parts.[126] The policy was adopted to provide the RAF with the necessary handling experience of atomic weapons and ensure that Bomber Command could adopt an optimum state of readiness at all times. To achieve this capability all atomic bombs held by the RAF were to be 'available for immediate operational use if required.'[127] This requirement proved difficult to accomplish, for reasons explained by the VCAS:

> One of the components, the 'initiator', is subject to decay, and has a service life of only fifty days after manufacture. For the time being we propose, therefore, to maintain only the first lift of bombs at a continuous state of readiness. In an emergency, initiators for a second lift can be provided at two days notice, and for a third lift after a further five days. Alternatively, if seven days' prior notice can be given, the three lifts can be made available simultaneously.[128]

The custodial system adopted by the RAF for storage of atomic weapons was based on two principles. First, in the absence of a core, the weapon casing was to be regarded as comparable to other modern weapons, such as guided weapons, and subject to existing security arrangements covering details of construction. Second, custody of the cores would be the responsibility of a separate security system established outside the framework of existing supply channels. In both cases, however, 'it was decided that the atomic bomb should be regarded as a normal weapon, and that no special posts should be created within the Air Ministry to deal with it.'[129] In 1953, storage arrangements were agreed: nuclear weapons (including cores) were to be stored in two separate compounds at each medium bomber airfield under the supervision of specially trained RAF personnel. To safeguard against unauthorized use, the two sections of the weapon were stored in different areas with the core contained within a specially designed and locked container.[130]

The imminent delivery of fully fabricated weapons to the RAF required a formal decision by HMG on deployment. In 1953, the Defence Committee agreed that:

> Responsibility for the storage, periodic testing, maintenance and the assembly of atomic weapons should be given to the Air Ministry but that nevertheless the Air Ministry would have no authority to move atomic weapons out of the United Kingdom without the express permission of the Government.[131]

Britain's first operational atomic bombs were delivered to RAF Wittering in November 1953. Although the RAF had no aircraft capable of carrying them, by the end of the year five weapons were under effective control of Bomber Command.[132]

CONCLUSION

In the immediate post-war years, while the overriding British priority was development of an atomic capability and the means to deliver it, British attitudes towards the command and control of nuclear weapons were characterized by two dominant themes. First, the endeavour to restore nuclear collaboration with the United States. Second, the absence of debate concerning the control of British nuclear weapons. Indeed, it could be argued that the primary objective of government policy during this period was not concerned with British issues *per se* but was directed instead towards establishing control over American nuclear forces stationed in Britain. A related theme concerns the extent of informal exchanges between the British and American airforces: a finding that confirms the growing belief that the scale of such contacts was more influential than previously believed.[133]

In the US, the Korean War, and in particular the behaviour of General McArthur, fuelled concern about military control of nuclear weapons. In Britain, in contrast, civilian control of atomic weapons was never a public issue. According to Sir Frank Cooper, later Permanent Under Secretary (PUS) at MOD, the custodial issue 'was treated simply as following the normal course of events surrounding any weapon in the inventory but with considerably greater emphasis placed on secure movement and storage.'[134] It is unclear why the question of civilian control over the atomic stockpile received far less attention in Britain than in the US. A possible explanation is that due to the small number of weapons and the lack of any viable delivery system the issue seemed largely irrelevant. Indeed, as shown above, while the control of British nuclear weapons was not a concern, the government's disquiet over possible American adventurism was a major factor in British-American relations. Alternatively, the British political system engendered greater mutual trust between the civilian and military establishments. In short, neither the government, the Ministry of Supply nor the RAF was anxious to create an additional bureaucratic structure to address a problem that was not apparent. Given the lack of debate, and the small size of the arsenal, the custodial procedures adopted were often *ad hoc* and largely pragmatic. Attention focused primarily on securing control of the allied air offensive. This challenges the presumption that 'young nuclear states' will exercise 'very tight assertive control' over their nuclear weapons.[135] By the early-1950s, Britain was about to become the youngest of the three nuclear states.

1. For details, see Margaret Gowing, *Britain and Atomic Energy, 1939-1945* (Macmillan, 1965).
2. PREM 3/139/10, Articles of Agreement Governing Collaboration between the Authorities of the USA and the UK in the Matter of Tube Alloys, August 1943.
3. PREM 3/139/10, Aide-Memoire of Conversation between the President and Prime Minister at Hyde Park, 19 September 1944.
4. CAB 101/45, John Ehrman, *The Atomic Bomb: An Account of British Policy in the Second World War* (Cabinet Office, 1953), p. 253.
5. Ibid. Tube Alloys was the British codename for the atomic bomb project.
6. PREM 3/139/11a, Anderson to Churchill, 2 May 1945; 29 June 1945.
7. PREM 3/139/11a, Churchill to Anderson, 21 May 1945.
8. Ehrman, *Atomic* p. 256.
9. Churchill to Anderson, 21 May 1945.
10. Winston Churchill, *History of the Second World War, Vol. VI, Triumph and Tragedy* (Cassell, 1953), p. 553.
11. Harry S. Truman Library, Berlin Conference File, Vol.IX, Correspondence of the President and Prime Minister Attlee, 1 August 1945. For further details see, Kenneth Harris, *Attlee* (Weidenfeld & Nicolson, 1984), p. 277.
12. Clement Attlee, 'The Hiroshima Choice', *The Observer*, 6 September 1959.
13. Martin Gilbert, *Churchill: A Life* (Heinemann, 1991), p. 857.
14. Christopher Thorne, *Allies of a Kind: The United States, Britain and the War Against Japan 1941-1945* (Hamilton, 1978), pp. 533-4.
15. Gowing, *Britain,* p. 370.
16. Bundy, *Danger,* p.70.
17. Richard Rhodes, *The Making of the Atomic Bomb* (New York: Simon & Schuster, 1986), p. 691. The directive was drafted by Groves and sent to Marshall at Potsdam on 24 July who, together with Stimson, approved the draft having appraised Truman of the details.
18. Harris, *Attlee,* pp. 277-8.
19. Stanley Goldberg, 'Nagasaki', in Kai Bird and Lawrence Lifschultz (Eds.), *Hiroshima's Shadow* (Stony Creek, Connecticut: The Pamphleteers Press, 1998), pp. 405-6
20. Rhodes, *Making,* p. 743.
21. Quoted in Brian Cathcart, *Test of Greatness: Britain's Struggle for the Atom Bomb* (John Murray, 1994), p. 38.
22. For discussion of post-war institutional arrangements for atomic energy, see Margaret Gowing, *Independence and Deterrence: Britain and Atomic Energy 1945-1952,* Vol. I (Macmillan, 1974), pp. 19-59.
23. PREM 8/116, The Atomic Bomb, Memorandum by the Prime Minister, 28 August 1945.
24. CAB 130/2, GEN 75, 4th mtg. 11 October 1945.
25. CAB 130/16, GEN 163, 1st mtg. 8 January 1947. GEN 163 met only once, with the specific purpose of authorizing nuclear weapons production.
26. *The Times,* 26 September 1947.
27. The Atomic Bomb.

28. Clark and Wheeler, *British*, p. 66; Baylis, *Ambiguity*, pp. 21-8.
29. AIR 2/1252, TWC(46)15(Revise), Future Developments in Weapons and Methods of War, 1 July 1946.
30. Gowing, *Independence*, Vol.I, p. 174.
31. Future Defence Policy, report by the Chiefs of Staff DO(47)44, May 1947, reproduced in Julian Lewis, *Changing Directions: British Military Planning for Post-war Strategic Defence 1942-47* (Sherwood Press, 1988), p. 375.
32. RG 341, Box 746, Programs of Special Interest No. 1 (England) 1943-1953, [hereafter PSI(E)] JIC(49)9(Final), Scale and Nature of Initial Air Attack on the United Kingdom - 1949/50, 1 February 1949, National Archives.
33. AIR 20/6745, ACAS(Ops) to D.of Pol, 18 August 1948.
34. DEFE 7/1889, JIC(50)89, Confidential Annex to COS(50)169th, 16 October 1950.
35. DEFE 4/25, COS(49)143rd, 28 September 1949.
36. F.H.Hinsley, *et al*, *British Intelligence in the Second World War*, Vols. 1-5, (HMSO), 1979-1990.
37. CAB 81/130, JIC(45)265(O), 7 September 1945.
38. Ibid.
39. Richard Aldrich, 'Secret intelligence for a post-war world: reshaping the British intelligence community, 1944-51', in Aldrich (Ed.), *British Intelligence, Strategy and the Cold War, 1945-51* (Routledge, 1992), p. 25; Nigel West, *G.C.H.Q. The Secret Wireless War 1900-86* (Coronet, 1987) p. 300.
40. R.V. Jones, *Most Secret War, British Scientific Intelligence 1939-1945* (Coronet, 1990) pp. 619-24.
41. Jones, *Most*, pp. 618-26 & *Reflections on Intelligence*, (Heinemann, 1989) pp. 7-34; Aldrich, 'Secret', pp. 15-49. Jones' public view was that 'in six hours the experience of six years was jettisoned', Herman, *Intelligence*, p. 262.
42. DEFE 11/349, COS(47)231(O), 8 November 1947, referred to in COS 852/5/7/50.
43. Ibid.
44. CAB 161/14, COS(41)251st.
45. Annex to JIC(45)265.
46. *Reaping the Whirlwind, A Symposium on the Strategic Bomber Offensive 1939-45*, (RAF Historical Society, 1993).
47. RG 218, Appendix to Memo by Scientific Committee, Development of New Weapons, ABCI 9/1, 14 September 1949, National Archives. For explanation of the ABCI papers see Chapter 7.
48. India Office Library and Records, JIC(48)9(O), Russian Interests, Intentions and Capabilities, 23 July 1948, quoted in Richard Aldrich and Michael Coleman, 'The Cold War, the JIC and British Signals Intelligence', *Intelligence and National Security* Vol.4, No.3 (July 1989), p. 538.
49. DEFE 13/414, Lloyd to Eden, 4 August 1955.
50. Kenneth Strong, *Intelligence at the Top* (Cassell, 1970), pp. 121-2.
51. DEFE 11/349, Strong to Shinwell, 17 May 1950.
52. Ibid.
53. COS(47)231(O), 8 November 1947, quoted in COS 852/5/7/50.
54. Strong to Shinwell, 17 May 1950.
55. COS 852/5/7/50.
56. Aldrich, 'Secret', pp. 25-7.
57. West, *GCHQ*, pp. 299-302.
58. Jones, *Reflections*, pp. 15-16
59. Richard Aldrich, 'British Intelligence and the Anglo-American "Special Relationship" During the Cold War', *Review of International Studies* Vol.24, No.3, (July 1998); Bradley Smith, *The Ultra-Magic Deals 1940-6* (Navato, California: Presidio, 1993), pp. 217-29; Jeffrey Richelson and Desmond Ball, *The Ties That Bind, Intelligence Cooperation between the UKUSA Countries - the United Kingdom, the United States of America, Canada, Australia and New Zealand* (Unwin Hyman, 1990), pp. 1-9, 135 et seq.; James Bamford, *The Puzzle Palace* (Sidgwick & Jackson, 1983),

pp. 309-37; Aldrich, 'Secret', pp. 35-40; and Christopher Andrew, *For the President's Eyes Only: Secret Intelligence and the American Presidency From Washington to Bush* (HarperCollins, 1995), pp. 136-7, 160, 162-3.
60. Smith, *Ultra-Magic*.
61. Ibid, pp. 221-5.
62. Richelson and Ball, *Ties,* p. 135.
63. Ibid, p. 141.
64. AIR 8/1852, COS(53)536, 2 November 1953.
65. DEFE 13/60, COS(53)389, 11 August 1953.
66. DEFE 13/60, G. Wheeler, Brief for MOD, on C(53)129 & 130, 27 April 1953.
67. If these links had not persisted there were voices in Whitehall who urged that British intelligence should target the US. In July 1945 Air Marshal Slessor argued that if close co-operation on scientific and intelligence development proved impossible then 'our Secret Scientific Intelligence organisation should be extended to cover the United States. The Americans are insecure people, and I do not believe we should have any serious difficulty in finding out all they are doing if we were prepared to spend the money to do so. Conversely their Secret Intelligence is amateur to a degree and I do not think we should have much to fear from them.' AIR 2/12027, Slessor to VCAS, 16 July 1945.
68. For discussion of the British role in the creation of US wartime and post-war intelligence organisations, see Thomas F. Troy, 'Writing History in CIA: A Memoir of Frustration', *International Journal of Intelligence and CounterIntelligence*, Vol.7, No.4 (Winter 1994).
69. R.V. Jones records his exasperation with these arrangements in *Reflections*, pp. 16-18. After 1954, following the Davies Report, atomic intelligence was gradually brought under the JIB's Atomic Intelligence Division. Richard J. Aldrich (Ed), *Espionage, Security and Intelligence in Britain, 1945-1970* (Manchester University Press 1998), p. 80.
70. Simon Duke, *US Defence Bases in the United Kingdom: A Matter for Joint Decision?* (Macmillan, 1987), pp. 20-5.
71. Frank Cooper, 'The Direction of Air Force Policy in the 1950s and 1960s', *Proceedings of the Royal Air Force Historical Society*, No. 11, 1993, p. 16.
72. RG 340, PSI(E), Discussions in London with the Royal Air Force Pursuant to the Provisions of Paragraphs 10, 11 and 12 of JSPC 877/4, 20 May 1948, National Archives.
73. RG 340, PSI(E), Notes of an informal meeting between VCAS and Major General Lindsay, USAF, 10 May 1948, National Archives.
74. Ibid.
75. Alan Bullock, *Ernest Bevin: Foreign Secretary, 1945-1951* (Heinemann, 1983), p. 576.
76. Walter Millis (Ed.), *The Forrestal Diaries: The Inner History of the Cold War* (Cassel, 1952), p. 428.
77. AIR 2/14027, Bevin to Douglas, 27 June 1948. The minutes of the Committee can be found in CAB 130/88.
78. Peter Hennessy, *Never Again: Britain 1945-1951* (Jonathan Cape, 1992), p. 354.
79. Bullock, *Bevin,* p. 577.
80. Hennessy, *Never,* p. 353.
81. RG 340, PSI(E), Notes of an informal meeting between ACAS(P) and Major General Lindsay, USAF, 11 May 1948, National Archives.
82. Ibid, Major General Lindsay was the USAF representative on the US Joint Strategic Planning Committee.
83. AIR 8/1796, Tedder to Medhurst, 18 November 1948.
84. Cooper, 'Direction', p. 16.
85. William Suit, 'Anglo-American Amity: Transferring B-29s to the Royal Air Force', *Air Power History* (Winter, 1994).
86. Ibid.
87. AIR 2/15917, Command Directive to Air Marshal Sir Hugh Lloyd, May 1950.

88. Peter Roman, 'Curtis LeMay and the Origins of NATO Atomic Targeting,' *The Journal of Strategic Studies*, Vol.16, No.1 (March 1993), p. 56.
89. Patrick Murray, 'An Initial Response to the Cold War: The Buildup of the US Air Force in the United Kingdom 1948-1956', in Roger Miller (Ed.), *Seeing off the Bear: Anglo-American Air Power Cooperation during the Cold War* (Washington: United States Air Force, 1995), p. 21.
90. Robert Wampler, *NATO Strategic Planning and Nuclear Weapons 1950-1957* (Center for International Security Studies at Maryland (CISSM), Nuclear History Program (NHP) Occasional Paper 6, 1990), p. 5.
91. David Rosenberg, 'The Origins of Overkill: Nuclear Weapons and American Strategy, 1945-60,' *International Security*, Vol.7, No.4 (Spring 1983), pp. 29-30.
92. *FRUS*, 1958-1960, Vol.VII, Pt.1, p. 435.
93. RG 218, 1951-53, CCS373.11(12-14-48), Sec.7, Eisenhower to Chairman JCS, 11 April 1952, National Archives.
94. Roman, 'Curtis', p. 67.
95. RG 218, CCS350.05(3-16-48), Sec.11, JCS2220/138, Report by the Joint Intelligence Committee, Release to SHAPE and Subordinate Commands on a Need-to-Know Basis, the Existence and General Purpose of Field Representative, Europe, 11 April 1958. CINCNELM (Commander in Chief, Northern and Eastern Atlantic and Mediterranean.)
96. Entry from General Leon Johnson's diary, cited in Miller, *Seeing*, p. 65.
97. Wainstein, *Evolution*, p. 31. Presidential authority to deploy the first fully assembled nuclear warhead in Britain was not granted until April 1954. Ibid., p. 33.
98. RG 340 PSI(E), Brief of MATS Operational Plan No. 33-50, 1 December 1950, National Archives.
99. RG 340, PSI(E), Report to the Commanding General Third Air Division, Strategic Air Command Forces in the United Kingdom, February 1951, National Archives.
100. The Quebec Agreement was replaced by the *modus vivendi*, which governed UK-US nuclear relations. For the full text, see *FRUS*, 1948, Vol.1, Pt.2, pp. 683-87.
101. RG 340 PSI(E), Johnson to Vandenberg, 26 May 1950, National Archives.
102. Ibid.
103. Whether details of Defence Committee meetings were exchanged on a regular basis is unclear. In this instance, Slessor's information to Johnson was given on the understanding that 'this is between us.' Ibid.
104. DEFE 4/34, Confidential Annex to COS(50)117th, 27 July 1950.
105. DEFE 4/38, Confidential Annex to COS(50)200th, 8 December 1950.
106. Gowing, *Independence*, Vol.1, p. 316.
107. RG 218, Memorandum for the Director, Joint Staff (Informally), The United States Military Position on the Employment of Atomic Weapons, 31 July 1951. National Archives.
108. Ibid.
109. RG 218, Memorandum for the Joint Strategic Survey Committee, US Military Position on Employment of Atomic Weapons, 1 August 1951. National Archives.
110. RG 59, London to Secretary of State, Texts of Basic Agreements, 6 January 1958. National Archives.
111. Slessor later informed Churchill that the US presentation 'told us considerably less than we already knew about the plan.' AIR 75/119, draft minute to the Prime Minister, 5 February 1952.
112. Duke, *US Defence*, p. 80.
113. Feaver, 'Command', p. 173.
114. AVIA 65/1155, Air Staff Requirements, 16 March 1955.
115. The work at Fort Halstead was transferred to Aldermaston in April 1950. For details, see Cathcart, *Test*, pp. 127-44.
116. Herod was an acronym for High Explosive Research Operational Deployment.
117. Wynn, *RAF*, p. 91.
118. AIR 2/13777, Memo on RAF assembly teams for atomic weapons, undated.

119. AIR 2/13777, Herod Committee, agenda for mtg, 24 January 1951.
120. AIR 2/13783, RAF Assembly Teams for Atomic Weapons, undated.
121. Herod, agenda for mtg, 24 January 1951.
122. For further details, see Cathcart, *Test,* pp. 137-9.
123. AIR 2/13783, Responsibility for Storage of Atomic Weapons, July 1949.
124. Ibid. To satisfy US concerns it was agreed that wherever possible British security procedures for storage of atomic weapons should be 'co-ordinated with that of the Americans.'
125. AIR 2/13777, Herod Committee, Minute of meeting, 11 June 1951
126. AIR 2/13783, The Introduction of Atomic Bombs into the RAF, July 1951.
127. Ibid.
128. AIR 2/13783, VCAS to Secretary of State, 15 July 1951. Composed of polonium and beryllium, the initiator was a small device, no bigger than a ball bearing, which sat in the centre of the plutonium core. On detonation, it emitted a pulse of neutrons that 'kick-started' the nuclear chain reaction.
129. AIR 2/13777, Herod Committee, Minutes of meeting, 11 June 1951.
130. Wynn, *RAF,* p. 91.
131. DEFE 32/3 D(53)3rd, 25 February 1953.
132. Wynn, *RAF,* p. 92.
133. For assessment of these informal military contacts, see Robert Hathaway, *Ambiguous Partnership: Britain and America, 1944-1947* (New York: Columbia University Press, 1981).
134. Correspondence, Sir Frank Cooper, August 1993.
135. Feaver, 'Command', p. 173.

CHAPTER 3

National Control 1953–1964

'The idea was to discourage the Ruskies from any hope that they could knock out Washington and yourself, sir, as part of a general sneak attack, and escape retaliation because of lack of proper command and control' (General Buck Turgidson, Chairman of the US Joint Chiefs of Staff, explaining the principle of delegated nuclear authority to the President).

In November 1953, Britain's first atomic weapons designed for service use were delivered to the Bomber Command Armament School at RAF Wittering. Although theoretically Britain was now a nuclear power, operationally this was not the case. Britain's first Valiant squadron was not established until January 1956 and it was not until October 1956 that the first live air drop of a Blue Danube weapon was successfully accomplished.[1] Confirmation of Britain's nuclear status - from the delivery of the first atomic weapon to the creation of a fully operational force - had taken three years. Ironically, Britain's nuclear ascendancy accompanied her political decline: October 1956 not only witnessed the attainment of Britain's atomic ambition but the diplomatic disaster of Suez. Furthermore, all defence decision-making and calculations of Britain's international authority occurred against a background of continuing economic stringency.

Following Eden's resignation, Harold Macmillan became Prime Minister with two main policy aims: to revive the British economy and to restore the British-American relationship. Domestically, the former entailed reduction in government expenditure, whilst the latter required realignment of British foreign policy more in accord with US strategic concerns. The impact of this dual policy had immediate and profound effects in the field of defence. The consequences were announced in the 1957 Defence White Paper, which placed greater emphasis on the deterrent effect of nuclear weapons at the expense of conventional forces. Largely driven by the economic demand of limiting defence expenditure to 7.5 percent of GNP, the paper announced the end of conscription and the goal of establishing all-regular services of 375,000 personnel by the end of 1962.[2]

To justify these reductions, the government placed considerable emphasis on Britain's independent nuclear deterrent. This chapter explores the growth of the British nuclear stockpile and the command and control arrangements for its use. Analysis centres on the evolution of strategy and measures to reduce the vulnerability of the V-force to Soviet attack. Further consideration is given to the deployment of nuclear weapons overseas and the subsequent establishment of a fully co-ordinated strike plan. To assess the impact of these developments on the British nuclear command structure, emphasis is placed on the constitutional position of the Prime Minister, the role of alternate command centres and the delegation of nuclear authority to the military.

STRATEGIC CONTEXT

In the wake of the Monte Bello test in October 1952, HMG initiated a 'radical review' of Britain's defence requirements. The aim was to reduce military spending by adopting a short-war strategy. A central assumption was the belief that, in the event of hostilities, SAC would launch a devastating nuclear offensive against the Soviet Union.[3] In June 1953, the government informed the Chiefs of Staff that, for planning purposes, only those forces relevant to the first six weeks of war should be maintained.[4] The RAF welcomed the directive: the creation of a strategic bomber force armed with nuclear weapons was now assured. The directive was not received with universal acclaim and both the Admiralty and General Staff were implacably opposed. Central to the debate were the strategic implications of thermonuclear weapons. Despite their differences over the length of a nuclear war, the Chiefs were convinced that the West should exploit its lead in the development of these weapons. Moreover, it was agreed that Britain should manufacture a stockpile of her own.[5]

To examine the consequences of thermonuclear weapons on British policy the Prime Minister, Sir Anthony Eden, initiated a defence review. Central to this was a report in June 1956 by the Cabinet Secretary, Sir Norman Brook, on 'The Future of the United Kingdom in World Affairs'. Written with minimal service involvement, Brook concluded that unless substantial economies were forthcoming Britain's influence abroad would be substantially reduced. To halt the decline, cuts in conventional forces were recommended with stronger emphasis on nuclear deterrence. The report confirmed the view that hydrogen weapons had revolutionized strategy and that Britain should concentrate resources on deterrence rather than a war fighting capability.[6] Brook's report formed the basis of a systematic review of defence policy. The government's response, however, was interrupted by the Suez crisis. On Eden's resignation, Duncan Sandys became Macmillan's Minister of Defence and immediately began to finalize and implement the defence review. Sandys' brief was to reshape the defence establishment on the basis of two overriding criteria: deterrence and economy.

To complement the defence reforms, Macmillan established the Committee on Future Policy to examine future defence commitments in the light of the smaller forces at the nation's disposal.[7] British interests were divided into three main areas: European defence, global commitments and nuclear weapons. In each area, however, no significant reduction in expenditure was considered possible. In short, to stabilize the defence budget a revision of national priorities was essential. The dilemma was conveyed to the Prime Minister by Sir Norman Brook, 'No further substantial savings can be looked for short of major policy decisions concerning withdrawal from Germany or abandonment of the nuclear deterrent or unless a comprehensive disarmament agreement is achieved.'[8]

The Future Policy Committee established two working groups to examine these issues in detail. The first under Sir Patrick Dean, Chairman of the JIC, reviewed Britain's political and economic interests. The second, under Sir Richard Powell, Permanent Secretary at MOD, examined nuclear policy and was known as the British Nuclear Deterrent Study Group (BNDSG). Completed in February 1960, the Future Policy Study stressed the unlikelihood of war in Europe but emphasized the potential for limited war in Asia, the Middle East and Africa. It further argued that if present commitments remained unaltered the defence budget would rise over the next decade by at least ten per cent. To contain the spread of communism in the developing world Britain required the active assistance of Europe, America and the Commonwealth.

The report laid down two guiding principles to govern future strategic planning. First, British interests in NATO would continue to be served by a contribution to both the Western strategic deterrent and the shield forces of the alliance. Second, forces were still required to safeguard British interests outside Europe. More problematically, to fulfil these objectives without increasing the defence budget, a balance had to be struck between maintaining the deterrent and modernizing conventional forces.[9] Opinion between these two alternatives was finely balanced. The majority view favoured less stringent criteria governing the 'independence' of the nuclear deterrent coupled with a gradual transfer of global commitments to the USA. Accepted in principle by ministers, the report's conclusions formed a significant part of the 1962 Defence White Paper. In line with its 1961 predecessor, the 1962 Paper also downplayed the deterrent effect of nuclear weapons. Acknowledging the growth of the Soviet nuclear arsenal, the paper contended that 'if we had nothing but nuclear forces' threats to respond to aggression would be incredible.[10]

The 1962 White Paper failed to address the central problem facing British defence planning: economies at the margin were no longer possible and a drastic reappraisal of Britain's defence commitments was long overdue. The scale of the problem was starkly underlined in a joint memorandum from the Minister of Defence and the Chancellor of the Exchequer:

> The truth is that we are overstretched. The attempt from a small island with limited resources to maintain our role in Europe, our contribution to the deterrent and a worldwide military presence is proving too much for us. To try to do all these things upon the scale already envisaged is plainly beyond our resources... for this reason we believe that radical review of these commitments is urgently needed.'[11]

The choice facing HMG was simple: accept the nation's existing commitments or withdraw from one of the key defence roles. Although the question was straightforward, the political ramifications were enormous. To significantly reduce Britain's contribution to NATO would 'convey the impression of political and military disarray', dislocate the entire military structure and lead to renewed pressure from West Germany for control over tactical nuclear weapons stationed on its territory. The consequences of abandoning the worldwide role were no more appealing. British withdrawal was expected to create a power vacuum and risk the spread of communism throughout the Middle East and Asia.[12] To relinquish control of the deterrent to the US was also considered. However, 'as it was by no means certain that British and US interests would always remain coincidental' there would continue to be a requirement 'for a strategic nuclear capability under British sovereign control.'[13] Daunted by the magnitude of the problem and given the imminence of a general election no firm decision was taken and it was left to the incoming Labour administration to embark upon Britain's withdrawal from East of Suez.

VULNERABILITY AND THE V-FORCE

The increased emphasis on deterrence, embodied in the 1952 Global Strategy Paper, had important implications for the RAF. The deterrent posture meant provision for a limited war capability was curtailed. A particular concern was the final size of the V-force. Initial plans approved by the Defence Committee in May 1955 sanctioned a force of 240 aircraft by 1958.[14] However, in May 1957, the new Macmillan government reduced this figure: the front line strategic bomber force would comprise not less than 120 and not more than 184 aircraft, of which at least 80 would be the Mark II type.[15] Macmillan also established three criteria on which future policy would be based. First, the V-force required a capability to independently inflict an unacceptable level of damage upon the Soviet Union. Second, it must convince the US that Britain was still a significant actor whose interests could not be ignored. Third, it was to reflect the financial limitations imposed by a diminishing defence budget. In August 1957, the Defence Committee agreed a front-line strength of 144 aircraft, of which 104 would be Mark II Victors and Vulcans. This was approved 'as an appropriate compromise between military and economic considerations.'[16]

To constitute an effective deterrent, the V-force was required to escape destruction on the ground. In the period before ballistic missiles, the primary threat came from the Soviet bomber force. It was assumed that in the event of global war, US and British nuclear forces stationed in the UK would be a priority target: the Soviets would have to neutralize these retaliatory forces with their first blow to escape a devastating atomic counterattack.[17] An effective air defence capable of destroying every Soviet bomber before it reached its target was impossible. Consequently, as preventive war with the Soviets had been ruled out, the only practical solution was to disperse the force in times of international crisis. Ideally, as the early Soviet hydrogen weapons were expected to devastate an area of 10-15 miles, optimum deployment could be achieved by spacing each aircraft 25 miles apart.[18]

The dispersal of the V-force during a crisis had important implications for operational control. First, crews would have to be fully briefed in advance for the atomic attack, thus making the force less flexible. Second, aircraft would have to be loaded at all times with their nuclear weapons, posing problems for political control. Third, some form of communication would be necessary between Group headquarters and the dispersed aircraft. Only arrangements for the first sortie were considered. To extend the plan to cover refuelling, rearming and rebriefing for a second sortie introduced too many complexities and was not a practical proposition, 'in view of the balance in numbers between atomic weapons and aircraft'.[19] The first detailed dispersal plan for the V-force was produced by Bomber Command in conjunction with the Air Staff and issued for service discussion on 17 January 1955.

The purpose of the dispersal plan was to guarantee an 'effective nuclear response' during times of political crisis. To ensure that the V-force was not destroyed on the ground, two measures were adopted. The Medium Bomber Force would be airborne within one hour of receiving the executive order. The force was as widely dispersed as logistic and administrative considerations would allow. The consequences were conveyed to C-in-C Bomber Command in the following terms:

> Your force must therefore be trained so that all serviceable aircraft could be airborne within one hour of receiving an executive order. This order would contain directions either to strike against pre-selected targets or to proceed to holding areas. These targets will in due course be given to you by the Air Ministry, after approval by the Chiefs of Staff. In the meantime you should assume for planning purposes that first priority will be given to the Soviet Long Range Air Force Bases.[20]

Implementation of the dispersal plan was heavily dependent on warning time. In conjunction with NATO early warning systems, aircraft approaching the UK were first sighted on radar one hour from the British coast. However, if reliance was placed solely on British based radars, this warning time was reduced to 25 minutes.[21] In peacetime, Bomber Command intended to concentrate the V-force on ten Class I airfields. Based on a warning period of one hour, however, only those aircraft already at readiness would become airborne in the event of a Soviet attack. To fully disperse the force a further period of warning was essential. This information was expected to be supplied by British and American intelligence sources. Ideally, a warning period of over 12 hours was required, enabling 75 percent of the V-force to be fully dispersed and at readiness.

The availability of suitable airfields on which to disperse the bomber force was a further problem. Under initial plans, single dispersal, for example, would require 180 airfields. The majority of suitable airfields, however, had been allocated to other RAF Commands.[22] Reviewing the issue in May 1955, the Air Council proposed that if a flight of four aircraft was based on each of the ten Class I airfields during the dispersal phase only 50 extra airfields would be required. Moreover, in combination with the American nuclear forces, such deployment would make no discernible impact on the overall effectiveness of the Western deterrent.[23]

Responding to these recommendations, the C-in-C Bomber Command, Sir George Mills voiced his complete opposition to the view that measured the effectiveness of the V-force against the combined capabilities of a joint Anglo-American deterrent. He firmly believed that all issues relating to the V-force should be approached from a purely national point of view:

> We recognize that militarily it is far and away the most important factor which gives us any stature in the world and thus any say in world affairs. We must therefore convince both potential enemies and present friends that so far as this force is concerned we can stand entirely on our own and would be able to operate it really effectively without reliance on anybody else.[24]

Mills main contention was that dispersal was an integral aspect of deterrence; limited deployment would either dramatically increase the probability of the V-force being destroyed in daylight operations over the Soviet Union or on congested airfields in Britain. Despite these concerns, financial limitations dictated that more emphasis was to be placed on Class I airfields. In late 1957 (after agreement on the ultimate size of the V-force), the Air Ministry sanctioned the following policy: on the declaration of an alert, the V-force would disperse in units of four aircraft to the dispersal sites with a squadron of eight aircraft remaining at each Class I airfield. On the assumption that Bomber Command retained seven Class I airfields, implementation of the dispersal plan required a total of 26 dispersal sites to accommodate a force of 144 aircraft plus two squadrons of the photo-reconnaissance force.[25]

The degree of readiness adopted by the V-force was not solely determined by Soviet strategy: the adoption of a co-ordinated strike plan with SAC was equally important. Moreover, as reports from the US indicated that the V-force was considered vulnerable, continued co-operation was placed in doubt. To counter this, Bomber Command was instructed to place increased emphasis on alert and readiness procedures. The 1958 Defence White Paper noted that, 'if the deterrent influence of the bomber force is to be effective, it must not be thought capable of being knocked out on the ground. Measures are accordingly being taken to raise its state of readiness.'[26] In July 1958, the C-in-C Bomber Command was directed to introduce a readiness capability into the medium bomber squadrons to meet the following conditions:

Strategic Warning—24 hours notice after which 75% of the force should be at readiness, armed and dispersed.

Tactical Warning—forty minutes, capable of being sustained for one month, and/or fifteen minutes sustained for one week.

On notification of an emergency the generation rate of all medium bomber aircraft on the strength of stations was to be 20% in two hours, 40% in four hours, 60% in eight hours, 75% in 24 hours.

The above conditions were to be met at any time of the day, weekends, or holidays, throughout the year. Six additional dispersal airfields were to be provided to bring the total number, including six operational Class I bases, up to 36 airfields.[27]

To attain this level of readiness Bomber Command formulated the 'Medium Bomber Force Alert and Readiness Plan'. Containing the alert phases, operational procedures and additional support required from other RAF commands, the plan was approved by the Air Ministry on 5 March 1959 and provided for five alert conditions corresponding to changes in international tension. These Alert conditions were defined as follows:

Alert Condition	Definition
5	Normal. Bomber Force in normal peacetime condition.
4	Precautionary Alert. Instituted during periods of political tension; specific action is ordered by Command or Group Headquarters.
3	Aircraft Generation. The maximum number of aircraft are to be made combat ready. At main bases, aircraft planned to operate from those bases are to be prepared for operational take-off; the remainder are to be armed and prepared for dispersal.
2	Aircraft Dispersal. The Dispersal Plan is to be implemented.
1	Partial Cockpit Readiness (25% of Force at five minutes readiness). Will be ordered when an imminent risk of attack exists and may be sustained for prolonged

> periods. Crews covering Alert Targets are to come to five minutes readiness (Cockpit Readiness) and 25% of the force will be so held. Continuous coverage of Alert Targets is to be maintained by substituting crews and aircraft on a rotational basis. If the number of aircraft and crews available allows more than one crew to be at five minutes readiness, priority is to be given to holding this state during the four hours before dawn.[28]

To ensure that Bomber Command was capable of converting forces from peace to emergency readiness and to control a nuclear strike if required, Bomber Command's Operation Centre was reorganized and upgraded with the latest communications equipment. In May 1959, a full scale practice of the Alert and Readiness Plan, including dispersal of the force, was conducted and 'demonstrated that the plan, with minor modifications was considered feasible.'[29]

Military preparedness was further reinforced by introduction of regular training exercises. These covered three distinct categories: No-Notice exercises which could be conducted within Bomber Command's own resources in order to practice the alert and arming procedures but without dispersal of the aircraft; Pre-Planned exercises which included all aspects of the dispersal plan up to and including scrambling but which had been planned for and known about prior to implementation; and No-Notice exercises covering dispersal of the entire force, a procedure that first required political approval.[30] In addition to regular training, procedures known as Quick Reaction Alert (QRA) were introduced to allow at least one aircraft from each squadron to be fully armed and at fifteen minutes readiness on a 24-hour basis.[31] However, the growing threat of Soviet missile attack meant that a reaction time of less than four minutes was essential. To achieve this, Operational Readiness Platforms (ORPs) were constructed at main bases and dispersal sites. Consisting of hardened standings located at the end of the runway, the ORPs permitted the dispersed force to sustain a readiness capability of less than five minutes. Construction of ORPs also allowed a continuous alert state to be maintained at Bomber Command's main bases.

The credibility of the deterrent, however, was equally dependent on the ability of the V-force to avoid destruction on the ground *and* successfully attack its assigned targets. The growing threat posed by Soviet missile systems dramatically increased the difficulties of mounting such an operation. The deployment of M/IRBMs made main airbases vulnerable to a disarming first strike whilst the increased lethality of Soviet air defences threatened the bombers' ability to penetrate Soviet airspace. By the early 1960s, intelligence estimates concluded that with advances in Soviet air defences only a small percentage of the Mk I bombers with free fall weapons would reach targets deep in Soviet territory.[32] To counter this, the BNDSG recommended development of a stand-off missile with a range of 100 miles.[33] It was nevertheless recognised that even with Blue Steel the V-force would become increasingly ineffective after 1965. Moreover, even if a longer-range weapon was developed (Blue Steel MkII) and put into production, it would only extend the effective life of the V-bombers by a further two years. In contrast, the US WS-138A Skybolt Air Launched Ballistic Missile (ALBM) would extend the effective life of the V-force until about 1970, when the front-line strength would begin to run down. Despite this, the Soviet missile threat was increasingly lethal. Four minutes were needed to get the V-bombers up and away from their dispersal airfields and clear of nuclear attack on their bases. Although missiles fired on depressed trajectories from East Germany could take as little as three minutes, the Air Ministry believed that reaction time could be improved. It was clear, as the BNDSG concluded: 'the V-bombers, irrespective of the weapons with which they are equipped, would be vulnerable to a Soviet pre-emptive attack on their bases, though part of the force would escape.'[34]

CUSTODY AND CONTROL

The dispersal plan had important consequences for the control and custody of British nuclear weapons. A particular concern was whether nuclear weapons would be released to the bomber force at their home bases or transported separately to the dispersal sites by road. The latter was considered more suitable as it reduced the time required to disperse the force, did not require the aircraft to carry nuclear weapons at all times, and decreased the number of nuclear weapons stored within the target area of the main base.[35] Given these considerations, the Air Ministry authorized the construction of two storage depots for nuclear weapons at four main airfields: Wittering, Marham, Honnington and Waddington. In addition two nuclear weapons storage sites were constructed away from the airfields, at Barnham in Norfolk and Faldingworth in Lincolnshire.

An additional constraint was the requirement that 'the plan should not depend on the atomic weapon cores being in position in the weapon at any stage until finally required for readiness for the operational mission.'[36] To meet this requirement, a procedure known as In-Flight Loading was adopted in which the bomb casing and nuclear core were physically separated within the aircraft's bomb bay. To arm the assembly, the core had to be remotely inserted into the casing prior to the aircraft entering enemy air space. This was achieved by a mechanical arming device that lowered and secured the nuclear core into an aperture situated on the upper face of the weapon. The requirement for In-Flight Loading was to guard against an atomic explosion in the event of the aircraft crashing on take-off. The development of the In-Flight Loading system proved difficult and by March 1954 had still to be perfected.[37]

In November 1955, Bomber Command was issued with a revised directive. This stated that until they possessed a nuclear weapon that could be loaded in flight, an attempt should be made to modify the existing Blue Danube weapon so that the core could be inserted manually from below whilst the aircraft was still at rest.[38] Known as partial In-Flight Loading, the procedure was to be achieved in either of two ways: by moving the aperture for the insertion of the core from the upper to the lower face of the weapon or alternatively 'turning the bomb upside down to insert the cartridge from below.'[39] However, as the core weighed 140 lb., such a manoeuvre required considerable dexterity.[40] Given these problems, it was agreed that insertion of the core from below would require a redesign of the original weapon and the production of a Mark II variant.

Prior to the introduction of the re-designed weapon, Bomber Command proposed that the practice of last minute loading on the ground should be adopted.[41] In this procedure, the weapon casing and nuclear core were stored separately alongside the aircraft. Only when warning of enemy attack was received would the two sections be brought together and the aircraft 'bombed up'.[42] It was further decided that in an emergency the requirement to inspect the weapon on a daily basis could be disregarded for a period of 28 days. This procedure was soon found wanting. In tests, it was discovered that the undercarriage of a fully armed bomber would only withstand the load produced from a 10,000-lb. weapon for a period of seven days. This operational factor, therefore, delineated the maximum time Bomber Command could be placed on full alert. On entering service with the RAF, the Blue Danube weapon was designated 'the 10,000 lb. H.E. M.C. bomb' with the ground-loading type the Mk I and the In-Flight Loading version called the Mk II.[43]

The size and weight of the atomic bomb had important consequences for the operation, radius of action and degree of dispersal of the bomber force. To become airborne, a fully fuelled aircraft carrying a 10,000-lb. bomb required a runway of over 2,000 yards. Many of the dispersal airfields had runways below this length. A reduction in fuel capacity would permit take-off but decrease the bomber's radius of action. Consequently, deep penetration targets within the Soviet Union would not be covered by all elements of the V-force. As maximum flexibility was a primary consideration, an alternative solution was required.

Various proposals were considered: increasing the length of all dispersal site runways; using only suitable runways; employing booster rockets during take-off, enabling bombers to generate the necessary thrust required to use all dispersal airfields; or assigning short-range targets to bombers operating from dispersal sites whilst employing Class I airfields for strikes against deep penetration targets.[44] The debate about these various options highlights the factors that were responsible for shaping the V-force and its future operational role during this formative period. The possibility of lengthening the runways at all dispersal sites was rejected on grounds of cost whilst concentration of forces on usable dispersal sites was discounted for reasons of vulnerability. The use of rocket boosters, however, was considered practical both on grounds of economy and operational feasibility.

The concept of employing Rocket Assisted Take-Off (RATO) to generate extra thrust on take-off had been in existence for several years. Research and development on external motors had been an important aspect of the British guided weapons programme and similar applications were being examined for fighter defence.[45] Initially, proposals were based on bombers arriving at dispersal sites with fully charged RATO units. Due to the dangers of crash landing with a large amount of volatile fuel on board this proposal was rejected. The alternative of pre-stocking RATO units at all dispersal sites was also explored. While this would have eliminated the hazards of crash landing and increased the capability of mounting subsequent strikes, it was considered too expensive.[46] In June 1956, the Bomber Command Dispersal Plan was put to the Treasury requiring a definitive decision on the employment of RATO. After protracted debate within the Air Ministry, it was proposed that, 'facilities for RATO would be provided only at the Class I airfields and that provision at each Class I airfield would be sufficient for one strike by one squadron'.[47]

This proposal underlines the conflict between credible deterrence and financial constraint: it was submitted despite recognition that provision of RATO on this scale would reduce the flexibility of the force and would be available only on those airfields where it was least required and which were most likely to be destroyed in a Soviet first strike. The policy was adopted for two reasons. First, it would act as an insurance against the Mk II bombers not achieving the desired performance. Second, it would enhance the deterrent value of the V-force; the ability to use RATO would leave the Soviets in doubt 'about its deployment and operational radius of action'.[48] The decision regarding RATO therefore was related primarily to its deterrent, rather than its operational, value. A direct corollary was that any decision to provide RATO purely to build up the deterrent value of the V-force would diminish the capability of the force to operate a 'war-fighting' role. The possible consequences of this were not lost on the Air Staff, who cautioned that:

> If we are prepared to base any part of our requirements for the deterrent on a purely 'shop window' basis, there is the obvious danger that the Treasury will seize on this to examine other requirements in the same light. In particular, any preparations to use the force for second and subsequent strikes would be in danger.[49]

This analysis was well justified. In July 1956, the Air Council concluded that the V-force would achieve its aim if, by its contribution to the overall deterrent, it prevented global war. This policy was adopted despite Bomber Command's contention that the ability to launch follow on strikes increased the value of the deterrent and that it was uneconomic to invest large sums of money on a one-shot force: resources were now to be allocated on the basis of maintaining deterrence rather than developing a war fighting capability.[50]

VIOLET CLUB

In addition to Blue Danube, custodial procedures were also required to accommodate the arrival of hydrogen weapons. Moreover, to bridge the divide before 'true' thermonuclear weapons came into service, the government sanctioned deployment of a high yield fission weapon with a yield of some 0.5 megatons.[51] Known as Violet Club, the 'interim' weapon consisted of a modified Orange Herald warhead, designated Green Grass, housed in a Blue Danube carcass. Although only twelve Violet Clubs were ever deployed, the episode raises important questions regarding British attitudes to both safety and custody of nuclear weapons. Central to an understanding of these issues was HMG's desire to demonstrate a thermonuclear capability at the earliest possible date. To achieve this, Violet Club was deployed at operational bases even though its development programme had yet to be completed. A vocal critic of the scheme was the Controller of Armaments in the Ministry of Supply who expressed his concern that the deployment of Violet Club violated the 1953 Cabinet ruling on nuclear custody:

> Throughout the discussions on this interim megaton weapon the general approach has been that, in the interests of providing a megaton capability to the RAF at the earliest possible moment, the Service is prepared to sacrifice rigorous testing, proofing and clearance of the weapon and to introduce special maintenance procedures in association with AWRE.[52]

Despite such reservations and the worry of the DCAS that the interim megaton weapon was 'rather delicate', the first Violet Club was delivered to RAF Wittering on 27 February 1958.[53] In the following six months an additional five weapons were assembled on Bomber Command stations. The operational effectiveness (and safety) of these weapons, however, remains in some doubt. Specifically, as Violet Club took a minimum of thirty minutes to prepare, it could not be placed on QRA unless safety measures were relaxed. However, once the safety device was extracted from the weapon, it immediately became live. Moreover, as the warhead contained 'enough U 235 to form an uncompressed super critical mass in the event of a mechanical deformation of the shere occurring', a small explosion or accident in which the weapon was dropped would result in a full yield nuclear explosion.[54] As a result of these considerations, it was agreed that 'Removal of the nuclear safety device must not occur except as the final act of weapon preparation before take-off.'[55] To officially sanction the deployment of Violet Club, the C-in-C Bomber Command was issued with the following directive:

> Violet Club is still in some degree experimental and will be subject to a number of serious handling restrictions. The extent of these... and their effect on operational readiness are still under discussion with the Ministry of Supply. Until Violet Club has been formally cleared by the Ministry of Supply and it is possible to issue specific instructions on storage, handling and transport, *the weapon is to remain exclusively in the custody and under the control of the Atomic*

Weapons Research Establishment... because of its experimental nature certain restrictions must be applied to the method of handling this weapon, the most important of these are as follows: (i) that it is assembled on the RAF station from which it would be used (ii) its road transport is limited to that necessary to convey it from its assembly point to its storage building.[56]

In addition to handling restrictions, Violet Club also exhibited serious design flaws. In late May 1958 'a crisis arose' over corrosion of the nuclear flask which resulted in the recall and breakdown of the No.1 Green Grass warhead. To monitor the remaining weapons each warhead was withdrawn for examination every six months.[57] As Limited Approval for Violet Club was only sought in February 1959, several months after initial deployment, there is *prima facia* evidence to suggest that in order to demonstrate Britain's thermonuclear capability, HMG was prepared to both compromise safety and sanction *ad hoc* custodial arrangements for nuclear weapons. Moreover, in authorizing these procedures, the government effectively reversed its own policy: operational nuclear weapons were to be retained under the civilian control of the AWRE, despite their deployment on RAF bases.

Due to the serious operational limitations of Violet Club, the RAF was anxious to acquire a true thermonuclear potential as soon as possible. However, whilst some of the worst features of Violet Club were ameliorated by the introduction of Yellow Sun MkI in 1959, it was not until mid-1961 that the service received its first thermonuclear weapon.[58] Designated Yellow Sun MkII, the weapon was a virtual copy of the US B-28 and used the megaton-warhead Red Snow. The introduction of the new weapon, however, presented fresh problems for both storage and custody. A significant feature of Red Snow was the encasement of the fissile material within the central core or 'pit' of the weapon. This made the removal of the core impossible without the total disassembly of the entire weapon. Consequently, the requirement for In-Flight Insertion was untenable. Storage of the weapon was also problematic. Facilities for kiloton weapons were based on housing the cores separately from the weapon. As this requirement was no longer possible, new storage procedures were required. Approved in September 1959, the revised storage plan authorized the following measures:

> Criteria for the storage of the present MT warhead for Yellow Sun MkI (Green Grass) calls for the holding of not more than one per building. The new warhead for Yellow Sun Mk2 and Blue Steel (Red Snow) will have fissile material built in and single storage will also apply. As to the planned KT weapons (Red Beard)

the fissile material is removable and stored separately. Four RBs can be held in the same space as one Yellow Sun.'[59]

OVERSEAS DEPLOYMENT

Although the mainstay of the British nuclear deterrent, the V-bombers were not the only aircraft capable of delivering a nuclear strike. The Canberra light bomber squadrons based in West Germany and Cyprus could also carry nuclear weapons. In the former, the Canberras were assigned to the 2nd Allied Tactical Airforce (2ATAF), whilst in the latter they came under operational control of the Near East Air Force (NEAF). Four squadrons of Canberras based at RAF Akrotiri provided CENTO with a nuclear capability.[60] Armed with Red Beards, the target list for the Canberras was co-ordinated between Bomber Command and SACEUR on the understanding that 'the use of this force would in effect amount to global war.'[61] In common with the V-force, the Canberra squadrons were also expected to disperse in times of crisis with elements operating from RAF Muharraq (Bahrain) and RAF Sharjah (United Arab Emirates). To guard against accidental explosion, insertion of the nuclear assembly was only to be undertaken after redeployment to the Persian Gulf and 'under no circumstances' were aircraft to conduct any exercise carrying nuclear weapons.[62]

Although conceived primarily for use with the Canberra, Red Beard was also capable of being delivered by the NA39 carrier-based bomber. The Admiralty's case for a nuclear-capable fleet was based on two distinct propositions. First, due to the increasing vulnerability of the V-force, a carrier-based contribution to the deterrent would both complicate any Soviet offensive and provide a means of engaging targets only accessible from carrier-based aircraft. Second, a British naval nuclear capability would constitute a significant deterrent against China and facilitate British participation in US strategic planning for the Far East.[63] To fulfil the Admiralty's nuclear requirement, a special variant of Red Beard was developed for naval deployment. Designed primarily for use against ships, submarines and harbour installations, the first Red Beard was deployed aboard HMS Hermes in November 1960.[64] The deployment of nuclear weapons aboard aircraft carriers had direct operational and political implications for command and control. The storage of such weapons raised issues concerning safety, whilst the 1953 ruling that the Air Ministry was alone responsible for the carriage of nuclear weapons was no longer applicable.

To address the issue of storage, the Defence Committee was presented with two alternatives: to keep the weapons on land or disperse them within the fleet. The land-based alternative was quickly dismissed as the weapons might not be available at short notice; the advantage of dispersal would be lost; and the decision to embark the weapons in time of crisis might dangerously exacerbate tensions. The storage of nuclear weapons aboard ships, however, raised further problems. A particular concern was accidental nuclear explosion. To guard against this, all naval nuclear weapons were stored in two pieces, in separate parts of the carrier. One section consisted of the bomb casing and high explosive, the other comprised the fissile component which was stored in a specially designed container. To further guard against accidental use, a variety of safety procedures ensured that a nuclear explosion could only occur after the weapon had been positively armed.[65] While the operational aspect of deploying nuclear weapons aboard aircraft carriers was resolved, the political ramifications proved more contentious. Two aspects were of particular concern. The first related to the passage of British ships carrying nuclear weapons in foreign waters. The second concerned the procedures to authorize a nuclear strike from a seaborne force.

The carriage of nuclear weapons in foreign waters presented HMG with an awkward problem: disclosing the presence and location of nuclear weapons would compromise security whilst failure or refusal to inform foreign governments that nuclear weapons were located in their territory was fraught with political repercussions. An example of the possible difficulties arose with newly independent Singapore, where it was noted that nuclear weapons had been stored but that 'Singapore Ministers had not been informed about this and under the constitution there is no legal need to do so.'[66] Whilst serving as a temporary expedient it was recognised that such clandestine arrangements were far from satisfactory. Consequently, until bilateral arrangements could be finalized, the government concealed the presence of such weapons by adopting the principle that for security reasons it could neither confirm nor deny the location of any nuclear weapon.[67]

Deployment of nuclear weapons aboard aircraft carriers also brought into question the chain of command covering the control of nuclear weapons. The difficulty stemmed from the 1953 Cabinet ruling that the Air Ministry was alone responsible for the storage, periodic testing, maintenance and assembly of atomic weapons. A review of the procedures was undertaken within MOD. To obviate detailed revision, it was decided to regard the 1953 ruling as 'no more than an "obiter dictum" of the Prime Minister that arose in the course of discussions about increasing the supply of fissile material.'[68] It was further agreed that any new procedures should be determined on their own merits. Informing his counterparts in Australia, Canada and New Zealand of the decision to employ nuclear weapons in aircraft carriers, the First Sea Lord explained: 'As regards operational control, there is an overriding rule that the bombs are not to be armed or flown in peace-time: and in fact, no naval aircraft may take off with a nuclear bomb aboard except on an operational mission authorized by the Prime Minister.'[69]

Britain's decision to deploy tactical nuclear weapons raised a number of questions concerning command and control. Foremost was the problem of co-ordinating nuclear strikes delivered by different Commands. To analyze the issue, concurrent studies of the European, Middle East and Far East theatres were undertaken.[70] A conclusion of all three studies was that 'in the tactical land battle the control of atomic weapons should be a joint Army/Air Force responsibility, with naval participation where necessary.'[71] It was realized, however, that once hostilities had started, control of tactical nuclear weapon raised problems, as:

> No legislation or directive can attempt to cover all the circumstances likely to arise in a battle, and no ruling can be made which would attempt to govern the exercise of a Commanders' discretion in the event of a breakdown of communications such as to prevent him adhering to the accepted principles for control and clearance of nuclear weapons.[72]

For a growing number of strategists, the inherent difficulty of controlling tactical nuclear forces was a compelling argument against their deployment. A prominent critic was Sir Solly Zuckerman, the MOD's Chief Scientific Advisor, who believed that military planners 'were living in wonderland' and did not seem to realize 'what a mess nuclear explosions would make of a battlefield; that all communications would be disrupted, so making command and control impossible.'[73] Zuckerman's hostility coincided with a review of NATO strategy initiated in 1960, which concluded that the function of tactical nuclear weapons within Europe was solely for deterrence and not to fight a battle aimed at retention of territory.[74] The number of tactical nuclear weapons required to implement the strategy would therefore be small. The decision had profound implications for continued development of Blue Water, Britain's independently developed battlefield nuclear system. Scheduled for introduction in 1964, Blue Water offered the British Army independent control over nuclear weapons in the tactical land battle.[75]

The decision to limit deployment of tactical nuclear weapons was conveyed to the CDS in guidelines from Harold Watkinson, the Defence Secretary. On Blue Water these stated that:

> It can be assumed that anything but the most limited exchange of tactical nuclear weapons would rapidly escalate to all-out nuclear war, and the issue would then be settled by the strategic nuclear forces. The main purpose of tactical nuclear weapons is therefore deterrence... Since Blue Water is a British weapon and since development of the low yield warhead for it is almost complete, some of these should be produced. Should NATO require us to have a higher yield warhead for this weapon in Europe, we should rely on the NATO stockpile provided by the Americans for our supply.[76]

In response, the Army Council maintained that for both national prestige and technological reasons, it was 'highly desirable that the British Army should have at least some nuclear weapons of British manufacture.'[77] The ideal system was Blue Water, which would allow the Army to deploy nuclear weapons outside Europe if necessary by withdrawing units from the two missile regiments currently planned for BAOR. The Army Council further argued that as development of the low yield warhead (RO 106) was almost complete, a stockpile of fifty warheads should be established under the control of the General Staff. Why this warhead was developed is unclear, especially in view of Macmillan's statement to the Defence Committee in early 1957, that Britain would never use tactical nuclear weapons without the US and therefore 'could rely entirely on American warheads for this purpose' [78]

In July 1962, the fate of Blue Water was sealed. In the ministerial changes following the 'Night of the Long Knives', Watkinson was replaced at MOD by Peter Thorneycroft. A former Chancellor with a strong reputation for fiscal restraint, Thorneycroft acted quickly. Barely two weeks in office and with 'practically no consultation, he cancelled the Army's pet project Blue Water.'[79] Presenting his case to Cabinet, Thorneycroft argued that as there was an 'urgent need for substantial economies' and it seemed 'increasingly doubtful whether the sort of campaign in which Blue Water would be used would ever take place' it should be cancelled.[80] Macmillan agreed with Thorneycroft, emphasizing that if nuclear weapons were to be used to enforce a pause in hostilities such a strategy would require 'no more than the provision of limited numbers of nuclear weapons under the direct control of the Supreme Commander'.[81]

NUCLEAR STRIKE CO-ORDINATING COMMITTEE

The deployment of nuclear weapons abroad brought to the fore the question of co-ordinating nuclear strikes conducted by a number of Commands. In the US, similar problems of target duplication were encountered and led to adoption of a Single Integrated Operational Plan in 1960.[82] Whilst the size, dispersal and target set of the British arsenal were considerably less than that of the US, a fully co-ordinated strike plan was still essential. In 1961, to meet this requirement, the Nuclear Strike Co-ordinating Committee (NSCC) was established.[83] Its purpose was to ensure that the nuclear strike plans of the Air Ministry and Admiralty were conducted on a co-ordinated basis which prior to the creation of the NSCC had been limited to the inclusion of a naval liaison officer on the Air Ministry's Targets Committee. The first task of the NSCC was to prepare a list of priority targets within the USSR and establish service responsibilities for a unified nuclear strike. To achieve this, the NSCC established three working groups with the following responsibilities:

(a) The Targets Working Party, to establish a list of targets in order of importance for a National Retaliatory War Plan in accordance with the target systems laid down by the Chiefs of Staff.
(b) The USSR Planning Team, to allocate targets in the USSR in accordance with the outline plan to the nuclear strike forces of the Royal Navy, Bomber Command and Near East Air Force to ensure the most efficient use of the weapons systems available for a National Retaliatory War Plan.
(c) The Far East Planning Team, to co-ordinate tactical nuclear strikes in support of SEATO and national retaliatory action against China and targets in the Soviet Far East.[84]

A major consideration addressed by the NSCC was the problem of maintaining close political control over the use of nuclear weapons in overseas theatres. The problem was particularly acute in the Far East. Specific instances of concern included lack of clearly defined procedures for obtaining political authority, unreliable communications and the absence of any system to authenticate a nuclear release message. To compound these difficulties, the question of whether a strategic nuclear strike against China would be mounted independently or in conjunction with the US had yet to be resolved.[85] Expressing disquiet, the NSCC made the following recommendations. First, as allied command structures in overseas theatres were not comparable with NATO, 'authority to use nuclear weapons should pass down exactly the same channels as would be used for all other orders for military action.'[86] Second, to enable a continuous exchange of intelligence between the overseas theatre and the government in Whitehall and to provide a means of conveying the political decision to initiate nuclear action, a secure and reliable communications system was essential. Third, to eliminate the risk that 'spurious instructions could be issued by an enemy possessed of the key to our cryptographic systems, or by a mentally deranged person with access to our communications' a secure system of authentication was imperative.[87]

In formulating their recommendations the NSCC was directed by the Chiefs of Staff to assume that the initial decision to use nuclear weapons would not be taken by a military commander without first receiving specific political authority.[88] The government's unwillingness to delegate such authority stemmed from the belief that even the most limited use of tactical nuclear weapons carried a grave risk of escalation to global war.[89] The government was adamant that 'there should be no delegation of authority to initiate the first strike'.[90] The Chiefs nevertheless continued to press for a more flexible interpretation of policy. It was argued that once the decision to use tactical nuclear weapons had been taken by HMG, the argument against delegating nuclear authority to the military lost much of its force. To balance the requirement to retain political authority with the need of local commanders to counter any immediate threat, the Chiefs recommended that:

> As strike planning proceeds, it should be possible for the three services jointly to classify targets in groups so that HM Government can give a degree of delegation in the continuation of nuclear operations. The machinery would then exist for putting the decision into effect quickly and effectively. We foresee that static targets and targets of opportunity could be graded according to the risk of escalation, and to the risk of injury to civilians. Graduated target lists in London and the Theatre Command would make it possible to retain effective political control without the need to sacrifice every tactical opportunity that occurs.[91]

Britain's decision to withdraw from East of Suez and rely on the supply of US tactical nuclear weapons in the event of global war removed many of these problems. The use of nuclear weapons on aircraft carriers, however, was a question still to be resolved. In addition, by the early 1960s, the targets to be attacked by British nuclear forces required clarification.

TARGET POLICY AND MINIMUM DETERRENCE

By the early-1950s, the centrality of the bomber force to British strategy and its role in counter-military targeting were firmly established - a position reflected in the 1952 Global Strategy Paper which endorsed the view that the V-force represented 'an essential defensive factor in the form of attack at source'.[92] Although measures to improve the air defence of the UK were not discounted, the counterforce role of the bomber was now integral to British strategy, a view firmly endorsed by the Chiefs of Staff:

> In the foreseeable future no purely defensive system will be effective against atomic attack. It is therefore imperative that every possible step should be taken to reduce the scale of attack to which the UK could be subjected. There is one way, and one way only, in which this can be done during the first critical days of war. That is by direct attack on the enemy air force and its bomber bases.[93]

Initial intelligence estimates indicated the existence of fifteen long-range air bases in western USSR.[94] Although the location of these main bases was well known, the number and position of possible dispersal sites was uncertain. Despite SAC's ability to destroy the majority of Soviet air bases, HMG was reluctant to be completely dependent on the US. This reflected the advice of the Chiefs of Staff who warned of 'strong political disadvantages' if the UK did not possess a stock of atomic weapons under its own control.[95] A particular concern was the disproportionate nature of the Soviet threat confronting Britain and the US. Specifically, as the Soviets did not possess an effective intercontinental delivery capability, the continued existence of the USA was not immediately threatened, a position not enjoyed by the UK. It was therefore considered essential for Britain's future security that an atomic bomber force was immediately available and under national control. The consequences of placing undue reliance on the US were starkly described by the Air Staff:

> If the Americans were the only Western power with a strategic bomber force, there would be nothing to prevent them from triggering off a war at any time they believed to be most advantageous to their national policy. In such an event this country would most certainly be at the receiving end of Russian thermo-

nuclear weapons, and we would be in no position to make any arrangement with the Soviets to stay out of a war which was not of our seeking. On the other hand, if we had a small but powerful bomber force, capable of delivering our own H Bombs on Russia, we might well persuade them to lay-off attacking our centres of population, in the event of us being in the war at the start, or not to bomb us at all should the Americans decide 'to go it alone'.[96]

These arguments were accepted by the Cabinet, who concluded that, 'since the very survival of Britain would depend upon the promptness and thoroughness of the counter-attack against these Russian air bases, it is essential that we should ourselves possess and control a bomber force capable of performing this vital task'.[97] Soviet acquisition of the hydrogen bomb, however, placed these plans in doubt. For Britain, the implications of the H-bomb were clear: a few weapons exploded over major population centres would result in the total devastation of the country.[98] The limitations of a counterforce strategy were further compounded by intelligence estimates. It was believed that by 1960, the Soviets would have 150 airfields from which they could mount nuclear strikes.[99] A significant threat was also anticipated from Soviet ballistic missiles. In short, as Bomber Command could not guarantee the complete destruction of every Soviet air base, it was recognised that counterforce would only be effective in combination with the superior strike power of the US.

The advantages of a coordinated offensive with SAC were outlined to the Prime Minister by the CAS, Sir William Dickson, in February 1955. However, 'in a matter so vital to our survival' doubts still remained on placing undue reliance on the Americans, especially 'in the first few days which are now of such critical importance.'[100] Moreover, while the Chiefs had rejected the concept of preventive war with the Soviets, they were careful not to rule out the possibility that in response to a conventional attack in Europe, the West would retaliate with nuclear weapons. The requirement to neutralize the Soviet atomic arsenal immediately at the outbreak of hostilities significantly increased the pressure 'to strike the first blow'.[101] Indeed, as long as the West possessed the capability to eliminate the Soviet nuclear threat in a first-strike, the temptation for nuclear pre-emption remained high.[102] Against this, however, was the realization that once the Soviets achieved nuclear parity with the West, a counter-military strategy alone could not save the UK from complete annihilation.[103]

In response to this assessment, the Air Staff re-examined targeting policy. For some such as Sir George Mills, the C-in-C Bomber Command, the growth of the Soviet arsenal confirmed the advantages of reverting to a counter-city strategy. On this Mills argued bluntly:

> Whoever would be afraid of launching a sudden attack if he thought the greater part of our retaliation would come back on his airfields? I am sure for the enemy's edification as well as our own we must be specific in saying that our aim in retaliation is to hurt him where it really hurts; I do pray we keep our minds absolutely clear on this issue.[104]

In contrast, a significant element within the Air Staff still favoured a counterforce role. It was argued that the recent Suez crisis and the uncertainty of US intentions provided strong justification for retention of an independent warfighting capability. This view was not shared by Prime Minister Macmillan, who sought to reduce the bomber force on the grounds that the only true deterrent to Soviet aggression was the US nuclear arsenal. That Britain required an independent force under national control was not in question—the difficulty was determining a suitable force level capable of both influencing the US and constraining the USSR. Macmillan's intentions were clear: 'we should have within our control sufficient weapons to provide a deterrent influence independent of the US.'[105]

In late 1957, two events led to a systematic reappraisal of strategic target policy. The first was the Cabinet's decision to establish the V-force at 144 aircraft. The second was the agreement to co-ordinate the nuclear strike plans of Bomber Command and SAC. To assess the consequences of these developments, the JPS produced a report 'Allied Strategic Nuclear Attack in Global War in 1957' which was to form the basis of strategic target policy for the UK.[106] The report estimated the scale of a fully co-ordinated nuclear assault on the USSR and assessed the damage to the communist bloc's war making capacity. The scale of attack was massive: a first wave strike of 1,500 bombers directed against 800 targets, including airfields, nuclear storage facilities, centres of administration and the transport system.[107] In relation to control and target selection, the report assumed that the operation and administration of the British strategic bomber force would remain the responsibility of the Air Ministry. However, as these forces were of supreme importance to the UK's position in world affairs, all policy decisions concerning their employment and readiness should be formulated by the Cabinet on advice from the Chiefs of Staff. To achieve this, the JPS argued that:

The responsibility for the selection of strategic targets is at present vested in the Air Ministry. The British strategic air forces are, however, the supreme instruments of national defence policy. We therefore consider that broad target policy should be decided by the Government on advice from the Chiefs of Staff. Detailed target selection would remain the responsibility of the Air Ministry. It would be essential for this target selection to cover two eventualities: (a) Co-ordinated action with the USAF; (b) Action on an emergency basis in a situation in which the UK was forced into unilateral retaliation.[108]

In September, the Chiefs accepted this and approved a dual targeting policy for the V-force: a unilateral strike plan aimed at Soviet cities and a combined offensive coordinated with SAC directed against a mix of urban and military targets. Later approved by the Defence Committee, these recommendations formed the basis of Bomber Command's Emergency War Plan, which came into operation on 1 October 1958.[109]

To help formulate detailed planning, the JIB established a target list of Soviet cities. The JIB estimated some 130 Soviet cities with a population over 100,000, of which 54 were targets of major importance. Of these major cities, ten were in the east of the USSR and outside Bomber Command's operational radius. Consequently, a target list of 44 major cities was established as Bomber Command's primary objective in an independent nuclear attack.[110] Britain's ability to achieve destruction on this scale, however, was open to doubt. In October 1958, Bomber Command's front-line strength was only 92 aircraft. Moreover, to ensure the successful destruction of the targets, Bomber Command planned to double up strikes on each city. Consequently, the maximum number of cities that could have been covered in a single strike was 46.[111] Given that a large percentage of the V-force would be destroyed prior to reaching their designated targets, the exact number of cities that would have been laid waste is a matter of speculation.

The issue of what exactly constituted an effective deterrent was also crucially dependent upon the perceptions of the Soviet leadership. The minimum level of destruction that would deter Soviet aggression was a matter of speculation. Indeed, in examining the issue, the BNDSG concluded that the exact scale of destruction required was largely arbitrary and depended ultimately on political judgement. Existing plans indicated that destruction of forty Soviet cities would 'render ineffective' over 38 million people or thirty per cent of the urban population.[112] For many, destruction on such a scale was excessive.[113] To provide a critical analysis of the issue, the JIC was requested to study the Soviets' ability to absorb damage. The main conclusion was that the destruction of forty cities was greater than necessary and that future policy should be based on the following criteria:

> For a British system to constitute an effective deterrent valid from a Russian point of view it is enough that the force should by itself be capable of significantly altering the balance of power between Russia and the US. We believe that the destruction of 20 of the largest cities in Russia (and even possibly the destruction of a much smaller number) would so alter the Russo/American balance that it would be unacceptable to the Russians and that a British force with this retaliatory capability would constitute an effective deterrent, provided that the Russians knew we possessed it and believed that in reprisal for damage to vital interests we would use it.[114]

The question of reducing the forty city criteria was discussed further by the Defence Committee on 7 March 1962. Intended primarily to review progress on the 1962 Defence White Paper, the Prime Minister used the opportunity to explore the implications of taking fifteen cities as the requirement for a minimum deterrent. Although it was emphasized that the review did not imply a change in government policy, it was considered essential 'as without a ministerial ruling on the vital issue of degree of damage', the Air Ministry would be unable to provide costings for Bomber Command's front-line strength.[115] In examining the implications, the BNDSG concluded that to successfully guarantee the destruction of fifteen Soviet cities would require a total of 128 Skybolt missiles on 72 Vulcan Mk II aircraft of which thirteen would be airborne during any period of continuous alert.[116] The fifteen city criterion was later approved by the Prime Minister and formed the basis of Bomber Command's strategic target policy which came into operation in May 1962.[117] Of the fifteen cities selected only Moscow and Leningrad were guaranteed as targets.

Fundamental to adoption of the fifteen city criterion was the expectation that Bomber Command would soon be equipped with Skybolt. The cancellation of the project in December 1962 placed the future effectiveness of Britain's nuclear deterrent in considerable doubt. The subsequent implementation of the Nassau Agreement obliged HMG to assign the entire V-force to SACEUR to be targeted in accord with NATO plans. To meet national requirements, however, HMG successfully argued for an exclusion clause that allowed the V-force to be withdrawn from NATO when supreme national interests were at stake. The implications of this arrangement were later spelt out to the new C-in-C Bomber Command, Sir John

Grandy:

> The force is assigned to SACEUR for targeting and the planning, co-ordination and execution of strikes in accordance with his Nuclear Strike Plan. Comply, as far as available resources permit. In all other respects, the force is under national control and you will inform the Air Ministry of any instructions you may receive from SACEUR that appear to conflict with this proviso.[118]

A further consequence of Skybolt's cancellation was that a minimum deterrent capability, as defined by the ability to destroy fifteen Soviet cities, was no longer credible. To ameliorate the gap in Britain's deterrent capability before the arrival of Polaris in the late-1960s, three alternatives were available: to leave the gap uncovered as a temporary necessity; to hire US Polaris submarines complete with missiles; or to further reduce the number of Soviet cities required for destruction.[119] In reviewing the various options, the latter was considered the most appropriate - a position supported by a JIC analysis that concluded: 'The current intelligence assessment was that the Russians would regard the certain destruction of five of their largest cities as an unacceptable risk.'[120] In the course of only six years, Bomber Command's ability to threaten the assured destruction of Soviet cities had decreased from over forty to five—a reduction that reflected Britain's growing inability to maintain a wholly independent second-strike capability.

HIGHER COMMAND AUTHORITY

In the immediate post-war years, the command structure of Bomber Command remained largely unchanged with operational control of the force vested in the Commander-in-Chief based at High Wycombe. Directly under Bomber Command HQ were two numbered Groups, No.1 Group with Headquarters at Bawtry and No.3 Group with Headquarters at Mildenhall. Executive control of the Command was the responsibility of the Chiefs of Staff in conjunction with the Defence Committee, chaired by the Prime Minister, with the Air Ministry designated as executive agent.[121] In the early-1950s, the development of nuclear weapons coupled with the reduction of response time led to revision of the command structure.

A firm proponent of adapting the higher command authority to the strategic imperatives of the nuclear environment was Kenneth Cross, a future C-in-C of Bomber Command. In 1953 Cross observed that:

Under the time scale given in Global Strategy, there will be no time for the ponderous machinery of the last war to take effect. You will remember that Bomber Command's operations were controlled then by means of directives to the C-in-C from the Air Ministry acting on behalf of the COS - the COS having previously reconciled the demands of the numerous other Ministries in Whitehall. This method was considered very unsatisfactory by the C-in-C, even in the slow time process of the last war.[122]

A particular area of concern was the procedure for issuing directives to Bomber Command. Indeed, as presently constituted, the war directive could only be issued by HMG after the declaration of war. Given the need for rapid response, such a process was inappropriate. In 1955, a new procedure was therefore adopted: the war directive governing the employment of the strategic bomber force would be approved by the Defence Committee during peacetime with the Chief of the Air Staff authorized to issue the directive immediately upon the outbreak of hostilities.[123] To maintain political control, however, it was considered essential that the order was confirmed at Cabinet level, 'before Bomber Command aircraft were committed to hostile actions.'[124] To further reduce the vulnerability of the V-force, authority was sought for C-in-C Bomber Command 'to order his available aircraft off the ground in case of surprise attack on the UK without consulting anyone.'[125]

In light of these considerations, the procedures for obtaining political approval to initiate nuclear war were re-examined. Indeed, with the introduction of the dispersal plan and the deployment of weapons overseas, the lack of clarity began to affect military planning. The Chiefs of Staff argued that, 'it was urgent that some progress should be made towards establishing the Government machinery for obtaining a decision to despatch the bomber force with the minimum of delay'.[126]

The Cabinet body responsible for examining the issue was the Defence (Transition) Committee (DTC) under the chairmanship of Sir Norman Brook.[127] The DTC set itself two main objectives: first, the scope of Emergency Powers that the executive would require in a future global war; second, how these powers should be implemented. Conducting its review in secret and assuming a warning period of seven days (a timescale corresponding to an increase in international tension to a nuclear attack on the UK), the DTC examined not only the Emergency Powers that would be needed after the outbreak of war, 'but also the powers required during the period when war appeared imminent in order to carry out certain precautionary measures.'[128] The powers required by the government during this precautionary stage were far-ranging and included evacuation of twelve million people from urban centres, dispersal of key workers, arrest and detention of suspected saboteurs, requisition of vehicles, and establishment of emergency hospitals. Despite the controversial nature of these measures it was regarded as essential that the government of the day possessed the necessary Emergency Powers immediately there was reason to expect an attack on the UK.

To implement the Emergency Powers, three courses of action were available: to introduce in peacetime a Bill enabling Defence Regulations to be brought into operation by Order in Council when war was considered imminent; to rely on enactment of an Emergency Powers (Defence) Bill when the necessity arose; or to rely on the exercise of the Royal Prerogative. All three proposals presented significant difficulties. Introduction of a bill in peacetime had the advantage that there would be no time constraint to enact the relevant legislation. Against this was the argument that Parliament would be reluctant to grant such draconian powers in peacetime. It was suggested that misapprehension would be removed if the government explained that placing the proposed legislation on the Statute Book merely represented 'a prudent measure of insurance in an age of megaton weapons when a devastating offensive could be launched at short notice and so great an advantage could be gained by a surprise attack.'[129]

The second option was to introduce a bill during a period of crisis when Parliament would be less inclined to oppose the emergency powers requested by the government. However, during a period of mounting international tension HMG would primarily be engaged in attempts to prevent the outbreak of war. Consequently, there might be delay in asking for Emergency Powers for fear of escalating the conflict. As the first few hours of a nuclear war would be decisive, any delay in taking precautionary measures before the initial attack could be catastrophic. The final option for the authorisation of Emergency Powers was to exercise the Royal Prerogative. To employ the Prerogative, the Executive was required to advise the Sovereign to approve Orders in Council authorizing the use of Emergency Powers including possible use of nuclear weapons. However, to invoke the Royal Prerogative before the actual outbreak of war was considered unconstitutional and would have required either an Act of Indemnity or retrospective approval from Parliament. In these circumstances, it was considered that the use of the Royal Prerogative should only be considered by HMG as a matter of last resort and the risks involved should be accepted until Parliament could pass the necessary legislation. How Parliament would function (or indeed survive) in the event of thermonuclear attack was not clear. Nevertheless, 'whatever the physical difficulties' some form of legislative body was regarded as essential.'[130]

LAUNCH ON WARNING

The review highlighted the constitutional problems in establishing agreed procedures for launching the deterrent. With a possible decision required in only fifteen minutes (and subsequently less), it was essential to possess such authority in advance to order nuclear forces into action with the minimum of delay. In early 1958, the higher command authority for launching the deterrent was formally agreed. Based on the assumption that the final decision to commit Britain's nuclear retaliatory forces would not be taken 'until there is confirmation that an attack has been launched by the Soviet Union', the agreed measures and procedures were as follows:

(i) On receipt by the Joint Intelligence Committee of Intelligence information which indicates that the Soviet Union is likely to launch an attack, certain designated UK Ministers, the Chiefs of Staff and the US Intelligence authorities will be informed.

(ii) The Chief of the Air Staff will immediately order all possible unobtrusive measures to bring the Royal Air Force to a state of operational readiness. Further measures which would inevitably involve publicity would be considered by the Cabinet under (iv) below. The Air Ministry will inform the Commander of SAC units in this country of the action that is being taken to improve the state of readiness of the medium bomber force.

(iii) A meeting of the Cabinet will be summoned at which the Chiefs of Staff will also be present.

(iv) The Cabinet will decide, in the light of the Intelligence information, what further preparatory measures should be taken.

(v) Arrangements will be made for the Prime Minister to speak personally to the President of the US.[131]

Once a decision to launch the deterrent had been taken, two options were available: the V-force could proceed directly to assigned targets if the executive order had already been issued or remain airborne and await further instructions. This latter option increased the flexibility of the force as it allowed bombers to be launched prior to the receipt of a strike execution order. To facilitate this, the CAS was authorized, 'at his discretion', to launch the bomber force if he considered such action necessary to avoid destruction on the ground.[132] The procedure known as 'Positive Control' or 'Fail Safe' required the aircrew to make radio contact with selected stations along the route in an attempt to receive the 'go code'.[133] A central feature of the procedure was that if the bomber force reached the fail safe line (approximately forty minutes after take-off) and no order had been received, the aircraft were to return to base or designated relocation sites—in no circumstances was the target to be attacked in the absence of an authenticated order.[134] Heavily dependent on reliable communications, the concept nevertheless reinforced the primacy of political control over nuclear forces.

In contrast to the bomber force, the ballistic missile offered no such flexibility. Once launched there was no means of recall. The implications had profound consequences for the future deployment of Blue Steak, Britain's independently manufactured IRBM. Intended to supplement and eventually replace the V-force as the main delivery vehicle for Britain's strategic nuclear deterrent, Blue Streak was powered by two liquid-fuelled engines. Designed to carrying a megaton warhead 2,000 miles, the missile was to be deployed at bases in both Britain and the Middle East with an initial operational capability scheduled for 1965. Regarded as the future cornerstone of Britain's deterrent policy, Blue Streak offered the hope of retaining an invulnerable megaton capability up to 1970. Symbolic of Britain's determination to retain an independent world role, the programme reflected the uncertainties at the heart of British strategic planning in the late 1950s.[135] Specifically, would it remain in Britain's interests to retain a strategic nuclear deterrent under undivided national control? Would the government be willing to sustain the cost of such a project? And in which circumstances and against which targets would such a weapon ever be used?

To answer these questions, the BNDSG reviewed the future of 'the British controlled contribution to the deterrent'.[136] Presented to the Cabinet in December 1959, BNDSG's interim report offered a critical assessment of Blue Streak and emphasized the vulnerability of a fixed-site liquid-fuelled missile. A particular concern was reaction time. Blue Streak could be kept indefinitely at four and a half minutes readiness, and if required, held at thirty seconds' readiness for ten hours. Two and half minutes were necessary to confirm radar identification of missile attack, communicate with the launch sites, and enable the missiles to reach a sufficient height to be invulnerable to a 3 MT ground burst attack on their launch-sites. Assuming all procedures worked perfectly, seven minutes would therefore be needed to launch the force after radar contact. With the missiles at thirty seconds' readiness, this would be reduced to three minutes. The report implied that that the successful launch of some missiles could only be guaranteed if they were kept at thirty seconds' readiness, but even then only 'very few' Blue Streaks could be launched.

The prospect of granting military commanders authority to launch the deterrent on radar warning alone, however, was discounted. Earl Mountbatten, the CDS, expressed his 'gravest doubts' whether any authority would order Blue Streak to be launched before nuclear missiles had landed in the UK.[137] This was later emphasized by the BNDSG:

> As ballistic missiles cannot be recalled once they have been fired, the political decision to retaliate must also have been taken before this means of evading a pre-emptive attack can be adopted. For this evasive tactic to succeed authority would need to be delegated to order nuclear retaliation on radar warning alone. We do not believe that any democratic Government would be prepared to delegate authority in an issue of such appalling magnitude.[138]

The report placed the credibility of Blue Streak in considerable doubt. From the perspective of deterrence it might be argued that 'whatever doubts the Soviet leadership might have about the UK retaliating on radar warning alone, they would always be conscious of a risk in assuming that delegated authority to fire in these circumstances had not been given.'[139] The BNDSG, however, recommended deployment only 'if a fire-first weapon was acceptable'. The Chiefs of Staff made clear that a 'second strike philosophy' was the only tenable position for control of strategic nuclear forces,[140] and on 5 February 1960, they unanimously recommended cancellation of Blue Streak.[141] In the Defence Committee on 24 February 1960, Defence Secretary Watkinson restated HMG's policy toward the strategic nuclear deterrent:

> We shall wish to continue to maintain under our undivided control the ability to deliver a significant number of megaton warheads. It is not, however, indispensable to our objective that the means of delivery should be of our own design or manufacture, provided we can buy what we want without political conditions.[142]

Reiterating the advice of the Chiefs, Watkinson declared that it was both militarily and politically unacceptable to rely on a fire-first weapon. The Cabinet agreed and cancelled the military deployment of Blue Streak, leaving the possibility of retaining the project as a space launcher for future study. Cancellation of the IRBM nevertheless effectively put Britain out of the ballistic missile business.

THE ROLE OF THE PRIME MINISTER

Authority to use nuclear weapons depends, *inter alia*, upon a state's constitution. In Britain, the ultimate decision is taken by the Prime Minister. Ideally, this would be supported by the full Cabinet and endorsed by Parliament, which constitutes the ultimate political authority in the country. Such a decision, however, would be likely to be taken during a period of crisis and confined to a small group of ministers acting as a 'war-cabinet'. Moreover, by the early-1960s, the deployment of Soviet M/IRBMs meant that a decision to launch the deterrent could be required in minutes. To clarify the chain of command in such an eventuality, the Chiefs of Staff requested that procedures contained in the government War Book for 'alerting and releasing our nuclear retaliatory forces... should be reviewed.'[143]

The body given responsibility for conducting the review was an *ad hoc* Cabinet committee known as GEN 743. All files relating to the committee's discussions are retained.[144] However, using related source material the committee's broad conclusions can be ascertained. The purpose of the review was twofold: to examine the procedures involved in the decision to authorize nuclear retaliation; and to determine the necessary communications required by the Prime Minister and others to achieve this objective.[145]

A primary consideration was given to the role of the Prime Minister in authorizing nuclear operations. Occupying the role of *primus inter pares* within the Cabinet, the Prime Minister's powers, though considerable, were largely undefined. The issue of the Prime Minister's authority now required clarification. A motivating factor in this was the 1958 Murphy-Dean agreement. The agreement, which covered the launching of US nuclear weapons based in the UK, stipulated that the decision to commit nuclear forces would be a joint decision reached between the Prime Minister and the President of the US.[146] Thus, while it was still possible to consult with the Cabinet, this decision rested ultimately with the Prime Minister. To sanction this role, the Prime Minister assumed the Royal Prerogative that granted the exercise of executive power without recourse to Parliament or the Cabinet.[147]

The privileged position of the Prime Minister to authorize nuclear attack raises a number of salient questions. First, what are the procedures for ensuring the safety of the Prime Minister and for maintaining communications in the event of attack? Second, who would assume authority in the event of the Prime Minister's death or incapacitation? Third, what safeguards exist to prevent the Prime Minister authorizing nuclear attack if the decision was strongly opposed by the Cabinet and/or military authorities? While at present these questions cannot fully be answered, the veil of secrecy that surrounded these issues has been partially lifted.

The procedures for obtaining political authority to launch nuclear weapons are contained in the Government's War Book. The function of the War Book and its circulation within government departments was explained by the Cabinet Secretary:

> Nuclear Retaliation Procedures: The arrangements (almost finalized, following discussions with SACEUR) are summarized in a Top Secret version of Chapter 1 of the Government War Book, copies of which are only held by Departments who 'need to know'. Other Departments are unaware of the existence of this version and are in possession of an expurgated version of this Chapter which is adequate for their purposes.[148]

In times of national crisis, the normal process of Cabinet government was expected to be dissolved and executive power transferred to an *ad hoc* group of ministers functioning as a 'war cabinet'. The formation of a war cabinet was expected to occur when 'serious military operations became imminent'. At this point the government would 'be moving into the strategic warning stage, which would bring War Book planning into operation including the possibility of a small War Cabinet.'[149] To serve the war cabinet, a Transition to War Committee was to be established. Comprising the Cabinet Secretary, the Permanent Secretaries of all Departments and the Assistant Chief of the Defence Staff, its primary function was 'to advise ministers, as required, on the implementation of the Government War Book, and to co-ordinate Departmental action in a national emergency.'[150]

The procedures contained in the War Book were based on a number of assumptions. The most important, in the case of nuclear retaliation, was that the arrangements assumed that 'the Prime Minister would be available at the centre of government to hold such discussions as are necessary and to give the order to retaliate.'[151] Given the deployment of Soviet M/

IRBMs, however, all assumptions concerning the immediate availability of the Prime Minister were placed in doubt. The issue was brought to the attention of Harold Macmillan by Sir Norman Brook:

> With the development of the missile threat, there may be only a few minutes interval before the bombs land. The US authorities have set up a special unit to provide the President with communications which are supposed to be 'instantaneous' at all times wherever he may be. But, even so, I do not see how we in this country can base any practical planning on the certainty that the Prime Minister, or a nominated deputy, would be available and able to undertake the appropriate consultations, e.g. with the President of the US, within an interval of this order; nor, frankly, do I see much advantage in doing so even if it were practicable. All that we can do against this situation is to ensure that our own deterrent forces cannot be annihilated by surprise attack and that procedures have been laid down under which the most competent surviving authority can order retaliation.[152]

Given this gloomy assessment, planning provisions for the Prime Minister's survival were 'confined to the arrangements already made for his speedy removal from London in an emergency.'[153] The procedures for contacting the Prime Minister in his absence from Whitehall were also examined. These were found to consist of attempting to communicate with the Prime Minister at known points along his route. To supplement this procedure, it was suggested that use should be made of the Automobile Association, 'by installing a radio in the Prime Minister's car that would permit messages to be relayed in plain language through the Automobile Association's radio network.'[154] The details of this and other ingenious solutions for maintaining communications with the Prime Minister are discussed more fully in Chapter 6.

The concentration of political authority within the office of the Prime Minister focused attention on procedural arrangements for maintaining political control in the event of the Prime Minister's death. Without a clearly defined procedure for the transfer of executive power, the death of the Prime Minister would render Britain's deterrent useless. In the US, succession of command was clearly delineated with power transferring to the Vice President, the Speaker of the House of Representatives, the President pro tempore of the Senate, and to members of the Cabinet in order of seniority.[155] In Britain, no such succession existed. On the death of an incumbent Prime Minister the successor was chosen by the Monarch in close consultation with Palace officials. Clearly, with the prospect of nuclear annihilation only minutes away such a protracted system was no longer applicable. To retain the primacy of political control, the prior appointment of a designated successor to the Prime Minister with authority to order nuclear retaliation was considered essential. Within the Cabinet Office, the position was described as follows:

> The principle aim is to consider alternative procedures for the release of nuclear forces if the basic procedure fails. One of the proposals is to nominate a Deputy to the PM for nuclear retaliatory purposes who would act in the PM's absence. He would not, perhaps, need to be nominated except in time of tension but his functions would have to be laid down in advance.[156]

This proposal was later accepted by Macmillan who added a significant amendment of his own. Not one but two deputies to the Prime Minister were to be appointed: one of them authorized 'to act as the Prime Minister's deputy for purposes of nuclear retaliation during any period, however short, when the Prime Minister was not immediately available.'[157] What remains uncertain is whether the designated deputy was chosen from the Cabinet's order of precedence or an individual personally selected by the Prime Minister.[158] The issue is unclear as the position of deputy Prime Minister did not then exist in the British constitutional hierarchy. Indeed, in 1951 George VI specifically refused to accept Anthony Eden as deputy Prime Minister.[159] The matter was raised again in 1962, when Rab Butler was appointed as Macmillan's deputy. Informing Parliament of his decision, Macmillan stated that, 'this is not an appointment submitted to the Sovereign but is a statement of the organisation of government.'[160] The constitutional position of the designated deputy is of more than academic significance. For, as discussed below, the delegated powers given to C-in-C Bomber Command were only to be exercised if communication could not be established with either the Prime Minister or designated deputy. Consequently, the identity of the designated deputy needed to be known to those requiring such information well in advance of the Prime Minister's death or incapacitation.

A question apparently not directly addressed by GEN 743, but which is nevertheless of concern, is what safeguards exist to prevent the Prime Minister authorizing nuclear attack if the decision was strongly opposed by both the Cabinet and military authorities? If a Prime Minister went 'bananas' what could prevent him/her unleashing a nuclear holocaust? The answer, it appears, lies in the peculiarities of the British constitutional system. Only the Prime Minister can authorize the use of nuclear weapons; only the military can legally issue the order to do so.[161]

To further safeguard against one individual acting in isolation, a 'two-person' rule was introduced throughout the nuclear command chain from the Prime Minister down to the bomber crew. The procedure ensured that '*all* the individuals who have access to, or an executive function in, the system are selected using the greatest possible care, and... since no known methods of selection are infallible, some form of insurance is required, such as multiple control at each executive level.'[162] As a result, the Prime Minister could not launch nuclear weapons alone but required the assistance of another individual, widely believed to be the Chief of the Defence Staff. Incomplete codes for carrying out a nuclear strike were held by both individuals. The section held by the Prime Minister granted authorisation, that held by the CDS carried the order. Only when the two sections were brought together could a fully authenticated launch order be transmitted to Britain's nuclear forces.[163]

ALTERNATE GOVERNMENT HEADQUARTERS

To ensure a prompt retaliatory response, knowledge of the exact location of the Prime Minister at any given time was vital. Loss of contact through communications failure or enemy action would seriously delay transmission of an authenticated launch order. In routine conditions, the Prime Minister's official residence at 10 Downing Street served as the focus of executive government within London. In direct communication with all government departments and linked to a number of underground operations rooms, authority to launch the deterrent could be issued by the Prime Minister directly from the Cabinet Office in Whitehall or the Air Ministry Operations Centre. In times of crisis, however, London was regarded as a major target for a Soviet nuclear strike. In the early-1960s, to provide a secure facility for the continuation of government in the event of a nuclear strike, the Prime Minister agreed to construction of an alternate seat of government located outside London. Known as Turnstile, the facility was constructed 100 feet beneath the ground and, according to press reports, extended over 54 acres of countryside close to the Wiltshire town of Hawthorn near Bath.[164]

The concept of an alternate seat of government located away from the nation's capital first began to receive close attention in mid-1950s. In the US, anxiety about a surprise Soviet missile attack on Washington led to development of an Alternate National Military Command Center (ANMCC) located underground near Fort Ritchie, Maryland. The facility was designed to operate in isolation for thirty days and to provide 'sufficient information for ordering the execution, redirection, or termination of strategic nuclear operations.'[165] In Britain, the idea of using an underground command facility also received close attention. The arrangements for central government in the event of thermonuclear attack were described as follows:

> Ministers have accepted the view that it would be extremely unlikely that central control would continue to operate from London after attack and that the government of the UK would be conducted by a central nucleus in protected accommodation in the country. It is planned to establish two seats of government, a main and reserve, to carry out only functions essential to the prosecution of the war and the survival of the UK. One centre is to be manned in advance of war as a reserve seat of government and the other is to be available for the use of those exercising supreme direction should they at any time decide to leave London.[166]

The decision to leave London in the event of an imminent attack was governed by the Prime Minister's directive on Turnstile planning and based on 'the principle that control should remain in Whitehall for as long as possible.'[167] If attack appeared imminent, a Precautionary Stage was to be declared with MOD given primary responsibility for co-ordinating military action to launch nuclear retaliation. It was further assumed that the Prime Minister would not move to Turnstile 'until a warning of nuclear attack on this country had been received and nuclear retaliation had been authorized.'[168] The directive also explained the functions of Turnstile: to act as the seat of Government in the period of survival and reconstruction; and to be an alternative centre to London for authorizing nuclear retaliation.

The integration of Turnstile into operational military planning proved difficult. If the purpose or location of the facility became widely known, it was expected to become a prime target for Soviet attack. For the same reason, severe difficulties were also experienced with communications and are discussed in Chapter 6. It is unknown whether the Prime Minister actually set foot in Turnstile. It is however evident that as part of Fallex 62 (a NATO Command Post Exercise conducted in September 1962) a simulation of the Turnstile procedures was undertaken. The scope of this exercise was described by the Minister of Defence:

> The Prime Minister has agreed that exercise planning for the Services should include the transition from Whitehall to an alternate seat of Government to be simulated in the exercise at Wilton Park near Beaconsfield; a Committee

of senior officials should also take part in the pre-exercise play to represent both the Cabinet and the Defence Transition Committee and take in the exercise the sort of decisions which would face the Cabinet in reality at a time when war was imminent.[169]

Despite construction of Turnstile and the appointment of a designated deputy, the Prime Minister remained vulnerable. It is also probable that senior political leaders would be collocated with the Prime Minister. A Soviet nuclear decapitation attack on both Whitehall and Turnstile could therefore have removed the entire political leadership responsible for authorizing nuclear retaliation. To guard against this possibility and ensure a nuclear response, it is now clear that political authority to initiate nuclear retaliation was delegated to military commanders.

DELEGATED CONTROL

The delegation of nuclear command authority to the military is one of the most contentious and politically sensitive areas of nuclear operations. The ability of the military to initiate nuclear war without explicit authority of the political leadership fits uneasily with the traditions of a liberal democracy. Moreover, in a society in which a significant part of the population is opposed to nuclear weapons, the knowledge that military leaders possessed such power would place the government under acute political pressure. As a consequence, the issue of nuclear pre-delegation has remained shrouded in government secrecy. Recently, however, with the end of the Cold War, a small but significant number of documents have been made available which for the first time shed light on British procedures for delegating nuclear control to the military.

As has been demonstrated, British procedures for restraining unauthorized military use of nuclear weapons relied exclusively on procedural mechanisms. Nuclear weapons were deployed in operational configuration near to or aboard their delivery systems. The only safeguard against unauthorized use was the allegiance of the military officers entrusted with their possession. Whilst it could be argued that the military demands dictated by a fifteen minute (or later four minute) response time militated against negative control, it must be recognised that HMG implicitly granted *de facto* control of nuclear weapons to the military. The introduction of the two-person rule did not fundamentally alter this relationship. The codes authorizing nuclear retaliation were not required to launch the force but only indicated that the originator of the order was indeed the Prime

Minister.[170] In short, while the two-person rule maintained control at the lower levels of the command structure, in the absence of any electronic locks, senior military officers possessed the ability to order a nuclear strike even without receiving direct instructions from the Prime Minister.

The ambiguity of the command arrangements were certainly not lost on senior members of the RAF who in the early-1960s began to press for more explicit and politically sanctioned procedures that directly addressed the extent of delegated powers available to senior commanders. A particular concern was the difficulty presented by a total breakdown of communications. In March 1960, in a candid recognition of the implications, the Director of Plans at the Air Ministry put forward the following recommendation: 'I think we must be prepared to seek political approval for the C-in-C Bomber Command to launch the retaliatory force under certain circumstances. I have in mind cases either, where time does not permit prior consultation, or where communications breakdown entirely.'[171]

In the early-1960s, the extent of C-in-C's delegated powers were determined by the alert conditions specified in the Bomber Command Alert and Readiness Plan. Under this, C-in-C Bomber Command was permitted on his own discretion to order Alert Condition 3. On declaration of this alert state, the maximum number of aircraft were to be loaded with nuclear weapons and made ready for immediate take-off. Authority to order Alert Condition 2 and disperse the force, however, was not to be undertaken without political authority. If this proved impossible, the Chief of the Air Staff was granted delegated authority so that, 'at his discretion, he may order the force into the air under positive control procedure, if he deems such action necessary to avoid loss on the ground by enemy action.'[172] At no point in these procedures was the authority to initiate nuclear retaliation explicitly delegated to military commanders. However, in private discussions between the Air Staff and the C-in-C Bomber Command, it was appreciated that 'circumstances could exist... under which you would have to assume responsibility for launching the attack.'[173]

While the political implications of formally delegating nuclear use authority to the military were contentious, the consequences of denying such a request were equally disturbing: a Soviet decapitation attack could so disrupt the command and control system that the nation's nuclear forces would be left paralyzed awaiting instructions that would never arrive. In these circumstances, delegation of nuclear use authority to military commanders had much to commend it: acceptance would largely address the perceived deficiencies in command vulnerability and ensure nuclear retaliation under all conditions. In addition, if the Soviets believed that command authority had been delegated to the military it would both lessen the incentive to mount such an attack and increase the credibility of deterrence. Against such a proposal was the concern that diffusion of authority within the command structure would free the military from political control and make negotiations leading to a cease-fire impossible.

These issues were discussed by Sir Norman Brook and a small group of senior officials in May 1961, who examined the question of what alternative procedures were required by Bomber Command to despatch nuclear forces in the event of communications with Whitehall having been destroyed by nuclear attack. In abstract terms, the answer was straightforward: the Commander-in-Chief was to seek instructions from the most competent surviving authority.[174] Specifying these individuals, however, was more problematic. The expectation was that in such circumstances, the C-in-C would: 'Seek instructions from the Prime Minister or his First or Second Deputy in that order; failing that, from any Minister (such as the Secretary of State for Air) with whom he may already be in touch and whom he can consult without loss of time.'[175]

It was also appreciated that whatever procedures were adopted, they could only be undertaken 'if telephone lines exist.' A particular concern was evidence from the JIC that the Soviets were training saboteurs to knock out vital communication links in the government's nuclear control system, and 'that the Russians would do their best to strike at these, by treachery or sabotage, should they find means to do so without prejudice to surprise.'[176] Given this assessment, it was conceivable that C-in-C Bomber Command would be unable to contact anyone in the event of a Soviet surprise attack. To guard against this, it was recommended that the War Book be amended and that the Prime Minister should authorize the C-in-C, in the last resort, to order on his own responsibility nuclear retaliation by all means at his disposal.

While issuing such a directive solved the problem at hand, it introduced others. A particular concern was nuclear inadvertence or, as it was termed within MOD, 'the destruction of Russia by mistake situation'.[177] One possible scenario was that:

> Egypt acquires a nuclear bomb somehow, drops it on London and C-in-C Bomber Command then ensures that Russia, the UK and the USA are all destroyed by bombing Russia... [We must be] very careful to tie down C-in-

C Bomber Command and give him very precise instructions e.g. about getting in touch with the Americans and doing his best, by contact with any surviving authorities in NATO, to discover whether Russia launched the nuclear bomb that destroyed Whitehall, before he has a go at Russia.[178]

This dilemma was never fully resolved. However, to ensure that C-in-C Bomber Command did not order British nuclear forces into action until absolutely necessary, the Prime Minister approved the following recommendation: in the event of a 'bolt from the blue' or a situation in which the Prime Minister was not immediately available, the C-in-C was authorized to order his bombers airborne under positive control; to seek contact with the Prime Minister, his deputy or American authorities; and in the last resort, when he had confirmed that nuclear weapons had landed in the country, to order nuclear retaliation on his own responsibility.[179]

These procedures were approved by Macmillan in August 1961, and later incorporated into a Supplementary Directive issued to Sir Kenneth Cross, C-in-C Bomber Command, on 25 September 1962. The directive granted 'certain delegated powers' in the event of a surprise nuclear attack and specified the circumstances under which they were to be exercised:

> When either (a) from all possible sources of information available to you, you judge that your force in this country is about to be attacked with nuclear weapons and there has been no preceding period of strategic warning that a nuclear attack is imminent, or (b) nuclear bombs from an enemy attack have burst on this country before you have been authorised to retaliate, you are authorised:-
>
> (i) To order all bomber aircraft within your Command to be airborne under positive control in accordance with the agreed plans covering this procedure.
>
> (ii) To seek contact by any means of communication open to you with the Prime Minister or his Deputy in London or at the alternate Government War Headquarters (Burlington), and to act in accordance with his instructions.
>
> (iii) To ascertain, if possible, what instructions the Commander, 7th Air Division, has received and if [the] action above proves abortive and enemy nuclear bombs have burst in this country, to co-ordinate with the Commander 7th Air Division instructions to release nuclear weapons under joint control.
>
> If enemy nuclear bombs have burst in this country and [the] action above has proved abortive, you are authorised in the last resort to order on your own responsibility nuclear retaliation by all means at your disposal.[180]

Despite delegation of nuclear use authority to C-in-C Bomber Command retaliation was not wholly assured. In the event of a Soviet nuclear attack, High Wycombe was expected to be a major target. The C-in-C may therefore have met the same fate as the Prime Minister or designated deputy. Although contingency plans existed enabling HQ No. 1 Group at Bawtry 'to assume command in the event of the destruction of HQ Bomber Command,' there is no evidence to suggest that command authority to initiate nuclear retaliation was explicitly delegated to Group Commanders.[181] Indeed, if the C-in-C considered it necessary to delegate the authority contained in his Supplementary Directive, 'this should be brought explicitly to the attention of the Prime Minister and the Directive amended as necessary.'[182] It was nevertheless noted that the directive did not debar the C-in-C from delegating this authority. This may not have been necessary. In the event of HQ Bomber Command's destruction, the Commander of No 1 Group would then become C-in-C Bomber Command and assume all his command directives including delegated authority to initiate nuclear retaliation. Thus a Soviet decapitation attack would have the effect of devolving nuclear command authority downward within the command structure.[183]

THE POST-CUBA REVIEW

Government procedures for launching the deterrent were almost exclusively based on the assumption of at least seven days warning of global war in which Britain and the US would be jointly involved. In the aftermath of the 1962 Cuban missile crisis, discussed in Chapter 4, it became apparent that little consideration had been given to circumstances 'when there was a confrontation between the US and Russia, in which the UK was not directly involved.'[184] For Macmillan, Cuba demonstrated all too clearly the need to modify British defence planning to take account of 'a sudden emergency, in which we might have no more than two or three days warning of the outbreak of war.'[185]

A particular concern was whether HMG had sufficient time to enact the necessary legislation to obtain emergency powers. As described above, plans for the introduction of emergency powers were based on the assumption that a bill would be introduced into Parliament early in the Precautionary Stage and passed through all its stages including the Royal Assent in one day. If this proved impossible, reliance was to be placed on use of the Royal

Prerogative. These measures were contained in the Government War Book which stipulated that authority to institute the Precautionary Stage could only be given by the full Cabinet. It was realized, however that,

> If news were received at night or over the weekend of a sudden deterioration in the international situation which seemed likely to call for urgent Government War Book action, the Prime Minister might wish to institute the Precautionary Stage on his personal authority without waiting for the Cabinet to come together.[186]

A Post-Cuba review group, chaired by the Home Secretary, Henry Brook, met on 30 July 1963. It noted that the Prime Minister had already authorized the Government War Book to be amended granting him these additional powers.[187] Indeed, Macmillan never attended the meeting—another example, in the words of Peter Hennessy 'of a premier simply adding to the reach of his office on his own authority without wider ministerial, let alone Cabinet approval.'[188]

CONCLUSION

During the mid-1950s, the operational role of nuclear weapons within British strategy was uncertain. Indeed, it was unclear whether operational requirements were determined by strategy or vice versa. Of central importance to this debate was the concept of deterrence, or more specifically its interpretation and implementation. As we have seen, to those within government who favoured reductions in defence spending, the concept of deterrence was embraced. Proponents of deterrence, however, tended to conceptualize both nuclear weapons and their associated control systems as unproblematic technological 'black boxes' around which a strategy could be easily constructed.[189] Contingent upon this belief was the assumption that the mere possession of nuclear weapons, in combination with a modern bomber force and the will to use them, would itself constitute an effective deterrent.

To those charged with implementing a strategy based on nuclear deterrence, this proposition was extremely dangerous. The Air Staff, for example, argued that 'strategy should not be based on the misguided idea of thinking that anything is a deterrent which is not absolutely sound operationally or accept a paper solution which would lead to a hollow "hotch potch" in practice'.[190] Although there was awareness of the extreme financial difficulties facing all the services, there was equal determination that this should not be used as an excuse for the introduction of unsound operational thought and practice. The debate over the dispersal plan for the V-force and the use of RATO clearly demonstrate these conflicting views and highlight the difficulties faced by HMG in its attempt to develop a credible deterrent within a limited defence budget.

A further issue that emerges from study of this early period is the problem of implementing a command and control system in a rapidly changing strategic environment. In the mid-1950s, the British nuclear arsenal was relatively small. Given an extended warning period and limited dispersal, continued political control in the event of enemy attack was considered largely unproblematic. Indeed, the command and control of nuclear forces during this early period was not a major concern within either government or military circles. This position is reflected in the 1953 political directive governing the use of nuclear weapons which merely stated that the Air Ministry could not remove atomic weapons from the UK without express permission of the Cabinet. By the late-1950s, however, the situation had changed: deployment of Soviet M/IRBMs reduced reaction time, increasing the vulnerability of V-force bases to attack, whilst Soviet missile defences threatened the ability of the bomber force to reach its assigned targets. To counter these developments a variety of measures were adopted. First, the alert and readiness procedures for the V-force were improved and additional dispersal sites made available. Second, the minimum deterrent capability was redefined and reduced from the destruction of forty Soviet cities to the more attainable goal of a fifteen and then a five-city criterion. Third, positive control procedures were adopted allowing the V-force to become airborne on radar warning alone. The capability of the V-force to be recalled in the event of a false alarm did not apply to ballistic missiles such as Blue Streak which, once launched, could not be recalled. To launch Blue Streak on radar warning alone would therefore have required the adoption of a hair trigger: a possibility ruled out by both the government and Chiefs of Staff. The Blue Streak episode clearly suggests that although financial considerations were important, the critical factor in the cancellation was the command vulnerability associated with a fixed-site missile. [191]

Reduction in warning time had important implications for custody and political control and raised unresolved constitutional issues that the government was required to address. Indeed, prior to the late-1950s command

and control issues were almost exclusively *post hoc* arrangements. This tendency was clearly apparent in custodial arrangements for Violet Club which were considered of secondary importance to the central political goal of demonstrating a megaton capability at the earliest possible opportunity: a finding that supports the view that newly emerging nuclear states will make weapons development a priority over nuclear safety because of limited financial resources and the technical complexity of safety systems.[192]

With the deployment of weapons overseas and response time reduced to minutes such arrangements could not continue. To ensure nuclear retaliation and eliminate accidental or unauthorized use a formalised command and control procedure was urgently required. To achieve this, a number of measures were adopted. First, to provide a unified nuclear strike plan and define service responsibilities, the Nuclear Strike Co-ordinating Committee was established. Second, to provide continuity of political leadership, the Prime Minister appointed a designated deputy with authority to launch Britain's nuclear forces. Third, to retain central command authority in the event of a decapitation attack, an Alternate Government Headquarters was constructed as an alternative centre to London for authorizing nuclear retaliation. Despite these measures transmission of the executive order could not be guaranteed. To ensure retaliation, nuclear authority was delegated to the military as a last resort. In the event of a Soviet nuclear attack and the destruction of Britain's political leadership, Bomber Command was directed to launch a nuclear assault on the urban population of the USSR by all means available.

1. In April 1954, No. 1321 Flight was established at Wittering to undertake armaments trials. In February 1956, 1321 Flight was renamed C Flight and established with six modified Valiants. Two of these were later assigned to Operation Buffalo (Britain's first airborne trial of an atomic bomb) that took place in Edinburgh Field, South Australia, on 11 October 1956.
2. Cmnd. 124, *Defence: Outline of Future Policy* (HMSO, 1957). For discussion, see Navias, *Nuclear*, Chapter 5.
3. AIR 8/1998, RR(Ad Hoc)(53)8, 17 February 1953.
4. DEFE 5/47, COS(53)328, 8 July 1953.
5. For details, see Lorna Arnold, *UK H-Bomb* (Macmillan, 1999 forthcoming).
6. CAB 134/1315, PR(56)3, 1 June 1956.
7. For details of the Future Policy Committee, see Michael Carver, *Tightrope Walking: British Defence Policy Since 1945* (Hutchinson, 1992), pp. 63-4.
8. AIR 4/86, T.C.G. James, *Defence Policy and the Royal Air Force 1956-1963*, (MOD, Air Historical Branch, 1987) p. 194.
9. The report was circulated as C(60)35, 29 February 1960 and is closed for 50 years. It is located at CAB 129/100.

NATIONAL CONTROL 1953-1964

10. Cmnd. 1639, *Statement on Defence 1962: The Next Five Years* (HMSO, 1962).
11. CAB 131/28, D(62)43, considered at D(62)12th, 31 July 1962.
12. DEFE 4/149, JP(62)Note 23, 5 November 1962; James, *Defence*, p. 222.
13. DEFE 4/150, JP(62)134(Final), 3 December 1962.
14. CAB 131/16, DC2(55)5, 2 May 1955.
15. For details, see Navias, *Nuclear*, pp. 165-70.
16. CAB 131/18, D(57)7th, 2 August 1957.
17. AIR 8/2238, Bomber Strategy, 24 November 1954.
18. AIR 8/1998, Size of the Medium Bomber Force, June 1954.
19. AIR 8/2238, Outline Plan for Dispersal of the V-Force, 24 November 1954.
20. Ibid.
21. AIR 20/10277, MBF, Readiness During a Period of Tension, 28 September 1956.
22. AIR 8/2313, Dispersal Plan for the V-Force, 17 January 1955
23. AIR 8/2313, Mills to Dickson, 23 May 1955.
24. Ibid.
25. AIR 8/2313, Medium Bomber Dispersal Airfields, 8 August 1957.
26. Cmnd. 363, *Report on Defence: Britain's Contribution to Peace and Security* (HMSO, 1958).
27. AIR 8/2238, MOM/44, Readiness of Bomber Command, 21 July 1958.
28. AIR 28/1657, Alert Measures and Readiness Procedures, June 1959.
29. AIR 8/2238, Progress Report on the Readiness of the MBF, 1 June 1959. This exercise was conducted under the codename HALBARB I and according to MOD officials highlighted the fact that 'the present War Book arrangements for launching the deterrent were relatively simple.' DEFE 25/49 Nuclear Retaliation Procedures, 13 March 1961.
30. Within Bomber Command these exercises were codenamed Mick, Mayflight, and Mickey Finn respectively.
31. DEFE 7/980, Medium Bomber Readiness and Dispersal, 21 October 1960.
32. AIR 8/2400, D(58)24, 5 November 1958.
33. DEFE 7/1328, BND(SG)(59)19(Final), 31 December 1959.
34. Ibid.
35. AIR 8/2313, Dispersal Plan for the V-Force, 17 January 1955.
36. AIR 8/2313, CAS to AMSO, 21 January 1955.
37. AB 16/545, Penney to Plowden, 31 March 1954.
38. AIR 8/2313, Dispersal of the MBF, 17 November 1955.
39. AIR 20/11447, 10,000 lb. H.E. M.C. Bomb, 23 November 1955.
40. AIR 8/2313, Mark 2 Atomic Weapon, undated.
41. AIR 8/2313, Mills to CAS, 17 December 1955.
42. AIR 20/11447, Medium Bomber Dispersal, 12 April 1956.
43. AVIA 65/1155, Progress Report on the 10,000 lb. H.E M.C. Bomb, 16 March 1955.
44. AIR 8/2313, Dispersal Policy, 28 November 1955.
45. Stephen Twigge, *The Early Development of Guided Weapons in the UK 1940-1960* (Harwood Academic Press, 1993), pp. 20-30.
46. AIR 8/2313, Brief for CAS, 12 April 1956.
47. AIR 8/2313, Note by VCAS, June 1956.
48. Ibid.
49. AIR 8/2313, RATO for the V-Force, 18 June 1956.
50. AIR 8/2313, The Dispersal and Operation of the Medium Bomber and Photographic Reconnaissance Force in the UK, 5 July 1956.
51. See Lorna Arnold, *The Third Power and the H-Bomb*, (forthcoming 2000).
52. Wynn, *RAF*, p. 245.
53. AVIA 65/774, Notes of Meeting, 17 April 1958.
54. AIR 2/13705, D.Ops to ACAS, 28 April 1959.

55. AIR 2/13705, D.Ops to ACAS(Ops), 18 June 1959. The 'safety device' appears to have entailed filling the warhead with ball bearings to prevent criticality; these could then be removed by opening a funnel on the lower side of the warhead. AVIA 65/1218.
56. Wynn, *RAF*, p. 248, emphasis added.
57. AVIA 65/1155, Examination of Blue Danube and Yellow Sun Warheads, 14 August 1959.
58. AVIA 65/774, Notes of Meeting, 29 April 1958. Initiated in July 1955, Yellow Sun Mk I was designed to meet Air Staff Requirement OR1136, and incorporated the Green Grass warhead. Developed for reliability, it met the requirements of OR1136, in contrast to Violet Club 'which had been accepted with the minimum of proof and clearance testing and fell short of OR1136 in many respects.' Wynn, *RAF*, p. 246.
59. Ibid., p. 266.
60. DEFE 7/2239, JP(60)122(Final), 2 December 1960. Under development since 1954, Red Beard was a small tactical nuclear weapon with a variable yield of between 1-10 kilotons.
61. DEFE 7/980, Watkinson to Macmillan, 21 June 1961. It has also been reported that in addition to Red Beard the RAF also stored Yellow Sun thermonuclear weapons at RAF Akrotiri.
62. AIR 8/2530, Policy Directive for Dispersal of the NEAF, 21 December 1964.
63. Eric Grove, *Vanguard to Trident* (Bodley Head, 1987), pp. 98-100, 108.
64. DEFE 32/6, COS(60)66th, Statement by FSL, 26 October 1960.
65. DEFE 7/1676, D(59)2, Minister's brief, 22 January 1959.
66. DEFE 7/679, The Implications of the Admiralty Proposal to Store Nuclear Weapons in Aircraft Carriers, 1 September 1958.
67. Malcolm Spaven, *Royal Navy Nuclear Capable Ships*, (ADIU, University of Sussex, 1985).
68. DEFE 7/679, Gough to Mottershead, 22 July 1958.
69. DEFE 7/1676, FSL to CONS of RAN, RCN, RNZN, 6 February 1959.
70. DEFE 11/311, COS(59)72, 25 March 1959; DCC(59)2, 18 February 1959; DCC(FE)(59)288, 3 September 1959.
71. DEFE 11/311, Annex to COS(59)72, 25 March 1959.
72. Ibid.
73. Solly Zuckerman, *Monkeys, Men and Missiles* (Collins, 1985), p. 294; see also his contribution to a SHAPE symposium in May 1961, revised and published in *Scientists and War* (Hamish Hamilton, 1966), pp. 101-21.
74. For details, see Chapter 5.
75. Initiated in 1956, Blue Water was a ground-to-ground artillery rocket able to deliver a nuclear warhead up to 300 km. Intended to replace the US-supplied Corporal missile, Blue Water was air transportable and used solid propellant. Possessing high operational mobility, the missile was intended for deployment with British forces serving in NATO, CENTO or the Far East. For details, see Peter Morton, *Fire Across the Desert: Woomera and the Anglo-Australian Joint Project 1946-1980* (AGPS: Canberra, 1989), pp. 345-6.
76. AVIA 65/1047, Watkinson to CDS, 26 February 1962.
77. AVIA 65/1047, AC/P(62)7, 9 March 1962.
78. CAB 131/18, D(57)2nd, 27 February 1957.
79. Zuckerman, *Monkeys*, p. 248
80. CAB 128/36, CC(62)53, 3 August 1962.
81. Ibid.
82. Scott Sagan, 'SIOP-62: The Nuclear War Plan Briefing to President Kennedy', *International Security*, Vol.12, No.1 (Summer 1987).
83. AIR 20/10056, COS(61)262, 10 August 1961.
84. Air 20/10056, Record of Meeting, 28 June 1961.
85. For UK/US planning in the Far East, see Chapter 4.
86. Air 20/10056, Record of Meeting, 6 February 1962.

87. AIR 20/10056, Initiation and Control of Nuclear Strikes in Overseas Theatres, 21 December 1962. Later circulated as COS 118/63. For details of communications, see Chapter 6.
88. DEFE 4/154, COS(63)29th, 25 April 1963.
89. DEFE 4/151, JP(62)110(Final), 17 January 1963, extract from JIC(62)70(Final).
90. COS(63)29th.
91. DEFE 4/155, COS 118/63, 10 May 1963.
92. CAB 131/12, D(52)26, 17 June 1952.
93. AIR 8/1998, COS(53)114, RAF Medium Bomber Policy, 21 February 1953.
94. AIR 20/7765, ACAS(I) Briefing, 10 February 1954.
95. DEFE 5/40, COS(52)361, 15 July 1952.
96. AIR 8/1998, ACAS(I) to CAS, 27 April 1953.
97. CAB 129/71, C(54)329, 3 November 1954.
98. See Baylis, *Ambiguity*, pp. 190-1.
99. DEFE 11/101, Secretary of State for Air to Minister of Defence, 23 March 1955.
100. PREM 11/1191, CAS to PM, 14 February 1955.
101. DEFE 5/49, COS(53)519, 21 October 1953.
102. Clark and Wheeler, *British*, p. 194; Baylis, *Ambiguity*, pp. 93-5, 376-7.
103. DEFE 4/70, COS(54)45th, 22 April 1954.
104. AIR 2/15917, Mills to ACAS(Ops), 13 April 1955.
105. CAB 131/18, D(57)2nd, Confidential Annex, 27 February 1957.
106. The report, JP(57)10, was reviewed by the MOD in 1994 but was still considered too sensitive to be released.
107. AIR 8/2400, ACAS(P) to CAS, 24 May 1957.
108. AIR 20/11338, Extract from JP(57)10, ACAS(P) to CAS, 15 May 1957.
109. Progress Report on Readiness of MBF.
110. AIR 8/2400, DB(58)10, 30 October 1958.
111. AIR 8/2201, COS(58)148, 5 June 1958.
112. AIR 19/999, BND(SG)(62)1, 22 January 1962.
113. For further discussion, see Clark, *Nuclear*, pp. 388-90.
114. AIR 19/999, BND(SG)(62)1st, 24 January 1962, extract from JIC(62)10(Final), 23 January 1962.
115. PREM 11/3716, Record of Meeting, 7 March 1962.
116. AIR 2/13714, BND(SG)/P(62)8, 10 April 1962. These figures were based on Moscow and Leningrad representing 4 and 2 targets respectively.
117. AIR 8/2530, Command Directive to Air Marshal Sir Kenneth Cross, 21 May 1962.
118. AIR 8/2530, Command Directive to Air Marshal Sir John Grandy, 15 October 1963.
119. AIR 19/999, BND(SG)(62)4th, 18 December 1962.
120. DEFE 4/160, Confidential Annex to COS(63)68th, Part 1, 3 December 1963.
121. AIR 20/10277, Bomber Command - Authority and Control, 19 November 1957.
122. AIR 2/15917, Cross to D.Ops, 10 July 1953.
123. AIR 2/15917, ACAS(P) to VCAS, 16 May 1955.
124. AIR 20/10277, MBF, Readiness During a Period of Tension, 28 September 1956.
125. AIR 20/10277, Bomber Alert and Readiness Plan, 12 December 1957.
126. AIR 20/11338, Confidential Annex to COS(57)72nd, 23 September 1957.
127. The DTC was assisted in its work by two further bodies: the Sub-Committee on Machinery of Government in War and the War Book Sub-Committee.
128. DEFE 7/728, Defence Committee, Emergency Powers, Memorandum by Chairman of the Defence (Transition) Committee, undated.
129. Ibid.
130. DEFE 13/321, Review of Government War Book Planning in the Light of the Cuba Crisis, 21 May 1963.

131. RG 59, Policy Planning Staff Records, 1957-61, Lot 67D548, Box 130, Great Britain, Launching of Nuclear Reprisal, Aide Mémoire, 14 May 1958, National Archives. We are grateful to William Burr for drawing our attention to this document.
132. DEFE 7/373, COS(59)1, 1 January 1959.
133. In August 1962, to increase reliability of communications, the Air Ministry authorised deployment of an airborne command post to ensure communications to the medium bomber force without recourse to landlines. After Skybolt's cancellation, the project was abandoned.
134. AIR 2/16433, Meeting with CAS, 15 January 1964.
135. For discussion of Blue Streak, see Baylis, *Ambiguity*, pp. 279-88, 377; Clark, *Nuclear*, pp. 157-190; Navias, *Nuclear*, pp. 119-124.
136. BND(SG)(59)19.
137. DEFE 25/13, Minute from CDS, 30 September 1959.
138. BND(SG)(59)19.
139. AIR 19/998, BND(SG)(59)9th, 19 November 1959.
140. DEFE 7/2228, Watkinson to CDS, 25 July 1960.
141. AIR 19/891, COS(60)28, 5 February 1960.
142. AIR 19/891, Memorandum by the Minister of Defence, 16 February 1960.
143. DEFE 32/6, COS(61)9th, 7 February 1961.
144. GEN 743 files remain closed, and are located at CAB 130/177. In 1964, its functions were transferred to the Cabinet Committee on Nuclear Retaliation Procedures. These files are also closed and are located at DEFE 24/228-30.
145. DEFE 25/49, GEN 743/10(Revise), 23 January 1962.
146. For details of the Murphy-Dean Agreement, see Chapter 4.
147. See Chapter 1.
148. CAB 21/4350, Brook to PM, 20 August 1960.
149. PREM 11/3815, Brook to Sir Frank Lee, 25 August 1961.
150. CAB 134/2554, Transition to War Committee, Terms of Reference, 24 November 1961. The committee absorbed the functions of the Defence (Transition) Committee.
151. AIR 2/16433, Extract from GEN 743/2, 23 August 1961.
152. Ibid.
153. DEFE 25/49, Brook to Mountbatten, 20 April 1961.
154. DEFE 25/49, Nuclear Retaliation Procedures: Communications, 30 January 1961.
155. For details, see Gregory, *Nuclear*, pp. 82-5.
156. DEFE 25/49, Brief for Brook, 3 May 1961.
157. GEN 743/10.
158. The Cabinet order of precedence was decided by the Prime Minister 'according to his wishes'. In 1958 the order was: Prime Minister, Home Secretary, Lord Chancellor, Foreign Secretary, Chancellor of the Exchequer, Commonwealth Secretary, Secretary of State for Scotland, Lord President, Minister of Defence, President of the Board of Trade, CAB 21/4326, Brook to Prime Minister, 6 January1958.
159. Vernon Bogdanor, *The Monarchy and the Constitution* (OUP, 1995), p. 87.
160. *HC Deb.*, Vol.663, Col.633, 19 July 1962.
161. For a discussion of this division, see Peter Hennessy, *The Prime Minister: The Office and its Holders since 1945* (Penguin, 2000, forthcoming).
162. AIR 20/1113, A Study of Human Factors in Strategic Deterrent Systems for the UK, May 1958. Emphasis in original document.
163. Gregory, *Nuclear*, p. 106.
164. Duncan Campbell, 'Maggie's Bunker', *New Statesman*, 24 September 1982. For details see, Nick McCamley, *Secret Underground Cities* (Leo Cooper, 1999). In its early stages, the complex was given the codenames Burlington and Stockwell.
165. Wainstein, *Evolution*, p. 315.

166. AIR 8/2376, CIC(56)26, UK Command Structure in War, 6 June 1956.
167. The Prime Minister's directive on Turnstile planning is contained in DH(O)(MG)(61)20. The document is still retained, extracts can be found in DEFE 4/152, Confidential Annex to COS(63)17th, 28 February 1963; DEFE 5/136, Annex to COS 96/63, 4 March 1963.
168. DEFE 25/49, Brook to Mountbatten, 20 April 1961.
169. CAB 131/27, D(62)10, 6 February 1962. Wilton Park was located 18 miles from Fighter Command HQ and 28 miles from London. In war it was designated to serve both as the Joint Headquarters for the UK C-in-Cs Committee and GHQ UK Land Forces.
170. Gregory, *Nuclear*, p. 106.
171. AIR 20/10620, D.Ops. to VCAS, 3 March 1960.
172. DEFE 7/373, COS(59)1, 1 January 1959.
173. AIR 8/2238, VCAS to Cross, 11 August 1959.
174. DEFE 25/49, Meeting with Brook, 3 May 1961.
175. DEFE 25/49, Playfair to Mountbatten, 26 June 1961.
176. GEN 743/10, extract from JIC(61)29(Final).
177. DEFE 25/49, Brief for Mountbatten, 13 March 1961.
178. Ibid.
179. Extract from GEN 743/2, 23 August 1961.
180. AIR 8/2530, Supplementary Directive to Air Marshal Sir Kenneth Cross, 25 September 1962. The directive is reproduced in full in Appendix 2.
181. AIR 19/964, Command Organisation, February 1960.
182. AIR 2/16433, Nuclear Release Procedures, 13 July 1965.
183. The delegation of nuclear command in Britain mirrored procedures adopted in the USA. Testifying to Congress in 1960, CINCSAC, General Power acknowledged that 'arrangements existed for him to launch a retaliatory strike after verifying that an enemy nuclear strike was under way in circumstances in which the President was not available.' Blair, *Logic*, p. 49.
184. DEFE 13/212, Record of Meeting between the Minister of Defence and Chiefs of Staff, 28 October 1962.
185. DEFE 13/321, Trend to Thorneycroft, 21 May 1963.
186. Ibid. Review of Government War Book.
187. DEFE 13/321, Trend to Macmillan, 1 August 1963.
188. Hennessy, *Prime*.
189. Steven Flank, 'Exploding the Black Box: The Historical Sociology of Nuclear Proliferation', *Security Studies*, Vol.3, No.2 (Winter 1994).
190. AIR 8/2313, Mills to CAS, 23 May 1955.
191. For further discussion, see Clark, *Nuclear*, pp. 176-89 and Baylis, *Ambiguity*, pp. 285-8.
192. Lewis Dunn, *Containing Nuclear Proliferation*, Adelphi Paper No. 263 (IISS, 1991), p. 20.

Chapter 4

Bilateral Control 1953–1964

'The officer exchange program does not give you any special prerogative to question my orders' (General Jack D. Ripper to Group Captain Lionel Mandrake, DSO, DFC, RAF exchange officer, Burpelson Air Force Base).

The 1950s were the period when Britain's political illusions were dispelled by economic and military realities. Yet nuclear weapons proffered some prospect of political power as well as military security. During the 1950s Britain pursued the development of an independent deterrent while seeking nuclear co-operation with the United States. A primary motive for this dual strategy was to gain access to US nuclear weapons prior to the completion of Britain's own indigenous weapons programme. This chapter explores the various political initiatives undertaken by HMG to attain this objective. Attention is first focused on the transfer of US nuclear weapons to the RAF with particular emphasis on development of bilateral control arrangements between the two countries. Co-ordination of nuclear strike plans between the two airforces and the deployment of US IRBMs in the United Kingdom are also explored. Particular attention is given to the Murphy-Dean agreement which established procedures for the use of nuclear weapons by US forces stationed in Britain and the Holy Loch agreement which allowed US Polaris submarines to operate in British territorial waters. The significance of these agreements is examined against the background of the Cuban missile crisis of October 1962. Finally, a detailed analysis is provided of the Nassau agreement negotiated between Macmillan and Kennedy in December 1962 and its consequences for the future command and control of the British nuclear deterrent.

For Britain, a prime objective was the creation of a genuine transatlantic nuclear alliance. To achieve this, Macmillan formulated the policy of interdependence, in which both countries would pool their nuclear resources for the common good. The policy had its limits as Britain's continued control of its nuclear deterrent was not negotiable. British policy was also motivated by the conviction that possession of nuclear weapons gave Britain an elevated international status and offered a restraint on possible American adventurism. Washington considered a nuclear duopoly divisive and remained committed to the creation of a fully integrated Europe and a more flexible NATO strategy. Formulated under Eisenhower, the policy was pressed with renewed vigour by the Kennedy administration. A dominant theme of the new strategy was both to raise the nuclear threshold and provide limited and controlled nuclear strikes. To do this required substantial increases in NATO's conventional capability coupled to a centralized command structure under US control. In this context, small national deterrents were viewed by the Kennedy administration as expensive, potentially destabilising and encouraging nuclear proliferation. The implications were clear. Britain's continued status as a nuclear power was placed under threat.

PROJECT E

The early-1950s were anxious and uncertain times for British defence planners. While Britain had demonstrated its ability to develop a nuclear weapon, full-scale production would take several years. Moreover, the RAF's strategic bomber force would not be ready until the mid-1950s. In the interim, Britain was without a deterrent against atomic attack: a vulnerability intensified by explosion of the Soviet H-bomb in 1953. Britain was therefore compelled to rely on the atomic strike power of the United States. A visible manifestation of this policy was the increase in American nuclear forces stationed in the UK, which by October 1953 amounted to twenty-seven bases occupied by the US Third Air Force and fifteen by SAC's 7th Air Division.[1] Despite the deployment of American nuclear forces in the UK, HMG was still refused access to US nuclear material, war plans and targeting.

Britain's desire for access to the US nuclear stockpile had been a persistent goal of successive governments after 1945. The terms of the 1946 McMahon Act, however, prohibited transfer of nuclear technology to foreign nationals. The election of Eisenhower in 1952 portended a change in American policy. More sympathetic to the British position, the new President had long disapproved of the McMahon Act. Meeting with Churchill at Bermuda in December 1953, Eisenhower proposed giving Britain details of the external characteristics of US nuclear weapons, information required by the RAF to carry US nuclear weapons in the event of global war.[2] Eisenhower also promised to amend the McMahon Act. Legislation detailing this policy was later included in the President's State of the Union message delivered to Congress. On 30 August, the 1954 Atomic Energy Act became law.[3]

Despite Eisenhower's more liberal attitude to nuclear sharing, progress remained slow. In an attempt to force the American hand, Duncan Sandys, the Minister of Supply visited Washington and bluntly told the President that:

> Our [Britain's] comparatively small output of atomic weapons would not justify a bomber force of the size which we had planned. Consequently, we should very likely feel obliged to reduce our programme substantially—unless, of course, the United States should decide to supply us with some of their bombs until such time as we had built up a sufficient stockpile of our own.[4]

In response, Eisenhower confirmed that in the event of war Britain would be allocated US atomic bombs. Churchill was delighted: Britain's nuclear ambitions would be realized prior to successful completion of her indigenous programme.[5] When the Defence Committee considered the proposal, it was informed that the RAF had already begun to convert their Canberra bombers to carry US atomic weapons, and that: 'The United States Air Force will maintain in the United Kingdom, at their bases, facilities for the storage, assembly and loading of United States atomic weapons on to British aircraft.'[6] The transfer of US atomic weapons to the British, however, was only expected to take place in war. As a consequence, it was considered imperative to preserve Britain's independence 'by continuing to produce our own bombs and the means of delivering them.'[7]

In December 1954, three USAF officers from the Pentagon's Special Weapons Center visited Britain to obtain specifications on RAF aircraft, suggest modifications and allocate the most suitable US nuclear weapon for each aircraft. The aircraft studied included the three V-bombers, the Canberra Light Bomber and the Javelin all-weather fighter.[8] The sensitive nature of the visit and the close co-operation of the two airforces is exemplified in a memorandum from the British Air Force Secretariat in Washington to the Air Ministry which stated that, 'USAF representatives will be coming to London regarding Project E, they will be in civilian clothes and do not wish to notify either the US Air Attaché or Embassy.'[9]

The US team submitted detailed modifications to the Air Ministry, which were used in a series of flight tests at RAF Sculthorpe. The transfer of US nuclear weapons to the RAF was more problematic. According to a review of the project by the Secretary of State for Air and submitted to the Prime Minister: 'There is a prospect that, *in war*, we may be able to obtain some nuclear bombs from the United States stockpile in this country. But I do not think we can count upon the Americans changing their present attitude so as to allow us to acquire physical possession of any of their bombs *in peace*.'[10]

Project E, as the programme came to be known, was specifically a British-American arrangement and outside the remit of NATO. The nuclear weapons covered by the agreement were to be stored under US custody and could only be transferred to the RAF after US custodians had received Presidential authority. However, in time of war the British government had agreed that Bomber Command's Canberra force should be deployed according to SACEUR's tactical requirements. The agreement was therefore divided into two parts. The first applied to the RAF Canberras based in the UK and West Germany and assigned to SACEUR, the second applied to arrangements for supplying US nuclear weapons to the V-force.

Domestic sensibilities also played a part in the development of Project E. The impact of the Suez crisis caused both parties to reassess the consequences of the deployment. For the UK, the project offered the opportunity of displaying solidarity between the two countries. In October 1956 (in an attempt to consolidate his precarious domestic position), Eden proposed a joint public statement regarding the existence of Project E. Eisenhower considered this inadvisable, as he was keen to distance his administration from the events in the Middle East during a US election period.[11] Eisenhower's refusal to sanction a public statement raised difficulties. To authorize modifications for the Canberra and V-bombers, the Air Ministry required Treasury approval. The Treasury, however, refused to sanction payment until formal agreement was reached. The response caused consternation within the Air Ministry who demanded that if detailed agreements were required in 'chapter and verse' it would need to be raised 'at the top political level.'[12]

THE CO-ORDINATION OF NUCLEAR STRIKE PLANS

The lack of any formal agreement concerning the supply of American nuclear weapons was soon rectified. In August 1955, CAS Sir William

Dickson, received a formal invitation from his opposite number, General Nathan Twining, to visit Washington 'to discuss certain matters with the USAF.'[13] Informing his fellow Chiefs, it was agreed that the primary objective of the talks should be to obtain American agreement that the strategic air offensive would be jointly conducted. Clarification was also required on the most effective command structure. The issue had been previously studied by the JPS who raised the following tentative suggestion, which echoed the arrangements of the Combined Bomber Offensive of 1944:

> There might be some advantage if our medium bomber force together with the United States Strategic Air Command was placed under a United States Supreme Commander, provided we could ourselves provide the Deputy Supreme Commander. We would still retain the actual control of the bombers and, at the same time, be able to obtain far more knowledge of US plans than we could at present.[14]

More contentious was the JPS's proposal to create a 'covert' combined Chiefs of Staff Committee to which the Supreme Allied Commander of the strategic air forces would be directly responsible. It was argued that only by such an arrangement in peacetime could the higher direction of the offensive be maintained 'especially for the critical phase when centralized control is likely to break down.'[15] Reviewing the proposal, the Chiefs of Staff concluded that, while 'a covert organisation was out of the question,' it might be necessary in war to appoint a Supreme Commander allied strategic air forces.[16] Aware of the benefits of a co-ordinated offensive, the Chiefs recommended that joint studies on the subject should be conducted between the two airforces provided 'they are under the general direction of the United Kingdom Chiefs of Staff and the United States Joint Chiefs of Staff.'

In his meeting with Twining, CAS was informed that real co-operation between the two airforces would only occur 'if the RAF had nuclear weapons; if the RAF had a bomber force; and if the RAF showed it was an effective operational force...because, whether it liked it or not, the US government would have to accept the reality of it.'[17] By mid-1956, the first Valiant squadrons armed with Blue Danube nuclear weapons were entering service with Bomber Command. Accepting that the RAF was now an operational nuclear force, the Americans sent a team of senior airforce officers to London to discuss future operations. The meeting between the two airforces took place in August 1956 and resulted in outline arrangements for co-ordination of nuclear strike plans, the provision of US nuclear weapons for the RAF in the event of war, a concept of Allied atomic air operations and a brief plan of action.[18] Writing to CAS (Sir Dermot Boyle), on 12 December 1956, Twining reiterated the proposal and confirmed that the measures had recently been approved by the Secretary of Defense and the US Joint Chiefs and requested formal approval 'at appropriate levels of authority within your government.'[19]

In early-January 1957, the Chiefs of Staff approved the American proposal with the following qualifications. First, the agreement would not prejudice Britain's right to determine the size of the V-force or the number of nuclear weapons produced. Second, Britain's national control of the RAF bomber force would not be relinquished by the co-ordination of nuclear strike plans.[20] In late-January, the newly appointed Minister of Defence, Duncan Sandys, flew to Washington. In an exchange of letters with his US counterpart, Charles Wilson, the proposals received government sanction. To facilitate agreement, approval was granted for Sir Dermot Boyle to initiate discussions with both General Twining and SACEUR General Norstad. Command authority governing the use of US nuclear weapons was also elaborated. The details were conveyed to Sandys in the following terms:

> With respect to measure No 1 [transfer of US nuclear weapons] the provisions of United States legislation must govern and that the United States cannot engage in a commitment to transfer custody of such weapons to the Royal Air Force other than by Presidential decision in strict accordance with his constitutional and legislative authority.[21]

Inter-service discussions on the practicalities of transferring US nuclear weapons to the RAF were initiated in March 1957.[22] The agreed conditions were in two parts. The first applied to the Canberra force assigned to SACEUR, whilst the second concerned arrangements for supplying US weapons to the V-force. Although similar storage conditions were required in each case, the command arrangements were treated separately. Modifications to the Canberras were designed to allow the aircraft to carry the US Mark 7 nuclear weapon, which had a variable yield of 9, 30 or 60 kilotons, depending on the core selected.[23] Initially, the weapon chosen for the V-bombers was the US Mark 5, with a yield of between 40-50 kilotons. The Mark 5 weapon had advantages for the

British: the same release gear was required for the carriage of US megaton weapons.[24]

The possibility of Britain acquiring US megaton weapons was one of the items discussed by the new Prime Minister, Harold Macmillan, and President Eisenhower at the Bermuda Conference in March 1957. The renewal of nuclear co-operation engendered at the conference proved fruitful for the British. In relation to the control and supply of US nuclear weapons, the President confirmed the following memorandum:

> The United Kingdom Government welcome the agreement to co-ordinate the strike plans of the United States and United Kingdom bomber forces, and to store United States nuclear weapons on RAF airfields under United States custody for release subject to decision by the President in an emergency. We understand that for the present at least these weapons will be in the kiloton range. The United Kingdom forces could obviously play a much more effective part in joint strikes if United States weapons made available to them in emergency were in the megaton range, and it is suggested that this possibility might be examined at the appropriate time.[25]

In July 1958, Macmillan and Eisenhower signed the *Agreement for Cooperation on Uses of Atomic Energy for Mutual Defence Purposes* which restored nuclear collaboration between the two countries.[26] The first fully co-ordinated strike plan between the two airforces came into operation on 1 October 1958. In the Plan, which was to be reviewed on an annual basis, Bomber Command was given responsibility for destruction of 106 targets, which included 69 cities, 17 airbases and 20 installations of the Soviet air defence system. To further integrate the two airforces, Bomber Command was authorized to work through the US Joint Co-ordination Center at Ruislip which housed the US Chiefs of Staff agency in the UK for the co-ordination of US atomic strike forces.[27]

The first nuclear weapon supplied to the RAF under Project E was the US Mk 5, with transfer to RAF bases occurring in October 1958.[28] To carry the weapons, nine squadrons of the V-force were modified and by 1 January 1959, 72 aircraft at three Bomber Command stations were capable of delivering US nuclear weapons.[29] Under US law custodial officers were required to 'retain physical possession and custody of all US atomic weapons,' with transfer to the RAF only occurring after 'authority was received from the US Chiefs of Staff, through HQ Strategic Air Command.'[30] The strict conditions of these custodial arrangements placed considerable constraints on the operational effectiveness of the V-force.

According to Sir Kenneth Cross:

> The security conditions under which American nuclear weapons are provided for this Command make it impossible to load and disperse these weapons on Medium Bomber aircraft, unless US presidential authority has been received to release the weapons for use by the Command. At present, this inhibits the use of American nuclear weapons in any precautionary phase where the Command is brought to a dispersed alert. The position has been discussed with the USAF Strategic Air Command and by the Air Ministry with the Pentagon. A remedy has been proposed whereby the present restrictions could be overcome under certain guarantees and this is at present the subject of discussions between the Pentagon and the US President.[31]

The 'remedy' alluded to by Cross involved maintaining US custody of the weapons but granting the RAF temporary possession under specific conditions and for specific purposes. A mechanism to achieve this was first suggested by General Blanchard, the Commander of SAC forces in Britain (7th Air Division) who disclosed 'verbally' to VCAS that should enemy attack appear imminent and dispersal of the V-force became necessary, his interpretation of the legal position would be satisfied if one of his representatives accompanied the weapons aboard the aircraft.[32] The issue was discussed further in correspondence with General Thomas White, USAF Chief of Staff, and in a meeting between the Secretary of State for Air, Sir George Ward, and his opposite number in the United States, James Douglas. The results were less than encouraging. The US authorities were unable to find a formula 'within US law whereby during a period of tension Bomber Command aircraft can disperse carrying a US Project 'E' weapon.'[33] In short, Blanchard's informal agreement on nuclear transfer was the only guarantee that Bomber Command would be able to fully implement its alert and readiness procedures in the event of possible Soviet attack.

The problems presented by the custodial arrangements for US weapons were not confined to the co-ordinated strike plan. The capability of Bomber Command to mount a unilateral retaliatory strike was also placed in doubt. Storage of Project E weapons on three Class I airfields meant that 'UK weapons are not disposed in the best locations to meet the unilateral strike plan, in which aircraft from E stations must be used.'[34] Due to these limitations and the expectation that the British stockpile of megaton weapons would soon match available aircraft, the Air Council recommended that 'Project E for the strategic bomber force should be phased out.'[35]

The British decision to discontinue Project E for the V-force was communicated to the US authorities in August 1960. To allay any possible repercussions, Sir Thomas Pike wrote personally to General White expressing both the gratitude of HMG and the hope that the end of Project E 'will not mean any slackening of the already close co-operation that exists between our two Air Forces'.[36]

The agreed schedule for the phasing out the weapons was July 1961 for Honnington and December 1962 for Waddington. Arrangements at Marham, however, were uncertain. The three Valiant squadrons based at the station were assigned to SACEUR and targeted in accordance with NATO plans. In this role, the Valiants were modified to carry two Mk 28 nuclear bombs with three aircraft on constant QRA status.[37] The weapons stored at Marham were covered under the terms of Project E. Consequently, phasing out Project E would leave a shortfall in SACEUR's requirements. The implications were not lost on the government. As Harold Watkinson, the Minister of Defence, informed Macmillan: 'we see no need to produce British bombs to replace American bombs for the forces assigned to NATO.'[38] In light of these arguments, Project E remained in operation at Marham until January 1965, when the Valiants were eventually withdrawn from service.

Co-ordination of nuclear strikes between Britain and America involved not only Soviet targets. With Britain's decision to station nuclear weapons in the Far East, planning was extended to cover a nuclear attack on China. The decision to base nuclear weapons in the Far East was taken by the Defence Committee in October 1960, who considered that a British contribution to the strategic nuclear deterrent against China, 'was vital to maintaining our influence with the Americans in the area.'[39] British plans covered two eventualities: a US/UK strategic attack on China and co-ordination of tactical nuclear strikes in support of SEATO.[40] The nuclear forces comprising the British contribution consisted of the deployment of three Victor Squadrons to Butterworth (Malaya) and Tengah (Singapore), one squadron of Canberras already stationed in the theatre and a Carrier Group deployed East of Suez.[41] HMG's intention to support SEATO with a nuclear capability was confirmed in late-1961. The agreement, however, contained a qualification: 'detailed nuclear planning would be conducted outside the military planning office in bilateral discussions with the Americans.'[42]

To co-ordinate joint action, nuclear strike plans were considered under two contingencies: a tactical nuclear response in defence of SEATO and a strategic attack against China. Responsibility for the former was vested on the US side with the Commander-in-Chief Pacific (CINCPAC) and on the British side with the Commanders-in-Chiefs Committee, Far East. Responsibility for the strategic deterrent, however, was considered to lie with the Joint Strategic Targets Planning Staff based at SAC HQ in Omaha. In October 1962, bilateral discussions covering a combined nuclear strike were initiated in Singapore. The outcome was described to the Prime Minister by the CDS:

> As you know, there are two aspects of nuclear strike planning in the Far East: that concerned with our contribution to the strategic nuclear deterrent against China, and our support to SEATO. Detailed development of the former concept is as yet incomplete, and we have so far not discussed matters with the Americans. As to our declared capability for tactical nuclear strikes in support of SEATO Plan 4, the Americans have asked us if we would take on targets in Burma, adjacent parts of China and in Hainan. This we could do reasonably with the Canberras now stationed in Singapore and the V-Bombers that we plan to deploy to the theatre in an emergency, and by stationing our strike carrier in the Indian Ocean.[43]

Although the documentary record on co-ordination of nuclear strikes in the Far East remains sketchy, there is strong evidence to suggest that a co-ordinated tactical nuclear response in support of SEATO was agreed between the two governments. The assumption is based on examination of the communications system adopted by Britain to relay nuclear release authority to commanders in the Far East. In reviewing the position, the Chiefs considered reliable communications essential to implementation of a co-ordinated plan, as 'provided there is agreement at Heads of Government level, authorisation becomes a straightforward matter between Whitehall and the UK Commander in the field'.[44] To fulfil these criteria two options were available: to rely on British equipment that was 'extremely vulnerable' or seek American assistance.[45] In the event, the latter option was adopted as is apparent in the following message from the JCS to the British Defence Staffs in Washington:

> ... the advice of CINCPAC was sought on this subject and he foresees no communications operational difficulties. Accordingly you will be contacted by the Director for Communications-Electronics Joint Staff for discussions on passing over the Defence Communications System alternate alerting and

executing messages from National Military Headquarters in London to Singapore for Nuclear Strike Operations in support of SEATO Plan 4.[46]

Given the American desire for centralized command and control it is inconceivable that the US would allow Britain use of its communications facilities to order a British nuclear strike independently of US forces. The only plausible explanation is that a co-ordinated nuclear strike was agreed between the two governments. To ensure that British nuclear forces received political authorisation, the Americans granted Britain access to their communications.

THOR

The supply of nuclear weapons to the RAF was not confined to Project E. In 1958, agreement was reached between the two governments to station 60 Thor missiles in the UK. To be deployed under dual control and operated by the RAF, the missiles carried a 1.45 megaton warhead to a range of 1,500 miles. Thor was deployed at four main bases: Driffield, Hemswell, Feltwell and North Luffenham. Surrounding each main base were four satellite stations, with missiles deployed at each location in groups of three. All squadrons were fully manned by RAF personnel, with the warheads under control of American custodial officers. In June 1959, Bomber Command declared an initial operational capability with full-scale deployment completed in April 1960.[47]

Operational control of Thor was covered by the basic understanding on joint decision, contained in the Memorandum of Understanding signed by the two countries on 22 February 1958.[48] In practice, this was achieved by a dual-key system (described below) which granted each government a physical veto over the launch of an armed missile. Operational orders were transmitted simultaneously through two channels. For the USAF, they would pass from HQ SAC through the 7th Air Division Headquarters and then to the squadrons. For the RAF, the orders would pass from the Air Ministry through HQ Bomber Command and then to the squadrons.[49]

Initial plans for the deployment of Thor were based on the assumption that the nuclear warheads would be stored centrally and only deployed operationally when the international situation deteriorated. Under these conditions, the time required to make Thor operational was estimated to be 57 hours if the warheads were stored at Lakenheath and 24 hours if warheads were stored at main bases.[50] This was in contrast to a readiness capability of fifteen minutes if the warheads were permanently installed on the missile. Opinion within the RAF favoured installation of the warhead: a position strongly endorsed by the Air Ministry, who argued that 'as far as the RAF is concerned the operational readiness of the weapons system demands that the warhead should be fitted.'[51]

HMG's position, however, remained equivocal. A particular concern was the risk of accidental explosion if the missile was struck by lightning. Although considered 'so remote as to justify disregarding it', the issue caused further delay.[52] Of greater significance was a JIC report that indicated HMG would only receive '24 hours strategic warning before any heavy Soviet attack on this country.'[53] In response to this assessment, it was concluded that 'if we only get 24 hours warning, Thor, without its warheads already fitted would be largely valueless.'[54] To permanently attach the warhead to the missile, however, raised questions concerning US custody. The implications of the proposal were described to US Secretary of State Herter in the following terms:

> It is difficult to understand how a nuclear warhead attached to and made part of a weapons' system (missile or otherwise) under the operational control of another nation can be considered within the exclusive custody or possession of the United States when the only real control is possession of one of the firing keys... With such a strained interpretation of exclusive custody, the co-operating ally also having possession of one of the firing keys likewise can claim exclusive custody.[55]

Despite this realization, and despite doubts about the legality of the situation in US law, and contrary to earlier assurances by the Pentagon to Congress that the custody of nuclear weapons would 'be maintained and protected separate from the carrying vehicle',[56] the decision to fit the warheads to the missile was taken in May 1960 and subsequently confirmed in a Bomber Command directive which stipulated that Thor was to 'maintain a capability to react within tactical warning at all times'.[57]

Control of the Thor squadrons was exercised from Headquarters Bomber Command. To monitor the readiness of the force, an extensive communications system was provided that enabled the launch order to be sent directly from the Bomber Command Operations Room to each missile squadron. To guard against breakdown or enemy action, alternate routes of communication were provided which allowed 'for command to be exercised by a subordinate formation in the event of HQ Bomber Command being destroyed.'[58] The anticipated launch procedure was described to Sir Kenneth Cross in the following manner:

The Air Ministry now have under urgent consideration the steps which are required to bring the political machinery into line with the readiness of the weapon. It is considered, however, that when the V-Force are dispatched on 'positive control missions' the Thor force should be brought to T-8 and, should current R&D studies prove it practicable, a proportion of the force should be brought to T-2. There is, in fact, no difference in the problems with the two forces; when the decision is made not to recall the manned bombers, we must simultaneously commit the Thor force. It is one and the same decision.[59]

In July 1960, initial plans for the readiness of the Thor missile squadrons were issued and directed that sixty per cent of the force was to be maintained at standby. In practice this was achieved by keeping forty missiles at thirty minutes readiness, ten available within six hours and the remainder operational within 24–48 hours.[60] On receipt of an alert, the maximum number of missiles was to be brought to fifteen minutes readiness and prepared for immediate initiation of the countdown. The launch took fifteen minutes to complete and, according to one Thor Launch Control Officer (LCO), consisted of five-phases:

Phase 1. All equipment and targeting data checked. Countdown sequence initiated.
Phase 2. Shelter retracted and missile erected. Targeting data entered.
Phase 3. Missile loaded with fuel. Target data and missile valves rechecked.
Phase 4. Missile functions transferred to internal power source. Missile topped up with liquid oxygen (LOX) if required.
Phase 5. Authenticated launch codes received. Keys turned and engine started.[61]

During the launch procedure, a phased-hold could be introduced leaving the missiles eight minutes from launch in the vertical unfuelled condition or two minutes from launch in the fuelled position.[62] In October 1961, the readiness capability of the force was revised with a minimum of 65 per cent of the force placed at fifteen minutes readiness.[63] To integrate Thor with the V-force, the Medium Bomber Alert and Readiness Plan was amended to incorporate the missile squadrons. Arrangements were also made to co-ordinate Thor with the combined strike plan immediately the squadrons became operational.

Launching the Thors under dual-key control involved a procedure in which RAF and USAF officers operated separate physical keys. The British key initiated the missile launch sequence and the American key armed the warhead.[64] There has been speculation about whether the American veto on the Thors could have been overridden *in extremis*. In a letter to *The Times* in 1974, a retired RAF officer recalled when a USAF launch officer did not arrive for a simulated launch a RAF counterpart inserted a screwdriver in the US key-hole to complete the count down.[65] Other RAF officers have discounted the suggestion.[66] Nevertheless, there may have been ways around dual control, certainly in the early stages of the deployment. Devising means of circumventing dual-key control, was, according to another NCO, 'a game we all played,' though the outcome was intended to be constructive rather than sinister.[67] In 1960, for example, a Thor was accidentally armed when a RAF NCO leaned on the USAF keyway.[68] When this was reported, Douglas Corporation and USAF personnel immediately set about rectifying the problem in all the missiles. Britain was later informed that 'at one time it had been possible for many American missiles to be simultaneously launched by a particular combination of accidents.'[69]

US Permissive Action Links (PALs) were never installed on the Thors, and it is not impossible that British crews could have armed their missiles during a crisis. Conversely, as only one American serviceman was involved in the launch procedure, it is virtually inconceivable that the British veto could have been overridden.[70] The dual-key system was designed to ensure that HMG could not launch the force as an act of national policy. While there is no suggestion that any RAF crew contemplated such action, fear of unauthorized use of Jupiter IRBMs in Turkey greatly exercised senior American officials including President Kennedy at the height of the Cuban missile crisis.[71]

Targeting Thor was covered by the terms of the combined strike plan in which joint target policy was decided by ministers on the advice of the Chiefs of Staff, leaving target planning to be co-ordinated by the USAF and RAF. The distinction between these two categories was defined by the Chiefs such that target policy was 'the definition given to the choice of a group or system of targets to be attacked', whereas 'target planning (i.e. targeting) includes operating techniques, operational capabilities and limitations, routes and selected targets.'[72] This division of responsibility left the choice of targets entirely at the discretion of the military with civilian oversight strongly resisted. Indeed, the Air Ministry was unaware 'what the specific selections are for either plan, since the Command does not divulge its plans as it is required to do under the terms of the C-in-C's directive. This also includes targeting for Thor and Blue Steel.'[73]

For Bomber Command, the favoured policy was to use Thor against cities, as 'to ensure the destruction of a pinpoint target, such as a missile site or a bomber base, considerably more than one missile per target is required.'[74] In contrast, SAC favoured a cross-targeting strategy in which weapons and delivery vehicles were selected from different types of bases and geographical locations to achieve the highest probability of delivering a weapon on any given target. In employing this policy SAC sought to ensure the complete destruction of the target irrespective of the survivability of any specified launch site.[75] The position at the beginning of 1959 was summarized by DCAS as follows:

> The targets of the Driffield squadron are partly cities and partly airfields. I have decided that they must be entirely cities. If we attack airfields we shall be doubling up with SAC and our chances of hitting airfields are low. Thor also has the advantage of getting there first. The cover of the 4 squadrons will be increased from 21 to 50 city targets.[76]

The new combined plan issued in mid-1961 gave Bomber Command responsibility for the destruction of 48 cities, six air-defence targets and three long-range airbases.[77] In comparison to previous plans, however, in which 106 targets were allocated to Bomber Command, a total of 57 targets was a marked reduction. This is especially the case, as the 60 Thor missiles were not included in the original plan. In the absence of detailed targeting documents this reduction is difficult to explain. One possibility is that the figure of 57 targets relates solely to the Thor force. Alternatively, the reduction represented no significant change in the overall plan with the allocation of targets decided primarily on tactical considerations. A further suggestion is that the new plan revealed the strong preference of the recently-elected Kennedy administration against city-strikes in the first wave. Indeed, it has been argued that the American preference for counterforce targeting was a significant factor in Britain's eventual decision to reduce the scale of its unilateral strike plan from forty city targets, so facilitating the introduction of Polaris.[78] This latter interpretation is partially borne out by Bomber Command's contribution to the subsequent combined plan issued in August 1962. In this plan, Bomber Command's target allocation was increased to 98 with the combined attack of the

V-force and Thor squadrons directed against sixteen cities, 44 airfields, 28 IRBM sites and ten air defence centres.[79]

There is also evidence that the Thor strike plan was co-ordinated with elements of the US tactical airforce stationed in the UK. Comprised of F-100 Super Sabres and armed with a 1.1-megaton warhead, these forces were assigned to cover priority targets contained in SACEUR's Atomic Strike Plan.[80] Apparently, the intention was to use the F-100s to deliver the primary nuclear strike, to be followed on to the target by a Thor missile operating in a secondary follow-on strike role.[81] The targets allocated to the F-100s were primarily command and control facilities in major metropolitan areas in non-USSR Warsaw Pact nations. In the case of East Berlin, one of the Warsaw Pact's main control centres, the cross-targeting policy was apparently employed to its limit, requiring the F-100 to deliver its weapon after the explosion of one Thor and before the arrival of another.[82] In contrast, the Jupiter IRBMs in Italy and Turkey were under control of SACEUR and 'targeted on 45 of the 129 Soviet MRBM-IRBM sites facing Europe'[83]

The apparent use of Thor in support of SACEUR's Atomic Strike Plan requires explanation. This is particularly the case as the deployment of Thor was based on explicit understanding that the missile was a strategic weapon and would be jointly controlled and targeted by Bomber Command and SAC. There are two possible explanations. One is that in response to American pressure to establish a NATO MRBM force, Britain agreed to target Thor more in line with SACEUR's wishes but on the understanding that Britain's involvement in target selection remained unaltered. It could be argued that such an arrangement was covered by the terms of the Thor agreement which obliged both governments to deploy the missile 'having regard to the undertaking' in Article 5.[84] Conversely, accepting the change of targeting, Britain might undermine SACEUR's requirement for a NATO MRBM force. While both alternatives are plausible, the former offers a more credible explanation. Indeed, taken in conjunction with the American decision to supply Britain with Polaris, the change in targeting helps to explain Britain's apparent willingness to assign Thor to the NATO multinational nuclear force agreed at Nassau. In short, Thor was already targeted to meet SACEUR's requirements.[85]

With the deployment of Thor complete, consideration was given to extending the duration of the original agreement. Scheduled to expire in November 1964, the matter was brought before the Air Council for detailed examination. The VCAS explained that Thor was a proven and efficient weapon, represented a large investment and should not be discarded lightly. Moreover, Thor would remain a valid deterrent from 1965 onward provided it could be held permanently at a high state of readiness and 'HMG was prepared to launch it on missile early warning'.[86] In response, the PUS at Air Ministry, Sir Maurice Dean, pointed out that the government had largely disowned a fire-first strategy and doubted whether 'an above-ground fixed-site missile' would fill a hypothetical gap in the UK's deterrent capability. The situation was made more difficult as the arguments in support of Thor's extension 'were almost exactly the converse of those that had led (with the concurrence of the Air Ministry) to abandonment of Blue Streak as a military weapon.'[87]

The Labour Party's opposition to Thor was a further factor against extending deployment. This was based on the firmly held belief that Thor was a first-strike weapon. The Party's hostility to Thor was articulated by John Strachey, a former Secretary of State for War, who described the missiles as 'large, clumsy, slow firing liquid fuel rockets... sitting targets for a pre-emptive strike.'[88] Given this criticism, any suggestion to extend the Thor deployment by adopting a fire-on-warning strategy would cause a political outcry. No firm decision was taken until April 1962, when CAS informed the Air Council that the proposal to extend Thor's deployment would almost certainly result in a concerted attempt to reduce the remainder of the deterrent.[89] The final decision to phase out Thor was taken by the Defence Committee in July. The run-down was strongly endorsed by the Defence Secretary:

> Thor is not part of our independent contribution to the deterrent and, with its operational limitations, can never be a satisfactory second-strike weapon. It is, relatively speaking, expensive in manpower and money and I have reached the conclusion that, in present circumstances our expenditure on Thor should be brought to an end.[90]

The first squadron to be released from operational responsibility was the Driffield complex, which was disbanded in January 1963. In the following months, Bomber Command's missile force was gradually reduced with the last Thor missiles taken off station in August 1963.[91]

THE MURPHY-DEAN AGREEMENT

The deployment of sixty Thor IRBMs heightened public concern over the use of American nuclear bases in the UK. The issue received further prominence with remarks by Secretary of State Dulles and CINCSAC, General Thomas Power, which were widely interpreted as sanctioning American determination to respond immediately with nuclear weapons should US forces come under attack.[92] Public unease was reflected in Parliament. Labour MPs subjected the government to a barrage of hostile questions concerning the extent of British control over US nuclear forces stationed in Britain and the consequences of a crash or accident involving US aircraft. When leaders of the Trade Union Congress (TUC) met the Prime Minister and Foreign Secretary in January 1958, the safety of these flights was an issue on which the TUC pressed the government.[93] To address these concerns, the government proposed issuing a White Paper 'designed to make more information available to the public and thereby to reduce domestic political interest in the subject.'[94] Bilateral discussions with US authorities began in January 1958 with Britain receiving details of US bomber movements and arming procedures. Informing Parliament of the outcome of these talks, the acting Prime Minister, Rab Butler stated that:

> It is necessary for the maintenance of the deterrent that aircraft of the Royal Air Force and United States Air Force should from time to time carry nuclear weapons over the United Kingdom. Bombs carried on such flights are never ready for instantaneous use. The process of arming would require an elaborate technical procedure by the crew of the aircraft and in no circumstances could bombs be armed in accident... The operational use of US bases in an emergency would be a matter for joint decision by Her Majesty's Government and the United States Government.[95]

In the following months, discussions were expanded 'to establish precisely what were the agreements on the use of US aircraft from bases in the UK in the case of emergency; and how to clarify the procedures by which the decision to use nuclear weapons should be taken.'[96] To elevate the status of these discussions, Macmillan wrote to Eisenhower on 30 April 'proposing a joint study of the procedural arrangements in our two countries for taking a decision to launch nuclear retaliation'.[97] In reviewing the British proposal, the US administration concluded that due to recent developments in the US-Soviet strategic balance 'a fresh examination of the desirability of reaching more specific agreements with the British regarding arrangements for the use of nuclear retaliatory forces' was essential. The major factors behind this decision were outlined as follows:

(a) The development of the Soviet atomic capability, including IRBM and ICBM, has created new and far more critical problems than those which confronted us at the time of the Korean War.
(b) Whereas only the US possessed atomic capability in 1948, the United Kingdom possesses a significant atomic capability of its own today.
(c) Considering the rapidly shrinking warning times, and the probability that a Soviet attack would consist of an attempt to knock out at once all British and US retaliatory capability, it is becoming increasingly clear that if there is to be co-ordination of US and UK decisions respecting launching of nuclear retaliatory forces, the procedures for such decisions should be carefully arranged in advance.[98]

In response, Macmillan forwarded an *aide-mémoire* that detailed British procedures for launching the deterrent and possible arrangements for an agreed understanding on joint control.[99] To represent American interests, Dulles appointed Deputy Under-Secretary of State Robert Murphy with Britain represented by Sir Patrick Dean, Chairman of the JIC. The outcome of these negotiations resulted in detailed proposals governing the launch of British bombers armed with American nuclear weapons, the Thor force and units of SAC located in the UK.

Although the text of the Murphy-Dean Agreement remains classified, significant details can be determined from early drafts and related documents.[100] The agreement consisted of three sections: a 'basic understanding' governing political consultation and two annexes which detailed the procedures governing the launch of British and American nuclear forces under various states of alert.[101] The agreement covering political authorisation repeated almost literally the language of the Truman-Churchill communiqué:

> The basic understanding between the United Kingdom and United States Governments, regarding the use of bases in the United Kingdom by United States forces, provides that such use in an emergency shall be a matter for joint decision by the two governments in the light of the circumstances at the time.[102]

In ratifying the basic understanding, it is evident that Macmillan did not receive any formal guarantee establishing a British veto. What is less clear, however, is whether any such binding agreement was sought. Indeed, to have pressed for a formal veto would have delayed ratification of the new Atomic Energy Act, a consequence HMG was eager to avoid. Moreover, in prior discussions it became apparent that Washington 'would not accept any limitation upon its freedom of action if circumstances should require that it act independently.'[103] Macmillan, later reflected that, 'so far as the bases are concerned, which the Americans have in England, this regular agreement replaces the loose arrangement made by Attlee and confirmed by Churchill.'[104] Undoubtedly misgivings remained, but as the Defence Committee had already concluded that, 'in practice, there might be little time for consultation between the two governments' no advantage was to be gained by prolonging the issue.[105] The Murphy-Dean agreement was signed on 7 June 1958 and initialled by Macmillan and Eisenhower on 12 June.[106]

In 1959, the procedures of the Murphy-Dean agreement were extended to cover nuclear-capable aircraft based in the UK and committed to SACEUR. The subsequent negotiations addressed two fundamental objectives. On one hand, SACEUR required a formal guarantee that once a joint decision had been taken to commit nuclear forces, there would be 'a clear and unequivocal chain of military command between himself and those forces assigned to his control.' On the other, Britain insisted on obtaining an absolute assurance that these forces could not in any circumstances be 'launched irrevocably' before a joint decision to do so had been reached between the Prime Minister and President.[107] In reviewing the position, the government concluded that Britain possessed four independent safeguards to guard against SACEUR's unauthorized employed of British nuclear forces.

First, SACEUR's assumption of full authority as Supreme Commander on the declaration of a reinforced alert could only occur after prior approval of HMG. Second, atomic weapons could only be employed within NATO after the announcement by SACEUR of the release of atomic warfare (R-hour). Moreover, R-hour could only be declared after SACEUR had obtained agreement from London and Washington. Third, SACEUR's orders to the assigned squadrons would not be given direct but would have to be relayed via Bomber Command HQ. Consequently, if C-in-C Bomber Command considered these orders to be at variance with national policy, he was authorized to consult with higher authorities.[108] Finally, the Murphy-Dean agreement itself stated that 'in addition, there are located in the United Kingdom certain UK and US tactical bomber units committed to SACEUR and having a nuclear retaliatory capability. The use of [which]... falls under the basic understanding'. As the basic understanding did not sanction the use of bases by US 'NATO-committed' units then *a fortiori* SACEUR could not order the UK 'NATO-committed' units to nuclear attack in advance of the joint decision.[109] This final point was considered to constitute a fundamental safeguard against SACEUR employing any 'NATO-committed' units based in the UK without first obtaining government approval. To meet SACEUR's requirements, the Murphy-Dean agreement was revised and later ratified by President Kennedy on 6 February 1961. In December 1963, these bilateral agreements were recomfirmed in an exchange of letters between Prime Minister Alec Douglas Home and President Johnson. It was also noted that these agreements were not legally binding but 'in the nature of personal assurances between successive Presidents and Prime Ministers.'[110]

THE HOLY LOCH AGREEMENT

A further issue affecting joint control that emerged during 1960 was an American request to establish a Polaris submarine base in British territorial waters. Initial discussions were conducted through naval channels with Macmillan receiving broad details of the proposal in December 1959. The matter was formally raised by President Eisenhower at the Camp David summit in March 1960, when Macmillan agreed 'in principle' to provide the US with facilities to berth Polaris submarines at Holy Loch in Scotland.[111] For the British, the Polaris agreement was only one aspect of a larger package that included an American guarantee to provide the RAF with Skybolt. Although not formally linked, the two elements became part of the complex diplomatic maneuvering that characterized the nuclear relationship between Britain and America during the early-1960s.[112]

From the beginning, the issue of control was central to the negotiations. The American position was most forcibly expressed by the US Navy who insisted that the SLBM force could not be placed under the same control procedures that applied to US bombers stationed in Britain. The procedure favoured by the USN was to allow joint control in territorial waters but once the ships were on patrol the sole provision covering the launch of the missiles was the general agreement on consultation reached between Eden and Eisenhower in 1953.[113] Presenting the proposals to the Defence Committee in late May, Watkinson summarized the position as follows:

> The American suggestion that a joint decision should only be necessary for launching missiles from United Kingdom territorial waters would be unacceptable... the Government would undoubtedly be subject to pressure for joint

control of the submarines and their missiles to be exercised under arrangements similar to those agreed with the Americans for United States aircraft based in the United Kingdom. The control of submarines, with their longer range and endurance, admittedly posed problems different from aircraft; the United States Government might be reluctant to accept that all specific orders to launch missiles from their United Kingdom-based submarines should be subject to a joint decision.[114]

To assess the policy options, Macmillan convened a ministerial meeting. Watkinson argued that it would be necessary to present the arrangements as a partnership and that in return for the base, Washington should first give a commitment to supply Britain with Polaris submarines, 'both as a measure of reinsurance in case Skybolt was a failure, and in order to influence United States policy as regards the control of their Polaris submarines.'[115] The Foreign Secretary, Selwyn Lloyd, pointed out that US submarines using the base would not be subject to joint operational control by the two governments. To allay public concern, he considered it essential that any future Polaris submarine force that Britain might obtain under the agreement was ultimately 'under sole United Kingdom control'. Summing up, the Prime Minister concluded that base rights should be offered to the Americans in return for two Polaris submarines, which would be 'operationally available to SACLANT on the understanding that we withdraw them and bring them under our own control if the situation requires it.'[116]

Macmillan wrote to Eisenhower at the end of June, suggesting that for 'presentational purposes' the area in which a joint decision would be required to launch the missiles 'should be extended to something like a hundred miles.'[117] Eisenhower was unimpressed and indicated that the US Navy was investigating other possible locations such as Bremerhaven in West Germany.[118] The implications were clear: if Britain overplayed its hand, America would review its requirements for berthing facilities, an outcome that would raise uncertainties over Skybolt. Sensing the possible dangers, Macmillan apologized to Eisenhower 'if there had been any misunderstanding' and expressed his regrets 'if such a valuable strategic plan had to be abandoned.'[119] In response, Eisenhower became more conciliatory and conceded that although dual control could not be extended to the hundred miles limit, additional co-ordinating measures would be considered.[120]

To explore further the American position, draft instructions were forwarded to the British Ambassador, Sir Harold Caccia, explaining HMG's position on control:

> Our main concern is to be able to say that the joint control arrangements for the United States submarines will be broadly as effective, though not the same as, for the United States Thors and bombers. We take it for granted that our two governments will be at one on the policy of using Polaris submarines operationally. But the formal position, to which attention has been closely drawn at this time, will be entirely different from that of United States bombers and Thors based in this country. Over these our control is formally complete; over submarines it would cease at three miles.[121]

To clarify the position, a discussion document was jointly prepared by Watkinson and Selwyn Lloyd that considered the possible methods for control of US Polaris submarines. The report was less sanguine than previous documents and ruled out as impractical 'any formal joint consultation prior to the firing of missiles by US submarines within a given radius of the UK or within a limited sea area.'[122] Despite this realization, it was nevertheless considered possible to secure an American agreement that went beyond a UK veto over missiles launched from British territorial waters. Although the precise details required further elaboration, the anticipated measures included American acceptance that UK naval authorities would at all times be informed of movements in and out of UK bases; that there would be consultation between the President and the Prime Minister before the order to fire was issued to Polaris submarines in the North Atlantic Ocean area; and that in times of tension or during a period of general alert, the 'flushing' of Polaris submarines from UK bases would be subject to consultation. It was also acknowledged that such agreements could not be included in a published document and would 'rely primarily on Anglo-American good relations.'[123]

Acceptance that arrangements for the control of Polaris submarines using UK facilities would be both general and secret presented the government with a political problem. In the absence of a formal agreement, any public statement was expected to raise parliamentary questions that could not be properly answered. To provide the basis for a public statement by the Prime Minister, a number of draft agreements were forwarded to Washington for consideration. The State Department stood firm and maintained that any public statement relating to control outside British territorial waters would have to be 'couched in general terms, not geared specifically to Polaris submarines.'[124] Discussion was effectively curtailed when the Pentagon refused to sanction any US public statement concerning control of Polaris submarines and 'would rather forego the facilities in the Clyde than make one.'[125] The diplomatic impasse presented HMG with two alternatives: persuade the President to overrule the Pentagon or omit all reference to control from the final text and work out some formula that could be used 'apparently off the cuff' in answer to a parliamentary question.[126] Aware that Eisenhower's tenure as President would soon come to an end, Macmillan reluctantly agreed to the second option: 'Although I would have liked to have got better terms, I agree that we may do better to rest upon a gentlemen's agreement than to try to tie the Americans up in a legal option which is in any case unenforceable upon a successor Government.'[127]

To establish the technical details and areas of responsibility, a Memorandum of Understanding was agreed between the two navies with the first submarine expected in mid-1961.[128] With the departure of Eisenhower, some doubt was raised about the continued validity of the Holy Loch Agreement. To confirm the understandings on nuclear use between the two countries, Macmillan wrote to President Kennedy on 26 January 1961.[129] Replying to Macmillan's telegram, the President gave the following commitment:

> Our understanding on the use of British bases is that the President and Prime Minister will reach a joint decision by speaking personally with each other before certain forces equipped with US nuclear weapons and operating from bases in the United Kingdom will use nuclear weapons, namely SAC, British Bomber Command (excluding aircraft of such Command equipped with British nuclear weapons but including the IRBM force) and SACEUR-assigned forces in the UK. (US Polaris submarines in British territorial waters should now be added to this list.)... With reference to the launching of US Polaris submarines, I give you the following assurance which of course is not to be used publicly. In the event of an emergency, such as increased tension or the threat of war, the US will take every step to consult with Britain and other Allies.[130]

Confirmation of the agreements on nuclear use confirmed the close nuclear and political relationship that now existed between London and Washington. In October 1962, this relationship was put to the test when the US discovered Soviet nuclear missiles in Cuba, and the world went to the brink of nuclear confrontation.

THE CUBAN MISSILE CRISIS

Evidence of Soviet MRBMs in Cuba was obtained by a U2 reconnaissance flight over the island on 14 October. President Kennedy was informed on 16 October.[131] The British government was formally briefed on the Cuban situation on 21 October, when President Kennedy personally informed the UK ambassador, Sir David Ormsby-Gore, on developments in Cuba and the US reaction.[132]

It is now evident that elements within the British government were aware of the situation in Cuba several days in advance of the ambassador's briefing.[133] What is not yet clear is if Macmillan learned of the missiles before he received Kennedy's formal message on the evening of Sunday 21 October.[134]

Given that in the absence of PALs, the Commander-in-Chief of Bomber Command had *de facto* control over Britain's strategic nuclear arsenal and the delegated authority to attack the Soviet Union under certain conditions, it is instructive to examine how Britain's command system functioned during the crisis.[135] In a similar analysis of the American system, for example, Scott Sagan has concluded that 'the US nuclear command system clearly did not provide the certainty in safety that senior American leaders wanted and believed existed.'[136] Given the more assertive nature of American C^{3}I, as compared to its British counterpart, is there any indication that inadvertent nuclear use was significantly greater in Britain than has previously been assumed?

The records of the Air Ministry show that Bomber Command HQ ordered Alert Condition 3 at 13.00 hours on Saturday 27 October and this remained in force until 5 November.[137] On 29 October orders were given to double the number of bombers on QRA. At most stations within Bomber Command this would have required six aircraft in total, although at RAF Waddington the number of QRA bombers was trebled by the station commander, resulting in nine fully-armed Vulcans at fifteen minutes readiness.[138] To arm the extra aircraft on QRA, additional Yellow Sun thermonuclear weapons were transported to all operational RAF bases from the Faldingworth nuclear storage site in north Lincolnshire. The proportion of Thor missiles at fifteen minutes readiness was increased, with 59 of the 60 missiles 'made serviceable and ready simply by use of the telephone.'[139] Preparations to disperse the V-force were also put in hand with the ADOC at Bentley Priory informed that Alert Condition 2 (dispersal of the force) would be 'flash' signalled by Bomber Command HQ 'to ADOC and dispersal stations, using the authenticating codeword FRAMEWORK.'[140] To provide early warning of Soviet missile attack, the Jodrell Bank telescope was prepared for use by the RAF on the declaration of a 'state of military vigilance'.[141]

The manner by which Bomber Command implemented these alert measures, raises salient questions about the command and control of British nuclear forces and the division of responsibility between civilian and military authorities. Speculation has also arisen whether ministers were aware of these events, a concern heightened by the account of Air Vice-Marshal Menaul that, *inter alia*, contends no more than 'a handful of people outside Bomber Command' was given full details.[142] In his own study on the issue, Sagan quotes Lord Zuckerman who recalls that within MOD, no orders were given to Cross to change Bomber Command's alert state. Sagan's tentative conclusion is that senior civilian officials (including the Prime Minister), 'were not fully cognizant' of events and that 'Air Marshal Cross's actions are another example of how the military commander's interests in combat readiness can cut against civilian authorities' interests in safety.'[143] This conclusion is contested by Ian Madelin, the head of the MOD's Air Historical Branch, who argues that Cross 'had already implemented the measures that could be done routinely and covertly. Anything beyond that would be overt and could be construed as provocative and destabilising... The steps he was taking were quite appropriate and, in retrospect, one would not say we should have done anything more or different.'[144] Given that key records have now been declassified, which account is the more appropriate?

MOD records recently released show that the first official instructions received by the military occurred at 11.00 hours on Saturday 27 October when Sir Thomas Pike, the Chief of the Air Staff, was summoned to Admiralty House by the Prime Minister.[145] Earlier in the week Macmillan had told General Norstad, that 'mobilization had sometimes caused war', reinforcing SACEUR's preference for discrete and limited preparations.[146] When Macmillan met Pike they 'discussed what measures might be taken to alert the United Kingdom forces' and the PM expressed his desire that overt preparations be avoided. 'Moreover, he did not wish Bomber Command to be alerted, although he wished the force to be ready to take the appropriate steps should this become necessary.' Immediately after meeting the Prime Minister, Pike contacted Cross to inform him 'that he should be on the alert and that his key personnel should be available on station.'[147] This chronology is corroborated by Air Ministry records that show Alert Condition 3 was ordered by HQ Bomber Command at 1300 hours.

Details of CAS's meeting with the Prime Minister (including his conversation with Cross) were given to the navy and army chiefs in a hastily convened meeting in MOD at 14.30 hours. In that meeting the Chiefs decided that 'at the moment no action was needed other than that of alerting key personnel.'[148] However, to maintain the credibility of the deterrent, it was essential that 'Bomber Command should be alerted and dispersed in the event of positive indications that the United States propose to operate against the Cuban mainland.'[149] The Chiefs were informed that the US invasion force would not be ready to operate until 29 October and HMG would be notified before any definitive action was taken though that 'this might take the form of information rather than consultation.'[150] The Chiefs set down their views (including the various alert measures that could be undertaken in a Precautionary Stage) in a brief for the Chief of the Defence Staff, 'in the event of a Cabinet meeting being called at short notice.'

There is therefore no evidence to support conjecture that Cross acted *ultra vires*. Declaration of Alert Condition 3 was specifically designed to be authorized by C-in-C Bomber Command without recourse to political authority.[151] Although there is some evidence to suggest that Cross 'had been badgering MOD, Air Ministry and Whitehall for the previous five days to be allowed to bring his command to 05',[152] there is no indication that measures were implemented against political wishes. Indeed, as Cross himself, was later to argue, political considerations were a constant worry as 'despite having everything ready to bring 75% of the aircraft in the Command to readiness, we could not give the order for fear of the effect it might have (if it became known) on the very tense negotiations being carried on by Mr Kruschev and Mr Kennedy.'[153]

The alert status of the Medium Bomber Force, however, represents only one aspect of the nuclear forces stationed in the UK during the crisis. Other elements included the Thor missile squadrons (under dual control), the NATO-assigned Valiant Squadrons (under SACEUR's control), and US Polaris submarines and tactical bomber forces (under US control and operating under the provisions of the Murphy-Dean agreement). To assess fully the efficacy of British command and control the activity of these forces must also be considered.

As noted above, 59 of the 60 Thors had been made 'ready'. Once alerted, the usual procedure was to place the Thors at the same readiness condition as the aircraft on QRA. Consequently, during the crisis Thor was at fifteen minutes readiness. In effect there was no significant change from normal operational conditions in which 65 percent of the force (39 missiles) was already at standby (i.e. about thirty minutes from launch) with the remainder available in 24–48 hours.[154] However, if the QRA force had been placed at 05 minutes readiness, the missiles would have been erected and held at Phase 2 hold, eight minutes from launch.

A more significant aspect of these procedures, however, is that the decision to fully alert the Thors was taken unilaterally by Air Marshal Cross apparently without consulting US authorities. As Thor was a dual-key weapon, 'he could not do this without 7th Air Division knowing, and he knew they were talking back to SAC.'[155] Exactly what the US authorities made of Thor's alert state is unclear. According to Sagan 'There is also no indication in the available records that high-level American political or military authorities in Washington were aware that Britain's nuclear forces were being put on a higher state of alert.'[156] Cross' own communications with SAC were surprisingly muted during the crisis: '...Once the Cuban missile crisis started, there was no one at the end of the phone and there was no one at the end of the phone until the crisis was over. [Cross] suspected that this may have been deliberate.'[157] For C-in-C Bomber Command, the performance of the Thors during the crisis reaffirmed the deterrent value of the missile. Outlining the advantages of Thor to the VCAS, he contended that 'this well proven weapon enables a high proportion of missiles to be brought to readiness at will.'[158] He further argued that in the 'eye of the American professional, as represented by SAC, it was systems at readiness that really counted.' Cross therefore recommended that phase-out of the Thors be 'retarded' and 'the reduction planned to start on April 1st 1963 be postponed until at least April 1964.' As noted earlier, the C-in-C's views were not shared by the Minister of Defence and the missiles were withdrawn on schedule.

US authentication officers were also stationed at RAF Marham to supervise the NATO-assigned Valiant squadrons. In peacetime, the aircraft came under operational control of the base commander. In war, they were to be armed with two American Mk 5 nuclear weapons and operate under SACEUR. The loading of the nuclear weapons was always supervised by USAF officers. In the case of the aircraft on QRA, control was maintained by locating the Valiants in a specially secure compound on the far side of the airfield. Release of the loaded aircraft to the RAF could only occur after an authenticated release message had been received by the American custodians. On 25 October, US forces in Europe were informed that 'Two-stage weapons may now be loaded on land-based alert strike aircraft on station in NATO. This decision shall be applicable to US forces as well as non-US forces when the specific QRA capability is achieved and dispersal authorization is granted.'[159] When the Valiants were being prepared, however, it soon became evident that the USAF custodial officers could not maintain physical control of all the nuclear weapons as they were only established with sufficient manpower to monitor the QRA compound and the nuclear weapons storage area. Therefore at the discretion of the Commanding Officer USAF, control of the weapons was handed over to the base commander. The result was 24 Valiant bombers (each armed with two US nuclear weapons) under the effective operational control of Bomber Command.[160]

The reasons why the US custodial officers adopted this procedure may be explained by the outcome of a Bomber Command alert and readiness exercise held between 20–1 September 1962. In the post-exercise report which was only circulated to the stations on 2 October, it was stated that:

> The present SACEUR release procedures are liable to impose such a delay on the scrambling of the SACEUR assigned force that it seriously risks being destroyed on the ground. This has been the subject of previous negotiations with SACEUR and is being taken up again.[161]

The exercise represented the first time weapons release procedures had been practiced by USAF custodians at RAF Marham. Consequently, new or modified release procedures may have been adopted between 2-25 October. There is also the possibility that the US custodial officer interpreted his mandate in very broad terms.[162] The final possibility is that *ad hoc* arrangements were implemented in the light of conditions at the time.

In addition to the NATO-assigned Valiant squadrons, US tactical bombers based in the UK were also placed on alert. The squadrons operated under two distinct categories of alert: 'overt', in which base klaxons would sound and all personnel would report to duty stations to upload weapons on all operationally available aircraft; and 'covert', in which only selected people on a duty roster would be contacted by telephone and told to report to their duty stations. It would appear that several hours prior to President Kennedy's public announcement, a 'covert' alert affecting all US tactical alert squadrons was initiated. As the crisis developed, a more advanced state of alert was adopted. Indeed, at the most critical point of the crisis, pilots adopted cockpit alert, with engines readied for immediate take-off.[163] In the case of the 20th Tactical Fighter Wing, target coverage was increased by fourteen with an additional two aircraft placed on tactical alert. This increase occurred after General Landon, the Commander of United States Air Forces Europe (CINCUSAFE), transferred responsibility for nuclear strikes to squadrons in the UK, allowing aircraft stationed in West Germany to implement contingency plans for the protection of Berlin.[164] In implementing these measures General Landon 'pushed his individual authority for alerting his forces to its limits'.[165] Indeed, the increase in alert status was at variance with Norstad's instructions not to implement all the measures required for a DEFCON 3 alert.[166]

A final area in which alert states were raised involved the US Polaris force at Holy Loch. As detailed above, the operation of US Polaris submarines from British waters was governed by the 1960 Holy Loch agreement. The United States Navy declared DEFCON-3 at 3–46 am on 23 October, at which point there was only one Polaris SSBN, *USS Abraham Lincoln*, in Holy Loch.[167] According to a US naval staff officer, Vice-Admiral Beshany, there were three Polaris submarines at Holy Loch at the start of the Cuban crisis, which were moved 'out of Holy Loch as a precaution without orders from above'.[168] The decision was then at once communicated to higher authorities and 'immediately endorsed, embraced, there was no argumentation'.[169] Both the submarines and the submarine tender, *USS Proteus*, were deployed from Holy Loch: 'The first ship went out almost immediately and the second one went out within 24 hours and then there was a third one alongside and she went out like 36 hours later, followed by the tender'.[170]

If this account is accurate, two of the boats were 'flushed' before the declaration of the DEFCON-3 alert state. The *USS Abraham Lincoln* left Holy Loch at 2pm on 23 October.[171] American political authorities were then informed of the deployments. The Joint Chiefs situation report to the White House and State Department for 25 October showed that 112 Atlantic Command SLBMs were on alert, indicating that all seven available SSBNs were on station; it was also made clear that the 'submarine tender Proteus is dispersing to Clyde Op[erational] Area'.[172] Hence, there was adequate time for the US authorities to meet the formal requirement to consult on the deployment of *Proteus* after the military decision to deploy the submarines. Naval channels of communication, and possibly the Royal Navy's own monitoring team at Holy Loch, presumably enabled the Admiralty to learn of events in the same way Bomber Command was told of changes in SAC's DEFCON alert state.

For those involved in providing a military and political response, the Cuban missile crisis consolidated the British-American relationship and 'brought the intimacy and trust between Macmillan and Kennedy to a new peak.'[173] This position was soon challenged when in November 1962, the American administration announced the cancellation of Skybolt. The decision threatened Britain's continued status as a nuclear power and set the stage for the 'angriest' Anglo-American summit since the war.[174]

THE CANCELLATION OF SKYBOLT

The Holy Loch agreement was only the first step in a series of complex negotiations ultimately linked to Britain's acquisition of the Skybolt missile. Indeed, the precise relationship between the Skybolt deal and the Holy Loch agreement has been the subject of considerable speculation.[175] The most authoritative account to date is provided by the US official historian Ronald Landa, who states that towards the end of the meeting at Camp David, Macmillan and Eisenhower drove by themselves to the President's farm at Gettysburg during which time the Skybolt and Polaris questions were raised.[176] That evening, a draft memorandum representing Macmillan's recollection was forwarded to the US delegation. The memorandum covered one subject: American willingness to extend the life of the V-force by supplying Skybolt, Polaris or both. No mention was made of either berthing facilities or the American proposal to establish a NATO MRBM force under SACEUR's control (discussed in Chapter 5).

The President's advisors believed the British memorandum did not fully represent Eisenhower's conversation and a completely new document was prepared. The President's memorandum came in three parts: the first reiterated American opposition to supply Polaris in a purely bilateral arrangement; the second outlined the position on Skybolt; and the third addressed the berthing of US submarines in Scottish ports. In response, the British produced a revision of Macmillan's original memorandum that was also rejected. Finally, a third version was prepared to which the American delegation agreed. This retained reference to the possible acquisition of Polaris, but without being specifically named, and loosely linked it to the MRBM proposal. The two memoranda consisting of Eisenhower's original and Macmillan's third version were exchanged and a 'gentleman's agreement consummated.'[177] In short, there was no single agreement or even a formal exchange of notes.

To clarify the details, Watkinson travelled to Washington and received a full account of Skybolt's development programme. A technical agreement between the two governments was subsequently agreed with Britain placing a provisional requirement for 100 missiles. Initially, progress proceeded smoothly but in October, Watkinson was told that Skybolt's development costs 'were turning out much higher than expected' and the project 'might be in real trouble'[178] Its future was placed in further doubt with the election of President Kennedy, who initiated a review of all major US defence programmes with Skybolt singled out for particular scrutiny. By common consent, Skybolt was the most daunting technological project yet attempted by the US and a figure of $500 million was eventually allocated to cover the development programme.[179]

Initial Bomber Command plans for the introduction of Skybolt were based on carriage of two missiles on each of the Mk II Vulcans and Victors. It was also proposed to maintain a proportion of the force on airborne patrol in times of international crisis, with the remainder brought to a maximum state of alert. Once launched, the aircraft would proceed under 'positive control' to designated holding areas. Suitable patrol areas included Central Norway, the Skaggerak, the Adriatic and the Aegean Sea. Alternatively, the aircraft could remain on patrol over the United Kingdom. The latter option was considered more suitable due to 'the complete certainty of VHF communications' with aircraft over the UK, in comparison to the low frequency required to reach aircraft patrolling outside enemy radar cover.[180] In both cases, however, the aircraft were expected to remain on patrol until they were either ordered to attack or endurance expired. It was also stipulated that the weapon could not be launched by accident and required 'at least one deliberate action by each of two separate crew members', one of whom was to be the first pilot.[181] An exercise to examine the feasibility of such an operation was conducted in July 1962 and demonstrated that, with tanker aircraft and bomber rotation, a weapons system could be kept airborne for a period of fourteen days.[182]

By the beginning of 1962, it was becoming clear to Washington that the original concept could not be completed within either its proposed budget or timescale. The first indication of Skybolt's impending cancellation was given to Ambassador Ormsby-Gore by Defense Secretary McNamara on 8 November. Reporting the details back to London, Ormsby-Gore concluded that although 'no decisions had yet been reached... the repercussions of such a decision by the United States would be extremely grave.'[183] He further described the three alternatives offered by McNamara:

to continue development of the project alone; to accept the Hound Dog missile as a replacement; or the provision of an alternate system such as Minuteman or Polaris. To confirm the details, the new Defence Secretary, Peter Thorneycroft, telephoned McNamara the following day. Emphasizing 'the grave repercussions for the British government if Skybolt was cancelled', he stressed the urgent need 'to consider alternative means of providing the British government with an independent deterrent' with 'the same degree of independence as Skybolt would have.'[184]

Thorneycroft initiated an urgent study to consider HMG's options. It concluded that if Skybolt was cancelled the government should initiate 'a crash programme to build nuclear-powered submarines armed with American Polaris missiles and British warheads; and/or acquire or borrow complete nuclear-powered submarines from the Americans, plus Polaris missiles, to be fitted with British warheads'[185] In both cases it was considered essential that Washington declare publicly its desire for Britain to maintain an independent strategic nuclear deterrent, and to provide the missiles 'without any conditions whatsoever upon their use.' Discussing the report with Macmillan, Thorneycroft expressed his belief that, 'the only efficient alternative to us is a submarine-borne Polaris weapon system.'[186] Details of the American position were also filtering back to London. The most optimistic report was presented by Ormsby-Gore who firmly believed that McNamara would offer 'whatever weapons system suited us'.[187] Aware of the debate within Whitehall, he considered that if Skybolt could not be saved 'this is certainly the moment for us to put forward whatever alternative demands we may wish to make.'

Thorneycroft and McNamara met on 11 December. The charged atmosphere was evident, the meeting being variously described as 'tense and dramatic', 'disconcertingly cool' and 'one of the bluntest talks ever within the Anglo-American alliance'.[188] Opening the discussion, McNamara set out the reasons why the US administration had arrived at the tentative conclusion that Skybolt should be abandoned. He then presented three options: Britain could continue to develop Skybolt alone; the American Hound Dog missile could be adapted for British use; Britain could 'participate in a seaborne MRBM force under multilateral manning and ownership.'[189] Thorneycroft considered all three alternatives unsatisfactory and would 'put the Government in an impossible position.' He further suggested that to fully satisfy British needs, 'the best alternative might be Polaris.' McNamara agreed to consider the proposal, but expected 'serious problems, both legal and policy-wise, in providing assistance to a UK constructed Polaris fleet'.[190] The meeting ended abruptly with Thorneycroft stressing that 'the political situation could not be held for long', emphasizing that a decision in principle would be required 'not later than the Nassau meeting between the Prime Minister and the President.'

In preparation for the Nassau summit both sides were keenly aware of the potential consequences for British-American relations. By now, the British position had moved firmly towards acquisition of Polaris. In briefing notes for the Prime Minister prior to the meeting, the objectives were clear:

> If the Skybolt programme is discontinued the United Kingdom Government have concluded that a submarine based rocket is the most suitable form for a British deterrent. For us missiles on fixed bases are unsuitable. To give our deterrent the best chance of survival against surprise attack it must be maintained on a mobile platform capable of a long endurance on station. Polaris missiles fired from submarines offer the best chance of achieving this purpose.[191]

To deploy Polaris it was intended to construct seven nuclear-powered submarines each armed with eight missiles. Completion of the submarine construction programme, however, was expected to take several years. In the interim, before the first submarine came on station, Britain could not claim with credibility to possess a true strategic deterrent. To maintain this, the government further proposed to hire from the Americans two or three complete submarines together with their missiles 'to cover the interval until our own new force was ready.' Informing Ormsby-Gore of the British position, Macmillan starkly underlined the implications of failure: 'if we cannot reach an agreement on a realistic means of maintaining the British independent deterrent, all the other questions may only justify perfunctory discussion, since an agonizing reappraisal of all our foreign and defence policy will be required.'[192]

The American negotiating position for Nassau also received close attention. On 16 December Kennedy met McNamara, Ball and Bundy to discuss the matter. McNamara reviewed the Skybolt project and the understandings reached with Britain, and in commenting on the British proposal to obtain Polaris, indicated his unwillingness to hire the submarines. On the other hand, he supported the sale of Polaris, provided that suitable control arrangements could be agreed.[193] McNamara's proposal was strongly opposed by Ball who explained that such an outcome would reverse current US policy, which was designed to remove Britain's status as an independent nuclear power.[194] He further argued that the administration should avoid any actions that strengthened the nuclear relationship with Britain and make clear its determination not to assist in the creation of a UK Polaris missile force. For the State Department, the preferred solution was to supply Britain with Polaris but solely within the context of a multilateral force. Concluding the meeting, the President approved the following measures: Britain would be supplied with Polaris missiles; the offer would be conditional on Britain's agreement to assign the eventual force 'to a multilateral or multinational force in NATO', Britain would further agree to build up her conventional forces to agreed NATO levels; the terms governing the use of Skybolt would also apply to Polaris; the new system would become effective in 1969. In short, despite later commendations of Macmillan's 'bravura performance' at Nassau, Kennedy arrived in the Bahamas with the expectation of supplying Polaris firmly on the US agenda.[195]

THE NASSAU AGREEMENT

The Nassau meeting was held between 18-21 December with cancellation of Skybolt the first item on the agenda.[196] Macmillan opened the discussions by expressing concern that the failure of Skybolt should not be used 'as a means of forcing Britain out of an independent nuclear capacity.'[197] Kennedy agreed and hoped that the US offer to pay half the further development costs of Skybolt would redress such misapprehensions. He believed, however, that a decision to supply Britain with Polaris was a different question and would be seen to invite the spread of further national deterrents. Macmillan then addressed the two options facing HMG. They could either abandon the deterrent altogether or continue 'no matter what the cost or effort required.' Continuing on this theme, Macmillan observed that:

> It was true that Britain had not at present got a submarine-fired missile in the development programme but they would if necessary be prepared to undertake this and to find the resources for the extra effort involved by making savings elsewhere in the defence programme. If they had to go ahead and develop a submarine-fired missile themselves this would lead inevitably to a deep rift in United States-United Kingdom relations. This was not to say that the government would in any way lessen their efforts to co-operate with the United States Government. But public opinion could not be controlled.[198]

The American response was delivered by Kennedy. The terms were contained in a draft communiqué that listed the offer of Hound Dog, the completion of the Skybolt programme on a 50-50 basis, or 'as an alternative', a joint study into the feasibility of a NATO missile force in which both countries would participate along with other members of the alliance. For Britain the proposal was wholly inadequate. Not only was no mention made of Polaris by name but the accompanying terms and press release were considered to make independent use of the force almost impossible. Reviewing the documents in private session, Thorneycroft stated that under the proposals Britain 'would not in fact have (nor could we claim to have) an independent nuclear deterrent.'[199] Given the circumstances, he reluctantly recommended to Macmillan that, 'with great regret', the talks should be abandoned. Macmillan stayed his hand. 'The Americans may give in to us', he replied, 'I have not given up hope.'[200]

To bridge the divide between the two positions, the issue of control was central. In short, America was determined to achieve centralized control of the West's nuclear forces, while Britain was determined to maintain an independent strategic capability. To accommodate both objectives, a form of words was required that allowed both parties to satisfy their domestic constituencies. The key to achieving this (and ultimately the preservation of the British-American alliance) rested on the interpretation of the word 'assign'. The resultant dilemma was succinctly encapsulated by Kennedy, who remarked that 'For their different reasons, the United Kingdom wanted the word "assign" interpreted as loosely as possible and the United States wanted it defined as tightly as possible.'[201] Expanding on the American position, Kennedy explained that it was important that Polaris submarines should be assigned to NATO, as this would protect the administration from any charge of inconsistency, particularly as a result of McNamara's Ann Arbor speech when he deprecated small national deterrents. He, however, appreciated Macmillan's position and conceded that the British Polaris force could be withdrawn from multilateral command if the very survival of the United Kingdom was at stake. Macmillan considered this interpretation too restrictive. He thought it essential that any British government should possess the unquestioned right to use Polaris as an instrument of policy in a serious national emergency and believed that a mechanism could be established for putting the force under NATO command while still preserving this right.

For HMG, this principle was a cardinal requirement of any eventual agreement: acceptance would have allowed the force to be used outside the NATO area and thus preserve Britain's status an independent nuclear power. Reporting developments back to his Cabinet colleagues in London, Macmillan expressed his concerns:

> I am afraid things are not at present going very well... So far, the Americans have felt unwilling to offer us the Polaris missile on terms that are acceptable to us. They wish us to assign the whole of the British Polaris force to NATO or a multilateral nuclear force. Such an arrangement would not give us an independent British contribution to the nuclear deterrent in any real sense of the word independent, since, under the American proposal we would only be able to withdraw the force from NATO in a dire national emergency. It would therefore not be available outside the NATO area or play a role in strengthening our foreign policy. Our feeling is that it would not be tolerable to British public opinion that we should pay about £300 million for a force which would then become, as it were, the property of NATO.[202]

Although events seemed to be slipping away, Macmillan trusted to his political instincts. Firm in the belief that 'unlike his high brow advisors', the President was 'a political animal' who would not ditch old friends lightly,[203] he made one last impassioned plea:

> Britain needed some independent deterrent in order to give their voice a legitimate authority and strength in international councils. Whether the force was committed or assigned or dealt with under some other phrase, in fact it must still be capable of being used by the British Government when they wished. This power would be exercised with the utmost sense of responsibility. But in the ordinary day-to-day diplomatic life and during periods of international stress people must know that the force could be used when the British government regarded supreme national interests as involved. Unless this principle could be accepted he would prefer to drop the whole idea of the Polaris system and find some other way. He would go a very long way to tie the force to NATO but in the last resort he would have to say that it was as much part of Her Majesty's Government's forces as were the Brigade of Guards.[204]

Concluding his remarks, Macmillan announced that if agreement were not reached HMG would be forced 'to make a reappraisal of their defence policies throughout the world.' To avert the imminent collapse of the talks, Kennedy signalled his intention to look again at the drafts and give more consideration to British concerns. The revised draft moved considerably closer to the British position. Of particular significance was paragraph 8 which granted Britain an 'opt out' from multilateral control whenever 'Her Majesty's Government may decide that supreme national interests are at stake'[205] In return for this American concession, Macmillan was required to provide a secret understanding which granted the American President 'as much notice as possible' before Britain withdrew its Polaris submarines from NATO command.[206]

Before accepting the revised text, Macmillan sought the view of the Cabinet. Drawing their attention to paragraph 8, he strongly advised acceptance: 'it gives us want we want... the sole right of decision on the use of our Polaris submarines and missiles as an independent force.'[207] Although in general, the Cabinet endorsed the Prime Minister's position, a number of reservations were raised. A particular concern was the open-ended financial commitment that was only acceptable 'if our independent control of the deterrent is clearly and unambiguously expressed.'[208] The Cabinet's anxiety stemmed from the wording of paragraph 8 which placed the commitment to use the force in defence of the western alliance before the 'opt out' clause and could have been interpreted as merely providing a British veto over the use of its own Polaris submarines rather than allowing the force to be used as an independent deterrent. To remove this ambiguity, the Cabinet recommended the following revision that was duly accepted by the Americans:

> The Prime Minister made it clear that except where Her Majesty's government may decide that the supreme national interests are at stake these British forces would be used only for the purposes of international defence of the Western Alliance.[209]

A further concern expressed by the Cabinet concerned omission of any reference to the hiring of American submarines to cover the expected gap in Britain's deterrent forces from the mid-1960s. Although Macmillan conceded the importance of the point, he thought it unwise to raise the matter at such a late stage in the talks. In contrast to the Cabinet's 'warm approval,' a disparaging note was delivered by the Conservative Chief Whip, Martin Redmayne, who thought the American offer 'no more than a sop' to British national pride and that under the present conditions, Polaris would provide 'little but prestige value'.[210] Voicing the concern of the party right, he strongly advised that Macmillan be recalled immediately 'to pause at leisure' and consider whether there were any 'practical alternatives which even if more costly might well be more acceptable politically'. In response, Macmillan considered the final agreement 'very satisfactory,' with Britain's continued possession of an independent deterrent 'quite unambiguously expressed'. While he recognised that the position would be criticized by both 'the extreme right and nuclear disarmers' he thought 'the whole of middle opinion will surely be favourable.'[211]

The agreed text was issued as a joint communiqué that has been described as 'a monument of contrived ambiguity'.[212] This is less than surprising. Working under pressure of a tight deadline and with inadequate staff support, the document attempted to reconcile Britain's demands for an independent strategic deterrent with the American concept of an integrated multilateral force.[213] Subsequent criticism centred on interpretation of paragraphs 6 and 8. Specifically, paragraph 6 sanctioned the development of a NATO nuclear force under multinational control, whereas paragraph 8 envisaged the creation of a multilateral force. To add further confusion, the British Polaris force referred to in paragraph 8 was to be 'assigned and targeted in the same way as the forces described in paragraph 6.'[214] The ambiguous language of the Nassau Agreement 'reflected two soliloquies rather than an understanding' and enabled both parties to claim success.[215] In a subsequent press briefing, Kennedy stressed the multilateral element of the deal with Macmillan informing Parliament with equal conviction of Britain's continued independent contribution to the Western deterrent.[216]

For many, the election of a Labour government in October 1964 was expected to herald the demise of Polaris. In opposition, the Labour Party leader, Harold Wilson, had been a severe critic of Britain's nuclear deterrent. Indeed, discussing Polaris as an independent deterrent, the 1964 Labour Party manifesto declared 'it will not be independent and it will not be British and it will not deter.'[217] In short, 'there was to be no nuclear pretence or suggestion of a go-it-alone British nuclear war against the Soviet Union.'[218] Despite such convictions, however, the only major change in policy from the previous Conservative government was to reduce the number of boats from five to four with the first 'R' class Polaris submarine entering Royal Navy service in June 1968.[219]

AN ASSESSMENT

The Nassau summit illuminates a number of themes in the nuclear relationship between Britain and America. The most apparent is the personal relationship between Macmillan and Kennedy that has been described as the intangible linkage in the special relationship.[220] This is clearly shown at Nassau where the two leaders' 'personal affection for each other was to have a decisive impact on the course of the conference'.[221] Indeed, it has been argued that it was the strong interplay of individual personalities that eventually persuaded Kennedy to 'overrule his subordinates in order to help

Macmillan'.[222] This portrayal of events is not shared by all participants. McGeorge Bundy offers a more realist interpretation: 'Macmillan could have been dull, and Ormsby-Gore just another diplomat, and the underlying imperative would still have been clear: Nothing could justify this kind of American damage to Anglo-American relations.'[223]

Whilst accepting such reservations, it is nevertheless evident from the preceding analysis that the full significance of the nuclear relationship between the two countries cannot be established from the documentary evidence alone: informal personal understandings developed at a variety of levels played an important role. Although by its very nature such a contention is difficult to substantiate, a number of intriguing vignettes have emerged. The informal understanding reached between Air Marshal Cross and General Blanchard on the use of Project E weapons in an emergency offers one example. Further examples are provided by the joint targeting arrangements initiated between Bomber Command and SAC and the 'gentleman's agreement' consummated between Macmillan and Eisenhower at the 1960 Camp David Summit.

A separate theme apparent at Nassau was Britain's growing inability to maintain nuclear control on a purely bilateral basis with the United States. This tendency first became apparent in the early-1960s when arrangements covering the transfer of Project E weapons to the V-force were expanded to cover NATO commitments. The increased emphasis on Britain's nuclear role within NATO was further strengthened by the re-targeting of the Thors and the revision of the Murphy-Dean agreement which was amended to incorporate nuclear forces assigned to SACEUR. At Nassau, the process reached its culmination: Britain's strategic nuclear forces would now be assigned to NATO and targeted in accordance with SACEUR's plans.[224] Although the British government retained the right to withdraw these forces when supreme national interests were at stake, 'what these could ever be, or whether, when it came to the crunch, we would be allowed by the Americans to fire a Polaris missile without them agreeing, was never discussed.'[225]

The acquisition of Polaris also marked the transfer of the British deterrent from the airforce to the navy. The consequences of this had direct implications for both targeting and command and control. In October 1963, Bomber Command was informed that target selection for the V-force would be determined by the requirements of SACEUR's Nuclear Strike Plan. Operational planning was to be undertaken at SHAPE and marked the end of direct target co-ordination between Bomber Command and SAC.[226] Targets for Polaris were compiled in two ways: for the 'NATO-assigned' boats, by the US Joint Strategic Planning Staff based at Omaha; and in its national role, by the Navy Department in conjunction with the Defence Intelligence Staff.[227] In comparison to airborne systems, however, the deployment of Polaris reduced the flexibility of Britain's nuclear response. Direct communication with submarines remained difficult and the missiles were relatively inaccurate. Faced with contraction of the Soviet target base, was it merely a happy co-incidence that by the end of 1963, the government had concluded that 'the Russians would regard the certain destruction of five of their largest cities as an unacceptable risk'? [228]

A final factor at Nassau was the realization that only through nuclear collaboration with America could the British deterrent be maintained at an affordable cost. To provide a comparable system to Polaris from British resources alone would have required a substantial increase in the defence budget, a burden HMG was determined to avoid. While reliance on US technology inevitably increased Britain's dependency on America, this was a price the government was willing to pay. Although it has been argued that the close relationship with the US made Britain reliant on American nuclear technology, Britain's declared policy objective was never one of total independence.[229] Indeed, it was believed that only by fostering an interdependent relationship with America would Britain retain any degree of influence over US policy and guard against a return to American isolationism.[230] Viewed in this context, the command and control arrangements governing US nuclear weapons in Britain were subordinate to the primary political objective of maintaining a strong security link with the United States. For America, the issues were more evenly balanced. On one hand, a preferential nuclear relationship with the UK would militate against closer European co-operation. On the other, refusal to co-operate with Britain could have jeopardized base rights, resulted in a duplication of effort and increased the potential for nuclear proliferation. To balance these opposing demands, Washington adopted a strategy of qualified engagement: Britain would be assisted in its nuclear programme on the understanding that the force was already in existence and would remain under national control but would be placed under US command in the event of general war. If this view is accepted, Nassau did not mark 'the total collapse of the government's defence policy'[231] but rather a continuation of British policy that stretched back to the mid-1940s.

BILATERAL CONTROL 1953–1964

1. Duke, *US Defence*, p. 95.
2. For more details, see Jan Melissen, 'Prelude to Interdependence: The Anglo-American Relationship and the Limits of Great Britain's Nuclear Policy, 1952-1957', *Arms Control*, Vol.11, No.3 (1990); Timothy Botti, *The Long Wait: The Forging of the Anglo-American Nuclear Alliance 1945-1958* (Greenwood Press: New York, 1987); John Young, 'Churchill, the Russians and the Western Alliance: the three-power conference at Bermuda, December 1953', *The English Historical Review*, Vol.101, No.3 (October 1986), pp. 905-6; John Baylis, *Anglo-American Defence Relations, 1939-1980: The Special Relationship* (Macmillan, 1984), pp. 68-72.
3. Simpson, *Independent*, p. 113.
4. PREM 11/1763, Sandys to Churchill, 15 June 1954.
5. According to Sandys, this was the first occasion when the President or any of his officials had definitely stated the intention to supply the UK with atomic bombs in the event of war. Ibid.
6. PREM 11/1763, DP(54)4th, 24 June 1954.
7. Ibid.
8. PREM 11/1763, Secretary of State for Air to Churchill, 10 January 1955.
9. AIR 2/13213, Washington to Air Ministry, 27 November 1954.
10. S of S for Air to Churchill, emphasis in original.
11. AIR 19/939, Eisenhower to Eden, 12 October 1956.
12. T 225/645, Bligh to Macpherson, 24 October 1956.
13. DEFE 4/78, COS(55)62nd, 3 August 1955.
14. DEFE 4/77, COS(55)34th, 29 June 1955.
15. DEFE 4/78, Annex to JP(55)48(Final), 28 July 1955.
16. DEFE 4/78, COS(55)62nd, 3 August 1955.
17. Cooper, 'Direction', p. 16.
18. The Terms of Reference covering the supply of US atomic weapons to the RAF and the co-ordination of nuclear strike plans are reproduced in full in Appendix 3.
19. AIR 20/11338, COS(56)451, 31 December 1956, Annex D, copy of letter dated 12 December 1956, General Twining to CAS.
20. AIR 20/11338, COS(57)3rd, 8 January 1957.
21. Wynn, *RAF*, p. 257.
22. AIR 20/11338, Co-ordination of SAC and Bomber Command Global War Nuclear Strike Plans, USAF/RAF Conference, Washington, May 1957.
23. PREM 11/1763, Brief for Macmillan, 20 March 1957.
24. For more information on the physical parameters of early US nuclear weapons see, Michael Yaffe, 'A Higher Priority than the Korean War!': The Crash Programs to Modify the Bombers for the Bomb', *Diplomacy and Statecraft*, Vol.5, No.2 (1994).
25. PREM 11/1763, Notes and memoranda - Bermuda, 23 March 1957.
26. *Agreement... for Cooperation on the Uses of Atomic Energy for Mutual Defence Purposes*, Treaty Series no. 41, Cmnd. 537 (HMSO, 1958).
27. AIR 8/2201, COS(58)148, 5 June 1958.
28. To accommodate the weapon, a number of Special Storage Areas (SSAs) were constructed at RAF bases at Honington, Waddington and Marham.
29. AIR 20/10061, AC(58)14, 17 February 1958.
30. AIR 20/11338, Memorandum of Understanding Between the USAF and RAF, 1 October 1958.
31. AIR 8/2238, Progress Report on the Readiness of the Medium Bomber Force, June 1959.
32. AIR 8/2201, Hudleston to Broadhurst, 7 July 1958.
33. AIR 19/939, Release of US Nuclear Weapons to Bomber Command, 24 April 1959.
34. AIR 20/10061, Future of Project E, 8 May 1959.
35. AIR 6/129, AC(60)10, 7 July 1960.
36. Pike to White, 5 September 1960, US Library of Congress, Manuscripts Department, Thomas White Papers, Box 29. We are grateful to William Burr for drawing our attention to this document.

BILATERAL CONTROL 1953–1964

37. Correspondence, Air Vice-Marshal Ian Campbell, July 1993.
38. Wynn, *RAF*, p. 267.
39. D(60)10th, 16-17 October 1960. The minutes of the meeting are retained and are located at CAB 123/28. The above extract is taken from James, *Defence*, p. 202.
40. AIR 20/10056, COS(61)32nd, 30 May 1961. The South East Asia Treaty Organisation (SEATO) was established in Manila in September 1954. Comprising Australia, New Zealand, the USA, Pakistan, Thailand, the Philippines, Britain and France, it provided for mutual collective action if any signatory was attacked or subject to internal subversion.
41. AIR 20/10056, COS(62)131, 27 March 1962.
42. AIR 20/10056, JP(62)Note 4, 26 January 1962.
43. AIR 20/10056, Macmillan minute, 13 November 1962. SEATO Plan 4 was designed to meet a direct attack from China on member states.
44. AIR 20/10056, Annex to DASB/7597, 16 November 1962.
45. DEFE 4/154, COS(63)29th, 25 April 1963.
46. AIR 20/10056, WASCOS 46, JCS reply dated 11 June, BDS Washington to MOD, 13 June 1963.
47. For details of the Thor negotiations, see Clark, *Nuclear*, Chapter 1; Wynn, *RAF*, pp. 280-97; Ian Clark and David Angell, 'Britain, the United States and the Control of Nuclear Weapons: The Diplomacy of the Thor Deployment 1956-58', *Diplomacy and Statecraft*, Vol.2, No.3 (November 1991); Jan Melissen, 'The Thor Saga: Anglo-American Nuclear Relations, US IRBM Development and Deployment in Britain, 1955-1959', *Journal of Strategic Studies*, Vol.15, No.2, June 1992.
48. *Exchange of Notes… Concerning the Supply to the United Kingdom of Intermediate Range Ballistic Missiles*, Treaty Series No.14, Cmnd. 406 (HMSO, 1958).
49. AIR 20/10300, Technical Agreement between USAF and RAF on the Establishment of IRBM (SM-75 Thor) Bases in the United Kingdom, 26 June 1958.
50. DEFE 13/394, MM7/59, 24 November 1959.
51. DEFE 13/394, Humphreys to Sabatini, 31 March 1960.
52. DEFE 13/394, Record of Meeting between Sir Richard Powell and Mr Gates, Deputy Secretary of Defense for International Security Affairs, 31 August 1959.
53. AIR 8/2239, Ward to Watkinson, January 1960.
54. Ibid.
55. Dwight D. Eisenhower Library, (DDEL), Anderson to Herter, 16 May 1960, White House Office, Office of Assistant for National Security Affairs, NSC Series, Box 14.
56. Feaver, *Guarding*, p. 176.
57. AIR 20/10620, Thor Strategic Missile Force, Readiness Policy, 25 July 1960.
58. DEFE 13/121, Progress Report on the Thor Project, 2 June 1958.
59. AIR 8/2238, Hudleston to Cross, 11 August 1959.
60. AIR 8/2307, AC(61)44, 2 August 1961.
61. Correspondence, Flt. Lt. George Stalker, November 1992. By August 1961 the actual countdown time was 13 to 14 minutes. Air 8/2307, The Future of Thor, Note by VCAS, AC(61)44, 2 August 1961.
62. To maintain Thor at two minutes readiness raised various technical problems. First, the missile was designed to be kept in the fuelled state for only two hours, after which various components became frozen through contact with the liquid oxygen. When this point occurred, the fuel was unloaded and the missile subjected to a six-hour recovery period. Consequently, to avoid the whole force becoming inoperable after two hours, only one quarter (i.e. fifteen missiles) could be held at two minutes readiness at any one time. Second, continuous loss of liquid oxygen due to boil-off was expected to increase demand for LOX by seventy times. Third, the current safety regulations prohibited the loading of fuel into a fully armed missile. The Future of Thor, ibid.
63. Wynn, *RAF*, p. 348.
64. For discussion of the Thor deployment, see ibid., pp 340-62.
65. Letter by Donald Hofford, *The Times,* 23 September 1974, discussed in Duke, *US Defence*, p. 233n.

66. Correspondence, Gp. Capt. K.W.T. Pugh, commander of the Driffield Thor Complex, November 1992; Flt. Lt. Dennis Moore, December 1992; Sqd. Ldr. Frank Leatherdale, December 1992.
67. Correspondence, Flt. Lt. George Stalker, November 1992.
68. Correspondence, Sqd. Ldr. Colin Burch, November 1992.
69. AIR 19/999, Minister of Defence's visit to the United States, 19 September 1962.
70. Normally the American key was kept locked in a safe, though during the Cuban missile crisis USAF authentication officers wore them around their necks, as was normal practice with their RAF counterparts. Correspondence, Stalker.
71. Sagan, *Limits*, p. 109.
72. DEFE 7/2018, COS(62)120, Control of Nuclear Weapons, 20 March 1962.
73. Notes on UK Target Selection and Co-ordination Developments over the past 10 years, 26 August 1960, cited in Wynn, *RAF*, p. 276.
74. Air Marshal Sir Kenneth Cross, 'Bomber Command's Thor Missile Force', *Journal of the Royal United Services Institute* (May, 1963), p. 136.
75. Sagan, 'SIOP-62', p. 46.
76. AIR 19/964, Minute from DCAS, 23 March 1959.
77. AIR 20/10056, ACAS(Ops) to CAS, Strategic Strike Planning by Bomber Command, 5 October 1962.
78. Clark, *Nuclear*, pp. 382-94.
79. Strategic Strike Planning by Bomber Command.
80. AIR 24/2688, Exercise Fallex 62, 2 September 1962. The units involved were the 20th Tactical Fighter Wing at RAF Wethersfield, the 48th Tactical Fighter Wing at RAF Lakenheath, and the 81st Tactical Fighter Wing at RAF Bentwaters.
81. Correspondence, Sgt (USAF) Sam Wein, July 1993.
82. Ibid.
83. RG 59, Rusk to Kennedy, Political and Military Considerations Bearing on Turkish and Italian IRBMs, 9 November 1962, National Archives.
84. Article 5 of the North Atlantic Treaty states that an armed attack against any signatory will 'be considered an attack against them all' and would result in collective action 'including the use of armed force, to restore and maintain the security of the North Atlantic area.' The North Atlantic Treaty, Washington DC, 4 April 1949, NATO Office of Information and Press, Brussels.
85. Against this, however, it is also apparent from an examination of readiness exercises that Bomber Command possessed *de facto* control of targeting such that during countdown 'two changes of target were ordered'. Given that the Launch Control and Authentication Officers at the individual Thor sites could not determine where these targets were located, Bomber Command had operational control to alter targets against US wishes. For further details, see Wynn, *RAF*, p. 353.
86. The Future of Thor.
87. AIR 8/2307, Air Council, conc. of mtg. 15(61), 7 September 1961. .
88. *HC deb.*, Vol.618, Col.1034-5, 1 March 1960.
89. AIR 8/2307, Annex B to conc. of mtg. 6(62)(Special), 9 April 1962.
90. CAB 131/27, D(62)40, 24 July 1962.
91. Wynn, *RAF*, p. 361.
92. At a press conference on 20 November 1957 Dulles was reported to have said that the US could not accept a veto by other governments over its right to use nuclear weapons. A week later General Power informed NATO parliamentarians that one-third of SAC was in the air, at all times carrying nuclear weapons.
93. National Museum of Labour History (NMLH), TUC International Committee, Summarised Reports of meetings between the Prime Minister, the Foreign Secretary and General Council Representatives, I.C. Special 2/5, 6 January 1958.
94. RG 59, Timmons to Murphy 711.56341/12-2657, National Archives.
95. *HC Deb.*, Vol.581, Cols.979-80, 4 February 1958.

96. RG 59, Whitney to Dulles, 711.56341/1-3158, National Archives.
97. RG 59, Dulles to Eisenhower, 611.4112/5-1558, National Archives.
98. RG 59, Kohler to Murphy, Letter from Prime Minister to President Proposing US-UK Talks on Procedural Arrangements Leading to Decision to Launch Nuclear Retaliation, 8 May 1958, Policy Planning Staff Records, 1957-61, Lot 67D548, Box 130, Great Britain, National Archives.
99. See Chapter 3.
100. The Murphy-Dean Agreement was re-examined by the Cabinet Office in November 1994, but was still considered sensitive and remains closed. It is located at CAB 21/4061. In July 1996, a sanitised version of the agreement was released in the US. We are grateful to William Burr for drawing our attention to this and related documents..
101. The two annexes and basic understanding are reproduced in full in Appendix 4.
102. DDEL, Report to the President and the Prime Minister, Procedures for the Committing to the Attack of Nuclear Retaliatory Forces in the United Kingdom, 7 June 1958, Ann Whitman File, Admin. Series, Box 5, AEC 1958 (2).
103. RG 59, British Proposal for Talks to Ensure US-UK Agreement on Procedure for Reaching Decision to Launch Nuclear Retaliation, 13 May 1958, Policy Planning Staff Records, 1957-61, Lot 67D548, Box 130, Great Britain, National Archives.
104. Harold Macmillan, *Riding the Storm, 1956-1959* (Macmillan, 1971), p. 294.
105. CAB 131/18, D(57)30, 31 December 1957.
106. AIR 8/2201, McLeod to Sandys, 23 January 1959.
107. Ibid.
108. AIR 19/690, Hudleston to Amery, 18 November 1960.
109. AIR 8/2201, Hooper to Orme, 22 January 1959.
110. PREM 11/5199, Home to Johnson, Prime Minister's Personal Telegram, T 70/63, 20 December 1963.
111. Alistair Horne, *Macmillan, 1957-1986: Volume II* (Macmillan: 1989), p. 276.
112. For the most comprehensive account of linkage between Skybolt and Holy Loch, see Clark, *Nuclear*, pp. 258-280.
113. PREM 11/2940, Watkinson to Macmillan, 14 December 1959. For details of the 1953 Eden-Eisenhower agreement, see Chapter 5.
114. CAB 131/23, D(60)5th, 25 May 1960.
115. PREM 11/2940, Notes of Meeting, 15 June 1960.
116. Ibid.
117. PREM 11/2940, Macmillan to Eisenhower, 24 June 1960.
118. PREM 11/2940, Eisenhower to Macmillan, 30 June 1960.
119. PREM 11/2940, Macmillan to Eisenhower, 2 July 1960.
120. PREM 11/2940, Eisenhower to Macmillan, 15 July 1960.
121. PREM 11/2940, FO to Washington, Tel. 3360, 22 July 1960.
122. PREM 11/2940, Joint Control over US Polaris Submarines Based in the UK, 28 July 1960.
123. PREM 11/2940, FO to Washington, Tel. 3522, 3 August 1960. Eisenhower's assurance concerning Polaris and his confirmation of the 1953 Eden-Eisenhower agreement are given in Appendix 5.
124. PREM 11/2941, Washington to FO, Tel. 1638, 16 August 1960.
125. PREM 11/2941, Washington to FO, Tel. 2086, 17 October 1960.
126. PREM 11/2941, Macmillan to Home, 18 October 1960.
127. PREM 11/2941, Macmillan to Watkinson, 18 September 1960. The establishment of the US Polaris base at Holy Loch was announced in the Queen's Speech to Parliament, see *HC Deb.*, Vol.629, Col.38, 1 November 1960.
128. Deployment of nuclear warheads to the UK for use by the US Navy was co-ordinated by the Admiralty under the codename 'Project Lamarchus'. All files relating to Project Lamarchus remain classified and are located at ADM 1/27199-203.
129. AIR 19/690, Macmillan to Kennedy, 26 January 1961.

130. AIR 19/690, Memorandum attached to President's letter of 6th February 1961.
131. For recent accounts of the crisis, see Ernest R. May and Philip D. Zelikow (Eds.), *The Kennedy Tapes: Inside the White House During the Cuban Missile Crisis* (Harvard University Press, 1997) and Aleksandr Fursenko and Timothy Naftali, *'One Hell of a Gamble': Khruschev, Castro, Kennedy, and the Cuban Missile Crisis 1958-1964* (John Murray, 1997).
132. PREM 11/3689, Ormsby-Gore to Macmillan, Tel. 2636, 22 October 1962, PM's Pers. Tel. T.495/62; Ormsby-Gore to Macmillan, Tel. 2650, PM's Pers. Tel. T.505/62, 23 October 1962.
133. Sherman Kent, 'The Cuban Missile Crisis of 1962: Presenting the Evidence Abroad', *Studies in Intelligence* Vol.10, No.2 (Spring, 1972), p. 24.
134. Macmillan, *End*, pp. 180-4. For discussion of Macmillan and Britain's role in the crisis see, L.V. Scott, *Macmillan, Kennedy and the Cuban Missile Crisis: Political, Military and Intelligence Aspects* (Macmillan, 1999).
135. For details of C-in-C's delegated powers, see Chapter 3.
136. Sagan, *Limits*, p.110.
137. AIR 25/1703, Operational Record Book, Headquarters No.1 Group, October 1962.
138. Correspondence, Air Vice-Marshal Arthur Griffiths, July 1993.
139. AIR 24/2689, Conference of Group, Station and Squadron Commanders, 14-15 November 1962.
140. AIR 24/2696, Appendix 71 to Form 540, Administrative Order No. 8/62, 24 October 1962.
141. Bernard Lovell, *Astronomer by Chance* (Macmillan, 1990), p. 322; see also Chapter 8.
142. Stewart Menaul, *Countdown: Britain's Strategic Nuclear Forces* (Robert Hale, 1980), p. 116.
143. Sagan, *Limits*, p. 110.
144. Group Captain Ian Madelin, 'Some Additional Comments on Command and Control During the Cuban Missile Crisis', in Miller, *Seeing*, p. 225.
145. DEFE 32/7, Record of a conversation between the Chief of the Air Staff, First Sea Lord and the Chief of the Imperial General Staff held in the Ministry of Defence at 1430, Saturday, 27 October 1962.
146. Macmillan, *End*, p. 190.
147. Record of conversation, CAS, FSL and CIGS.
148. Ibid.
149. Ibid.
150. Ibid.
151. For details of Alert Conditions, see Chapter 3.
152. Correspondence, Air Vice-Marshal Michael Robinson, August 1993.
153. AIR 20/11371, Cross to Kyle, 31 October 1962.
154. The Future of Thor.
155. Madelin, 'Additional', p. 224.
156. Sagan, *Limits*, p. 113; see also Raymond L. Garthoff, *Reflections on the Cuban Missile Crisis* (Washington: The Brookings Institution, 1989), p. 208n. The only British forces whose alert state the President was notified of were three SACEUR-assigned Valiants and four Canberras. John F. Kennedy Library (JFKL) JCS to Secretary of State, NSF Cuba Cables, 10/25/62 Box 41. Kennedy was notified of the alert state of the Jupiters but not the Thors.
157. Madelin, 'Additional', pp. 223-5.
158. AIR 20/11371, The Thor Strategic Missile System, 31 October 1962.
159. RG 273, Records of the NSC, National Security Action Memorandum (NSAM) No.199, Loading of SACEUR Land-based Alert Strike Aircraft, October 25 1962. National Archives.
160. Correspondence, Air Vice-Marshal Ian Campbell, July 1993.
161. AIR 24/2688, Post Exercise Report on Exercise Micky Fin II, 2 October 1962.
162. According to Major-General Coiner, the Assistant Deputy Chief of Staff/Operations for Atomic Energy at SHAPE: 'there were two possibilities. 1) Maintaining US custody by having one US airman in the vicinity of the aircraft. 2) Maintaining US ownership but not custody. The US act required ownership but did not specify custody. US Department of Defense lawyers took an optimistic view of this possibility.' AIR 8/2201, Note of discussion, 2 April 1959.

163. Correspondence, Wein.
164. Impact in the USAFE Area, 28 February 1963, National Security Archive, *The Cuban Missile Crisis, 1962*, Microfiche collection (Washington: Chadwyk-Healey, 1990), Doc. 02973.
165. Sagan, *Limits*, p. 104.
166. When the US JCS ordered all US forces worldwide to DEFCON-3 on 22 October Norstad was given discretion in implementing the command. He decided to take less obtrusive action, so as not to alarm western Europeans and undermine political support for the US. Ibid, p. 103.
167. CINCLANT Historical Account of Cuban Crisis, 1963, p. 133 (NSA:CMC), Doc. 03087.
168. Oral History Interview, Vice-Admiral Philip A. Beshany, 8 November 1977, pp. 526-7 (NSA:CMC), Doc. 03275.
169. Ibid, p. 528.
170. Ibid., pp. 526-7. The movement of submarines from the base during the crisis was public knowledge; see, for example, Frank Allaun, *HC deb.*, Vol.666, Col. 95, 30 October 1962.
171. CINCLANT Account, p. 133.
172. JCS to Secretary of State, JCS 6968, Situation Report as of 0400 October, 25 October 1962 (NSA: CMC), Doc. 01325.
173. Horne, *Macmillan*, p. 385.
174. JFKL, Richard Neustadt, *Report to the President: Skybolt and Nassau*, 15 November 1963, NSF, Box 322, p. 88.
175. Clark, *Nuclear*, pp. 264-70; Baylis, *Anglo-American*, pp. 98-102; David Dimbleby and David Reynolds, *An Ocean Apart*, (Hodder and Stoughton, 1988), p. 226; Neustadt, *Alliance Politics*, pp. 33-4; A.J.R. Groom, *British Thinking about Nuclear Weapons* (Pinter, 1974), p. 535.
176. Ronald Landa, 'The Origins of the Skybolt Controversy in the Eisenhower Administration', in Miller, *Seeing*.
177. Both documents are contained in Wynn, *RAF*, pp. 410-11.
178. PREM 11/2941, Record of Meeting, MM46/60, 21 October 1960.
179. Zuckerman, *Monkeys*, p. 245.
180. AIR 20/10925, Introduction of Skybolt, 10 March 1960.
181. AIR 20/11493, Air Staff Requirement No. 1187, 29 August 1962.
182. AIR 28/1657, Operational Order No.5/62, Airborne Alert Phase 2, July 1962.
183. DEFE 13/409, Ormsby-Gore to FO, Tel. 2832, 8 November 1962.
184. DEFE 13/409, Hockaday to Samuel, 9 November 1962.
185. DEFE 13/410, Scott to Thorneycroft, 3 December. 1962.
186. DEFE 13/410, Thorneycroft to Macmillan, 7 December 1962.
187. DEFE 13/410, Ormsby-Gore to Home, Extract from a letter, 8 December 1962.
188. Zuckerman, *Monkeys*, p. 250; David Nunnerley, *President Kennedy and Britain* (Bodley Head, 1972), p. 146; Andrew Pierre, *Nuclear Politics: The British Experience with an Independent Nuclear Force, 1939-1970* (OUP, 1972), p. 230.
189. DEFE 13/410, Record of Conversation, 11 December 1962.
190. RG 59, McNamara to Kennedy, 741.5612/12-1162, National Archives.
191. DEFE 13/340, Brief for Macmillan, Talks with President Kennedy, December 1962.
192. PREM 11/4229, Macmillan to Ormsby-Gore, 14 December 1962.
193. *FRUS*, 1961-63, Vol.XIII, Memorandum of Conversation, p. 1089.
194. American policy concerning Britain's continued nuclear status was contained in NSAM 40 approved by the President on 24 April 1961, which stated that 'Over the long run it would be desirable if the British decided to phase out of the nuclear deterrent business.' For details, see *FRUS*, 1961-63, Vol.XIII, p. 1073.
195. For an account of Macmillan's oratory on the US delegation, see Horne, *Macmillan*, pp. 437-9.
196. For other accounts of Nassau, see Baylis, *Ambiguity*, pp. 320-6; Clark, *Nuclear*, 374-5, 412-21, 434-5; Mark Smith ' "Oh Don't Deceive Me": The Nassau Summit' in David Dunn (Ed.),

Diplomacy at the Highest Level: The Development of International Summitry (Macmillan, 1996); Jan Melissen, 'Pre-Summit Diplomacy: Britain, the United States and the Nassau Conference, December 1962', *Diplomacy and Statecraft*, Vol.7, No.3 (November 1996).

197. PREM 11/4229, Record of meeting held at Bali-Hai, the Bahamas, at 9.50 a.m. on Wednesday, December 19, 1962.
198. Ibid.
199. DEFE 13/410, Watkinson to Macmillan, 19 December 1962.
200. DEFE 13/410, Macmillan to Watkinson, 19 December 1962.
201. PREM 11/4229, Record of Meeting held at Bali-Hai, the Bahamas, at 4.30 p.m. on Wednesday, December 19, 1962.
202. PREM 11/4229, Nassau to FO, T 623/62, 20 December 1962.
203. Ibid.
204. PREM 11/4229, Record of a meeting held at Bali-Hai, the Bahamas, at 12 Noon on Thursday, December 20, 1962.
205. PREM 11/4229, Joint Draft Statement on Nuclear Defence Systems, 20 December 1962.
206. PREM 11/4229, Memorandum by the Prime Minister, 20 December 1962. The full text of the British commitment is reproduced in full in Appendix 6.
207. PREM 11/4229, Nassau to FO, Tel. 24, 20 December 1962.
208. PREM 11/4229, FO to Nassau, Tel. 62, 21 December 1962.
209. Ibid.
210. PREM 11/4229, FO to Nassau, Tel. 63, 21 December 1962.
211. PREM 11/4229, Nassau to FO, Tel. 43, T 632/62, 22 December 1962.
212. George Ball, *The Past has Another Pattern: Memoirs* (Norton: New York, 1982), p. 268.
213. For further details, see Baylis, *Ambiguity*, pp. 324-5.
214. For full text of the final agreements, see *Bahamas Meeting, December 1962: Texts of Joint Communiqués*, Cmnd. 1915 (HMSO, 1962).
215. Alastair Buchan, 'The Multilateral Force: A Study in Alliance Politics', *International Affairs*, Vol.40, No.4, October 1964, p. 626.
216. President Kennedy, Press Interview, Palm Beach, 31 December 1962, cited in Ian McDonald, *Anglo-American Relations Since the Second World War* (David & Charles, 1974), pp. 189-93; *HC Deb.*, Vol.670, Cols.1251-53, 31 January 1963.
217. David Butler and Anthony King, *The British General Election of 1964* (Macmillan, 1965), p. 130.
218. Harold Wilson, *The Labour Government 1964-1970* (Wiedenfield & Nicolson, 1971), pp. 68-9.
219. Lawrence Freedman, *Britain and Nuclear Weapons* (Macmillan, 1980), p. 39.
220. Henry Kissinger, *White House Years* (Boston: Little, Brown, 1979), p. 90.
221. Horne, *Macmillan*, p. 438.
222. Neustadt, *Report*, p. 91.
223. Bundy, *Danger*, p. 492.
224. Prior to Nassau, Britain's strategic nuclear forces were described as being in support of NATO and under the control of HMG.
225. Zuckerman, *Monkeys*, p. 257. To stop the UK firing Polaris without US consent, the Johnson administration briefly entertained the possibility of stationing 'veto-squads' aboard British submarines. For details, see *FRUS*, 1964-68, Vol.XIII, p. 99.
226. AIR 8/2530, Command Directive to Sir John Grandy, 15 October 1963.
227. Lawrence Freedman, 'British Nuclear Targeting', *Defense Analysis*, Vol.1, No.2 (1985).
228. DEFE 4/160, COS(63)68th, Part I, 3 December 1963; for discussion of targeting criteria, see Clark, *Nuclear Diplomacy*, pp. 384-94.
229. David Reynolds, *Britannia Overruled: British Policy & World Power in the 20th Century* (Longman, 1991), p. 181.
230. Lawrence Freedman, Martin Navias and Nicholas Wheeler, *Independence in Concert: The British Rationale for Possessing Strategic Nuclear Weapons* (CISSM: NHP, Occasional Paper 5, 1989).
231. George Brown MP, acting leader of the Labour Party, *HC Deb.* Vol.670, Col.979, 30 January 1963.

CHAPTER 5

Alliance Control 1953–64

'We are all in this together' (President Muffley).

The onset of the Cold War led to unprecedented accumulations of military (including nuclear) forces in Europe. Political and military structures were cemented, with Germany rearmed within NATO from 1955 and a Soviet-dominated Warsaw Treaty Organisation established in response. Diplomatic progress, such as the withdrawal from Austria was more than offset by turbulence within Eastern Europe, culminating in Soviet repression of the Hungarian uprising in 1956. The continuing problem of a divided Berlin was one factor in the Soviet-Amercian confrontation, culminating in the Berlin crisis of 1961 and the Cuban missile crisis of 1962. The associated risks of nuclear war, apparent at these moments of greatest Cold War peril, added further impetus to the search by governments for credible nuclear policies that would reassure allies, deter adversaries, and maintain effective command and control over their nuclear weapons.

In its formative years, military planning and force structure within NATO centred primarily on countering Soviet predominance in ground forces. Initially, NATO intended to match these levels. By the mid-1950s, however, it became apparent that many alliance members were neither willing nor able to support such a large-scale conventional build up. In 1954, NATO approved the deployment of tactical nuclear weapons within Europe. These served two specific purposes. First, by increasing the firepower of the alliance, they enhanced the credibility of forward defence. Second, the requirement to match Soviet force levels was no longer necessary. Underpinning the strategy was the continued belief that a Soviet attack on Western Europe would be met with an immediate and overwhelming nuclear assault on the Soviet homelands by the US Strategic Air Command. This strategy and associated force structure became official NATO doctrine in April 1957, when the North Atlantic Council approved MC 14/2, otherwise known as 'Massive Retaliation'.

No sooner had Massive Retaliation been adopted, however, than the strategic assumptions on which it was based were brought into question. In August 1957 the Soviets tested an ICBM and in October launched the *Sputnik* satellite. The development of ICBMs directly threatened the USA and raised European doubts about American willingness to sacrifice US cities for the defence of Europe. The British remained outwardly confident that the Americans 'would not shrink from using either strategic or tactical weapons if it was necessary to do so', but recognised that existing arrangements did not satisfy the Europeans.[1] The credibility of the US nuclear guarantee dominated alliance politics and arguably became the principal factor in both intra-alliance relations and the development of strategic doctrine within NATO. At the heart of the debate was the question of who controlled the nuclear weapons protecting the alliance? To address this, two distinct approaches were available: a hardware solution, concerned with ownership and possession; and institutional procedures, related to deployment, planning and potential use. The former approach was reflected in proposals to establish a NATO nuclear stockpile and the Multilateral Force, while the latter came to partial fruition with the Athens guidelines of 1962, culminating in the creation of the Nuclear Planning Group in 1966.

A common feature of both approaches was the growing American desire to move away from Massive Retaliation and towards a more flexible strategy based on a centralized command structure under US control. The Europeans strongly resisted this tendency but were frustrated by their failure to adopt a unified position. The divergent objectives pursued by Britain, West Germany and France compounded the difficulty. For Britain, anxious to preserve an exclusive nuclear relationship with America, wider alliance control was unwelcome. West Germany, on the other hand, determined to remove her status as a secondary power, demanded greater participation in NATO's nuclear planning. France, meanwhile, resented Britain's nuclear status, feared German resurgence and distrusted American domination, a position that fostered isolationism and facilitated development of a French independent nuclear deterrent.

MC 48 AND THE POLITICS OF PREDELEGATION

The centrality of nuclear weapons to British strategy was affirmed in the 1952 Global Strategy Paper. Throughout 1953, the British government used the arguments in the paper to urge a similar reappraisal of NATO strategy. The objective was to shift resources from a forward strategy and towards development of a smaller nuclear deterrent force. Substitution of tactical nuclear weapons for a proportion of more expensive conventional forces also provided a means of stabilizing NATO's expenditure.[2] These proposals, however, tended to treat conventional and nuclear forces as waging separate battles. Consequently, the overall significance of tactical nuclear weapons was difficult to assess.

In June 1953, this shortcoming was partially addressed by the Ridgway Report. Prepared under the aegis of SACEUR General Ridgway, this was the first detailed attempt to incorporate nuclear weapons within NATO strategy. For the British, the outcome was disappointing: the force goals of 96 divisions recently agreed at the Lisbon conference remained unaltered. The report also contained important political consequences. To implement the plan, Ridgway advocated that SACEUR be granted peacetime predelegated authority both to establish a nuclear weapons stockpile and to launch the atomic 'counter-offensive' immediately after the outbreak of hostilities.[3]

Increased emphasis on nuclear weapons within NATO coincided with a review of national security policy by the new Eisenhower administration. This resulted in approval of two policy documents pivotal to NATO's formal adoption of a strategy based on nuclear weapons: NSC 162/2 was a restatement of national security policy; NSC 151/2 proposed a greater degree of openness in sharing US atomic information with NATO allies. NSC 162/2 was unequivocal in elevating nuclear weapons to a predominant role within US strategy: 'In the event of hostilities the United States will consider nuclear weapons to be as available for use as other munitions.'[4] To buttress this resolve, tactical nuclear weapons were made available for deployment in NATO Europe. The first 280 mm nuclear artillery was deployed in West Germany in October 1953.[5]

Prior to NATO's embrace of a nuclear defence policy, Washington had to convince its allies that deployment of tactical nuclear weapons would increase Western European security. This was essential, as agreement was necessary to station, and possibly launch, US nuclear weapons from allied territory. Anxious to retain political control over the use of nuclear weapons, HMG sought safeguards. In March 1953 in a meeting with President Eisenhower, the Foreign Secretary Sir Anthony Eden, received the assurance that 'the United States would of course, in the event of increased tension or the threat of war, take every possible step to consult with Britain and our other allies.'[6] Fully appraising NATO allies of US intentions, however, implied disclosure of atomic information restricted under the terms of the 1946 McMahon Act. In December 1953, these provisions were partially removed when Eisenhower approved NSC 151/2, allowing NATO allies to participate in joint military planning.[7]

Expectations concerning the broad direction of NATO strategy had been conveyed to Churchill earlier in the year by Lord Ismay, NATO's Secretary General. Ismay warned Churchill of the difficulties that would soon face member governments:

> We have for some time been working away at the arrangements that are necessary to enable a general alert to be given at the earliest possible moment; but I confess that, however, simple and sensible these arrangements may be, it will be difficult to get governments to take the plunge if and when the time comes.[8]

In July 1954, two reports were submitted to NATO's Standing Group. The first was SACEUR's capabilities study for 1957; the second focused on the most effective deployment of NATO military strength over the next three years. On one issue, both reports were emphatic: to counter a Soviet surprise attack, SACEUR required an integrated atomic force capable of immediate response. A strategy based on rapid response, however, required resolution of politically sensitive issues first raised in the Ridgway Report: in the event of a surprise attack, SACEUR required the political authority to use nuclear weapons. This requirement was defined in the following terms: 'His [SACEUR's] authority to implement the planned use of atomic weapons must be such as to ensure that no delay whatsoever will occur in countering a surprise attack.'[9]

In general, HMG welcomed the nuclear emphasis now placed on NATO strategy and sought to amend NATO planning to provide alliance members with immediate access to US nuclear weapons in time of war, and authority to use them at the start of hostilities.[10] Nevertheless, the government remained reticent to endorse delegation of nuclear use authority to SACEUR. This was particularly the case as nuclear weapons would be required not only in support of ground forces but 'for air attacks upon targets in enemy territory.' In August 1954, to address these concerns, the RAF established a liaison office within SHAPE, to 'act as a link for the issue of operational orders from SACEUR to Bomber Command for such proportion of the medium bomber force as may from time to time be made available to him by the United Kingdom Chiefs of Staff.'[11] A major area of contention concerned responsibility for target selection. In SACEUR's view, once the medium bomber force had been placed under his operational control, targets would be issued by SACEUR, via the liaison officer, direct to Bomber Command. The British Air Staff contested this interpretation. They insisted that all targets should be passed to Bomber Command from the liaison officer via the Air Ministry. The Air Ministry considered this essential, as despite a slight time penalty, it would prevent confusion if a target of prime national importance was suddenly established.[12] To accommodate these concerns, the Chiefs of Staff agreed that they would not allocate any part of the medium bomber force to SACEUR without first considering the relative merits of the targets selected. These planning assumptions were later incorporated into the 1954 command directive issued to Air Marshal Sir George Mills, C-in-C Bomber Command:

> The medium bomber squadrons will be based mainly in the UK and will be under national control, but the force may, at the request of Supreme Commanders and at the discretion of the Chiefs of Staff, be directed in whole or in part to support of other forces in specific theatres of war. The force may also from time to time, at the discretion of the Chiefs of Staff, be placed in whole or in part, under the operational control of SACEUR.[13]

Despite these safeguards on SACEUR's nuclear use authority, the British government remained concerned that under the proposed recommendation, 'it would be possible for SACEUR to begin thermonuclear war in certain eventualities without reference to governments'.[14] Indeed, the Chiefs of Staff concluded that political issues were central to such a strategy and doubted whether agreement could be reached with all NATO members to implement the plan effectively.[15] In response, the proposal was amended and simply stated that 'NATO forces must be able to use nuclear weapons from the outset of an attack, and SHAPE must be authorized to plan on this assumption.'[16] Although Dulles conceded that the recommendation was 'somewhat ambiguous', he stressed that the related political problem was so difficult that considerable time would be needed to find a perfect solution.[17] To emphasize the importance the US placed on the decision, he further stated that if NATO was prevented from planning on the most efficient basis, 'the United States government would want to reconsider their decision to maintain forces on the European continent.' Dulles concluded by describing the central dilemma now facing NATO:

If the council were faced with this political problem, each of fourteen Governments would find it difficult, if not impossible, to delegate its authority. But it was hardly realistic to conceive that this vital decision about the use of atomic weapons should depend on a procedure involving the concurrence of the fourteen Governments. Such a procedure would render ineffective our most potent weapon, both as a deterrent and as a defensive asset. If we wrapped our deterrent up in red tape, it would cease to be a deterrent.[18]

The issue was partially resolved in December 1954. The planning assumptions contained in MC 48 (which placed NATO strategy on a firm nuclear basis) were formally adopted with the qualification that approval did not delegate government responsibility for putting plans into effect in the event of hostilities.[19] Despite these semantic elaborations, it was recognised that once SACEUR had been authorized to plan on the use of nuclear weapons, the political latitude of member governments would be almost minimal: the options would be unconditional surrender or atomic retaliation.

MC 14/2 AND THE CONTROL OF NATO NUCLEAR FORCES

In authorizing MC 48, member governments had assumed that deployment of tactical nuclear weapons would make the retention of large-scale conventional forces unnecessary. A firm proponent of this view was the UK government, who in mid-1955 sought to introduce a political directive reducing NATO's conventional force levels. The British directive was based on two underlying principles. First, strategic planning should be reoriented to take more account of the change in Soviet tactics away from military confrontation and towards greater economic and political competition. Second, to bolster the economic potential of the Western alliance, military resources should be directed towards the strategic deterrent which was the main check against Soviet military expansion.[20] The policy was starkly underlined: 'If the Soviet Government do commit an identified act of aggression against NATO territory it must be understood that the West would at once launch a full scale attack on Russia with thermonuclear weapons.'[21] In short, the British directive was designed to reduce NATO force requirements to the minimum necessary required to identify large-scale Soviet aggression and to hold these forces until the allied counter-offensive became effective.[22]

In advancing this strategy, HMG attempted to retain the decision for launching the nuclear counter-offensive to the governments of the US and

UK who would then inform SACEUR of their joint decision.[23] Although the Americans were sympathetic to British concerns, Dulles confirmed that the US would not support the 'trip wire' concept favoured by HMG (and the RAF). The problem now facing NATO members was to agree the balance between conventional and nuclear forces. In December 1956, after a series of discussions described by Dulles as 'serious and controversial', a new political directive for NATO was finally agreed.[24] In essence the directive was a compromise between military aspiration and economic reality.

The adoption of a new political directive for NATO was only a first step in reforming alliance strategy: completion required translating political aspirations into the realities of military planning. The document that attempted to bridge this divide was MC 14/2—'the Overall Strategic Concept for the Defence of the North Atlantic Treaty Organisation Area', approved by the NAC in April 1957. The main conclusion was that NATO would be unable to resist a concerted Soviet attack unless both strategic and tactical nuclear weapons were employed from the outset of hostilities. It was further stated that this response was irrespective of Soviet use of nuclear weapons. A rapid response was therefore imperative for the successful implementation of SACEUR's plans.[25]

A constant sub-theme within NATO planning was that the military logic underpinning instant retaliation considerably enhanced, and may have even necessitated, the pre-emptive use of nuclear weapons. Although evidence on this matter is difficult to obtain, all NATO studies from the Ridgway report onwards placed heavy emphasis on the need to counter a Soviet attack with immediate nuclear retaliation. The time-urgent nature of these targets, comprising mainly Soviet tactical and strategic airfields, made it essential that targets were destroyed immediately at the start of hostilities. Indeed, military logic also dictated that optimum strategic benefit would accrue from the destruction of the airfields *before* any aircraft had taken off. However, a strategy based on forestalling attack would have required the preventive use of nuclear weapons, a policy discounted by both Presidents Truman and Eisenhower. It would also have demanded the predelegation of nuclear use authority to SACEUR in conditions where imminent Soviet attack was considered highly probable.

Although preventive war was ruled out as a policy option, the debate concerning nuclear pre-emption remained a significant feature of US nuclear strategy. Indeed, throughout his tenure as Commander of SAC, General

Le May was firmly committed to a pre-emptive strategy, believing that 'if the US is pushed into a corner far enough we would not hesitate to strike first.'[26] At present, the documentary evidence concerning SACEUR's delegated powers is limited. However, certain discernible trends are apparent. First, SACEUR's discretionary powers appear to have become more formalised with the passage of time. In 1954, SACEUR was granted authority to act 'when appropriate'. By 1956, however, he was given delegated authority to act without first seeking political guidance: 'in cases of emergency where the degree of emergency precludes following the full procedures'.[27] General Norstad has also suggested that during his time as SACEUR, he was given pre-delegated authority to launch nuclear weapons under certain established circumstances.[28]

Second, to assure the survival of NATO's nuclear forces, SACEUR required the implementation of alert measures including authorisation for dispersal of nuclear weapons. Although the NATO Alert Plan remains classified, it is known to consist of five separate levels:

> Alert Condition 5 – Peacetime Readiness
> Alert Condition 4 – Military Vigilance
> Alert Condition 3 – Simple Alert
> Alert Condition 2 – Reinforced Alert
> Alert Condition 1 – General Alert[29]

The main purpose of these alert conditions was to provide NATO with the means of orderly transition from peace to war. Through the alert system 'Governments delegate progressive authority to Supreme Commanders to put in hand the military measures needed to put their forces on a war footing' culminating in 'giving the Supreme commanders full operational control of their forces and at General Alert to use them in warlike operations'.[30] Authority to raise these alert levels lay with the NAC. The agreement of all member governments, however, was expected to take several hours. To guard against possible delay, SACEUR proposed augmenting the NATO Alert Plan with a system of purely military alerts 'capable of implementation by military commanders and not subject to prior political or national agreement'.[31] This involved three additional states of readiness: the State of Military Vigilance and the Counter-Surprise Military Alert System, which comprised 'State Orange' that allowed certain defensive measures to be taken if enemy attack was expected within 36 hours; and 'State

Scarlet' when hostilities were expected within a few minutes.[32] The British government gave SACEUR authority to order these alert states 'on his own authority for the United Kingdom forces under him'.[33] Although the exact content of these measures remains classified, it is claimed that SACEUR was granted the authority to disperse the nuclear stockpile and launch NATO-assigned forces under positive control.[34]

The procedure for obtaining nuclear release was further elaborated in SACEUR's 1957 Emergency Defence Plan. This was the first document to specifically mention the concept of 'R-Hour'—the moment when nuclear release authority would be granted to SACEUR.[35] Implementation of nuclear release procedures, however, was compounded by related political problems. Of particular concern to European members of NATO was American insistence on maintaining nuclear weapons employment strictly within the US chain of command. To reassure the European NATO members of US intentions and increase allied involvement in nuclear planning, the Eisenhower administration agreed to establish atomic information exchange agreements with all NATO allies. These bilateral agreements, known as Programs of Co-operation, committed the US to 'cooperate in the operation of atomic weapons for purposes of mutual defense.'[36] This process was broadly welcomed by European members of NATO as the agreements appeared to increase their control over the US nuclear forces stationed in Europe and further coupled the US deterrent to the defence of the European mainland.

The American decision to increase nuclear co-operation with NATO allies was tempered by realization that the US still retained the ability to act unilaterally if it so desired. On this point, Dulles was emphatic that in no circumstances would the US administration sanction any agreement that mandated prior consultation with its allies. Eisenhower further stated that political considerations should not be allowed to block SACEUR's military plans and that the US would always retain the right to initiate unilateral nuclear action if time or circumstances did not permit either agreement or consultation with the NAC.[37] The ability to unilaterally employ nuclear weapons rested in large part on SACEUR's dual role as CINCEUR in which position he commanded all US forces in the European theatre including those systems with a nuclear capability. In this role, CINCEUR was granted predelegated release authority and enabling codes to ensure that 'nuclear weapons could be used in the absence of a direct, timely order from the President or his successor.' In short, America possessed the ability to use nuclear weapons in ACE without seeking alliance approval.

To allay European fears on this, the US administration suggested the establishment of a NATO atomic stockpile. President Eisenhower personally proposed this at the 1957 NATO meeting in Paris. A consequence of the stockpile plan was that although the US still retained custody of nuclear warheads, NATO allies were given greater responsibility for their storage and transportation. In addition, under specified alert conditions, SACEUR was given authorization to release live nuclear weapons to those NATO allies included in his atomic strike plan.[38] In issuing this authorization, it is claimed that the JCS violated the US Atomic Energy Act, which stipulated that at all times the US should retain possession and not merely custody of its atomic weapons.[39]

The creation of a NATO stockpile had direct consequences for Britain's deployment of the Corporal missile.[40] Preliminary negotiations had been initiated with the US authorities in late 1955 with final agreement to deploy Corporal with British forces reached between Macmillan and Eisenhower at Bermuda in March 1957.[41] The agreement consisted of two elements. First, the UK Corporal missiles would be committed wholly to SACEUR. Second, HMG would devote the Sterling equivalent of the Corporal programme 'to finance projects for the modernisation of the Royal Air Force to be jointly agreed upon.'[42] The technical aspects of the Corporal deployment were agreed in June 1957. The Americans were anxious to obtain procedural agreements similar to those between the RAF and USAF. Command procedures for the missiles stated that the nuclear warheads would remain under custody of US custodial officers and be released to the unit on the instructions of SACEUR.[43]

Ratification of this bilateral agreement, however, became entangled with the wider issue of a NATO atomic stockpile. The main concern came from the State Department who expressed fears that bilateral agreements with the British would undermine the stockpile concept.[44] Norstad regarded the establishment of a NATO atomic stockpile as essential. He therefore regarded the bilateral agreement with Britain as subordinate to a fully established NATO stockpile. As he explained to the new Secretary of Defense, Neil McElroy:

> There have recently been indications of sensitivity on the part of other NATO nations, particularly France, to special US-UK arrangements in the atomic field. I believe that this sensitivity would be considerable lessened here if other nations

were assured that the US is prepared to endorse in principle some form of NATO stockpile arrangement along the lines I recently suggested to the JCS. I strongly urge that no information concerning further US-UK agreements in this field be released pending decision and appropriate announcement by US authorities on the question of a NATO atomic stockpile.[45]

Final agreement covering the terms of the NATO atomic stockpile was reached in 1958 and Corporal missiles were eventually deployed with the 47th and 27th Guided Missile Regiments, based near Dortmund, in early 1959. In addition to Corporal, by the end of 1960, BAOR also fielded 12 nuclear-capable 203mm howitzers and a regiment armed with the Honest John Rocket.[46]

To integrate the NATO atomic stockpile into alliance planning and develop a strategy based on MC 14/2, Norstad initiated a review of future NATO requirements. The central premise of Norstad's study was to determine the relative importance of conventional and nuclear forces within the strategic framework laid down by MC 14/2.[47] The main conclusion of these studies strongly reflected Norstad's view that creation of a strong SHIELD force was essential for NATO's security. Norstad stressed that in the event of Soviet hostilities, a token SHIELD force would allow no flexibility in the level of NATO's response. The choice was both limited and stark: nuclear holocaust or capitulation. Norstad believed that NATO governments should be fully aware of this situation and its possible consequences on future stability within Europe.[48]

Concern over the inflexible nature of NATO strategy was conveyed to a wider audience by an article in the October 1957 edition of *Foreign Affairs* by Secretary of State Dulles. Dulles proposed a shift in NATO strategy away from massive retaliation and towards a force structure more suited to fighting a limited nuclear war.[49] The European members of NATO who viewed it as a possible prelude to US retrenchment from Europe greeted this proposal with apprehension.[50] Concern was heightened by the launch of *Sputnik*, the realization that the US mainland was now more vulnerable to nuclear attack, and the fear that the US would not sacrifice American cities in the defence of Europe.

These developments accentuated the strategic asymmetry between the US and European members of NATO. For the Europeans, limited nuclear war in Europe would be as devastating as a total nuclear exchange. From this perspective, the primary purpose of nuclear weapons was not to grant NATO a war fighting capability but to deter war. Proposals to control the flexibility of nuclear options were therefore unwelcome, as they were perceived to weaken deterrence and increase the probability of limited war in Europe. Conversely, growing opinion in the US viewed the controlled escalation of nuclear force as increasing the credibility of the deterrent. Selective nuclear strikes would both demonstrate political intent and create a pause in which the Soviets could reconsider the implications of continuing the offensive.[51]

NUCLEAR WEAPONS AND COLLECTIVE CONTROL

To implement 14/2, SHAPE planners were directed to prepare a long-range requirements study for the period 1958–63. The document, Minimum Essential NATO Force Requirements (MC 70), was formally adopted at the NAC on 12 June 1958. MC 70 addressed two main problems: the need to modernize NATO forces and the failure of national governments to meet previously established requirements. To resolve these concerns, the document envisaged reducing the Lisbon force goals to 30 active divisions with nuclear capable forces compensating for conventional reductions. MC 70 also proposed introducing MRBMs into the European theatre to counter Soviet missile deployments.[52] Although not stated explicitly, deployment was to be undertaken within the framework of the recently established NATO stockpile.

The intention of deploying M/IRBMs on the European mainland became public at the 1957 December meeting of the North Atlantic Council. The communiqué stated, *inter alia*, that 'In view of the present Soviet policies in the field of new weapons, the Council has decided that IRBMs will have to be put at the disposal of SACEUR.'[53] The deployment, however, was contingent on establishing an agreed method of control. This process was regarded by Washington as already covered by the existing stockpile agreement. In the ensuing months, US optimism was tempered as the conflicting demands posed by SACEUR's military requirements and the need to assuage national sensibilities became apparent.[54] A particular problem was presented by the bilateral control arrangements for the Thor IRBMs in the UK.

The Thor agreement established a precedent for subsequent negotiations. The declared intention of deploying IRBMs in Europe was to increase NATO's military capability. Britain, however, was adamant that the IRBMs stationed in the UK would not come under the control of SACEUR.[55] From the perspective of other NATO countries, this meant that Britain had a degree of control not enjoyed by other alliance members. Consequently, at an early stage in negotiations, the control and deployment of IRBMs within Europe became inextricably linked.

The difficulty of reconciling national demands and alliance objectives was reflected in the position subsequently adopted by the French government. Initially, deployment of IRBMs within France received the broad support of the Gaillard government. The publication of the British-American Thor agreement, however, increased demands for a bilateral understanding on an equal basis to the British. The JCS were determined that all future IRBM deployments on the European continent would be under the direct control of SACEUR. Negotiations with the French became deadlocked and in May 1958, in the wake of the Algerian uprising, were abruptly cancelled. The ascendancy of Charles de Gaulle to the Presidency reinforced French nuclear ambitions and increased demands for bilateral control of *all* NATO forces stationed on French soil. To forestall any further demands, Norstad informed de Gaulle that the three IRBM squadrons earmarked for deployment in France would now be located in Italy and Turkey.[56]

Despite Norstad's attempts to placate de Gaulle, relations were further strained when French participation within NATO was made conditional on creation of a tripartite organisation composed of the United States, Britain and France.[57] Specifically, de Gaulle demanded joint agreement on global security, strategic planning and the employment of nuclear weapons. To emphasize his determination, he threatened to withdraw the French Mediterranean fleet from NATO's integrated command. De Gaulle's *demarche* placed both Britain and the United States in a serious dilemma: to accommodate the French demand would exacerbate relations with the remaining NATO members, while outright rejection would give de Gaulle the opportunity for a fundamental realignment of French foreign policy. Paul Henri Spaak, NATO's Secretary General, confided to Dulles that if de Gaulle pressed his proposal it would be the end of NATO.[58]

In informal discussions in Washington with the French and British Ambassadors, the US agreed to discuss with France and others future US policy in non-NATO areas. However, Dulles was adamant that Washington would never participate in any new organisation that placed a veto over US freedom of action. The British attitude towards French demands was more ambivalent. Although Britain was prepared to countenance tripartite discussions on an informal basis, HMG was unwilling to institutionalize the procedures.[59] Fundamentally, however, London was determined to preserve the joint targeting agreement, recently ratified with the US, and viewed French nuclear ambitions as a possible prelude to the dissolution of the British-American axis. Britain's position was further strengthened by the secret protocol of the 1957 Bermuda agreement in which both Britain and the United States agreed that neither power would assist France in the development of her nuclear programme.[60]

The problems of developing a tripartite strategy, however, were soon apparent. At the UN General Assembly both Britain and the United States abstained on a resolution recognizing the right of the Algerian people to self-determination, provoking a furious de Gaulle to withdraw the French fleet from NATO command. The continued participation of France within the NATO alliance was also placed in considerable doubt with de Gaulle's statement that:

> France feels it is essential that she participate, if the case were to arise, in any decision which might be taken by her allies to use atomic missiles or to launch them against certain places at certain times. Until she has been able to conclude with the United States and with Great Britain the agreements which seem necessary to her on this subject, she cannot consent to such projectiles being stored on her territory and used from there unless she herself has complete and permanent control over them.[61]

In issuing the ultimatum, it became apparent that de Gaulle's ultimate objective was to acquire a veto over US nuclear weapons, a position Washington was not prepared to accept. Consequently, Norstad recommended redeployment of the nine USAF nuclear capable squadrons from France to Britain. In accepting this decision, the State Department hoped to discretely impress upon de Gaulle that although French co-operation was desirable their real estate was not indispensable.[62]

The resultant dislocation of NATO's chain of command in both the Mediterranean and Allied Air Forces Central Europe (AIRCENT) led Britain to re-examine SACEUR's powers over subordinate commanders. As the subject of NATO authority had recently been raised in Parliament and was becoming a matter of public concern, the issue required urgent clarification.[63] The subsequent review initiated by the COS addressed the central question now facing NATO: how to retain the primacy of national governments whilst maintaining a strategy based on immediate nuclear response.

As shown, the procedures whereby SACEUR was granted authority to employ nuclear weapons were largely fudged. The agreed 'guidelines' governing nuclear release within NATO were designed to cover two distinct categories: a massive pre-emptive nuclear attack and a large-scale conventional engagement. In the former, SACEUR was delegated authority to respond with nuclear weapons; whilst in the latter, nuclear weapons could only be employed after declaration of R-hour. However, once R-hour had been declared, SACEUR was empowered to use all nuclear weapons under his command. Consequently, continued political control was extremely limited. In effect NATO possessed a control switch that could only be set at two positions: off and fire at will.

In March 1960, British and American officials met in Washington to address the 'button pushing' issue within NATO. The outcome was less than encouraging with Britain presenting two alternatives 'neither of which seemed very desirable.'[64] The first was to prepare a 'contingency directive' which detailed SACEUR's pre-delegated powers. However, as all contingencies were difficult to anticipate, preparation of such a document was problematic. Moreover, if it became public knowledge that such a document existed, the political consequences would be acute. The second option was to arrive at a procedure by which the use of nuclear weapons could be made by the NAC or subsidiary body. However, 'this raised the question as to whether a decision could be made effectively by such a body.' For America, the readiness of the deterrent was paramount. A simple release procedure was therefore the preferred option. To maintain this position, 'it was most undesirable for the Military Committee to become involved in the political aspects of the decision to use nuclear weapons and that steps should be taken to insure that this did not occur.' To reaffirm the primacy of political control, it was suggested that British officers serving in NATO should follow SACEUR's commands only after receiving ratification from Whitehall. The Chiefs of Staff flatly rejected the idea:

> To instruct a UK Commander of NATO assigned forces not to take action on SACEUR's orders until he had confirmation that SACEUR had been given HMG's authority would be a negation of the principle of military command and indicate an utter lack of faith in SACEUR. Furthermore, if a leak occurred it would undermine SACEUR's position and precipitate a general debate on exactly how political approval in NATO is given, a subject which has deliberately not been ventilated.[65]

There was, nevertheless, growing realization that SACEUR's planning was based on immediate authorisation. To address the issue, British commanders serving in NATO were issued with the following rules of engagement:

> NATO major Commanders have no authority to order United Kingdom forces to open fire until a General Alert has been declared, which requires the express permission of Her Majesty's Government. When Her Majesty's Government give their agreement to the declaration of a General Alert you will be notified, for information, through Service channels, in parallel with the notification given to our Permanent Representative on the NATO Council. Should you receive orders to open fire from a NATO Supreme Commander before the receipt of this parallel notification, you will assume that the NATO Supreme Commander is acting with the approval of Her Majesty's Government and you will obey him.[66]

This directive did not cover British naval commanders whose forces were earmarked for, but not assigned to SACLANT, who at this stage lacked SACEUR's additional alert scheme and an R-hour.[67] The directive nevertheless reflected the government's acceptance that 'we must trust NATO commanders to obey the political rules, just as we trust our national commanders.'[68] In accepting this principle, the British position was tempered by the strongly-held belief that the use of tactical nuclear weapons would be concurrent with the initiation of global war. SACEUR possessed only tactical nuclear weapons and the control of the strategic deterrent was independent of NATO. Consequently, as long as Britain perceived that the US would not initiate a strategic nuclear offensive without the close co-operation of the UK, the continued control of tactical weapons in Europe 'would be of quite secondary importance and would depend on the circumstances at the time.'[69] In short, control of strategic nuclear forces was the only control that mattered. Any strategy that attempted to advance the concept of limited nuclear war was strongly opposed by the British: such a doctrine would effectively decouple tactical nuclear weapons from strategic forces, with control of the former assuming fundamental importance. Second, as tactical nuclear weapons were already deployed within ACE, the control mechanism would require active participation of all alliance members, thus negating Britain's secret understandings on nuclear use with both the US and SACEUR. Significantly, the proposal to deploy MRBMs under SACEUR's control was increasingly regarded by Britain as a prelude towards the implementation of such a strategy.

MRBM DEPLOYMENT

Preliminary studies on the deployment of MRBMs within Europe were initiated by SHAPE planners in late-1957. Designed to accommodate both military and political objectives, the proposal received the strong support of SACEUR. Militarily, MRBMs fulfilled the dual function of countering similar Soviet deployments and modernizing NATO's interdiction force, some of whose strike aircraft were becoming obsolete. Politically, deployment of MRBMs was intended to address growing concerns over nuclear use. To be deployed under the NATO stockpile, the MRBMs would grant the European members of the alliance a significant increase in both NATO decision-making and nuclear use.[70]

For many Europeans, the Soviet ability to significantly strike the American mainland placed the US nuclear guarantee for the defence of Europe in question. European concerns were further exacerbated by remarks of Christian Herter (Dulles' replacement as Secretary of State) who, in March 1960, told the US Foreign Relations Committee, 'I can't conceive of the President of the United States involving us in an all-out nuclear war unless the facts showed clearly that we are in danger of devastation ourselves, or that actual moves have been made toward devastating ourselves.'[71]

Advocates of a strong Atlantic relationship feared that doubts about the US nuclear commitment would force European members of the alliance to pursue either a neutralist foreign policy, an independent nuclear programme or both. Within this context, and to counter such trends, the MRBM proposal could be attractive: it helped re-affirm the credibility of extended deterrence and addressed the need for national nuclear programmes. This analysis was confirmed in the US by the Draper Committee, which recommended that the Polaris missile, currently under development in the US, should be offered as a land-mobile MRBM to fulfil SACEUR's requirements.[72]

In October 1959, Norstad formally proposed creation of a NATO MRBM force under control of SACEUR. Eventually entailing 655 missiles with a maximum range of 2,800 km, and delivering a one-megaton warhead, half the force was to be combat-ready by 1965.[73] The control arrangements for launching the force were also addressed: the MRBMs would be operated under the command of SACEUR, be targeted as an integral element of SHAPE planning, and launched by the Supreme Commander under the authority of the US President.[74] Approved by the Military Committee, the proposal formed the basis of discussions held by NATO Defence Ministers meeting in Paris on 1 April 1960.

Central to the negotiations (and a question that remained largely unresolved) was the US veto. Specifically, retention of the veto would allow the US to maintain negative control of the force and thus encourage the drive for national capabilities. Conversely, to remove the US veto over missiles supplied to host countries would create further tensions, especially to those countries who considered that SACEUR's veto in isolation was an inadequate safeguard against irresponsible or unauthorized use by national crews. This problem was expected to be particularly acute if missiles were stationed in West Germany.

This ambivalence went to the heart of the programme and largely explains the disparate response from various European governments. Led by West Germany, the non-nuclear members supported the scheme, in contrast to France who strongly opposed it. Although publicly the British government preferred to remain non-committal, in private London shared Paris' reservations.[75] As the proposals neither allowed the Europeans to employ NATO nuclear weapons without US consent nor restrained independent US action, officials in MOD dismissed the scheme as 'a piece of eyewash, so far as control is concerned.'[76] The Foreign Office was more circumspect, 'though in direct relation to control, they think [eyewash] is an apt description.'[77]

The MRBM issue also generated dispute between the Chiefs of Staff on the range of ballistic missile that SACEUR should be given. The army and navy chiefs argued that missiles supplied to SACEUR should be limited to 200 miles, as above this range SACEUR would possess the means of starting global war. In contrast, the Chief of the Air Staff believed that, 'the question of starting a war will in any case be decided by the President and Prime Minister and consequently SACEUR should have 1000 mile missiles for the specific purpose of knocking out enemy airfields.'[78] It was conceded, however, that whatever the Chiefs decided was unlikely to be conclusive, as the whole question of MRBM deployment was primarily political. A significant consideration was whether NATO MRBMs would be matched by the Soviets. The COS argued:

> It is improbable that the American proposals in their present form would cause the Soviet Government to make similar arrangements with their satellites or with the Chinese. In view of their own reluctance to give nuclear weapons to the East Germans or the Chinese, they might be cautious in claiming that the

Americans had given the West Germans full control over their own nuclear weapons.[79]

To consolidate support for the scheme, Norstad floated the possibility of NATO's eventual emergence as a 'fourth nuclear power', a proposition first publicly advanced at a meeting of NATO Parliamentarians in November 1960. Norstad's suggestion entailed creation of a multilateral control organisation responsible for all nuclear warheads within ACE, including those currently under exclusive US control. Specifically, the proposal if implemented would remove the US veto and grant NATO 'the power of decision as to their use'.[80] The proposal attracted Norstad primarily as a political alternative to the development of national nuclear forces operating outside NATO's control. The emergence of NATO as a fourth nuclear power was totally rejected by the Chiefs of Staff. Fundamental to their concern was the inadequacy of command and control:

> SACEUR was at present entitled, once NATO governments had authorized him to declare R-hour, to implement his atomic strike plan. This meant that his whole nuclear power could immediately be released. The current United States proposals for a NATO MRBM force would entitle him to go even further, by providing him with more powerful weapons of greater range, and by authorizing him, without reference to NATO governments, to fire these weapons in the event of a nuclear weapon being delivered against NATO Europe. This would amount to SACEUR having full control of a fourth deterrent. The United Kingdom's misgivings did not arise so much from the weapons at SACEUR's disposal or the targets at which he proposed to direct them, but rather from the inadequate political control over the moment at which he might use them. Ministers were unlikely to accept that he should have authority to initiate a major nuclear exchange in advance of the decision to release SAC and Bomber Command.[81]

THE BOWIE REPORT

Within the State Department, the possible consequences of Norstad's proposals were viewed with increasing alarm: MRBMs would allow West Germany access to nuclear weapons and exacerbate relations with both France and the USSR. To regain the initiative and develop an alternative strategy, the State Department turned to Robert Bowie. A former Director of the Policy Planning Staff, Bowie sought to accommodate specific European concerns within the broader framework of US foreign policy objectives. His report affirmed the recommendations of MC 70 and called for a Shield force of thirty active divisions. A significant reduction in the nuclear capability of the Shield force and a strong rejection of limited nuclear war were also highly prominent:

> By admitting the concept of a nuclear war restricted to Europe, the United States would be renouncing the threat inherent in current strategy to broaden the area of major European hostilities to the USSR. Thus it would be giving the Soviet heartland sanctuary status in order to preserve North American Sanctuary. There can be little appeal to our allies in this most divisive of strategies... It would shatter rather than rebuild European confidence and invite a spread of neutralism.[82]

Bowie realized that for the Europeans, tactical nuclear warfare was tantamount to a general holocaust. He consequently sought a greater conventional capability to raise the nuclear threshold. This would reduce the probability of limited aggression spiralling into general war and lessen the compulsion to move from non-nuclear to nuclear hostilities. In effect, the report extended Norstad's 'pause concept' in that the decision to embark on general war would not be automatic but a controlled response delineated by definable criteria.

A more radical aspect of the Report (which departed from Norstad's preferences) was its treatment of the NATO deterrent force. In a concerted attempt to reduce national programmes, advance European integration and avoid host country problems, the report recommended a sea-based, veto-free NATO strategic force under the command of SACEUR. Ultimately, 'so that no ally could withdraw units and employ them as a national force', the proposal envisaged the creation of a multilateral force under common financing and ownership, operated by mixed crews.

To safeguard design data, however, the US would retain formal custody of the warheads. Although primarily concerned with preserving security, the proposal provided a potential mechanism for the US to reimpose a veto on nuclear use. To specifically address European anxieties about the dependability of the force in a crisis, the report advocated granting SACEUR pre-delegated authority to 'use the force against key Soviet strategic targets in the event that the Soviets initiate major nuclear attack on the Treaty area.'[83]

As the development programme was expected to take several years, deployment would be in two phases. First, to reaffirm the US commitment to European defence, an interim force of US-manned Polaris submarines would be deployed in European waters. Under full operational control of

SACEUR, the force would launch a nuclear strike under three contingencies: a direct order from SACEUR, a decision by the North Atlantic Council or, *in extremis*, the US President. In the first two cases, the US would commit itself to comply with the decision, while in the latter scenario, the US retained its authority to initiate a nuclear strike without NATO approval.

The second phase of deployment represented the crux of the report: the creation of a truly multilateral sea-based strategic nuclear force. To be manned by a multilateral crew from at least three countries, each unit would be invulnerable to direct control from a single government. Envisaged as a natural successor to the interim programme, the operational advantages were considered to be its relative invulnerability and avoidance of host country difficulties. Although collective control was problematic, the proposal strongly reinforced Washington's objective of undermining support for national nuclear programmes.

Overall, the Bowie Report sought to assuage European anxieties on the use of nuclear weapons at both the tactical and strategic level. At the tactical level, where Europeans were more concerned with ensuring negative control (i.e. that nuclear weapons would not be employed without their consent) the substantial increases proposed in conventional capability were expected to enable a non-nuclear defence to be sustained for a period of days. Consequently, the nuclear threshold would be raised. The Soviets would therefore have time to reconsider their offensive and a conscious decision to continue hostilities would equate with the initiation of general war, at which point tactical nuclear weapons would be employed to retard the Soviet advance.[84]

By adopting a more conventional defence posture, the European members of the alliance could secure greater control over the initiation of nuclear war. First, raising the nuclear threshold would allow time for a considered response and militate against hasty or ill-considered action. Second, NATO would be under less compulsion to move from non-nuclear to nuclear hostilities so establishing an inherently more stable environment that would reduce the likelihood of enemy nuclear pre-emption. Finally, to facilitate the new strategy and increase alliance cohesion, structural changes were also anticipated, including the creation of a Steering Group to develop joint proposals and policies, and an Atlantic Planning Group, for long term planning.

Paradoxically, at the strategic level, the situation was reversed. To ensure that Soviet cities could be credibly threatened and hence guarantee a continued US commitment to the defence of Europe, the Europeans wanted positive control (i.e. the removal of the US veto). The creation of the NATO deterrent force was intended to substantially address this requirement. First, by agreeing to establish the force, the non-nuclear members of NATO would be granted a degree of control over the launch of strategic weapons. Second, the commitment to predelegate launch authority in the event of a Soviet first-strike against Europe 'would clearly involve the US in nuclear war.'

American concerns over the removal of the US veto were also addressed. For although non-nuclear members could now determine the circumstances in which the weapons would be used, their launch was largely constrained by the requirement to establish the unanimous agreement of all NATO members. As a further safeguard, the provision of the NATO deterrent force was contingent on substantial increases in conventional defence. As Bowie explained: 'The risks of giving our partners a trigger on nuclear war demand that they join with us in reducing the likelihood that it need be pulled because of Soviet provocations in Europe.'[85]

By employing an admixture of strategic reappraisal, procedural safeguards and predelegated authority, the report sought to accommodate legitimate European concerns over the initiation of nuclear war and decrease the incentives for national strategic deterrents. In retrospect, the Bowie report marks the transition between the defence policies associated with the Eisenhower administration and the new strategic objectives of crisis management and conflict resolution pursued by President Kennedy and his Secretary of Defense Robert McNamara. Completed in August 1960, the recommendations were presented to the December meeting of NATO Ministers by the outgoing Secretary of State, Christian Herter.[86]

THE BRITISH RESPONSE

In advance of the December meeting, Britain once again re-examined the political and military consequences of revising NATO strategy. While British antipathy towards existing NATO strategy was well known within the alliance, the presentation of new ideas required careful handling. Consequently, in August 1960, two concurrent studies were initiated: a political assessment under the tutelage of Richard Chilver, a senior MOD official, and a military analysis undertaken by the JPS.

A common theme underpinning both approaches was the growing realization that a 'middle course' had to be found between conventional conflict and nuclear holocaust. Moreover, to achieve this middle course, a fundamental revision of NATO strategy was essential. In short, as the British government rejected the concept of winning a nuclear war, preparations for fighting such a war were considered unnecessary: 'The consequences of an all-out nuclear exchange would be so catastrophic that what happens after it is irrelevant. Preventing it is so immeasurably more important than 'winning' it that the West cannot afford to allot resources or effort to the latter.'[87]

Central to British concerns was the significant increase in the Soviet nuclear stockpile and the resultant disparity between NATO strategy and military reality. The most important consequence of this new environment was that for the first time the continental United States was now exposed to direct Soviet attack by ICBMs and SLBMs. Consequently, the original NATO concept of deterring the Soviets by threatening Massive Retaliation was brought into question. Commenting on these developments, the JPS noted that 'as both sides face the possibility of nuclear devastation, a state of mutual deterrence has come about.'[88] Accordingly, the JPS recommended wholesale revision of NATO strategy predicated on acceptance of the principles that prevention of war was now of cardinal importance, and second, that the concept of a shield force which was able, even after a strategic nuclear exchange, to maintain territorial integrity and sustain operations 'until the will and ability of the enemy to pursue global war is destroyed', was no longer valid.[89]

The difficulty for HMG in advancing these proposals was considered to be more psychological than strategic. For if continental Europeans accepted that SACEUR could not prevent their territories being overrun, the cohesion of NATO would be jeopardized. To retain the political integrity of NATO, SACEUR was obligated to plan to win a nuclear war. Further, to achieve this aim with credibility, SACEUR required a war fighting capability, including provision of MRBMs.

For the British government, deployment of MRBMs was a further example of the consequences inherent in public acceptance of a strategy that in private they fundamentally rejected. Both politically and militarily, the British regarded the MRBMs as both unnecessary and potentially destabilising. Politically, the host country problem was expected to exacerbate intra-alliance strains, whilst militarily they heightened the risk that a minor conflict would develop uncontrollably into all-out warfare. The additional deterrent value afforded by deployment was also dismissed:

> if the Russians are not frightened by the prospect of thousands of megatons on their cities they will not be frightened by threats to airfields and railway junctions. Since the missiles would only be fired after, or concurrently with, all-out attack, their military capability is unimportant.[90]

To argue this within NATO, however, was both problematic and far-reaching: acceptance of the British position would place in doubt most of SACEUR's current planning and the very existence of SACLANT. Despite expected opposition from other NATO members and the realization that a satisfactory resolution would involve 'the key problems of the control of nuclear weapons', Britain was determined to press its case and advanced the concept of 'discriminate nuclear response'. The essence of the strategy was that if a Soviet attack was too strong for NATO conventional forces, nuclear weapons would be used, but primarily as political rather than military instruments. Discriminate nuclear use would send a strong signal to the Soviet leadership that NATO possessed the will to resist and that continued aggression would escalate to all-out war. To implement the policy successfully, political control over the timing, location and size of any nuclear explosion was essential. Although it was realized that escalation to all-out war was still possible, it was no longer considered inevitable, provided neither side believed that a decisive advantage could be gained by escalating the conflict.[91]

Although in broad agreement with the strategy, the Chiefs of Staff remained cautious. They believed that such a proposal would both seriously weaken Britain's position within the alliance and significantly undermine NATO's cohesion and military resolve. Noting the advice offered by the Chiefs, the government was not prepared to accept the status quo. Embroiled in a balance of payments crisis, Macmillan argued that to continue paying lip service to a policy in which it patently did not believe had destroyed confidence at home in the government's wisdom and abroad in its sincerity. Henceforth, Britain's policy towards NATO would be predicated on three objectives: to establish due limits and control over the substantial nuclear forces deployed by SACEUR; second, to ensure that NATO's strategic plans were revised to take account of mutual deterrence; and third, to avoid providing SACEUR with a strategic deterrent capability.[92]

THE KENNEDY ADMINISTRATION

On assuming office in January 1961, President Kennedy initiated a major review of US defence policy, with particular emphasis on the role of nuclear weapons within overall strategy. The review was based on the assumption that US strategic forces were now vulnerable to a Soviet surprise nuclear attack. Consequently, continued reliance on Massive Retaliation was no longer credible.[93] A further concern was the inflexible nature of the Single Integrated Operational Plan (SIOP). Developed at SAC Headquarters during 1960, the SIOP was in key respects the Schlieffen plan of the thermonuclear age. Once in motion, the SIOP would run its course. After transmission of an authenticated execute order there was no way to stop it.[94] Characterized by massive overkill, the SIOP envisaged delivery of 3267 nuclear weapons against 3729 targets in the Sino-Soviet bloc.[95]

Uneasy with the prospect of sanctioning destruction on such a massive scale, the new administration sought a more flexible strategy that would limit hostilities at the lowest possible level. At the theatre level this implied maintaining conventional defence for as long as possible, and if tactical nuclear weapons were to be used, they would be employed in limited numbers and with the specific aim of restoring deterrence. At the strategic level, this entailed adoption of a counter-force policy that spared Soviet cities as hostages and providing an incentive for terminating hostilities on terms favourable to the United States. To decrease the vulnerability of US strategic forces, Kennedy placed a proportion of the B-52 bomber force on continuous airborne alert and announced improvements in both warning and command and control facilities.[96] In April 1961 Kennedy addressed the NATO Military Committee and assured allied leaders that America intended to maintain responsible command and control over all US nuclear weapons.[97]

The renewed focus on command and control was a major aspect of the Kennedy defence review. The reason was simple: the system developed under Eisenhower placed the political leadership under great compulsion to launch the entire US nuclear force in one single attack. For in the event of a Soviet decapitation attack, failure to launch the force could result in virtual elimination of US retaliatory power. It was estimated that by the destruction of only 14 facilities the Soviets would achieve a 90 per cent probability of eliminating the entire US higher political-military command structure.[98] It was largely in response to this vulnerability that the SIOP was developed. Briefing President Kennedy on the SIOP options, the

Chairman of the Joint Chiefs, General Lemnitzer, stressed that a Soviet first-strike would so disrupt US command and control that there was an overriding requirement for simplicity of military response: immediate launch of the entire force.[99]

The solution to this problem was as simple as it was intractable. To provide the flexibility demanded by the political leadership required a command and control system invulnerable to nuclear attack. Without such a capability it would be impossible for the leadership to ensure that the response was appropriate to the threat; that action was undertaken by the duly constituted authority or that war was not precipitated by accident or miscalculation. In short, a fully responsive and survivable system was fundamental to the successful implementation of the new strategy. The policy implications were spelt out to Congress in the following terms: 'more flexible, more selective, more deliberate, better protected and under ultimate civilian authority at all times... a truly unified, nationwide, indestructible system to insure high-level command, communication and control and a properly authorized response under any conditions.'[100]

In conjunction with these developments, the US commitment to NATO was once again re-examined. To undertake the review, Kennedy assembled a small team of influential strategists headed by Dean Acheson, the former Secretary of State. In a conclusion reminiscent of NSC 68, the final report recommended a concerted increase in NATO's conventional forces coupled to reimposition of centralized US control over all NATO nuclear forces. Centralization of command and control was considered essential: it would ensure that NATO nuclear forces stationed in Europe could not follow a strategy at variance with the political objectives of the United States. In relation to nuclear use, there were three main implications: the US strategic arsenal would not be subject to a European veto; second, the nuclear forces of both Britain and France should be subject to US veto and control; and third, increased conventional forces would significantly raise the threshold for nuclear use.[101]

In Europe, the proposal met a largely hostile response. It was argued that the build-up of conventional forces would undermine the credibility of the nuclear deterrent by implying an unwillingness on NATO's part to resort to nuclear weapons. To assuage European concerns, it was explained that the primary purpose of raising the threshold was not to decrease the US nuclear guarantee to Europe but rather to increase US control and ensure that these weapons were not used by accident or miscalculation.[102]

FLEXIBLE RESPONSE AND TACTICAL NUCLEAR WEAPONS

McNamara's ambition to establish a more centralized command structure had direct implications for both the deployment and control of tactical nuclear forces stationed in Europe. Based primarily on the concept of escalation control, the new strategy rested on the ability to conduct successful military operations at a series of levels through non-nuclear, tactical and strategic nuclear war—a posture that required the alliance to maintain an appropriate range of capabilities at all levels of conflict. Since escalation control demanded a single focus of authority and exclusive control over nuclear forces, implementation would further reduce alliance participation in questions of nuclear use and reinforce US nuclear monopoly.[103] Further, as battlefield nuclear weapons were difficult to control centrally, the numbers deployed in the NATO stockpile were expected to be reduced substantially. McNamara's strategy reinforced the Acheson proposals: tactical nuclear forces could no longer substitute for shortcomings in conventional forces.

For HMG, these developments were unwelcome, as implementation would considerably increase the level of British conventional forces stationed on the continent. This would require a greater financial commitment at a time when domestic political pressure demanded reductions in government spending. Reviewing the possible implications, the Chiefs of Staff stated bluntly that Acheson's proposals could not be accepted 'without a complete reappraisal of our defence policy.'[104] To counter the Acheson proposals, Britain required a strategy that did not entail a substantial increase in conventional forces. The key to unlock this problem was provided by tactical nuclear weapons, or more specifically their perceived military role within overall NATO strategy. As has already been shown, government concerns about the credibility of NATO strategy had already compelled Britain to advocate a policy of discriminate nuclear response. However, due to the transition in the US administration, the British proposals had yet to receive close attention. To advance its position, the government established an interdepartmental working party with the specific aim of shifting NATO's agenda away from the increasingly sterile discussions on force levels and towards the more general issue of nuclear first use.[105] The approach had two basic aims: to provide an alternative to the Acheson proposals, and second, by offering a procedural mechanism for increasing alliance participation in nuclear use, to diminish European aspirations for a NATO MRBM force.

The Mottershead Report (as the proposals came to be known) was formally presented to NAC in May 1961.[106] Largely consisting of a series of questions and answers, the report sought to outline a rational policy for the deployment of tactical nuclear weapons. In Britain's view, provision of tactical nuclear weapons was exclusively for the purpose of deterrence and not for fighting a battle to retain territory. In this capacity, tactical nuclear weapons were the link between initial conventional resistance and actions requiring withdrawal or escalation to global war. In advocating discriminate nuclear response, Britain sought to restrict tactical nuclear weapons to the specific role of signalling NATO's intent to escalate to global war if aggression continued:

> [tactical] nuclear weapons would be used in the first instance under strict limitations of numbers, target, yield and type of burst and, although they would be directed against military targets, they would be intended at this stage primarily to influence the Soviet Government rather than to achieve strictly military aims.[107]

As escalation was regarded as highly probable if there was anything more than the most limited nuclear exchange, the provision of tactical nuclear forces to sustain a war fighting capability was consequently dismissed: 'There is no need to provide [tactical] nuclear weapons for any protracted nuclear exchange: the period would be days rather than weeks'. Specifically, the function of tactical nuclear weapons was to serve political rather than military goals. In short, Britain was advocating intra-war deterrence in which the use of tactical nuclear weapons would deter the Soviet Union from continued aggression by threatening a strategic nuclear exchange. Politically, the proposal was adept, inasmuch as HMG now had a rationale to reject both the increase in conventional forces and the deployment of MRBMs. As long as the West retained a credible strategic deterrent, substantial increases in both conventional and tactical nuclear forces were no longer required. The dynamics of intra-war deterrence, however, demanded effective command and control.

THE ATHENS GUIDELINES

The requirement for close political control ran counter to the military imperative for rapid response. At the beginning of 1961 the matter came to a head when General Norstad issued a request to the Council seeking 'rules of engagement' by which SACEUR would be authorized in advance to use nuclear weapons in specific ways in certain defined circumstances.[108]

Under Massive Retaliation this had been largely fudged with SACEUR granted predelegated authority to use nuclear weapons only in the case of a massive Soviet nuclear attack. In all other eventualities, such as Soviet conventional attack, SACEUR was expressly forbidden to employ nuclear weapons until nuclear release (R-hour) had been declared. This procedure was incorporated into SACEUR's formal alert measures that stated that 'Under General Alert operational plans will be fully implemented, except for atomic operations that will not be initiated until R-hour is declared by SACEUR.' Once R-hour had been declared, however, SACEUR was authorized to employ nuclear weapons at his own discretion.[109] The mechanics whereby political authorization was granted to SACEUR, however, had not been worked out. Within Whitehall it was recognised that while SACEUR had stated he required political authority before ordering the use of nuclear weapons, 'he has never specified which authority':

> There is no obligation on SACEUR to obtain the approval of the North Atlantic Council to R-hour. We have assumed that SACEUR would consult the President and that the President would, in turn, consult the Prime Minister whenever possible under the special secret US/UK consultative procedure. It is not clear whether SACEUR would regard the President's authority to him to release American warheads to NATO forces gave him authority to use nuclear weapons thereafter at his discretion, or whether he would require further authority from the President before authorising the use of the weapons.[110]

The lack of clarity in procedures is both apparent and intriguing:

> There is a secret agreement whereby SACEUR will consult HMG before ordering nuclear strikes by aircraft under his command operating from the UK. It seems highly probable that there are similar agreements between SACEUR and the Federal German Government, the French Government, the Italian Government and perhaps other Governments equipped with other nuclear delivery vehicles before SACEUR can authorise the use of these vehicles in nuclear war. It seems probable, therefore, that the authorisation for the use of nuclear weapons would follow the same procedure as the authority required by SACEUR before he can commit national forces under his command to warlike operations i.e. it is a question of bilateral negotiation between SACEUR and the Government concerned. The North Atlantic Council is not directly involved and there is no question of the need for a unanimous decision.[111]

Reflecting on the possible role of the NAC, it was noted: 'if one thing is clear, it is that the North Atlantic Council itself is the last body to be entrusted with reaching decisions of that kind'.[112]

It was clear that to accommodate a strategy based on discriminate use of nuclear weapons such an inflexible release procedure was no longer appropriate. A procedure was needed that would allow both flexibility of response and satisfy European aspirations for control, while simultaneously avoiding the impression that the weapons might be used aggressively or not at all. In an attempt to reconcile these demands, the Military Committee approved and forwarded to NAC a paper originally prepared by the Standing Group entitled *The Military Control of Nuclear Weapons in NATO (MC-95)*. A significant aspect of MC-95 was the proposal to pre-delegate nuclear use authority to Supreme Commanders in the following circumstances and subject to the following conditions:

(a) In the case of an unmistakable Soviet nuclear attack. It was stressed that this authority applied solely to the actual launching of the attack and specifically prohibited a pre-emptive strike in response to strategic warning.
(b) The employment of nuclear weapons under pre-determined rules of engagement against specific hostile acts. This was intended to cover circumstances in which it would be militarily desirable to use nuclear weapons quickly and in a defensive role. Specific examples included the destruction of aircraft before bomb release, the retardation of an enemy advance by the deployment of atomic demolition mines or the defence of vital naval units from submarine attack.
(c) In the event of a Soviet conventional attack which threatened the integrity of the forces and territory under attack, and which could not be curtailed with the available conventional forces. Under these conditions nuclear weapons would be employed selectively according to military requirements and against military targets either exclusively on their own territory or limited to the tactical battlefield.[113]

The conclusions of MC-95 proved contentious. A particular concern was pre-delegation and the belief that if adopted, MC-95 would invest too much authority in the hands of the Supreme Commanders. The political difficulties surrounding the issue had been foreseen by the British Chiefs of Staff who highlighted the central dilemma:

> In the event of a massive nuclear attack by the Soviet Union (which would mean nuclear war) it would not matter whether SACEUR had been given this authority or not. But it is very doubtful whether politically the UK government

could agree to give SACEUR the authority to use any nuclear weapons in any circumstances, without prior political authority.[114]

The policy adopted by the British government strongly reflected this view. The Cabinet was in full agreement that matters of war and peace should remain wherever possible under national civilian control. The British position was that: 'Her Majesty's Government cannot agree that the power to decide to employ nuclear weapons in any circumstances should be delegated to military commanders. Governments must reserve to themselves the heavy responsibility of any decision to employ nuclear weapons.'[115]

To reconcile these differences, an agreed set of political guidelines covering nuclear release was considered essential. The Secretary-General, Dirk Stikker, was authorized to examine the political implications governing nuclear release. Stikker's report, *The Political Control of Nuclear Weapons (NDP 62/2)* was submitted to the Council on 23 January 1962.[116] Consisting of a series of procedures and guarantees, it sought to address four specific areas of concern within the alliance:

(a) The determination of the US to use nuclear weapons for the defence of Europe.
(b) The perceived lack of consultation within NATO over nuclear use.
(c) Delegation of political authority.
(d) The absence of European involvement in the selection of targets.

Stikker proposed that the US maintain in Europe a certain number of nuclear warheads that could not be withdrawn without the unanimous approval of all member states.[117] By consenting to this the Kennedy administration hoped to impress upon Europeans that US nuclear disengagement from Europe was not an option. To provide further reassurance (and for the first time in NATO's existence), Washington offered a formal commitment covering the US nuclear guarantee to Europe. Thomas Finletter, the US NATO representative, told the Council that: 'The President wishes to make clear his intention to direct or authorise, as appropriate, the use of nuclear weapons in the event that the Alliance is subject to an unmistakable nuclear attack or that NATO forces are subjected to a non-nuclear attack with which they cannot cope.'[118]

At first sight, the American nuclear guarantee appeared to accommodate European concerns. In practice however, it only served to highlight further areas of contention—namely, which members of the alliance would be consulted and how would the decision be reached? In an attempt to answer these questions, the US formally agreed to the following commitments:

- to consult the Council, time and circumstances permitting, before using nuclear weapons anywhere in the world.
- to undertake in the event of unmistakable nuclear attack to respond as appropriate with nuclear weapons.
- to consult the Council, time and circumstances permitting, in the event of other forms of attack.[119]

Subsequently the British provided a similar set of assurances to the NAC and also undertook to 'consult with the North Atlantic Council, if time permits, concerning the use of nuclear weapons, anywhere in the world'.[120] Although the US was now willing to consult with its partners, the procedures for authorizing nuclear release remained unresolved. Several suggestions were advanced, including the formation of a NATO 'war cabinet', the delegation of responsibility to the country attacked and the US, and some system of weighed voting within the NAC. However, as the US was unwilling to relinquish its veto, discussions proved sterile and counterproductive. To consolidate progress and allow for continued discussion the British proposed establishing a NATO Peacetime Nuclear Administrative Committee. To consist of the Standing Group plus those countries in which nuclear weapons were stored, the function of the committee was twofold: to allay Continental anxieties regarding the US nuclear guarantee and develop a greater sense of allied participation in the whole range of NATO military planning.[121] To support these aims, information relating to the location, quantity and yield of nuclear warheads (including plans for their use) was to be made available. These measures, however, were largely symbolic. The prospect of granting the allies control over nuclear weapons was never the intention. Britain was particularly concerned that accepting such a principle would inevitably 'lead to renewed pressure for control over the use of nuclear weapons in wartime.'[122]

A further concern to HMG was the prospect of granting the alliance increased involvement in the selection of targets. Underlying this concern was the belief that such demands would inevitably compromise the British-American secret agreements on nuclear use and weaken bilateral targeting policy, recently ratified between Bomber Command and SAC, the preservation of which was regarded as central to strategic British interests.

British anxiety was further aroused when NATO's Secretary General requested a formal assurance from both Washington and London that the operational plans of their strategic air and naval forces took full account of the missile launching sites beyond the range of the nuclear forces available to SACEUR and SACLANT.[123] In discussing the request, the Chiefs of Staff made clear their strong opposition to the release of such information, for if compromised, 'it would seriously prejudice the deterrent value of the Atomic Strike Plans'.[124] To reassure NATO members, however, the Council was assured that there was 'complete co-ordination in the operational planning of both British and American nuclear forces, including targeting. This means that the British force covers targets of general importance to the defence of Europe, not just the targets essential for the security of the United Kingdom.'[125] It was also agreed that while the proposed NATO Peacetime Administrative Committee should be given details on target policy (the definition given to the choice of a group or system of targets to be attacked) details on target planning (including operating techniques, operational capabilities and limitations, routes and selected targets) should not be disclosed.[126]

Despite these guarantees and assurances, however, there was still no political agreement within the alliance covering the decision to use nuclear weapons. In a final attempt to reach some form of accommodation, Stikker proposed a set of procedures based largely on MC-95 but containing qualifications consistent with civilian control. In short, the procedures detailed situations in which the use of nuclear weapons would be seriously considered whilst upholding the principle that the Council would be consulted wherever possible. Formally adopted in May 1962 at the Athens meeting of NATO foreign and defence ministers, the guidelines covered the following:

As regards the possible recourse by NATO to nuclear weapons in its self-defence:

(a) in the event of an unmistakable Soviet attack with nuclear weapons in the NATO area, the forces of the alliance should respond with nuclear weapons on the scale appropriate to the circumstances. The possibilities for consultation in this context are extremely limited.
(b) In the event of a full-scale attack by the Soviet Union with conventional forces, indicating the opening of general hostilities on any sector of the

NATO area, the forces of the alliance should respond with nuclear weapons on the scale appropriate to the circumstances. It is anticipated that time will in this case permit consultation.

(c) In the event of a Soviet attack not fulfilling those conditions described in a) and b) above, but which threatened the integrity of the forces and the territory attacked and which could not be successfully held with the existing conventional forces, the decision to use nuclear weapons would be subject to prior consultation.[127]

The guidelines were part of a package of measures designed to reassure the Europeans about the US commitment and provide a greater sense of participation in the alliance. Other issues included the level of nuclear forces in Europe, the targeting plans of SAC and Bomber Command, and the provision of nuclear information though a NATO nuclear committee. Negotiations within NATO were intensive and imposed a strain on the Secretary-General. At one point in the NAC, 'his emotion overcame him and he had to leave the meeting'.[128] The Kennedy administration also undertook a concerted campaign to educate the non-nuclear members of NATO in the 'realities' of nuclear policy. This process reached its culmination at Athens where McNamara delivered 'the fullest statement the Alliance has ever received on the content of US nuclear strategy.'[129] In the address, McNamara argued that Massive Retaliation was simply not credible and should be replaced with a controlled response capable of dealing with any level of Soviet conventional aggression short of all-out attack. In spite of this pressure, and in the face of considerable French resistance, the results were mixed. While the Council accepted the guidelines, the anticipated agreement on conventional force levels was not forthcoming. Although this was considered a set-back this was not quite the case. It is now evident that although Kennedy's preferred policy was to achieve unanimity within the alliance, the administration was prepared to 'set aside' the Political Directive and act unilaterally to achieve a 'constructive interpretation' of NATO strategy.[130]

This is apparent in the formulation of SACEUR's Emergency Defence Plan. Undertaken on an annual basis, the formulation of the EDP was largely an American concern.[131] Its real significance however, lay in the ability to implement the plan solely through the US chain of command. Central to this were the NATO nuclear custodial units. Composed entirely of US personnel, the units were 'double-hatted' and could release nuclear weapons either through NATO channels via SACEUR or through a dedicated national channel under the control of USCINCEUR. In short, there were no physical restrictions to stop the US from initiating a nuclear exchange.[132]

In 1962, this capability was utilized to the full. The policy of flexible nuclear response was incorporated into the EDP. The result was profound and far-reaching. By simply amending the EDP, SACEUR (in his capacity as USCINCEUR) was granted *de facto* authorisation to develop a concept of limited nuclear use without the requirement to seek a revision of MC 14/2 'which provided very little direction in this respect.'[133] This is less than surprising as a cardinal aspect of MC 14/2 was its explicit rejection of limited war. It is also now apparent that the authority to employ nuclear weapons in limited war rested almost entirely on 'the statement of strategic guidance' issued personally by Norstad in December 1960. Using this 'guidance' SACEUR reserved to himself 'the sole military authority to direct the use of nuclear weapons under conditions less than General War'.[134] To implement this capability, a new S-Hour procedure was introduced into the EDP which authorized SACEUR to selectively employ nuclear weapons 'singly or in limited numbers for specific purposes and in specific areas'. Significantly, as the S-hour release procedure was to be conducted solely through the US chain of command, overall NATO approval was not required.[135]

The revised EDP also modified SACEUR's release authority for the use of nuclear weapons in General War. Whereas formerly the use of any nuclear weapons in ACE required SACEUR's specific approval, this procedure now only applied to weapons with a yield of more than ten kilotons. In addition, the use of air defence nuclear weapons of any yield was now authorized 'in accordance with approved rules of engagement'. The succession of military command within SHAPE was also addressed, with SACEUR nominating Deputy SACEUR as his successor, to be followed in order of rank and seniority by his Air or Naval Deputies, CINCENT or the Chief of Staff, SHAPE. Further, if SHAPE was destroyed or communications disrupted, operational control would transfer to HQ Allied Forces Central Europe (AFCENT).[136]

Critically, the provisions of SACEUR's EDP still left unresolved one important issue—the threshold at which general nuclear release would be declared. To resolve this question satisfactorily agreement on the fundamentals of NATO strategy was essential. It rapidly became evident, however, that no such consensus was possible and the issue threatened to split the alliance. For both Britain and the continental Europeans who were determined to avoid a limited war in Europe, the nuclear threshold was expected to be reached 'sooner rather than later'. On the other hand, the US (reluctant to commit strategic forces until absolutely necessary) demanded a considerably longer period. McNamara argued that conventional forces, assisted by an air-interdiction programme using conventional munitions, would be able to hold a Russian conventional attack for a period of 'weeks rather than days'.[137]

By early 1963, the divergence of views between the Americans and the Europeans was considerable. The inevitable breakdown occurred during the course of NATO's Force Planning Exercises, when the French government bluntly refused to discuss proposals to increase NATO conventional forces.[138] Fundamental to French concerns was the role of tactical nuclear weapons within NATO strategy. By now, the American position was explicit. Should deterrence fail, the function of tactical nuclear forces was 'to increase the flexibility of response to aggression by providing the capability to conduct any desired level of nuclear operations and thus to provide options to limit nuclear warfare below the general war level.'[139]

For the continental Europeans this came dangerously close to limited nuclear war, which was both unacceptable and incompatible with even the most 'constructive interpretation' of existing NATO strategy. The French argued forcibly for the retention of a simple trip-wire strategy. In contrast, the West Germans favoured a 'ladder of escalation' in which Soviet conventional attack would be met by conventional forces with nuclear weapons employed on a limited and strictly selective basis.[140] The various national positions on the use of tactical nuclear forces can be summarized as follows: for the Americans, as late as possible; for the French, as early as possible; and for the Germans, as early as necessary. Anticipating the possible dangers for NATO cohesion, the British attempted equidistance between these various positions. The concept of Massive Retaliation strongly advocated by France (and once favoured by the British) was rejected, as was any determination to match Soviet force levels. The resulting dilemma was encapsulated by the JPS:

> A trip wire strategy is not credible... and provides no room for either political or military flexibility. At the other end of the strategic alternatives, any attempt by NATO to base its strategy for the defence of Central Europe primarily on matching Soviet and satellite forces by conventional means is impossible, unless the Western nations drastically lower their living standards.[141]

The 1962 British Defence White Paper acknowledged that if the West had nothing but nuclear forces, threats to respond to aggression would be incredible. Accordingly, the paper called for a 'flexible' strategy representing a 'balance... between conventional and nuclear strength'.[142] There would be no protracted conventional war in Europe. In the event of large-scale conflict nuclear weapons would be used within days. Whatever the public pronouncements, in private HMG was fundamentally opposed to McNamara's ambitions. For the British, it was becoming increasingly clear that the concept of a war of movement in Europe using tactical nuclear weapons, but without recourse to strategic nuclear weapons, was untenable: the scale of devastation would be comparable to a strategic nuclear exchange.[143] In accepting this view, the Defence Committee concluded that the only plausible function for tactical nuclear forces was discriminate nuclear response. As implementation of such a strategy would require only a limited number of weapons under the direct control of SACEUR, it was further agreed that continued development of Britain's independent battlefield weapon, Blue Water, was no longer necessary.[144] To emphasize the level of Britain's dissatisfaction with current NATO strategy and to express his own personal disquiet, Macmillan wrote to Kennedy:

> I am increasingly concerned about the immense diffusion of so-called tactical nuclear weapons in NATO Europe. According to my information there are many thousands of these weapons, and their total capacity amounts to scores of megatons... I believe that we must take a fresh look at this dangerous situation. It seems to me that there would be great advantage if we could work toward the concept of a tactical nuclear command directly under SACEUR having the tactical nuclear weapons under his own control, instead of leaving them dispersed through the various national contingents. The strategic concept underlying the establishment of such a command would be different from that currently favoured in NATO. It would mean that, instead of preparing to fight a tactical battle with nuclear weapons, we were aiming to make such discriminatory use of those weapons as might be necessary to impose a pause or to demonstrate our will to use our strategic nuclear strength if fighting continued. I am convinced that on this point the current NATO strategy is misconceived; and I believe that in the months ahead, we shall have to try to get it modified along the general lines I have indicated.[145]

The President remained largely non-committal to Macmillan's request for revision of NATO strategy, and continued to argue that large-scale conventional forces were essential to European security. On the question of achieving greater control over the nuclear weapons stockpile, however, the two leaders were in broad agreement. Kennedy informed Macmillan that the administration had taken the decision to install Permissive Action Links (PALs) on all nuclear weapons, which would enable the US to exercise centralized control over their use.[146] Macmillan's suggestion for a tactical weapons command, however, was considered inappropriate, as its composition would raise complex questions about the organisation of NATO requiring further discussion. For Macmillan, Kennedy's reply was disappointing and characterized Britain's growing inability to influence the direction of NATO policy through bilateral agreement alone. The diminished status of Britain's world role was further reinforced by the policy of the US State Department with its 'messianic zeal' to foster closer European integration.[147] A policy agenda where this tendency became most apparent was the discussions surrounding the creation of the NATO Multilateral Force.

THE MULTILATERAL FORCE

First suggested by the Eisenhower administration in late-1960, the main purpose of the NATO Multilateral Force (MLF) was to allay European anxieties over the credibility of extended deterrence. Within the Kennedy administration however attention focused on the Acheson proposals and MLF received a low priority. Nevertheless, in Ottawa in May 1961, President Kennedy reaffirmed the US commitment to establish a Multilateral Force under virtually the same conditions foreshadowed in the Bowie report. It was stressed, however, that implementation would only occur after the conventional force goals had been achieved and an agreed method of control established.[148] These conditions placed the Europeans in a difficult position. To achieve some control over the launch of strategic nuclear forces the Europeans had first to adopt a strategy with which they strongly disagreed.

The stringent preconditions of Kennedy's Ottawa statement also served to reconcile a divergence of opinion concerning the MLF within Washington. For the Pentagon, the MLF was of minor importance. The main objective was to build up NATO's conventional forces in line with the Acheson report. Furthermore, the prospect of granting the Europeans some degree of control over the launch of strategic nuclear forces threatened to violate the requirement for a centrally controlled, unified nuclear arsenal, which formed the basis of McNamara's approach to strategic planning.[149] In short, McNamara considered the MRBM a military irrelevance and felt that advocates of the MLF 'indicated a lack of understanding of the nature of the nuclear control problem which was in itself dangerous'.[150] In light of these reservations, McNamara was adamant that the MLF should only be considered after the preconditions set forth in the Ottawa statement had been fulfilled, a situation that was not expected to arise. In contrast, the State Department adopted a more flexible approach. Whilst accepting that from a military viewpoint the provision of MRBMs was not urgent, the State Department considered the MLF proposal a potential alternative to national nuclear programmes.[151] It was hoped that by providing a strategic nuclear force at NATO disposal would contain French nuclear aspirations, curtail German dissatisfaction and eventually over time allow Britain to abandon its independent deterrent. The potential of the MLF to constrain nuclear proliferation was therefore seen as considerable. Despite the obvious advantages, significant difficulties remained, the most intractable being control. On one hand, to insist on retention of the US veto would not satisfy the Europeans, whilst on the other, agreement to relinquish control would largely undermine McNamara's entire strategy.

To reconcile these two positions President Kennedy sanctioned NSAM 147, which formed the basis of future negotiations with the NATO allies. This reiterated the administration's long-term objective to establish a modest-sized (200 missile) sea-based NATO MRBM force under full multilateral ownership, control and manning. Second, authorisation was granted for US officials to consider proposals for some form of NATO multilateral control over Polaris submarines committed to NATO. It was emphasized, however, that this condition should not be volunteered by the US and should serve only as an interim political measure to defuse future demands for increased alliance control over MRBMs in Europe. Third, to control the force, the US proposed a set of guidelines covering launch procedures. The basis of these were:

(i) Advanced delegation to some person or group of authority to order use of the MRBM force (in conjunction with other nuclear forces available to NATO), in the clearly specified contingency of unmistakable large-scale nuclear attack on NATO.
(ii) Agreement that the decision to order use of the force in other contingencies should be based on a prearranged system of voting in the NAC, which a majority of our allies will almost certainly wish to provide for voting by unanimity or by a group including the US.[152]

Viewed from Europe, the strength of the US commitment to MLF was seen with growing scepticism. This perception was vindicated by McNamara's subsequent pronouncements at both Athens and Ann Arbor. To reassure the Europeans that the MLF was still under active consideration, Kennedy authorized Ambassador Finletter to present the NAC with a sanitized version of NSAM 147. In private correspondence with Finletter, however, Kennedy conceded that due to its high cost, unproven military need and unresolved political difficulties 'the probability of final affirmative action for the MRBM force is low'.[153] Despite such reservations, discussions were continued, as this would encourage greater European understanding of current NATO strategy.

For NATO military commanders (particularly the planners at SHAPE) the continued vacillation of Washington towards the MRBM force proved frustrating. Concern over the lack of clear direction was stridently conveyed to President Kennedy by General Norstad. A less than wholehearted supporter of Kennedy's new strategy, Norstad's position was undermined by Finletter's statement to the NAC about which he had not been consulted.[154] Norstad's advocacy of a NATO MRBM force was well known within the alliance, and was forcibly restated to the Council in October 1962. The central thrust of Norstad's concern was that an MRBM force was required immediately to enable SACEUR to carry out his directives from both the Military Committee and the Council.

To support this contention, Norstad revealed that there were a variety of targets that in present circumstances could not be attacked effectively by any other weapon except an MRBM. These targets were contained in SACEUR's Atomic Strike Plan, composed of 603 priority targets in the USSR and Eastern Europe, designated as the 'fixed nuclear threat' (missile sites, light and medium bomber airfields) and 1300 contingency targets (airfields, bridges, road and rail centres) against which strikes might have to be mounted at the outbreak of hostilities.[155] Although Norstad accepted the vital part that external strategic nuclear forces had to play in the maintenance of deterrence, he doubted whether they would be launched until NATO had already reached a condition of general war. For Norstad, the position was clear: 'without the deployment of MRBMs there would be no defence of NATO Europe and consequently no NATO within a relatively few years'.[156]

To address Norstad's concerns and to brief more fully the Europeans on current US thinking a delegation jointly headed by Admiral John Lee of the Pentagon and Gerard Smith of the State Department visited Europe. The proposals which they eventually presented to European leaders envisaged a surface fleet of 25 vessels, each armed with eight Polaris MRBMs. To be owned and controlled on a strictly multilateral basis, each vessel would have a mixed crew of at least three nations. Although initially the US would retain a veto over the launch of the force, the possibility was held out that the US would review the situation if NATO considered alternative arrangements more suitable.[157]

In late-1962, two high-level policy conferences were convened between the Departments of State and Defense to review progress on the MLF. McNamara's main contention was that present US policy was ambiguous for whilst some officials were actively engaged in promoting the scheme others discounted the whole idea. In response, Rusk stressed that the allies had not yet faced up to the problem of command and control and if this issue was not soon resolved great difficulties lay ahead. Underpinning McNamara's argument, however, was the belief that continued prevarication was weakening the US position within the alliance and that NATO could not afford both a conventional build-up and an MRBM force.[158] For a time it appeared that McNamara's opposition had proved successful. The two departments agreed to abandon the MLF pilot scheme and it was widely believed that after a suitable period of mourning the whole idea would be quietly buried. Unfortunately, for McNamara, the MLF had a life of its own, and following the serious breach in British-American relations brought about by the cancellation of Skybolt the entire enterprise was resurrected again.

NASSAU AND AFTER

The crisis in British-American relations brought about by the cancellation of Skybolt had its origins in 1960 when the Macmillan government abandoned Blue Streak, Britain's independently developed IRBM. To retain a national nuclear capability HMG opted to purchase the Skybolt ALBM from the US. Skybolt would prolong the life of the V-Force and provide a credible national deterrent into the late-1960s. Due to protracted technical difficulties, however, Skybolt's development programme experienced a severe budget overrun and was eventually cancelled in November 1962. In Britain, the decision caused uproar. It was widely believed that the Americans had engineered the whole affair in a crude attempt to force

Britain out of the nuclear club (even though the British were aware of the technical and financial difficulties of the programme).

Aware of the possible consequences for future British-American relations Macmillan and Kennedy met at Nassau in December 1962, where Britain secured the purchase of US Polaris missiles.[159] Under the Nassau agreement, Britain was obliged to participate in the development of MLF. The commitment was received with little enthusiasm. Indeed, it has been suggested that Britain only agreed to this condition in the belief that MLF would never materialize.[160] In general, the government viewed MLF as a military irrelevance, while the CDS described the scheme as 'the greatest piece of military nonsense he had come across in fifty years.'[161] To advance the multinational dimension of the agreement, the government quickly announced plans for the formation of the 'Inter Allied Nuclear Force' (IANF) to which Bomber Command and three US Polaris submarines were to be allocated, though these each remained under national command.[162] To provide political control, the Foreign Office recommended a NATO Nuclear Trusteeship Group, comprising the US, UK and possibly France together with all states owning nuclear delivery systems, whose functions would encompass monitoring guidelines, discussing strategy and possibly making recommendations on the use of nuclear weapons.[163]

Despite the creation of the IANF, the State Department was still anxious to pursue a truly multilateral control arrangement. It was argued that as Nassau had only further demonstrated Germany's inferiority within NATO, implementation of the MLF was now more important than ever. In response, Kennedy sanctioned NSAM 218 and authorized Livingston Merchant, a career US diplomat, to intensify discussions with the Europeans on establishing some form of MLF. Whilst the proposals Merchant presented to the Europeans were essentially the same as those contained in the Smith-Lee briefings of the previous October, they also reflected an important shift in emphasis within Washington. Specifically, the MLF negotiations were not to be linked to NATO's conventional force build-up and the US would agree on unanimity of voting to launch the force.[164] In short, Kennedy abandoned the preconditions set out at Ottawa. In spite of this relaxation, the proposals elicited little enthusiasm within Europe and only Bonn offered any active support.

The lack of any concerted European support for MLF was due to several disparate factors. First, for a variety of domestic political reasons, Canada, Denmark, France, Portugal and Norway announced immediately that they were not interested in participating in the scheme. Second, general elections were imminent in both Italy and Holland, which precluded a rapid response. Third, as shown above, Britain was promoting its own proposal. For West Germany, however, the MLF proved attractive: deployment was seen to increase the security of the Federal Republic and provide an American counterbalance to an exclusively Franco-German military relationship.[165]

The increased emphasis now placed on MLF in Washington presented the British with a dilemma. Of the three policy options available none were particularly attractive. Outright rejection would place considerable strain on British-American relations and possibly jeopardize the supply of Polaris missiles. Failure to participate fully would curtail British influence on deployment of the force and prejudice the right to a full share in the formulation of NATO policy that possession of an independent deterrent had so far secured. However, acceptance would impose a significant burden in both finance and manpower to sustain a force whose overall militarily significance was regarded by the Chiefs of Staff as 'entirely superfluous'.[166] The Cabinet was presented with two divergent perspectives. The Foreign Secretary, argued that for wider political considerations Britain's participation within MLF was essential, both to maintain influence in Washington and sustain the impetus of Britain's policy towards Europe. In contrast, the Minister of Defence was implacably opposed to any British involvement: the force had no military requirement, was both expensive and vulnerable to attack, and would further divide the alliance.[167] To reconcile these positions, the Cabinet sanctioned a dual-track strategy. First, to move the policy agenda away from MLF, attention again focused on the multinational dimension of NATO's nuclear forces by the proposal of a Nuclear Control Commission that would:

(a) provide SACEUR with political guidance on nuclear affairs.
(b) approve SACEUR's targeting and operational plans.
(c) establish guidelines for the employment of nuclear weapons in certain defined circumstances.
(d) authorise SACEUR to execute NATO war plans, including the decision to release nuclear weapons.
(e) provide contingency planning for the possible use of nuclear weapons outside the NATO area.[168]

The Commission would comprise five permanent members from the US, Britain, France, Germany and Italy. To satisfy the non-nuclear members the Commission would have two additional representatives selected on a rotational basis. Bearing a remarkable similarity to the eventual composition and function of the Nuclear Planning Group formed in 1966, the proposal was forwarded to NATO for discussion in late 1963.[169]

The second strand of British policy was quite simply to do nothing, or, more accurately, to pursue a policy that did not formally bind the government to participate in the creation of any mixed-manned force. This aspect of British policy became apparent during Kennedy's talks with Macmillan in June 1963. Although a primary aim of the meeting was to gain a British commitment for MLF, Macmillan steadfastly refused to issue any such statement. The final communiqué reflected British concerns by stating firmly that HMG would continue to participate in discussions for a multilateral sea-borne force 'without prejudice to the question of British participation in the force'.[170] In short, British policy towards MLF was characterized by passive engagement. Unwilling to reject the proposal out of hand for fear of US recrimination, HMG was nevertheless prepared to persist in negotiations as the best hope of maintaining British influence while avoiding the political and military risks that deployment of such a force would entail. Implicit throughout, however, was the attendant hope that continued delay and uncertainty would gradually reduce the political momentum and lead to eventual cancellation of the entire project.

With the assassination of President Kennedy in November 1963, MLF faded from the political agenda, a decline compounded by events in Europe. In October, Konrad Adenauer relinquished his ten-year grip on the German Chancellery, whilst in Britain Macmillan was replaced as Prime Minister by Alec Douglas Home. The advocates of multilateralism were further hampered by the lack of experience in foreign affairs of Kennedy's successor, Lyndon Johnson, who entered the presidency largely ignorant of the complex negotiations surrounding the MLF issue. Fearing a collapse of the entire project, the State Department intensified diplomatic efforts. A tangible manifestation of this renewed diplomatic effort was confirmation that MLF would form a major aspect of President Johnson's forthcoming European tour.

The negotiations were thrown into further confusion by a British proposal for an alternate MLF scheme incorporating land-based missiles and aircraft. The proposal, first advanced by the Minister of Defence, Peter

Thorneycroft, at the NATO ministerial meeting in December, envisaged a force comprising British Canberras and V-bombers, US and West German F104s and Pershing surface to surface missiles, plus the projected British TSR2 and US F111. To be placed under SACEUR, the force was to be mixed-manned wherever possible and capable of providing NATO with both a strategic and interdiction capability.[171] Compared to the original MLF scheme, the 'Thorneycroft proposals' offered HMG three distinct advantages. First, as the force comprised existing weapons systems, the overall cost would be greatly reduced. Second, exclusion of the Polaris submarines enabled Britain to retain its commitment to an independent deterrent. Third, the absence of a fleet component deflected criticism from the Admiralty whilst inclusion of the TSR2 pacified the RAF who were anxious to acquire government support for a project whose future seemed in some doubt.[172]

In Washington the British proposals were greeted with little enthusiasm, being widely perceived as a calculated attempt to delay the proceedings. If this was indeed the purpose the objective was fulfilled. Discussion of the British proposals meant that ratification of the MLF treaty would not be reached before the end of the year. To circumvent the deadlock, the State Department initiated private discussions with West Germany in pursuit of a purely bilateral solution. The requirement to keep the negotiations secret soon proved counter-productive. In October 1964, the talks collapsed with Dean Rusk forced to issue a statement precluding a bilateral MLF agreement with West Germany alone.[173] The same month also marked the election of a new Labour government strongly opposed to the MLF programme.

THE ATLANTIC NUCLEAR FORCE

In 1964, defence policy and nuclear weapons were issues in the election campaign. The new Prime Minister, Harold Wilson, made clear his opposition to MLF, which he saw as a major obstacle to the successful conclusion of a disarmament treaty with the Soviet Union: 'so long as Western ideas about nuclear sharing were concentrated on proposals for a Multilateral Force, Russian opposition was implacable.'[174] Labour's Defence Minister, Denis Healey, also a vociferous critic, later described MLF as a 'military monstrosity'.[175] Meeting at Chequers soon after the election, the two men agreed to oppose both the mixed-manned fleet and any bilateral arrangement between the United States and West Germany as this was considered a possible mechanism for German acquisition of nuclear weapons. Policy now determined, the next objective was to obtain the desired result without unduly antagonizing Washington. To achieve this, Healey advanced a different proposal: the 'Atlantic Nuclear Force' (ANF).

To consist of the British V-bombers, British and US Polaris submarines, an unspecified French contribution and a jointly owned mixed-manned component, the ANF would be controlled by a Nuclear Control Commission linked to NATO and containing representatives of all contributing countries. Each participating nation would have a veto on the launch of the force. Comprised of existing or soon to be deployed units, ANF reflected elements of the earlier 'Thorneycroft proposals'. A new aspect was the inclusion of the British Polaris force. It was made clear, however, these elements would remain a nationally owned and manned contingent and capable of independent national control.[176] The advantage of the proposal was the expectation that a unified control system would 'bind the US still more closely into Atlantic defence and prevent the proliferation of national nuclear weapons, whilst ensuring that Germany remains satisfied with her share in the control'.[177]

The ANF proposal was formally presented to Johnson during Wilson's Washington visit in December 1964. It is now apparent that a firm but unspoken intention behind ANF was to block agreement on MLF. British opposition was further strengthened by the cordial reaction of Johnson and the mounting opposition now shown by the French. The reason for Washington's change of heart was due to several factors: lack of Congressional support, growing divisions in the Bundestag, the open hostility of the French and concerted opposition from the Soviets. Underlying the reverse however was Johnson's judgement that MLF would ultimately founder and that close personal association with a foreign policy failure would discredit his domestic political agenda. To further consolidate his position, Johnson authorized a decision document, which suspended the MLF negotiations until the Europeans arrived at a common position. Although the State Department continued to claim that the MLF/ANF proposals were still under active consideration, it was evident that a hardware solution to the question of alliance control was effectively dead. The project was finally abandoned by mutual consent in September 1966.[178] Franz Josef Strauss apparently quipped that the ANF was the only fleet in history which had not been created, yet torpedoed another fleet which had never sailed.[179] As a hardware solution was now discredited, attention focused on establishing a procedural mechanism that would grant the alliance a greater participation and control in nuclear issues. The process eventually resulted in the creation of the Nuclear Planning Group in December 1966, whose purpose, McNamara explained to Johnson, was 'to give the more important non-nuclear members of the Alliance a sense of involvement in the planning of nuclear strategy and deployment. Hopefully, it will be an adequate substitute for MLF type hardware arrangements.'[180]

CONCLUSION

Throughout the late-1950s and early-1960s the control of nuclear weapons dominated alliance politics and raised complex political and military issues central to NATO's role. On one level, the debate can be seen as a division between Europe and America, with extended deterrence and the US guarantee for the defence of Europe a dominant theme. On another level, the question of control exposed divisions within Europe with Britain, France and West Germany forced to balance domestic political agendas against wider alliance commitments. At yet another level, the issue caused division within government with defence and foreign ministries often pursuing separate and divergent policy objectives. The complexity was further compounded as the control issue itself possessed two separate elements. At the strategic level, the issue centred on assuring positive control, whilst at the tactical level negative control was the dominant factor. To satisfy these various objectives two solutions were advanced: a hardware solution concerned with ownership and possession; and procedural arrangements related to deployment planning and potential use.

Under the Eisenhower administration, the Americans favoured a hardware solution, resulting in the creation of the NATO atomic stockpile and proposals to establish the MLF. The outcome satisfied neither Kennedy's requirement for centralized control nor European aspirations for greater participation in nuclear planning. To accommodate these, the hardware solution was eventually abandoned and replaced with procedural innovations that increased alliance involvement in nuclear policy decisions. This process was reflected in the adoption of the Athens guidelines and the creation of the NATO Nuclear Planning Group in 1966. The general political guidelines covering nuclear release were the only mechanism to guard against unilateral use of US nuclear weapons in NATO Europe. Yet despite these arrangements, America maintained the operational capability to control nuclear release in Europe solely through the US chain of command. It is now evident that this capability was used by the Kennedy administration to develop a concept of limited nuclear war without the need to revise MC 14/2. Indeed, with the minimum of alliance consultation, SACEUR's Emergency Defence Plan was amended to grant SACEUR (in his capacity as CINCEUR) authorisation to employ nuclear weapons selectively and in limited numbers.

For Britain, the question of controlled nuclear response raised a political problem: agreement would increase alliance participation but diminish the perceived effectiveness of the British-American relationship. Consequently, Britain's aim to revise NATO strategy became directly linked to the command and control of nuclear weapons. The implications were noted by the Foreign Office who cautioned that, 'the doctrine of discriminate nuclear reaction would bring to the fore the intractable problem, which it has been HM Government's desire to keep shelved, of who are the political authorities that should control the use of nuclear weapons.'[181] Moreover, by refusing to address the issue directly, Britain increased Washington's dilemma over nuclear proliferation by continuing to believe that the fourth-country problem could be solved by provision of US nuclear weapons under SACEUR's control, a solution that Britain was absolutely unwilling to have applied to itself.[182]

The divergent nature of Britain's foreign policy objectives soon became apparent. On one hand, HMG sought to maintain an exclusive nuclear relationship with Washington. On the other (and at variance with the first) there were equally compelling economic arguments for closer integration with Europe. In short, economic and strategic pressures pulled in different directions, and although the government sought to separate security issues from economic policy the linkage could not be ignored. Macmillan's failure to resolve these conflicts and construct a coherent response eventually proved disastrous: the British-American relationship was almost severed whilst Britain's European ambitions were thrown into chaos. These results were not unforeseen. The political discussions surrounding the multilateral force highlighted these various tensions and indicated that Britain's privileged position within the alliance would not be accepted indefinitely.

1. DEFE 7/2018, FO to Certain HM Reps., Intel. 57, 5 April 1962.
2. CAB 129/62, C(53)234, 17 August 1953.
3. DEFE 5/49, COS(53)490, 2 October 1953. The study assumed SACEUR would have 1,000 tactical nuclear weapons of which 850 would be delivered in the first 30–day period. See Wampler, *NATO Strategic Planning*; David Yost, 'The History of NATO Theatre Nuclear Force Policy: Key Findings from the Sandia Conference', *Journal of Strategic Studies*, Vol.15, No.2 (June 1992); David Elliot, 'Project Vista and Nuclear Weapons in Europe', *International Security*, Vol.11, No.1 (Summer 1986).
4. NSC 162/2, 30 October 1953, *FRUS*, 1952–1954, Vol.II pp. 583–93.
5. For details of US tactical nuclear deployments, see Matthew D. Bird, *Political Firepower: Nuclear Weapons and the US Army 1945–1973*, (PhD, University of Wales, Aberystwyth, 1998).
6. AIR 19/690, Understandings with the British on the Use of Bases and Nuclear Weapons, 6 February 1961.
7. For further details, see Alan Macmillan and Stephen Twigge, 'Past, Present and Future? Tactical Nuclear Weapons in NATO Strategy', *War Studies Journal*, Vol.2, Issue1 (Autumn 1996).
8. Cited in Robert Wampler, *Ambiguous Legacy: The United States, Great Britain and the Foundations of NATO Strategy, 1948–1957* (PhD, Harvard University, 1991), p. 603.
9. DEFE 6/26, JP(54)76(Final), 2 September 1954.
10. RG 218, JCS to Wilson, 27 September 1954, Chairman's File 1953–57, Box 23, NATO, National Archives.
11. AIR 2/15917, Coordination of NATO and National Bombing Tasks, 16 August 1954.
12. AIR 2/15917, ACAS(Ops) to ACAS(P), 8 September 1954.
13. AIR 2/15917, Command Directive, August 1954.
14. PREM 11/849, FO to Washington, Tel. 5964, 3 December 1954.
15. DEFE 4/72, COS(54)98th, 13 September 1954.
16. DEFE 6/26, JP(54)86(Final), 21 October 1954.
17. PREM 11/849, Jebb to FO, Tel. 816, 16 December 1954.
18. Ibid.
19. PREM 11/849, Steel to FO, Tel. 262, 17 December 1954.
20. CAB 129/84, Annex to CP(56)269, 28 November 1956.
21. AIR 41/86, C–M(56)138(Final), 13 December 1956. The Political Directive is reproduced in James, *Defence*, Appendix C.
22. For further details, see Stephen Twigge and Alan Macmillan, 'Britain, the United States and the Development of NATO Strategy, 1950–1964', *Journal of Strategic Studies*, Vol.19, No.2 (June 1996).
23. AIR 8/2065, Draft directive to SACEUR, 5 September 1956.
24. *FRUS*, 1955–57, Vol.IV, p. 162.
25. DEFE 4/95, JP(57)11(Final), NATO – Overall Strategic Concept, 5 February 1957.
26. For details of the US debate, see Rosenberg, 'Origins of Overkill', pp. 33–5; Richard Rhodes, *Dark Sun: The Making of the Hydrogen Bomb* (Simon & Schuster, 1995), pp. 563–9.
27. DEFE 5/71, COS(56)377, 11 October 1956.
28. Bracken, *Command*, p. 198.
29. Gregory, *Nuclear*, p. 75; see also Paul B. Stares, *Command Performance: The Neglected Dimension of European Security* (Washington: Brookings, 1991), pp. 114–21.
30. DEFE 7/2019, The Initiation of War and Nuclear Operations by NATO, Sabbatini to Mottershead, 16 May 1963.
31. DEFE 4/93, JP(56)177(Revised Final), 16 November 1956.
32. AIR 19/690, VCAS to Amery, 18 November 1960.
33. DEFE 7/2016, Extract from COS(59)40th, 25 June 1959.
34. Carnovale, *Control*, p. 41.
35. DEFE 4/90, JP(56)133(Final), SACEUR's Emergency Defence Plan—1957, 28 August 1956.

36. Carnovale, *Control*, p. 38.
37. *FRUS*, 1955–57, Vol.IV, p. 185.
38. Wampler, *Ambiguous*, p. 1044.
39. Peter Stein and Peter Feaver, 'Assuring Control of Nuclear Weapons: The Evolution of Permissive Action Links' (Harvard University, Center for Science and International Affairs, Occasional Paper No. 2, 1987), p. 27.
40. Initial plans for Corporal were based on the assumption of fitting a British–developed nuclear warhead based on a modified Red Beard assembly and known as Violet Vision. DEFE 13/189 Brundrett to Minister, 18 January 1957.
41. RG 59, Memorandum of Conversation with Roger Makins, 741.5612/11–2255, National Archives.
42. RG 59, Memorandum of Conversation between the President and Prime Minister, 22 March 1957, National Archives
43. RG 59, West (EURCOM) to Wolfe, 711.56341/8.2057, National Archives.
44. Timmons to Guthrie, 5 September 1957, in National Security Archive, *Nuclear Non–Proliferation, 1945–1990* Microfiche Collection (Washington: Chadwyck–Healey, 1992) Doc. 437.
45. RG 218, JCS 1957, CCS 350.05 (3–16–48) Sec 10, Norstad to Secretary of Defense, 17 October 1957, National Archives.
46. Philip Karber et al. *Trends in the Deployment of Nuclear Weapons in Central Europe: 1948–1988*, Nuclear History Program Data Base Series (Washington: NHP, July 1989), pp. 95–7. The British were also offered the use of the Davy Crockett nuclear bazooka.
47. DEFE 5/79, COS(57)245, 14 November 1957.
48. *FRUS*, 1955–57, Vol.IV, pp. 170–71.
49. John Dulles, 'Challenge and Response in United States Policy', *Foreign Affairs*, Vol. 36 (October 1957).
50. European fears were initially aroused in mid–1956 by the leak of the Radford Plan, which suggested that America was planning to withdraw the majority of its conventional forces from Europe. This was indeed subsequently suggested by George Kennan in his 1957 Reith Lectures, see George Kennan, *Memoirs 1950–1963* (Hutchinson, 1973), pp. 229–66.
51. David Schwartz, *NATO's Nuclear Dilemmas* (Washington: Brookings, 1983), pp. 57–9.
52. *FRUS*, 1958–1960, Vol. VII, Pt. 1, pp. 386–402; DEFE 5/82, COS(58)70, MC–70, 11 March 1958.
53. Department of State, *Bulletin*, January 6, 1958.
54. Jan Melissen, 'Nuclearizing NATO, 1957–1959: the 'Anglo–Saxons', nuclear sharing and the fourth country problem', *Review of International Studies*, Vol.20, No.4, (July 1994).
55. AIR 8/1956, COS(58)12, 22 January 1958.
56. *FRUS*, 1958–1960, Vol.VII, Pt.1, pp. 354–5; Vol. VII, Pt 2, Doc. 34.
57. *FRUS*, 1958–1960, Vol.VII, Pt.2, pp. 81–3.
58. *FRUS*, 1958–1960, Vol.VII, Pt.1, pp. 359–60.
59. FO 371/159668, The Problem of France and the Emergence of Further Nuclear Powers, undated.
60. FO 371/159668, Shuckburgh to Brook, 8 February 1961.
61. *FRUS*, 1958–1960, Vol.VII, Pt.2, Doc. 117.
62. *FRUS*, 1958–1960, Vol.VII, Pt.1, pp. 459–64.
63. *HC deb*. Vol.607, Cols.1024–5, 23 June 1959.
64. RG 59, First Round US–UK Talks on Nuclear and Strategic Weapons in NATO, March 11 1960, Bureau of European Affairs, Office of European Regional Affairs, Records of the NATO Adviser, 1957–61, Box 1, TS Master File, 6/57–1/61. A second round of talks occurred on 18 March.
65. AIR 2/2247, COS 825/12/6/59, 24 June 1959.
66. Ibid., Annex A.
67. DEFE 7/2016, COS(59)40th, 25 June 1959 and COS(59)41st, 2 July 1959.
68. AIR 2/2247, Meeting with the Minister, 17 July 1959.

69. CAB 131/25, D(61)2, Annex A, 13 January 1961.
70. Robert Osgood, *NATO: The Entangling Alliance* (University of Chicago Press, 1962), p. 221.
71. *FRUS*, 1958–1960, Vol.VII, Pt.1, p. 466.
72. Schwartz, *Dilemmas*, pp. 76–7.
73. Christian Tuschhoff, *Causes and Consequences of Germany's Deployment of Nuclear Capable Delivery Systems 1957–1963* (CISSM, NHP, Occasional Paper 9, 1994), pp. 32 *et passim*.
74. Bluth, *Britain*, p. 66.
75. CAB 131/23, D(60)5th, 25 May 1960.
76. DEFE 7/2228, Memorandum by the Minister of Defence, 16 September 1960.
77. AIR 8/2288, COS. 1284/30/9/60, Collective ownership of NATO nuclear weapons, 30 September 1960.
78. AIR 8/2288, NATO MRBMs – Report for the UK Delegation to NATO, 1 October 1960.
79. Air 8/2288, COS1394/26/10/60, US Proposals for a NATO MRBM Force, 27 October 1960.
80. Speech by General Norstad to the NATO Parliamentarians' Conference, Paris, 21 November 1960, *Documents on International Affairs 1960* (OUP for the RIIA, 1964), pp. 124–30.
81. DEFE 32/6, Confidential Annex to COS(60)68th, 1 November 1960.
82. Robert R. Bowie, *The North Atlantic Nations Tasks for the 1960s: A Report to the Secretary of State, Aug. 1960,* (CISSM, NHP Occasional Paper 7, 1991).
83. Ibid.
84. *FRUS* 1958–1960, Vol.VII, Pt.1, pp. 611–14; 628–32.
85. Bowie, *Report,* p. 37.
86. *FRUS*, 1958–1960, Vol.VII, Pt.1, pp. 674–82.
87. DEFE 7/2888, The Reform of NATO Strategy, Memorandum by Richard Chilver, 8 August 1960.
88. DEFE 7/2888, JP(60)63(Final), August 1960.
89. Ibid.
90. Chilver Memorandum.
91. Ibid.
92. CAB 131/23, D(60)31, 8 July 1960.
93. Bundy, *Danger*, pp. 352–7.
94. Wainstein, *Evolution*, p. 284.
95. Rosenberg, 'Origins'; Sagan, 'SIOP–62'.
96. John F. Kennedy, 'Special Message to the Congress on the Defense Budget', 28 March 1961, in *Public Papers of the Presidents of the United States, John F. Kennedy, 1961* (Washington: USGPO, 1962), pp. 229–40.
97. JFKL, Speech to the NATO Military Committee, 10 April 1961, NSF, RS, Box 220.
98. Wainstein, *Evolution,* p. 242.
99. Sagan, 'SIOP–62', p. 37.
100. Kennedy, 'Special Message', pp. 230–2.
101. 'NATO and the Atlantic Nations', for full text see, *FRUS,* 1961–1963, Vol.XIII, pp. 285–91.
102. *FRUS,* 1961–1963, Vol.XIII, p. 315.
103. For discussions of the Kennedy/McNamara aims, see Jane Stromseth, *The Origins of Flexible Response* (Macmillan, 1988) and John S. Duffield, *Power Rules: The Evolution of NATO's Conventional Force* (Stanford, Stanford University Press, 1995).
104. DEFE 4/135, Annex to JP(61)Note 11, 28 April 1961.
105. CAB 131/25, D(61)2, 13 January 1961.
106. For a fuller account of the 'Mottershead Working Party' see Beatrice Heuser, 'The Development of NATO's Nuclear Strategy', *Contemporary European History,* Vol.4, No.1 (1994), pp. 61–4.
107. CAB 131/25, D(61)23, 1 May 1961.
108. AIR 8/1956, Brief on MC 95, 26 February 1962.
109. CAB 130/176, GEN. 734/1st, 27 April 1961.
110. Sabbatini to Mottershead, 16 May 1963.

111. Ibid.
112. Ibid.
113. AIR 8/1956, Annex to COS 258/26/2/62, 26 February 1962; *FRUS*, 1961–63, Vol.XIII, p. 374; Tuschhoff, *Causes*, p. 53.
114. AIR 8/2288, COS 1394/26/10/60, 27 October 1960.
115. Brief on MC 95.
116. AIR 8/1956, FO to UKDEL NATO, Tel. 312, 16 February 1962; *FRUS*, 1961–63, Vol.XIII, p. 359.
117. Tel. 312, ibid.; Tuschhoff, *Causes*, p. 39.
118. Tel. 312, ibid. Finletter's statement was made on 26 April 1961.
119. Ibid.
120. FO 371/166970, Evelyn Shuckburgh, Cuba and Anglo–American Consultation, 6 November 1962, reproduced in J. Baylis (Ed.), *Anglo–American Relations since 1939* (MUP, 1997), p. 127.
121. AIR 8/1956, FO to UKDEL NATO, Tel. 313, 16 February 1962.
122. Ibid.
123. AIR 8/1956, COS(62)20th, 15 March 1962.
124. DEFE 7/2018, COS(62)120, 20 March 1962. The NATO atomic strike plan consisted of three elements. 1) E–Hour – the time when the external strategic nuclear forces (i.e. SAC and Bomber Command) would attack targets in the Soviet Union. 2) The Scheduled Programme – which contained nuclear strikes automatic on the declaration of R–hour, targeted against Soviet atomic delivery capability and key control centres. 3) Regional Programmes – prepared by NATO Major Subordinate Commanders and approved by SACEUR. They consisted of high priority targets which were automatically attacked on R–Hour and targets of opportunity which were subject to pre–strike reconnaissance. ibid.
125. Ibid.
126. COS(62)120.
127. The 'Athens Guidelines' remain classified. The above is the revised draft of Stikker's proposal to the Athens meeting, UKDEL to Tomlinson, Tel. 62, 2 April 1962, DEFE 7/ 2018.
128. DEFE 7/ 2018, UKDEL NATO to FO, Mason, Tel. 61, 31 March 1962
129. *FRUS*, 1961–1963, Vol.XIII, p. 392; for full text of the address, see Robert McNamara, 'Speech to NATO Council, Athens', in Philip Bobbitt, Lawrence Freedman and Gregory Treverton (Eds.), *US Nuclear Strategy: A Reader*, (Macmillan, 1989), pp. 205–22.
130. *FRUS*, 1961–1963, Vol.XIII, p. 397
131. As the EDP was an Emergency Defence Plan, it did not require prior approval of either the Standing Group or NAC.
132. Carnovale, *Control*, pp. 108–10.
133. DEFE 6/78, Annex to JP(62)18(Final), SACEUR's Revised Emergency Defence Plan.
134. AIR 20/10056, COS(62)262, 21 June 1962.
135. When the British Chiefs of Staff approved the plan they noted that 'these documents are not subject to national approval', ibid.
136. The nuclear release procedures adopted in the EDP are reproduced in full in Appendix 7 .
137. DEFE 13/254, Record of meeting between Watkinson and McNamara, 11 December 1961.
138. Duffield, *Power*.
139. DEFE 4/157, Annex to JP Note 26/63, 15 August 1963.
140. For West German views on TNF, see Bluth, *Britain*, pp. 109–30.
141. DEFE 4/151, JP(62)110(Final), 17 January 1963.
142. Cmnd 1639, *Statement on Defence 1962, The Next Five Years*, (HMSO, 1962).
143. CAB 128/36, CC(54)62, 7 August 1962.
144. CAB 128/36, CC(53)62, 3 August 1962.
145. DEFE 13/254, Macmillan to Kennedy, 3 August 1962.
146. DEFE 13/254, Kennedy to Macmillan, 8 August 1962.

147. Pierre, *Nuclear*, p. 251.
148. *Public Papers of the Presidents*, p. 385.
149. Schwartz, *Dilemmas*, p. 94.
150. *FRUS*, 1961–1963, Vol.XIII, p. 368
151. John Steinbruner, *The Cybernetic Theory of Decision: New Dimensions of Political Analysis* (Princeton: Princeton University Press, 1974), pp. 225–6.
152. Ibid.; Steinbruner contends that these proposals, drawn up by State Department official Henry Owen, eventually evolved into the 'Athens Guidelines'.
153. *FRUS*, 1961–1963, Vol.XIII, pp. 407–11.
154. Ibid., p. 431; In light of these disagreements, Norstad offered his resignation which was accepted by President Kennedy on 19 July 1962. Owing to the Cuban missile crisis Norstad was asked to remain until the crisis was resolved, and was eventually replaced by General Lemnitzer in December 1962.
155. DEFE 4/150, JP(62)140(Final), 29 November 1962.
156. Ibid.; *FRUS*, 1961–1963, Vol.XIII, pp. 447–8.
157. Schwartz, *Dilemmas*, p.92; to defuse the control issue, Bowie suggested that the US should adopt the term 'joint control' rather than veto in all future negotiations.
158. *FRUS*, 1961–1963, Vol.XIII, pp. 446–7
159. See Chapter 4.
160. Buchan, 'Multilateral', p. 627.
161. Philip Ziegler, *Mountbatten* (Collins, 1985), p. 597.
162. *HC deb.*, Vol.670, Cols.955ff, 30 January 1963; *FRUS*, 1961–1963, Vol.XIII, pp. 559–60.
163. DEFE 7/2019, NATO Nuclear Force – Political Control, Memorandum by the Foreign Office, INNA(WG)/P(63)8(Revised), 4 February 1963
164. *FRUS*, 1961–1963, Vol.XIII, pp. 493–511; CAB 129/112, C(63)44, 11 March 1963.
165. For West German policy on MLF, see Bluth, *Britain*, pp. 93–5.
166. CAB 129/114, C(63)103, Annex A, 21 June 1963.
167. CAB 129/113, C(63)95 & C(63)96, 28 May 1963; CAB 128/37, CC(63)36th, 30 May 1962.
168. CAB 129/114, C(63)121, 9 July 1963
169. CAB 128/37, CC(63)44th, 12 July 1963; for details of the NPG, see Bluth, *Britain*, pp. 179–201.
170. CAB 129/114, C(63)151, 16 September 1963.
171. DEFE 7/2028, DP135/63(Final), Variants to the Multilateral Force, 22 January 1964.
172. John Baylis, *Anglo–American Defence Relations 1939–1984* (Macmillan, 1984), p.139.
173. Catherine Kelleher, *Germany and the Politics of Nuclear Weapons* (Columbia University Press, 1975), pp. 247–54.
174. NMLH, Box 328.662, *Controlling the Nuclear Arms Race*, 20 March 1967.
175. Healey, *Time*, p. 304.
176. *Statement on the Defence Estimates 1965*, Cmnd. 2592 (HMSO, 1965); Sir John Slessor, 'Command and Control of Allied Nuclear Forces: A British View', *Adelphi Paper*, No.22, August 1965.
177. DEFE 25/33, Misc 17/4, Atlantic Nuclear Force, Report by the Defence and Overseas Policy (Official) Committee, 18 November 1964.
178. Wilson, *Labour*, pp. 48–51.
179. Healey, *Time*, p. 305.
180. LBJ Library, McNamara to Johnson, 12 April 1967, NSF, Box 36, NATO, Vol.V.
181. DEFE 7/2228, The Reform of NATO Strategy, 29 August 1960.
182. Clark, *Nuclear*, p. 12.

CHAPTER 6

Defence Communications 1945–64

'I'm afraid we are unable to communicate with any of the aircraft' (General Turgidson explaining to President Muffley that the 843rd Bomb Wing, *en route* to starting a nuclear war with the USSR cannot be contacted).

The increased emphasis on nuclear weapons within both Britain and NATO resulted in substantial numbers of nuclear forces stationed in Europe and overseas. To decrease vulnerability, these forces were also widely dispersed. Such deployment, however, placed heavy demands on support facilities, and in particular communications. Communications perform two basic functions in the command and control of nuclear weapons: they provide warning of attack to the National Command Authority (NCA) and they relay an appropriate response to the state's nuclear forces. To maintain political control over the use of force, continuity of communication between the NCA and the military is essential. In the absence of communications, nuclear forces are either unable to respond due to lack of political authorisation or retaliate in an uncoordinated and uncontrolled response. Even if appropriate authorisation is received, the continued command of nuclear operations is not guaranteed. Indeed, as General Thomas Power, C-in-C of SAC, once remarked 'without communications all I command is my desk, and that is not a very lethal weapon.'[1] This chapter examines the development of Britain's defence communications infrastructure and discusses the difficulties faced by HMG in acquiring a secure and reliable system to ensure a co-ordinated nuclear response under all conditions.

To function effectively, the British nuclear deterrent required the close integration of three separate elements: tactical early warning intelligence (provided by the Air Defence Operations Centre); assessment and response (undertaken at the Air Ministry Operations Centre or the Alternate

Government Headquarters); and execution (relayed via Bomber Command's Operations Centre). To establish a unified structure, each centre was linked in a triangular relationship that formed the basis of a communications network for the command and control of Britain's nuclear forces. This communications network is examined under two broad headings: government communications to and from Whitehall, and military communications with particular emphasis on Bomber Command. Britain's alliance commitments are also discussed including the development of communications within NATO.

GOVERNMENT COMMUNICATIONS

Within Whitehall, prior to creation of a unified Defence Ministry in 1963, the control of Britain's nuclear forces was conducted from the Air Ministry Operations Centre, situated in the basement of the Air Ministry. To receive instructions from government-dedicated communications links were established with Downing Street and other designated ministries. The Air Ministry was located in King Charles Street in the 'New Public Offices' adjoining Parliament Square. Occupying the same building was the Home Office (at the front of the building in Parliament Square) and the Cabinet Office (situated to the rear facing St James's Park). Concealed beneath St James's Park was the Cabinet War Room that in WWII housed the Chiefs of Staff HQ.[2]

Designed to provide protection under conventional attack, the wartime shelters were inadequate to withstand an atomic bomb. To guarantee the maintenance of government, a deep-level shelter system was constructed below Whitehall. At the heart of the complex stood 'Montague', a nuclear bunker 100ft below the Air Ministry. Completed in October 1954, communication within the system was provided by an underground telephone exchange called Kingsway which was linked to similar underground exchanges, named Guardian and Anchor, in Manchester and Birmingham respectively.[3]

To operate under conditions expected in a nuclear attack, the exchanges required a survivable communications infrastructure. To fulfil this requirement, the Backbone programme was initiated. Details were first announced in the 1955 Defence White Paper:

> The maintenance of communications would be vital, not only to meet the operational needs of the fighting services and of civil defence, but also to make possible the organisation of supplies and movement and to disseminate essential

information. The Post Office are, therefore, planning to build up a special network both by cable and by radio, designed to maintain long-distance communications in the event of attack.[4]

A central feature of Backbone was the construction of microwave relay stations that linked the four major English cities: London, Birmingham, Manchester and Leeds. The system provided an alternative to underground cables that were considered vulnerable to nuclear attack or sabotage. The network also contained bypass switches enabling communications to be maintained even if one or more cities were destroyed. Additional features were incorporated into the network. These included the Telephone Preference Scheme, in which non-essential traffic could be disconnected from the system; the Emergency Manual Switching System, which consisted of a network of manual switchboards in semi-hardened sites within major telephone exchanges; and Federal, a private exchange located below Whitehall that linked ministers and senior civil servants.[5] The primary function of the network was to provide the government with secure and reliable communications in the event of enemy attack.

Installation of the system was overseen by the British Joint Communications-Electronics Board (BJC-EB). Established in 1949, the Board was responsible to the Chiefs of Staff for providing technical advice 'in global war, in emergency or limited war, and in day-to-day peacetime communications.'[6] Policy for the BJC-EB was determined by two high level Cabinet committees: the Official Committee on Communications (chaired by the Cabinet Secretary) and the London Communications Electronics Security Board, responsible for security and cryptographic systems.[7]

A primary requirement of the communications system was to provide early warning of enemy attack. Without this, the bomber force could be destroyed on the ground. A comprehensive network of landlines and radio transmitters was therefore provided to link the Air Defence Operations Centre (ADOC) at Bentley Priory to the radar stations and Royal Observer Corps. Designed to function independently of manual exchanges, the system was nevertheless provided with a radio back-up to guard against communications failure. To alert central government, ADOC was provided with a dedicated speech facility to Whitehall. Additional landlines were also provided for liaison officers to pass information directly to High Wycombe and Royal Navy HQ at Portsmouth. These facilities were later expanded to include direct links with the US Third Air Force, the 7th Air Division (SAC), SACEUR and Bomber Command Group HQs.[8]

The Soviet deployment of ballistic missiles in the late-1950s significantly reduced warning time. In response, government communications and procedures were re-examined. The Chief of the Defence Staff described the position as follows:

> Lord Mountbatten said that he had recently discussed with Sir Norman Brook the communications requirement for alerting and releasing our nuclear retaliatory forces, and especially the general arrangements needed to enable the Prime Minister to receive up-to-date information and to take the necessary action within the requisite time. He had suggested to Sir Norman Brook that the existing arrangements should be reviewed and that the Chiefs of Staff should be represented in the conduct of the review, which should then serve as the basis for detailed planning.[9]

As described in Chapter 3, the body responsible for the review was GEN 743. A primary concern was the realization that, in the event of a surprise missile attack, it might not be possible to establish contact with the Prime Minister. In these circumstances, the only practical option was to delegate nuclear retaliation to the military, details of which are discussed in Chapter 3. The prospect of the Soviets mounting a surprise attack, however, was considered unlikely. This view was supported by the JIC who concluded in January 1961 that the Soviet Union would not, as an act of policy, launch a surprise nuclear attack and only use nuclear weapons, 'if they considered themselves to be unacceptably threatened.'[10] Given this assessment, which was accepted by the Defence Committee, planning for the improvement of the Prime Minister's communications was based on the following assumptions:

- There would be a period of international tension before an attack;
- The Centre of Government, including the Prime Minister, would remain in Whitehall during the Precautionary Period, though the alternative seat of Government and the Regions would be manned by selected Ministers and officials;
- Two Deputies to the Prime Minister would be appointed in peacetime and one of them would be available to act as the Prime Minister's deputy for purposes of nuclear retaliation when the Prime Minister was not immediately available.[11]

Arrangements for recalling the Prime Minister to London in an emergency were also reviewed. At present, these depended on communicating with known points on his route and intercepting him with the aid of police or railway authorities. To provide permanent contact with the Prime Minister, it was suggested that 'these arrangements might be supplemented in this country by installing a radio in the Prime Minister's car that would permit messages to be relayed in plain language through the Automobile Association's network.'[12] The exact role of the AA in launching Britain's deterrent is less than clear. It is nevertheless intriguing that the Headquarters of the AA were situated directly opposite the Air Defence Operations Centre in Stanmore.

In an emergency, it was assumed that the Prime Minister would work from either Downing Street or Admiralty House and require secure communication with senior officials and intelligence sources. The main channels for this information were the Foreign Office, the Commonwealth Relations Office, the Ministry of Defence, the Joint Intelligence Committee (in conjunction with the Joint Intelligence Room in the Cabinet Office) and the Air Ministry Operations Centre which would act as the link between Whitehall and Bomber Command.[13] The communication facilities required for these departments included: the PICKWICK telephone system (see below); a teleprinter system based in both the Cabinet Office and Ministry of Defence capable of passing short War Book messages to over thirty departments; and closed circuit television, including a teletalk facility, that linked the Prime Minister's office to the Air Ministry and which in the event of enemy attack was 'to be pushed into the Cabinet Room on a trolley.'[14]

The Prime Minister's communications with the US President were also examined. An important consideration was the recently ratified Murphy-Dean agreement covering the use of British and American nuclear weapons. The agreement required a secure speech link between the Prime Minister and President.[15] An initial proposal to provide such a link centred on installation of a transatlantic cable called MILTAT.[16] Designed for both civil and military use, MILTAT was vulnerable to disruption and considered unsuitable for private political discussions. The project was eventually abandoned in 1959.[17] Other options included the Foreign Office teleprinter facility that linked the JIC both to its counterpart in Ottawa and the National Indications Center, Washington; and a teleconference facility linking MOD to the British Defence Staff at the UK Embassy in Washington.

For various reasons, these facilities were not considered suitable for discussions between the Prime Minister and President. To provide a secure speech link, Britain initiated development of the Sorcerer network. The results were disappointing. The system 'produced synthetic speech which was not easily recognisable.'[18] A second project was more successful and resulted in the TWILIGHT communications system. As an interim measure (before TWILIGHT became operational) the US offered the Prime Minister the use of the direct link between the Pentagon and the US base at Ruislip.[19] This requirement soon became unnecessary. In 1960, the US introduced the newly developed KY-9 communications system. Analogous in function to TWILIGHT, KY-9 allowed a secure speech link between the President, designated heads of state and military commanders.[20]

In November 1962, TWILIGHT became fully operational. Similar in operation to the already established PICKWICK telephone system in Whitehall, it relied on the use of individually issued key cards in combination with a specially encrypted telephone.[21] Under normal conditions, the time taken to set up a TWILIGHT call was two hours, but under 'crash conditions' this could be reduced to 30 minutes.[22] Despite the length of time required to operate the system, TWILIGHT was considered technically superior to the American KY-9. To integrate communications between Britain and America and to provide redundancy both systems became operational. It was envisaged that during an international crisis, the President and Prime Minister would talk on the KY-9 whilst the Foreign Secretary and US Secretary of State would use TWILIGHT. These procedures were soon put to the test. In October 1962, during the Cuban missile crisis Macmillan and Kennedy discussed developments on an almost daily basis.

In establishing transatlantic communications, a particular concern was the consequences of a complete breakdown of the system. For under such circumstances, the US President would be unable to release either American nuclear forces stationed in Britain or US nuclear weapons intended for use by British forces:

> The chances of a complete failure of trans-Atlantic communications may be remote, but the possibility should be considered. It might be desirable to seek an assurance from the President that in the event of such a failure, a suitable United States authority in this country would have the power to release United States weapons and warheads to us, preferably before attack, for use at the Prime Minister's discretion . . . it is doubtful whether this is a subject to raise with the Americans. In any case, we could get hold of the bomb even if it meant shooting the American officers concerned.[23]

From available documents, it is not yet known whether such a request was ever made and the response (if any) of the US President. Nevertheless, the fact that senior MOD officials were prepared to discuss shooting American custodial officers to gain access to nuclear weapons raises intriguing issues for the Special Relationship .The issue, however, highlights the difficulties faced by Britain in establishing reliable long distance communications. The decision to deploy nuclear weapons outside the UK exacerbated this problem and confirmed a dilemma already apparent: projection of force on a global scale was not commensurate with Britain's resources. For the control of nuclear weapons, the lack of a fully developed control system was potentially disastrous. Lack of communications could lead to inadvertent or unauthorized use.

OVERSEAS MILITARY COMMUNICATIONS

In January 1958, the Cabinet approved development of the Services' global strategic wireless network with responsibility for installation given to the GPO and Cable and Wireless.[24] Designed to carry military traffic, the reliability and security of the system was paramount. The network was therefore placed under government control with all staff subject to official discipline. Specific agreements were also established to ensure that essential military communications were not subject to interference by foreign governments. All installations were also required to operate for a period of fourteen days without outside support.[25] The need to maintain every element of the network under national control excluded use of commercial cables and American satellite systems.[26] In November 1962, however, in a review of defence communications, the Chiefs agreed to place more reliance on the use of such facilities and sanctioned discussions between the BJC-EB and the newly established US Defence Communications Agency.[27]

The existing communications network between Whitehall and the Far East Airforce in Singapore was also re-examined. A particular concern was the requirement to establish a 90 per cent reliability factor for authentication of nuclear strike messages. The present network was vulnerable to both natural and other forms of interference. An alternative method of communication was considered vital. The position was described to Macmillan by the Minister of Defence as follows:

> It is clear that, if communications remain open, a decision to use nuclear weapons in both limited and global war would be reserved to Heads of Governments. The communications with overseas theatres essential for this,

however, are extremely vulnerable and not only to hostile action. I am therefore inviting the Foreign Office, in conjunction with the Nuclear Strike Co-ordinating Committee and my Ministry, to study how the use of nuclear weapons in overseas theatres should be initiated and controlled in all circumstances.[28]

A possible solution was to rent a commercial radio circuit. However, as these circuits were liable to fail in the same way and at the same time as military circuits, no obvious advantage was apparent. The only method to significantly improve communications was to install a direct link between London and Singapore. The requirement for a direct link coincided with development of the Commonwealth ('Round the World') Telephone Cable System. Under construction since the mid-1950s, the system was intended to improve communications within the Commonwealth (the link to Australia being completed by 1964).[29] Therefore, as cable links from Australia to Singapore were already in existence, a direct cable circuit from London to Singapore would soon be available. Despite these improvements, and the possible use of US systems, it was recognised that in the event of global war, communications with overseas theatres would be extremely vulnerable—a situation that posed considerable problems for the control of nuclear weapons.

In reviewing the various contingencies, the Chiefs of Staff were presented with three possible options in the event of a communications breakdown:

(a) to allow total delegation for the deployment of nuclear weapons to the theatre commander;
(b) to grant partial delegation sanctioning retaliation only after nuclear attack;
(c) to provide no delegation, with authority for the use of nuclear weapons remaining solely within Whitehall.[30]

After considering the options, the Chiefs of Staff recommended that, 'despite the unreliability of communications, there should be no delegation of authority to initiate the first [nuclear] strike.'[31] Whether this implicitly sanctioned the use of nuclear weapons in a retaliatory role is unclear. Policy guidance issued to British Commanders overseas was less than forthcoming. Addressing the issue in late 1963, the Chiefs concluded that 'the question of the control of nuclear forces in the event of communications with the UK breaking down following the outbreak of global war has yet to be resolved.'[32]

THE INTEGRATION OF MILITARY COMMUNICATIONS

To establish a global communications network, the Chief of the Defence Staff proposed integration of all government communications, creating a network combining both military and civil traffic. To examine the practicalities, a steering committee was established under Foreign Office guidance, 'to consider the organisation of, and policy for, static communications by HM Government worldwide, with a view to increasing efficiency and economy, by inter-service integration, integration between service and civilian facilities, and to make recommendations.'[33]

Various recommendations were submitted but it was not until reorganization of the central defence structure in 1963 that substantial progress was achieved. A significant development was the creation of an integrated Defence Traffic Centre (DTC) within MOD. The previously independent service cryptographic centres were also combined within the DTC forming a fully integrated military communications network serving both the UK and overseas. The various signals staff were also integrated, creating a unified Defence Signals Staff under control of the Assistant Chief of the Defence Staff (ACDS). A single unified Defence Operations Centre combining the functions of the three services was also proposed. However, the proposal was rejected, as it was not considered possible to combine within one single operations room the diverse functions that would be required to establish effective control. Consequently, the system of tailoring operation centres to fulfil specific functions was maintained. This resulted in the formation of an integrated Defence Operations Centre (responsible for general policy and strategic decisions) supported by several smaller satellite centres responsible for specific service functions.[34]

To control Britain's nuclear forces, a joint Navy/Air Force Control Centre was established with the specific function of launching the deterrent. Historically, the Air Ministry Operations Centre performed this function, and it was decided to base the joint control centre within the newly formed Air Force Operations Centre, incorporating a naval cell on the introduction of Polaris. The location of the Air Force Operations Centre posed several problems. Specifically, as the new Ministry of Defence was to occupy the Air Ministry building in Whitehall, the location of the AMOC in the basement proved unsatisfactory. The Air Force Operation Centre was relocated to the upper floor and given additional communications, including a closed circuit television link to both the Defence Operations Centre and Downing Street.[35]

TURNSTILE PLANNING

In the event of thermonuclear attack, maintenance of communications within Whitehall was considered untenable. The existence of an Alternate Command Centre (ACC) outside London was therefore essential for the conduct of operations in the trans- and post-attack periods. Construction of the Turnstile complex was designed to meet this requirement. To successfully conduct operations from the ACC, a comprehensive and survivable communications facility was imperative. Due to the specialised and secretive nature of the ACC, however, the development of a viable communications system was hampered by a series of stringent demands unique to the facility.

Turnstile planning was governed by the Prime Minister's directive which stated *inter alia* that its functions were to act as the seat of government in the period of survival and reconstruction, and second, to be an alternative centre to London for authorizing nuclear retaliation.[36] A fundamental principle governing all ACC planning was the overriding need to maintain absolute security. If the location and purpose of the ACC were compromised, it would almost certainly become a primary target in a Soviet first strike. A particular concern was communications. In short, if communications were used for operational purposes, it was believed that within 48 hours, both the location and purpose of the ACC would be known to the Soviets. It was therefore essential that no plans should be made for the exercise of operational control from the ACC during the pre-attack period. This, however, was in direct conflict with the need to establish reliable communications. In reviewing the provisional arrangements, the Chiefs of Staff were informed that existing plans required the signals centre to be established at the same time as the military staffs were relocated to the ACC. For reasons of security, the line communications being installed by the GPO were unlikely to be operational within 48 hours. The only long-range radio equipment presently available at Turnstile consisted of surplus hand-operated sets limited to a Morse capability.[37]

The provision of suitably qualified staff to operate the various communications facilities was also totally inadequate. This situation was eventually remedied by the creation of the Defence Communications Network (DCN) which provided a unified strategic communications system for the three services and other relevant government agencies.[38] Prior to the creation of the DCN, communications at Turnstile were semi-autonomous with each service deciding its own requirements. As the RAF was responsible for launching the deterrent, it was also given the task of manning the Central War Cabinet Communications Centre with GCHQ responsible for intelligence traffic.[39]

In finalizing their review, the Chiefs concluded that under existing arrangements communications at the ACC were unlikely to be sufficient or fully operational in time. Consequently, it was recommended that if the ACC was to fulfil its designated role, 'it must be capable of being functional within 72 hours from the declaration of a Precautionary Alert.'[40] To provide an efficient system, a regular nucleus of personnel was permanently deployed at Turnstile on a 24-hour basis. The Chiefs also recommended that during a crisis, control should remain in Whitehall for as long as possible. Consequently, throughout the Precautionary Stage, command would continue to be exercised through MOD and associated operations centres: only when the powers of central government were transferred from London would control of the deterrent switch from Whitehall to Turnstile.

BOMBER COMMAND COMMUNICATIONS

Whether the order to retaliate came from Whitehall or Turnstile, maintaining communications with High Wycombe was essential. Equally important was the ability of Bomber Command to contact each individual aircraft, especially if the V-force had already been launched under positive control procedures. This requirement was described by GEN 743 in the following terms:

> The reliability of communications between Bomber Command and the aircraft is therefore vital to the certainty of nuclear retaliation and hence the effectiveness of the deterrent. There has been duplication and re-duplication of the channels of communication and of the necessary telephone, telegraph and wireless installations on which they rely.[41]

The result was a communications infrastructure that linked together in a single network the operational centres of the Air Ministry (AMOC), Bentley Priory (ADOC) and High Wycombe (BCOC). Installed by RAF No. 90 Group (later to become RAF Signals Command) and based on dedicated trunk cabling, the system allowed direct two-way communication between the Chief of the Air Staff and the C-in-Cs of both Bomber Command and Fighter Command (the latter in his capacity as the Air Defence Commander). The communications system also reflected the functional position of the various participants. At the apex was the Cabinet (more specifically the Prime Minister) who communicated directly with the CAS from either Downing Street or Turnstile. In employing this procedure, the communications system mirrored the constitutional position in that the decision to authorize nuclear retaliation was to be taken by the Prime Minister and executed by the CAS through C-in-C Bomber Command on behalf of the Chiefs of Staff.[42] The procedure was described as follows:

> Information of an impending raid is passed as soon as possible to the Operations Room at HQ Bomber Command from the ADOC. The MBF would then be ordered to take off, on retaliatory raids, by the Duty Operations Officer at Bomber Command. It would be necessary for this order to be confirmed before BC aircraft were committed to hostile actions. Confirmation could only come from Cabinet level and via either CAS or C-in-C Bomber Command.[43]

Once the decision authorizing nuclear retaliation had been received at High Wycombe, C-in-C Bomber Command was responsible for executing the order. Consequently, a secure and rapid means of communication was essential to transmit the authenticated launch order from BCOC to individual aircraft. Primary importance was placed on ensuring rapid transmission of the executive order. Secondary considerations were to enable elements of the dispersed force to report back on their states of readiness and inform the C-in-C of the status and disposition of the forces under his control.[44]

Initial criteria governing Bomber Command's communication policy was based on three requirements:

(i) To control deployment of the force in peacetime.
(ii) To mount the initial nuclear strike.
(iii) To maintain control of the remaining force during subsequent operations.[45]

To comply with these conditions required a communications system that would withstand a Soviet first-strike. This could only be guaranteed by construction of hardened command posts, transmission sites and landlines capable of withstanding thermonuclear attack. These facilities could not be developed within the budget and timescale available. By contrast, installation of a communications system capable of controlling a single retaliatory strike was not required to survive a nuclear attack. Its primary function was to ensure rapid transmission of the authenticated launch order to the bomber force. Moreover, provided transmission had occurred before the initial attack, continued communication between High Wycombe and the dispersal sites was not essential for the dispersal plan. Due to these constraints, Bomber Command's communication system was based on controlling the initial strike. The decision meant Bomber Command was a hostage to fortune: reduction in warning time or failure to respond would negate the validity of a land-based deterrent.

To disseminate the launch order throughout the Command, two methods were available: landlines and radio. The relative merits of these two systems depended on various factors. Installation of a radio network, for example, required continuous operation of the system during peacetime, as otherwise, in the event of surprise attack, the operators would be unfamiliar with the system and the equipment either mistuned or unserviceable. Yet to operate the network on a 24-hour basis raised several objections. First, Soviet interception of transmissions could not be completely discounted and continuous operation would reduce the security of the dispersal scheme. Second, such a system required permanent staff at every reception site. This was considered unacceptable in peacetime due to considerations of cost, manpower and practicality. However, without a permanently manned communications system, the dispersal plan would be of 'no value without an alert period and would be useless against a "Pearl Harbour".'[46]

The decision not to employ a continuous radio broadcast was in direct contrast to the 'Full Pipeline Philosophy' operated by SAC. By adopting this approach (which was at variance with USAF policy) SAC's communication lines were fully loaded at all times. The purpose was to familiarize operators with the conditions that would be encountered in an emergency. Two further advantages were also apparent: there would be no detectable increase in traffic if SAC was ordered to a higher state of alert and Soviet traffic analysis of communications would be difficult due to the vast quantity of material transmitted.[47] In later years, with increased co-ordination between the two airforces, Bomber Command adopted a similar procedure.

Operation of landline communications also presented problems. The cost of providing dedicated cabling between each dispersal site and Headquarters Bomber Command was prohibitive. Moreover, the time taken to individually contact every airfield would have exceeded ten minutes. This was the maximum acceptable time between the decision at HQ Bomber Command to issue the order and its reception at all airfields. In light of this, the only practical method to issue the launch order within ten minutes was the private operational speech line (i.e. the internal telephone). The system possessed advantages. The expected operational conditions arising from a surprise attack were also those most conducive for the successful transmission of the launch order over the network: communications traffic would be relatively low and none of the network would have been destroyed.

If the attack were preceded by a long period of alert, however, these conditions would no longer apply. In this event, the volume of traffic was expected to increase dramatically and overload the system. Consequently, even with priority clearance, Bomber Command could not guarantee that the launch order would reach the V-force within ten minutes. To ensure transmission, Bomber Command required the combined use of a radio broadcast system to augment the peacetime landline network. A dual system had advantages: it provided redundancy (in that whichever system was in use the other could be employed as a back-up); it created a more integrated command structure; and enabled rapid dissemination of the launch order by radio followed by acknowledgement of its receipt by telephone.[48]

The provision of the dual system was also required to conform to various operational criteria. In relation to the radio broadcast element, requirements included:

(a) Full coverage of the UK.
(b) Minimum susceptibility to jamming and interception.
(c) Complete independence of relay stations.
(d) Direct control of transmitters by Bomber Command.

All these requirements could not be met in full. To obtain full coverage of the UK a combination of frequencies covering the long, medium and high range wavelengths was necessary. Due to the long ranges available on both high and low frequencies these wavelengths were susceptible to jamming and interception. Soviet ability to jam allied communications was considerable:

> Intelligence assessments of probable Russian doctrine towards communications jamming, supported by specific evidence of their ability to jam military frequencies, revealed that the USSR has a potential capability to jam our strategic long distance radio communications circuits. The Russians are well versed in

the techniques of jamming as demonstrated by the effectiveness of the jamming efforts directed against the BBC and Voice of America in the high frequency bands. It is to be expected that the USSR will have considerable capability for jamming our vital radio communications circuits.[49]

Medium wave broadcasts were less susceptible to jamming but did not cover the whole of the UK. To obtain nationwide coverage, a network of medium frequency transmitters was needed. To activate the network, Bomber Command would issue the launch instruction on its own transmitter which would be intercepted by an adjacent relay station and re-broadcast. This process would be repeated until the whole of the UK had been covered. It was estimated that the time taken from the original broadcast to receipt by the last station would be no more than five minutes. Requiring only seven transmitters for complete coverage of the UK, the proposal was incorporated into Bomber Command's dispersal plan. The sites chosen for the transmitters were High Wycombe, Western Zoyland, Syerston, Dishforth, Acklington, Leuchars and Kinloss. In addition, two mobile transmitters were obtained and provision made for the installation of transmission facilities at each Group's Headquarters at Mildenhall and Bawtry to enable them to 'exercise control' in the event of High Wycombe's destruction.[50]

A strong alternative to this system was the BBC broadcast network, which already provided full coverage of the UK on medium wave. A further advantage was that the network consisted of 70 transmitters all broadcasting a common programme. By installing a simple switching mechanism, Bomber Command would be able to interrupt or impose on the programme a short executive instruction. Relying on the BBC network, however, meant that Bomber Command would not have direct control of the transmitters. Nevertheless, the fact that the network was in almost continuous operation, and required no special equipment or staffing, was a strong advantage. The use of the BBC network by Bomber Command would have required the approval of the Home Defence Committee.[51] It is uncertain whether such a request was approved. Significantly, however, in a review of procedures to be undertaken in the event of Soviet bomber attack in the early-1950s, the Defence Transition Committee authorized Fighter Command to assume control of the entire BBC transmitter network:

> From the moment the executive message is received by the BBC Senior Control Room Engineer, control over BBC medium wave and long wave transmitters will be exercised by Fighter Command Headquarters at Stanmore.[52]

It has also been suggested that to ensure transmission of the launch order to Britain's Polaris submarines, 'the Royal Navy had plans to use the British Broadcasting Corporation LF transmitters (which usually transmitted BBC Radio 4) at Droitwich in an emergency.'[53]

The difficulties encountered with the radio network were mirrored in the development of the landline system. The most important requirement was the ability to transmit the launch order with the minimum of delay. As shown earlier, this together with cost, prevented each dispersal site being contacted individually. A landline network was therefore developed with one designated station in each area acting as a control centre. To activate the network, Bomber Command HQ would originate ten calls (one to each area control airfield) which in turn would contact each of the airfields in its designated area. Conversely, if the launch order had been transmitted by radio, the system was capable of operating in reverse. The operation of the system was as follows:

> The sequence of events at stations would therefore be a warning from ADOC by telegraph circuit followed shortly by a W/T broadcast from Bomber Command Operations Room and an audible warning by private operational speech line from Bomber Command through Groups and Regional Headquarters. Finally executive instructions would be passed through Groups and Regional Headquarters over the private operational speech line.[54]

COMMUNICATIONS AND POSITIVE CONTROL

By the late-1950s, it was becoming apparent that attempts to harden facilities, re-route landlines or provide multiple circuits would only provide marginal advantage. Moreover, any significant improvement in provision of secure communications was either ruled out by prohibitive cost or nullified by the expected increase in the yield of Soviet weapons. The effects of electro-magnetic pulse (EMP) presented additional worries. In 1959, the implications were described by VCAS, Sir Edmund Hudleston: 'high altitude atomic explosions could create sufficient ionization of the atmosphere to interfere not only with radio, but also with landline communications. If this were so, the military implications would be extremely serious.'[55]

In response, Bomber Command's communications system and operating procedures were subjected to detailed review. This centred on four major requirements. First, the deployment of Thor required installation of a new communications system. Second, the construction programme for phase I of the dispersal airfields was nearing completion. Third, nuclear weapons were soon to be deployed overseas requiring transmission of authentication orders over long distances. Finally, the introduction of Soviet M/IRBMs was expected to reduce reaction time to a matter of minutes.

To guard against pre-emptive attack and possible destruction on the ground, it was recognised that the V-force might have to launch prior to receipt of the executive order. To maintain political control, the aircraft were required to operate under positive control, which required receipt of the 'go-code' by the time the fail-safe point was reached. The capability to maintain communication with an airborne force was therefore a fundamental prerequisite of a credible second-strike capability. To meet this requirement and increase reliability, teleprinter facilities and a new high frequency (HF) broadcast system were installed at all dispersal sites and main bases. In addition (to specifically counter the missile threat) the Air Ministry approved the following improvement programme:

(a) Telescramble direct from BCOC to aircraft held at cockpit readiness.
(b) Improved conference facilities between the Air Ministry, Bomber Command and Air Defence Operations Centres.
(c) Installation of a conference facility between C-in-C Bomber Command and the two Group Commanders.
(d) Transmission of alert messages from the BCOC 'bridge' rather than the Bomber Command W/T cabin.[56]

In adopting these measures, the medium bomber force was expected to become airborne within four minutes of receiving the launch order. The emphasis on communications at High Wycombe was also mirrored in the bomber force. To ensure communication with ground stations, all aircraft were equipped with radio telephonic (R/T) equipment in the HF, VHF and UHF bands, and wireless telegraphy (W/T) in the HF band. The allocation of radio frequencies for essential military traffic was also expanded. Nine additional VHF frequencies were transferred to the RAF of which five were designated for the V-force. Bomber Command also adopted an alert posture in which dummy traffic was transmitted on two frequencies throughout each 24-hour period with discreet channels remaining closed.[57] To supplement the speech broadcast system, hand-operated HF W/T transmitters were developed. Indeed, the reception at airfields in the

Near and Middle East was sufficiently clear to recommend their use as 'a primary means of control, both for scrambling aircraft and for releasing them from positive control.'[58]

Procedures for releasing the aircraft were also reviewed. Warning of attack would first be confirmed by receipt of positive radar evidence at the ADOC. Immediately this occurred, C-in-C Fighter Command (in his capacity as Air Defence Commander) was to directly inform the following individuals in order of precedent:

1. Air Ministry / CAS.
2. C-in-C Bomber Command.
3. Commander, 7th Air Division, SAC.
4. Commander, Third Air Force.
5. SACEUR.

Employing the conference facility, both CAS and C-in-C Bomber Command would be informed of events simultaneously. Therefore, on receipt of positive radar confirmation, CAS would order C-in-C Bomber Command to launch the force under positive control. To ensure the aircraft were not destroyed on the ground, C-in-C Bomber Command was also authorized to scramble in the event of surprise attack. Once airborne, the decision would be relayed to the Prime Minister, other designated Ministers and the Chiefs of Staff. Finally, the Prime Minister would consult the US President regarding a joint decision to authorize nuclear retaliation and inform CAS of the decision. The executive order to commit the force would then be relayed to C-in-C Bomber Command who would attempt to contact the squadrons before the fail-safe point was reached or the communications system destroyed.[59]

Provided the V-force had been launched under positive control during the warning period, the sole requirement for a post-strike communications system was the ability to contact the force once airborne. Subsequent developments in the communications infrastructure were largely directed towards establishing this capability. In general, the reliability of the system was ultimately dependent on adequate provision of three key variables: redundancy, delegation and survivability.

To increase the redundancy of the system required a variety of geographically dispersed transmission facilities operating over a wide spectrum of frequencies. Therefore, in addition to the main HF transmitter at High

Wycombe, alternate facilities were provided at the Headquarters of both No 1 and No 3 Group. To guard against possible disruption or jamming, existing radar transmitters were also modified to allow modulation on VHF frequencies. The proposal offered three significant advantages. First, the radar network used high power transmitters and would be difficult to jam. Second, no major construction was required and development costs would be kept to a minimum. Third, full coverage of the UK and its approaches could be provided by modification of only four stations. For Bomber Command, the provision of a VHF network was considered essential, as it would provide 'complete certainty of communication with aircraft patrolling over the United Kingdom in comparison with the relative uncertainty of lower frequency communications.'[60]

Development of the VHF Forward Relay was approved by the Air Council. The four ground stations chosen for modification were Saxa Vord, Neatishead, Buchan and Chenies. These were primarily responsible for providing early warning and the VHF Forward Relay network was only to be activated at high states of alert. It was estimated that the transition period would take less than fifteen minutes. Once alert conditions had been established, no broadcasts were to be made on the VHF Forward Relay until the scramble order had been issued on the HF frequency. This measure was adopted to limit radio interception, conceal the wavelengths of essential military traffic and prevent jamming.[61] In accepting this procedure, it is evident that the Forward Relay was specifically designed for only one purpose: transmission of the executive order to the retaliatory forces operating under positive control.

High Wycombe was considered a major target in a Soviet nuclear strike. In August 1961, the Air Ministry recommended development of a communications system that would remain operable in the event of the complete destruction of High Wycombe. Alternate control provisions were therefore established at each Group Headquarters. The completed system consisted of dual landlines linking all three HQs in a single network with dual ring routing connecting the three HQs to all Class I and dispersal sites. The radio broadcast net was also enhanced. Automatic failure alarms were installed at all communications terminals and alternate broadcast facilities provided at both Group HQs. Arrangements were also made to enable the VHF Forward Relay to be modulated independently by both Bawtry and Mildenhall.[62] Taken together, these improvements created an interlocking network that connected the various fixed command posts. This enabled transition of command to be mediated between the various sites with one centre succeeding another in the event of destruction.

Despite these improvements, misgivings remained. A concerted Soviet attack targeted against the transmitters, the command posts or switching stations would disrupt the entire system. Moreover, the majority of these facilities were housed in unhardened fixed-site locations. There was no guarantee that the V-force could be contacted before communications ceased. To address this problem, two alternatives were proposed: a mobile transmitter that would be difficult to target or a concealed hardened site that would be difficult to locate. In the event, both options were pursued. The former resulted in deployment of an airborne command post whilst the latter was realized in the construction of Turnstile, discussed above.

AIRBORNE COMMAND POSTS

The concept of employing a mobile command post to ensure survival and continuity of command was first established in the US. In a series of studies on the vulnerability of the US command and control system, a major conclusion was that mobile command centres would survive better than a fixed hardened site. To fulfil such a requirement, each service advanced its own preference. Various options were therefore pursued. In March 1961, the JCS concluded that airborne and sea-based systems were feasible and authorized a preliminary development programme.[63] To control US nuclear forces based in Europe, airborne command posts were deployed in both Britain and ACE (the former to control the strategic nuclear forces operated by SAC, the latter for tactical nuclear weapons assigned to SACEUR). Given that British nuclear forces were both co-ordinated with SAC and assigned to SACEUR, the advantages of adopting a similar system within Bomber Command were considerable. In January 1961, Bomber Command sought approval for 'a senior officer in a Valiant with authority to transmit the Go-Signal should he observe more than a pre-determined number of explosions in this country'.[64] At present, it is unclear how this request was received. However, In August 1962, the Air Ministry approved deployment of an airborne command post 'to ensure an alternative means of passing release messages to the Medium Bomber Force without recourse to landline communications.'[65]

To establish an airborne command post, a flight of Valiants was transferred from the tanker squadron and fitted with UHF transmission equipment. Operation of the system proved problematic. Joint exercises with SHAPE revealed that UHF transmission failed to meet required standards of reliability. However, if High Frequency Single Side Band (HF SSB) radio sets were used, no such difficulties existed. Moreover, as all SAC and SHAPE airborne command posts were fitted with HF SSB, provision of similar equipment for the Valiant force was considered essential. Differences also existed in the planned deployment of the aircraft. The SHAPE operations centre, SILKPURSE, was to be continuously airborne while the Bomber Command post would only become airborne at heightened states of alert. Consequently, for most of the time, communication with SILKPURSE could only be maintained from UK ground stations. To guarantee continuous communications with SHAPE, HF SSB equipment was installed at the Bomber Command Operations Centre and the alternative control organisations at Nos. 1 and 3 Groups.[66]

Provision of HF SSB also enabled Bomber Command to establish reliable communications with SAC, a process that had been underway since 1950. The co-ordination of strike plans also increased the need to standardize communication equipment and allocate common frequencies. Deployment of airborne command posts by both SAC and Bomber Command consolidated this process. Moreover, the use of SAC's worldwide communications network offered significant advantages over the limited capabilities of a purely national system.

SAC communications were based on two separate networks: a combined service channel called GLOBECOM (later renamed STRATCOM) available to all USAF traffic and a dedicated system consisting of UHF and VHF channels in combination with a HF SSB network. In 1958, the capital investment in the programme was over a third of a billion dollars and allowed communications to be established on a worldwide basis.[67] In principle, the development of compatible communications allowed Bomber Command to establish contact with the V-force even if national communications became disrupted. Significantly, as the network was controlled by SAC, its use by Bomber Command increased US control over the deployment of British nuclear forces. As a consequence, a dual operational policy was established for Bomber Command communications. This required an ability to use the SAC network in a co-ordinated strike whilst maintaining under undivided national control a minimum communications network capable of mounting a unilateral strike if so required.

NATO COMMUNICATIONS

In parallel with national requirements, British nuclear forces were also assigned to NATO. To facilitate nuclear release within NATO, a reliable communications system was therefore essential. To meet this requirement, the North Atlantic Council approved development of a military owned, operated and controlled communications system called ACE HIGH Troposphere Forward Scatter.[68] Prior to introduction of ACE HIGH in 1962, SHAPE communications relied on landlines leased from commercial sources supported by a radio relay network. The system linked SHAPE to all subordinate commands and SACEUR's atomic strike forces. Using this, senior commanders could be contacted within one minute, but fifteen minutes were required for orders to reach some of SACEUR's atomic strike forces. A primary reason for the delay was that SACEUR's release orders were not sent directly to the atomic strike forces but routed through NATO subordinate commanders. In 1961, to increase response time, the landline communications network was linked directly to the atomic strike bases.[69] In authorizing this procedure, NATO's command structure became more centralized: SACEUR now possessed the capability to order nuclear release without recourse to subordinate commanders. Moreover, as the majority of these subordinate commands were headed by European officers, the procedure increased American control over nuclear forces stationed in ACE.

To consolidate the command structure, SACEUR (General Norstad) advanced two further proposals: a Command and Control Communications System for ACE retaliatory forces, an Automatic Nuclear Weapons Detonation Reporting System. In advocating these, Norstad expressed his continued concern over the lack of a rapid, dependable and secure means of communication with the nuclear strike forces within ACE. Given the deployment of Soviet missile systems, the situation was expected to deteriorate unless remedial action was undertaken. The problem was further compounded as the nuclear forces were unable to relay tactical intelligence back to SACEUR. Consequently, SHAPE was unable to establish an accurate estimate of the ACE alert status. Introduction of a Command and Control Communications System was expected to remedy these deficiencies: implementation would allow SACEUR direct and instantaneous control of both the weapons custodial units and atomic strike forces down to the level of the launch vehicle.[70]

Communication delays also affected the existing system of reporting nuclear detonations that relied on human assessment. Given human fallibility and the resultant need for secondary confirmation, the decision to release nuclear forces was subject to delay. To eliminate this uncertainty, SHAPE proposed deployment of an automatic Bomb Alarm System at selected sites throughout Europe capable of providing unambiguous evidence that a nuclear explosion had occurred on NATO territory.

Despite SACEUR's argument that both systems were complementary and should be considered together, the Chiefs of Staff judged each project on its individual merits. The need for reliable and rapid communications within NATO was considered essential. Consequently, the NATO Command and Control Communications System received qualified approval. The problem, as perceived by the Chiefs, was the requirement to link SACEUR directly to the military units. If the scheme was implemented as proposed, SACEUR would be able to issue orders directly to the assigned Valiant squadrons without recourse to British authority. This decision might be against the wishes of HMG. To preserve negative control over the 'NATO assigned' Valiant squadrons, the Chiefs considered it essential, 'that Headquarters Bomber Command was incorporated in the Command and Control Communications System during the planning stage. This would ensure that, in the fully developed system, orders emanating from SHAPE could not be passed to stations other than through Headquarters Bomber Command.'[71]

British support for a Bomb Alarm System was less forthcoming. Indeed, the Chiefs were not convinced that deployment would produce any advantages over the present system. Doubts were also expressed over the use of the information and the exact concept of warfare to which it was to be applied. In short, the Chiefs regarded deployment as a means of controlling limited nuclear war—a development they could not support. Until these reservations were addressed (and the Chiefs were convinced that the proposal contributed to the deterrent), they refused to support SACEUR's proposal.[72]

By the mid-1960s, the communications facilities available to NATO had developed into a comprehensive and integrated network. The composition of the system was as follows:

(a) Tropospheric Scatter. This system was considered the most reliable within ACE and was the primary means of communication for early warning, the control of strike forces and vital command and liaison.

By using this, SHAPE was also directly linked to both Bomber Command and SAC.

(b) Radio Relay. This network was established to link AFCENT with the major subordinate commanders and main NATO formations in Central Europe and provided an additional communications link with SHAPE. The system could also be supplemented by capacity on the US national network. It was considered both reliable and not susceptible to major disruption.

(c) Landlines. In peacetime, a comprehensive net of rented landlines linked SHAPE with all subordinate headquarters. Procedures also existed to provide additional circuits in an emergency. As the landline communications network was mainly unhardened, it was regarded as both vulnerable to sabotage and various forms of attack.

(d) HF Radio. By using HF Radio Teletype and/or CW broadcast SHAPE was able to communicate with all main formation Headquarters 24 hours a day. Both systems were considered reliable but were vulnerable to atmospheric interference and high altitude nuclear explosions.

(e) Mobile HF SSB Radio. As a final insurance against the failure of all the above systems, SHAPE possessed a truck-borne HF SSB radio facility called LAST TALK. Only deployed in an emergency, it fulfilled the same function as the static HF system but due to its mobility was considered less vulnerable to attack.[73]

Through the development of these various systems, the SHAPE communications infrastructure possessed a high degree of redundancy. Although each system was individually vulnerable, a complete breakdown in all systems was highly unlikely: a total communications blackout could only be achieved by a large-scale pre-emptive nuclear attack aimed specifically against NATO communications.

SILK PURSE

To counter a possible Soviet decapitation attack on NATO communications, SACEUR proposed deployment of an airborne command post. This was considered essential for two specific purposes:

> The first and the most important was to relay SACEUR's orders to those locations from which operations must emanate; and secondly, as a last resort, to act for SACEUR as authorized by higher authority in the continuing conduct of operations in the event all other designated means of command and control had been destroyed.[74]

SHAPE contended that an operational capability would require deployment of seven modified aircraft and 270 personnel. It was argued that these were essential to ensure continuous airborne alert. To allay European concerns regarding finance, the US agreed to contribute 75 per cent of the overall cost. To staff the aircraft, SACEUR proposed establishing joint NATO/US control teams each containing one NATO and one US General. The Chiefs of Staff expressed strong reservations. Of particular concern was ambiguity concerning delegation of command:

> We cannot foresee the circumstances, in view of the present arrangements for the delegation of command in ACE, in which command of ACE could be delegated to a two-star general acting as SACEUR in an Airborne Operations Centre. Assuming, therefore, that there is no SHAPE requirement for an airborne emergency command post, we confine our examination of the Airborne Operations Centre to its role as an additional communications link.[75]

Notwithstanding their concerns over delegation, the Chiefs were less than convinced over the advantages of an airborne operations centre. They argued that the diverse communications system already available was sufficient to permit effective command and control of NATO forces. Although it was agreed that communications could be disrupted by massive pre-emptive nuclear attack, the likelihood of the Soviets employing this strategy was considered remote. It was further believed that even if such a strategy was adopted, communications from an airborne operations centre could be disrupted by high-altitude nuclear explosions. As a consequence, the proposal received low priority.

In August 1964, SACEUR submitted a revised concept for an airborne command post within ACE.[76] Under the new concept, SACEUR redefined the mission of the post to fulfilling the following three objectives:

1. Provision of an alternate release authority for the declaration of R Hour/General Alert in the event that SHAPE Main War HQ, SHAPE Mobile War HQ, or AFCENT War HQ (functioning as SHAPE) were destroyed or rendered incapable of performing this function.
2. Monitoring the execution of SACEUR's Scheduled Programme as far as the resources of the facility permitted.
3. Utilisation as a communications relay only in exceptional circumstances, and then only on a limited basis.[77]

It was further proposed that the senior NATO officers designated for duty on board the aircraft should be delegated 'specific authority under certain predetermined circumstances to declare R-Hour and General Alert.' The circumstances when this authority would be used covered three eventualities. First, if no radio contact could be made with either SHAPE HQ or the alternate command centres but contact remained open with SACLANT. Second, authenticated reports had been received that confirmed Soviet nuclear weapons had been used, or that SACEUR had been granted authority to declare R-Hour. Third, authenticated information had been received which indicated that US authorities had released US nuclear weapons to NATO for use in approved strike plans.

Reviewing the revised proposal, the Chiefs of Staff concluded that the airborne command post would diversify SACEUR's command and control facilities and increase reliability of the R-Hour message reaching NATO strike forces. The question of delegation proved more problematic. In short, the approval of such powers was 'contrary to the declared policy of HMG that British Commanders should not launch nuclear weapons without its prior approval.'[78] Given this position, the Chiefs considered it unlikely that the North Atlantic Council would be prepared to authorize the delegation of such authority 'which is in excess of that given to SACEUR.' In light of these reservations, the Chiefs re-affirmed their conclusion that the project remain a low priority. Despite these arguments, the first US Airborne Command Post was deployed to Europe in 1965. Known as SILK PURSE and based at Mildenhall in the UK, the aircraft was nominally independent of NATO and intended as a survivable headquarters for SACEUR (in his capacity as CINCEUR) and capable of directing US nuclear forces in Europe.[79] This distinction was largely semantic: as we have seen in Chapter 5, release authority could be transmitted to US nuclear forces in Europe wholly within the existing US chain of command.

CONCLUSION

Prior to the creation of the Defence Communications Network in the early-1960s, Britain's military communications were determined by individual Service need. The resultant networks were often diverse and located in a variety of unprotected sites. To compound the problem, overseas communications were developed in conjunction with commercial telecommunications companies. Designed for public use, the networks were vulnerable and insecure. To develop a global communications system capable of withstanding a nuclear attack required alternate command posts, hardened communications, re-routed landlines and satellite technology - developments that could be defeated by advances in Soviet capability or proscribed by prohibitive cost. In short, a communications system that incorporated such a capability was incommensurate with Britain's resources. This point was forcibly brought home to Macmillan at the Nassau conference, where McNamara revealed that the US were already spending $100 million on military communications and 'it would be ridiculous for the UK to duplicate facilities that the Americans already had.'[80]

To address these deficiencies, Britain adopted a dual strategy: to use US and NATO communications in the event of global war and retain (under national control) a residual communications infrastructure capable of directing a unilateral retaliatory strike. By adopting this policy, national requirements became more attainable. In short, a retaliatory nuclear strike did not require hardened communications. Once the executive order had been transmitted, its purpose had been served: a 'one shot war' was matched by a 'one shot' communications system. Despite this limited requirement, transmission of the executive order could not be guaranteed. A Soviet decapitation attack could destroy the entire political leadership prior to transmission of the executive order. Given this possibility, two options were available: to accept a limited deterrent capability or delegate nuclear authority to the military. Britain chose the latter. In the event of nuclear attack and communications blackout, Bomber Command was authorized to retaliate by all means at its disposal. It has been argued that such command vulnerabilities bolster deterrence as the attacking state 'cannot know precisely to whom authority has been predelegated, or if some innocuous communications link is a covert system that would be used to order nuclear retaliation in the event of an attack.'[81] Nevertheless, it must be recognised that to compensate for the deficiency in communications and ensure retaliation, Bomber Command was granted *de facto* control over Britain's nuclear weapons.

1. Carl Berger, *USAF Strategic Command and Control Systems, 1958–1963* (Historical Division Liaison Office, USAF, November 1964), p. 37.
2. Dennis Richards, *Portal of Hungerford* (Heinemann, 1977), p. 173.
3. Duncan Campbell, *War Plan UK: The Truth about Civil Defence in Britain* (Paladin Books, 1982), p. 230.
4. *Statement on Defence 1955*, Cmd. 9391 (HMSO, 1955).

DEFENCE COMMUNICATIONS 1945–64

5. Campbell, *War*, pp. 240–8. For details of Backbone's construction, see COU 1/38, Proposed Relay Station Sites for the GPO 1956–62.
6. DEFE 11/308, COS(58)90, 28 March 1958.
7. For terms of reference and committee structure, see CAB 134/2283 and CAB 161/14. The Official Committee on Communications was later renamed the Official Committee on Communications Electronics and Space.
8. Derek Wood, *Attack Warning Red: The Royal Observer Corps and the Defence of Britain 1925–1975* (MacDonald and Jane's, 1976), pp. 225–7.
9. DEFE 32/6, COS(61)9th, 7 February 1961.
10. DEFE 25/49, Nuclear Retaliation Procedures: Communications, 30 January 1961.
11. DEFE 25/49, GEN 743/10(Revise), 23 January 1962.
12. DEFE 25/49, Prime Minister's Communications in a Period of Emergency, April 1961.
13. Nuclear Retaliation Procedures.
14. GEN 743/10 (Revise).
15. See Chapter 4.
16. CAB 131/20, D(58)73, Memorandum by the Postmaster General, 28 November 1958.
17. We are grateful to Nigel Wright for this information.
18. CAB 134/2283, CCE(58)1st, 6 August 1958.
19. DEFE 4/152, COS(63)11th, Extension of the Twilight System, 11 January 1963.
20. PREM 11/4460, Operating Instructions for Private and Secured Voice System, 6 September 1961.
21. PICKWICK was introduced in Whitehall in the mid–1950s to provide secure communications between senior civil servants and ministers.
22. PREM 11/4460, Proposed Drill for Setting up the KY–9 link from Admiralty House to the State Department, undated.
23. DEFE 25/49, Brief for Secretary, 13 March 1961 covering Nuclear Retaliation: Alternative Procedures, March 1961.
24. Although Cable and Wireless was taken into public ownership in 1947, the company's assets and operations outside the UK were never absorbed into the GPO and it operated like any other company even though its facilities were closely co–ordinated and integrated with those of the GPO.
25. DEFE 4/150, JCE(62)19(Final), 19 November 1962.
26. DEFE 4/151, GSS(62)4(Final), Military Satellite Communications Capability, 27 December 1962.
27. The Defense Communications Agency was established in 1960 with the aim of co–ordinating all service communications support for the joint operational use of the JCS.
28. DEFE 7/980, Watkinson to Macmillan, 21 June 1961.
29. DEFE 4/154, COS(63)29th, 25 April 1963.
30. AIR 20/10056, NSCC, Initiation and Control of Nuclear Strikes in Overseas Theatres, 21 December 1962.
31. COS(63)29th.
32. DEFE 5/139, Annex to COS 185/63, Policy Guidance for Military Commanders Overseas in Global War, 15 September 1963.
33. DEFE 19/7, The Integration of Government Communications, 13 December 1960.
34. DEFE 13/316, DOS/P(63)12(Revise), Defence Organisation Steering Committee, 24 April 1963.
35. DEFE 5/139, COS193/63, Defence Reorganisation – Interim Report, 29 May 1963.
36. DEFE 5/136, COS96/63, 4 March 1963.
37. DEFE 4/152, Confidential Annex to COS(63)17th, 28 February 1963.
38. P.M. Ford, 'The Defence Communications Network', *Journal of the Royal Signals Institute* (Summer, 1989).
39. DEFE 4/142, PPO/P(61)45, Communications Staff for Cabinet Office and Burlington, 21 November 1961.
40. COS 96/63.

41. GEN 743/1 (Revise).
42. AIR 2/15001, Direction and Control of Strategic Bomber Forces, May 1958.
43. AIR 20/10277, MBF, Readiness During a Period of Tension, 28 September 1956.
44. AIR 8/2313, Dispersal Plan for the V Force, 17 January 1955.
45. AIR 8/2313, ERPC/P(55)5, Note by DCAS, 29 April 1955.
46. Ibid.
47. Wainstein, *Evolution*, p. 159
48. As the radio broadcast system did not incorporate a two way speech facility, use of this network alone would have left the central command uncertain as to whether the launch order had been successfully received, ERPC/P(55)5.
49. RG 218, Joint Strategic Communications Plans Panel, J/SP 103/20, Safeguarding of Allied Long Distance Wireless Communications, 10 August 1953. National Archives.
50. ERPC/P(55)5.
51. Ibid.
52. CAB 21/3396, DTC(CRT)(51)5, 29 March 1951.
53. Gregory, *Nuclear*, p. 114.
54. AIR 20/10277, AOC–in–C Bomber Command to Under–Secretary of State, 14 February 1957.
55. DEFE 32/6, COS(59)23rd, 2 April 1959.
56. AIR 20/10618, Six Monthly Progress Report on the Readiness of the Medium Bomber Force, Report No. 2 – Period 1st July, 1959 to 31st December, 1959, January 1960.
57. AIR 24/2724, Headquarters Bomber Command Signals Plan No. 1/63, 22 March 1963.
58. AIR 2/15605, Bomber Command Deployment, undated.
59. See Chapter 3.
60. AIR 20/10925, D.Air Plans/1559, Appendix B, 10 March 1960.
61. AIR 24/2688, Bomber Command VHF Forward Relay Stations, undated.
62. AIR 24/2689, Notes of meeting, 1 November 1962.
63. Wainstein, *Evolution*, pp. 232–4.
64. AIR 2/17801, Effects of the Missile Threat, 24 January 1961.
65. AIR 24/2689, High Frequency SSB Radio Equipment for Airborne Command Post, 22 November 1962.
66. Ibid.
67. Wainstein, *Evolution*, p. 161.
68. AIR 19/690, COS(61)79, 7 March 1961. For details of ACE HIGH, see Gregory, *Nuclear*, p.63.
69. AIR 8/1956, Annex to COS1458/30/11/61, 30 November 1961.
70. AIR 19/690, COS (61) 164, NATO Basic Military Requirements, 12 May 1961.
71. AIR 19/690, Extract from COS(61)30th, 12 May 1961.
72. For details, see Chapter 8.
73. DEFE 5/139, Annex to COS.220/63, Airborne Operations Centre for ACE, 19 June 1963.
74. DEFE 4/149, COS(62)10th, 10 February 1962.
75. Annex to COS220/63.
76. Annex to COS2719/18/8/64, 18 August 1964.
77. DEFE 6/92, DP101/64(Final), Airborne Command Post for Allied Command Europe, 23 September 1964.
78. Ibid.
79. William Arkin and Richard Fieldhouse, 'Nuclear Weapons Command, Control and Communications', in *World Armaments and Disarmaments: SIPRI Yearbook 1984* (Taylor & Francis, 1984), p. 465.
80. PREM 11/4429, Record of Meeting, 19 December 1962.
81. Thayer, 'Risk', p.473.

CHAPTER 7

Atomic Intelligence: Operations and Estimates 1945–1964

'Mister President, we must not allow a mine-shaft gap' (General Turgidson).

Strategic surprise has been a primarily twentieth century development, in which the application of military technologies has frequently been crucial and on occasions decisive. The development of weapons of mass destruction and the means of delivering these over inter-continental distances in very short periods of time fundamentally changed the context and prospects of surprise in modern warfare. In particular the development of ballistic missiles that were invulnerable to interception portended a revolution, arguably as significant as the development of the atomic and thermonuclear weapons they were designed to carry. Whole societies could be destroyed in the time taken for ballistic missiles to reach their targets. Moreover, until survivable weapons systems (and the means to control them) were developed the capacity to deter such attacks was put in jeopardy. Knowledge of an adversary's nuclear capabilities, and the likelihood and imminence of attack became of paramount importance to national and international security in the nuclear age.

The advent of weapons of mass destruction and the collapse of East-West relations after 1945 meant that Soviet capabilities and intentions were overriding targets for British intelligence during the Cold War. Assessing intelligence estimates presents considerable challenges to the historian. Systematic evaluation of British estimates of Soviet capabilities and intentions, for example, would require detailed study of Soviet records.[1] A second fruitful method is by way of comparison with American evaluations, and in particular US National Intelligence Estimates (NIEs). However, given the limited availability of British sources these comparative analyses cannot yet provide firm conclusions. Nevertheless, on the available evidence it seems clear that British estimates were generally less alarmist than their American equivalents, which tended to exaggerate Soviet technological and production capabilities. On the other hand there were occasions where the British appear to have underestimated Soviet capabilities and capacities. It is also clear that for both intelligence communities there was value in having separate expert evaluations of similar sources.

In comparing British and American estimates one question is how far these were based on different sources or whether they reflected different analytical techniques and judgements. There is clear evidence that in some areas the British reached different conclusions from the same raw data. Given the importance of American intelligence appreciations for American policy and the resulting Soviet-American 'arms race', the fact that British officials reached different conclusions is therefore particularly interesting. A second important question is how far intelligence appreciations informed British decisions on strategy or policy. The conclusions proffered below are preliminary, and aim to provide a framework for future research.

OPERATIONS

According to Sun Tzu, foreknowledge (of the enemy's intentions and dispositions) 'cannot be obtained inductively from experience, nor by deductive calculation'.[2] Yet for British and American officials after 1945 the paucity of available intelligence inevitably meant that analysis assumed a critical role. As MOD's Chief Scientific Adviser, Sir Frederick Brundrett, explained to the Defence Secretary in 1955:

> The real difficulty, of course, underlying the whole of this business is the fact that the Russian Security is at a higher level than has ever previously been known in the world, and, consequently, the information from which the Intelligence Authorities draw their conclusions is extremely sketchy.[3]

British secret intelligence about the Soviet Union in the period 1945–1964 came from a variety of sources, most of which remain veiled by official secrecy. The following discussion, while drawing upon published, and American archival, sources is based on limited British records. The files of GCHQ and SIS are not released to the Public Record Office as a matter of policy, and the government remains unwilling to release details of operations that might illuminate sources or methods of intelligence gathering.[4] Details of some operations, mainly of a scientific kind that did not entail intrusion into Soviet sovereignty, such as the Music programme (see below) have been released. And while specific espionage operations remain closed, the singular circumstances of the Penkovsky case allow for scrutiny of intelligence gathering (though not analysis) on the British side. The following section illuminates various aspects of British intelligence operations against the USSR, and proffer insights and opinions, which may be subjected to further inquiry in due course.

AERIAL RECONNAISSANCE

Administered through Bomber Command, the British Strategic Reconnaissance Force supplied aerial intelligence to the Chiefs of Staff and other government departments. Priorities for the force were allocated through the Joint Air Reconnaissance Intelligence Board (JARIB), a subordinate committee of the JIC. Chaired by the Assistant Chief of the Air Staff (Intelligence) (ACAS (I)), the Board comprised representatives of the three services, the JIB, the Directorate of Scientific Intelligence and the Joint Air Reconnaissance Intelligence Committee (JARIC).[5] Stationed at RAF Wyton, the scale and extent of British aerial reconnaissance remains unclear.[6] Equally important, the scope and significance of the material provided has not yet emerged.

Details of RAF involvement in any clandestine overflight programme remain sparse. The evidence suggests that for much of the 1950s overflights were few and far between. This is in contrast to the programmes of the USAF and the CIA, details of both of which have emerged.[7] Various accounts suggest British involvement in USAF and CIA overflight programmes, which is a further dimension of the 'special relationship' in the intelligence field.[8] Such involvement took various forms. After January 1952 US RB-45s were flown in RAF markings with mixed RAF/USAF crews.[9] In March, the RAF began a series of RB-45C operations from RAF Sculthorpe involving overflights of Soviet territory.[10] One account indicates that a RB-45C flown by a RAF crew overflew Moscow on the night of 29 April 1954.[11] Other accounts detail the involvement of RAF pilots in the CIA's U-2 programme.[12] It is also clear that the RAF undertook several missions involving various degrees of penetration of Soviet air space, and involving radar and photographic reconnaissance, as well as electronic intelligence gathering. In May 1953, according to various accounts, an RAF Canberra overflew the missile-testing centre at Kaputsin Yar at the behest of the United States.[13]

The need for knowledge of Soviet production capabilities was one key mission for aerial reconnaissance. Identifying potential targets, in peace and war, was a further requirement. While the targets remained cities and large towns this could be more easily achieved. Targeting Soviet air bases, missile sites and other installations, presented greater challenges. The 'lack of adequate target intelligence' required the exploitation of 'all conceivable sources, including defectors, public libraries, commercial and cultural records... for bits of information that might add to the little already known concerning most targets.'[14]

The issue of whether post-strike reconnaissance was required was closely involved with nuclear strategy, and whether there was value in planning for limited or protracted nuclear exchanges. The role, size and shape of the British strategic reconnaissance force became a matter of some debate toward the end of the 1950s.[15] In 1958, the RAF's target information consisted mostly 'of predicted radar pictures made up from extremely out of date photographic cover'.[16] It was believed that the 'effectiveness of a nuclear attack on this type of target could be increased by a factor of two if up-to-date and more accurate targets and route information could be provided'. Such information was necessary in peacetime, 'and this can only be done by clandestine flights'. This 1958 analysis by the Central Reconnaissance Establishment (CRE) at Brampton strongly implies that the RAF had not engaged in systematic clandestine overflights, nor had it acquired the necessary targeting and routing information from the US. Indeed when President Eisenhower launched his Open Skies initiative in 1955 the RAF simply did not have an effective reconnaissance capability to overfly the Soviet Union, even in the absence of Soviet air defences. The CRE concluded that:

> The possibility of being allowed to fly penetration sorties with our present and future reconnaissance aircraft is so remote it can be discounted. However, flights could be made around the fringes of USSR and the satellites from which a wealth of route, target and mapping material could be obtained.[17]

Whether or not the RAF developed its own overflight programme, it is clear that collaboration with the United States was an important source of intelligence. The CIA initially promised that 'all the intelligence from the operation [of U-2 overflights from British bases] would be shared with the British authorities.'[18] And when Eden withdrew his approval for the operation, the Americans nevertheless passed 'a great deal of useful intelligence' providing 'up to date information on the Soviet Air Force which we could not get in any other way in present circumstances'.[19] The American U-2, introduced in 1956, could operate above 70,000 feet, which made it invulnerable to Soviet air defences (until 1960 when the Soviets introduced a new Surface to Air Missile). Details of British co-operation in the U-2 missions flown from British bases both in the UK and abroad, are beginning to emerge, together with details of political authorisation. British participation in the U-2 programme was conducted under the codename Aquatone (later amended by the Americans to Chess) and was one of the issues discussed between Macmillan and Eisenhower at the 1957 Bermuda Conference, by when Macmillan had reversed Eden's prohibition on the overflights. [20]

Overflights were one element in aerial intelligence. Other important aspects were signals and electronic intelligence-gathering missions, flown along the periphery of Soviet air space. These were conducted by No. 51 Squadron, based at RAF Wyton. Similarly air-sampling missions to detect and monitor Soviet nuclear tests were undertaken. The RAF operated a squadron of Canberras (Squadron 76) for this purpose, which, for example, attempted to gather material on the French atomic tests.[21] Doubts about the cost-effectiveness of this squadron eventually led to its abolition. American operations flown from British bases certainly provided a much more cost-effective option for the RAF, as information from these operations was shared with the British.[22] In July 1960, however, a RB-47H, operating from Brize Norton, was shot down over the Barents Sea. So soon after the Gary Powers U-2 incident, the episode caused the Macmillan government acute political embarrassment.

To ensure the episode was not repeated, urgent talks were initiated between the two governments. In September 1960, agreement was reached on terms covering the use of US bases in Britain for aerial reconnaissance missions. The agreement comprised two documents. The first was a service-to-service agreement that required the USAF liaison officer at the Air Ministry 'to make available to the Royal Air Force information concerning reconnaissance flights around the periphery of the Soviet Bloc to or from airfields on British territory.'[23] The second covered political authorisation:

> By approximately the 15th of each month, the Assistant Chief of the Air Staff (Intelligence), Royal Air Force, Air Ministry, London, will be provided through appropriate liaison channels with a schedule of such flights planned for the following calendar month. The Air Ministry will pass this information to the

Foreign Office. If the Foreign Secretary should wish to make any representations concerning any of these projected flights, the Foreign Office will instruct Her Majesty's Embassy to approach the State Department and the Air Ministry will simultaneously inform the US service involved through the appropriate liaison channels.[24]

In the autumn of 1961, following requests from the USAF, procedures for authorizing these flights were changed. The USAF requested blanket rather than individual flight clearance. Macmillan agreed that once he and the Foreign Secretary had given general approval, the individual flights would only need to be cleared though the Secretary of State for Air, unless special circumstances warranted higher approval.[25] Subsequently, the VCAS, Air Vice-Marshal Kyle, recommended that he should retain the responsibility for obtaining authority for the individual flights and for granting it where the Secretary of State was not readily available.

In the autumn of 1962 the Soviets resumed their nuclear test programme in the Barents Sea, and from August to November the USAF conducted various intelligence-gathering operations. These involved daily flights of KC-135 aircraft from Brize Norton and an operation mounted from Upper Heyford involving a detachment of three USAF U-2s.[26] Their mission was to sample the upper air for radioactive material from Soviet nuclear tests. The Defence Secretary, Peter Thorneycroft, was concerned at the possible loss of such aircraft, as had happened when a 'Chinese nationalist' U-2 was shot down over China.[27] The operations, however, were flown over international waters, and the USAF 'have specifically undertaken that they [the U-2s] will not infringe the danger areas declared by the USSR for nuclear tests or fleet exercises, and will keep at least 100 miles away from any Soviet territory.'[28] In addition, the USAF undertook one specific mission, involving a KC-135 flight within the test area (though still over international waters):

> The object is to obtain high-speed photographs and optical telescopic measurements of the first few micro seconds after the detonation. The information obtained will provide accurate measurements of the yield of the weapon as well as valuable data on its construction; it will also give an important yardstick for the interpretation of information collected from more distant flights.[29]

This is a further illustration of RAF-USAF collaboration. How far the American authorities provided useful intelligence is an important question. In 1948 the USAF and the RAF reached a joint agreement to co-operate on target intelligence 'to ensure full exploitation of intelligence, maximum target coverage, compete standardization, and minimum duplication of effort.'[30] In November 1953 the Chief of the Air Staff was reminded that 'there is at present, and has been for some time, complete exchange and co-ordination with the Americans of tactical and strategic target material, in which field intelligence liaison was probably been better than in any other.'[31] Indeed when, in 1954, the US Joint Chiefs reviewed the participation of British and Canadian officers in US military intelligence activities, the USAF argued that:

> A large percentage of the factual data concerning Soviet aircraft, air equipment, and guided missiles is derived from the British. British and Canadian contributions to United States intelligence in the fields of Soviet Air Order of Battle, aircraft production and electronic development have been very substantial. At the present time the USAF and the RAF are cooperating very closely in a global targeting program.[32]

USAF exchange officers were 'given a greater measure of freedom and almost complete access to British intelligence files.'[33] This collaboration, it should be noted, preceded inter-governmental agreement on an integrated strategic plan, and underlines the observation of Sir Frank Cooper that personal relationships between senior RAF and USAF figures 'continued both within and without the laws of both countries.'[34] At the beginning of 1957 the formal agreement to co-ordinate the nuclear strike plans required the exchange of target intelligence.[35]

ESPIONAGE

In addition to the closed nature of Soviet society and the vast expanse of Soviet territories, British and western intelligence gathering faced other challenges in the espionage war. The resources and expertise of Soviet counter-intelligence presented formidable challenges to operations mounted in the Soviet Union. The successful espionage operations run by Soviet intelligence in Britain and North America were also a significant advantage for the Soviets. Both Kim Philby and George Blake, Soviet agents working within SIS, were able to compromise western operations. Furthermore, when the scale and seriousness of Soviet penetrations came to light, the ensuing search for further Soviet agents had a deleterious effect on intelligence gathering. The climate of suspicion, and the search for 'moles' who sometimes did not exist, provided a further handicap, especially in the CIA where 'molehunts' within the CIA's Soviet Division had a debilitating effect on operations during the 1960s.[36]

Soviet penetration of western governments reflected careful long-term planning dating back to the 1930s. One further disadvantage suffered by the British and the Americans were the wartime decisions by Churchill and Roosevelt not to spy on their ally. Work by the Government Codes and Cypher School (GC&CS) on Soviet codes and cyphers stopped on 22 June 1941 (though the Soviet meteorological cypher was read again after October 1942).[37] Some wartime intelligence was gained indirectly through GC&CS decrypts of German intelligence appraisals of Soviet strength.[38] It is not clear when the British resumed intelligence operations, though within SIS planning for the post-war intelligence and counter-intelligence operations against the Soviet Union was under way by 1944.

Human source intelligence (or HUMINT) took various forms. The debriefing of German rockets scientists, who had been co-opted onto the Soviet guided weapons programme, was of particular importance.[39] Published (and American) sources suggest that the British were able to recruit a variety of defectors (and some defectors-in-place), though the scope and value of the intelligence they produced is not yet clear.[40] The importance of recruiting defectors and defectors-in-place, was recognised within Whitehall, and in 1954 a sub-committee of the JIC, the Sub-Committee on Defectors (SCD) was established to 'recommend, and where appropriate, decide the policy for the handling and encouragement of defectors.'[41]

The most significant agent run by the British (in co-operation with the CIA) was Oleg Penkovsky. Between April 1961 and August 1962, Penkovsky, an officer of the Intelligence Directorate of the Soviet General Staff (GRU), supplied SIS and the CIA with information and documents from the files of the Soviet General Staff to which he had access.[42] He also provided details of GRU and KGB personnel, and high-level gossip gleaned from his cultivation of senior general staff officers, including the head of the GRU. Penkovsky's espionage was conducted from the heart of the Soviet military establishment. It was soon clear that he had access to high-level officials and could provide information on Khrushchev's attitudes and intentions, and the views of members of the Soviet General Staff. Moreover, Penkovsky's espionage came at a very significant moment. Khrushchev's adventurist foreign policies posed great challenges to the west. The threat of Soviet missiles was a serious problem for western planners and leaders, and Khrushchev's 'success' in helping convince the American of his nuclear strength was of great significance in the Cold War.

Penkovsky supplied information on various Soviet intentions and capabilities, including information on Khrushchev's aims in Berlin in 1961, and on relations between Khrushchev and his generals. Some of the potentially most significant intelligence concerned the Soviet ICBM programme. The American intelligence community had remained divided over Soviet ICBM capabilities and production plans, and Penkovsky's intelligence cast considerable doubt over the principal Soviet ICBM system. The significance of Penkovsky's intelligence on Soviet missile capabilities is discussed below.

THE SOVIET BOMB

It is clear that the explosion of the Soviet atomic bomb took the British and American scientific and intelligence communities by surprise. In 1945 informed opinion had been divided over when the Soviets would have the scientific knowledge and technological ability to construct an atomic bomb, though no-one seriously doubted that they would.[43] The first official British estimate in November 1945, concluded that the Soviets would be able to produce a bomb, perhaps in as few as three years.[44] By 1947 the planning assumption of the Chiefs of Staff was that the Soviets would probably have atomic (and biological) warfare capabilities by 1956/7:

> All our intelligence sources indicate that Russia is striving with German help, to improve her military potential; and to catch up technically and scientifically. We must expect that from 1956-57 Russia will probably be in a position to use some atomic bombs and biological warfare; that she may have developed probably with German advice and technical assistance, rockets, pilotless aircraft, a strategic bomber force and a submarine force; and that she will continue to maintain very large land forces, a considerable proportion of which may be equipped and trained up to Western standards.[45]

In 1948 the JIC believed that while it was possible the Soviets might have a bomb by January 1951, the tentative prediction was that January 1954 was the earliest likely date.[46] Ironically, shortly before the discovery of the Soviet test in August 1949, senior British, American and Canadian intelligence officials, meeting in Washington[47] were briefed by their scientific advisers that the earliest date by when the Soviets might explode their first test bomb was mid-1950, while the probable date was mid-1953.[48] President Truman publicly announced that the Soviets had tested an atomic bomb on 26 September, immediately casting doubt on the assumptions and work of the planning conference.

Evidence that the Soviets had tested a bomb coincided with the confession and exposure of Dr Klaus Fuchs, a German-born scientist who had worked on the British and Manhattan atomic projects, and who had volunteered information to Soviet intelligence from 1942 until his arrest. Assessing how far this information had accelerated Soviet research was an immediate worry, though for the British Chiefs of Staff a more practical concern was whether Fuchs' espionage would seriously damage British-American co-operation in atomic energy.[49] The MOD's Chief Scientific Adviser, Sir Henry Tizard was so skeptical of Soviet scientific and technical abilities, that not only did he attribute the Soviet test to the acquisition of 'absolutely full details of the whole US process' but he wondered whether the Soviets had simply stolen some plutonium from the Americans.[50] The fact that the Soviets had achieved the atomic bomb before the British challenged prevailing assumptions and caused much concern.[51]

Monitoring development of Soviet atomic and thermonuclear weapons presented formidable problems to western intelligence. In 1949 American aircraft discovered radioactive particles that enabled scientists at Los Alamos and the US Naval Research Laboratory to establish that the Soviets had tested an atomic bomb toward the end of August.[52] British officials were informed of the explosion on 10 September and were requested to monitor the radioactive cloud as it passed over Western Europe.[53] Air samples obtained from the cloud using a modified Halifax bomber confirmed American suspicions: the Soviets had detonated a nuclear device using plutonium as its fissile material.[54] Subsequently the British and Americans co-operated in monitoring radioactive gases created in Soviet plutonium production.[55] The radioactive emissions enabled calculations about the size of the Soviet plutonium stockpile that were in turn crucial to estimating how many weapons the Soviets could build. In 1953, the collaboration led to a joint British-American project known as the MUSIC programme. The validity of the project was a matter for speculation and by 1955 British officials expressed 'considerable doubts whether the programme continues to be worthwhile in view of the margins of error in assessments resulting from it.'[56]

There was nevertheless concern in Whitehall when the American authorities announced the detection of Soviet atomic explosions in October 1954. The Defence Secretary, Harold Macmillan, was worried about potentially embarrassing public questions concerning Britain's ability to detect such explosions and stressed to the Prime Minister that, 'it is important that nothing should be said which could lead the Russians to deduce the geographical positions of our stations.'[57] He was particularly anxious that if 'we were to reveal knowledge of a comparatively small explosion it might jeopardize the security of our very favourable forward position, the whereabouts of which you know.'[58] The nature and location of these stations is not clear. R.V. Jones explains one idea developed by Dr J.H. Lees (of the JIB) for detecting nuclear tests involved long-range detection of the pulse of radio energy or 'radioflash' created in an atomic explosion.[59] Whether this technique of detecting electro-magnetic pulse (EMP) was the one to which the Defence Secretary was referring, and indeed the extent to which GCHQ stations were a principal means of detecting Soviet testing remains unclear.

The size of the Soviet atomic stockpile was a crucial factor in estimating Soviet capabilities. These estimates were tentative, as were those of Soviet fissile material involved in development of thermonuclear weapons. The estimate produced in December 1950 by the US Joint Intelligence Indications Committee gave the expected growth of the Soviet atomic stockpile as follows[60]:

Mid-1950	30 bombs
Mid-1951	50 bombs
Mid-1952	120 bombs
Mid-1953	205 bombs
Mid-1954	315 bombs

By May 1952 the agreed British-American estimate of the Soviet atomic stockpile had been reduced to 70–100.[61] Interestingly, the Prime Minister held a different view of the Soviet arsenal than his advisers. Churchill credited the Soviets with only some 50 to 60 atomic bombs.[62] Official Whitehall thinking was more cautious. Commenting on Churchill's estimate, the Director of the JIB noted that: 'the evidence on which this intelligence estimate has been based is inferential, and the P.M.'s figures may be nearer the mark'.[63] By November 1952, British and American weapons evaluators placed the Soviet stockpile by mid-1954 at 190. Yet, illustrative of the margins of uncertainty, was the caveat that 'The actual stockpile may be as low as one-half or as high as twice that figure'.[64] These variations may well also indicate differences between British and American estimates, which continued over time.

It was not until the early 1960s that the British and Americans agreed on the Soviet stockpile: 'Our exchanges with our estimates in the U.S. are now so good that for the first time for some years British and American estimates of the amounts of Soviet produced plutonium and U-235 are as nearly identical as it would be reasonable to expect.'[65] As Strong noted 'for some years past the CIA estimate has been considerably greater than the British one.'[66] Translating these figures into estimates of weapons required various assumptions and calculations. The British believed that the Soviets could double their stockpile in about the next four years, while the Americans calculated it could double in three.[67] Given the US capacity for fissile production Strong concluded that it was 'apparent that the Soviets are making no extraordinary efforts to overtake the U.S. in this respect.'[68]

Soviet nuclear development was the predominant concern for the British authorities, though possession of nuclear weapons by other states was also a priority. Estimating when others would join the nuclear club became a matter of great significance to diplomatic efforts to constrain the proliferation of nuclear weapons. In September 1961 the JIC concluded that India could explode a nuclear device by 1964/5.[69] The JIC also estimated that China was the only 'fifth country' within sight of a nuclear test, which was believed to be likely by 1962/3.[70] Both these estimates, while correct in predicting testing of an atomic capability, were somewhat pessimistic with regard to timing (China tested in 1964; India in 1970). The advent of US satellite photography provided a significant improvement in monitoring Chinese progress.[71]

THE SOVIET BALLISTIC MISSILE PROGRAMME

While atomic and particularly thermonuclear weapons portended a revolution in warfare, the development of ballistic missiles was of enormous importance. Nuclear weapons could now be hurled hundreds and thousands of miles within minutes, and without possibility of interception. The capacity to strike at the United States threatened enormous political and strategic consequences. It was recognised as early as 1949 that the Soviets had bombers capable of reaching American territory. The TU-4 was capable of striking American (and Canadian) targets using either air refuelling or on one-way missions.[72] In 1949 western intelligence believed that the Soviets possessed 150 TU-4s, the only Soviet aircraft with a combat radius over 650 nm that could carry an atomic bomb.

The development of Soviet long-range strategic bombers and ICBMs became the major concern of American officials. American misperceptions of Soviet strategic nuclear capabilities, the so-called bomber and missiles 'gaps' of the 1950s, were of crucial importance to intelligence assessments and policy prescriptions, and indeed to the diplomatic conduct of the Cold War.[73] For British (and other European) governments the vulnerability of American targets to Soviet attack was also of enormous importance. Soviet perceptions of likely American reactions were the crux of the problem. As Chief of the Defence Staff Mountbatten told the Chiefs of Staff in 1960:

> It was important to look at the problem from the Russian point of view. The United States had for the first time in history become open to a large measure of destruction, which, when the time came, they might not be prepared to accept. The Russians might therefore think that the firmness of purpose shown by the United States Government at present or in the future might not be shared by the American people in the event. The Russian assessment of the firmness of purpose of the Americans and in particular of the U.S. Congress and the American people was more important than the actual American attitude.[74]

The British were also naturally concerned with Soviet forces that could attack the United Kingdom. Medium and long-range bombers were initially the main problem, though the scale and extent of the Soviet bomber threat would depend on whether and when the Soviets had overrun Western Europe.[75] By the mid-1950s British planners worked on the assumption of a Soviet force comprising manned aircraft, ballistic missiles and 'powered bombs' launched from aircraft.[76] The development of Soviet ballistic missiles meant that warning time was reduced dramatically.[77]

Initial estimates of Soviet ballistic missile capabilities reflected the important role of German scientists co-opted by the Soviets. The expectation was that early Soviet models would be variations on German weapons. The paucity of intelligence on which such estimates were based was nevertheless apparent. In November 1952 the US JCS were told that:

> There is insufficient information on which to base an estimate of the number of guided missiles the Soviets may be expected to have in stock by mid-1954. It is known that they have carried forward experimentation in the field, particularly in those items of German origin.[78]

Although German expertise provided the Soviets with a good start, it was also believed that the Soviets were well behind in the electronics necessary for a successful ballistic missile programme.[79] In the early to mid-1950s British estimates nevertheless differed from those of the Americans. The US NIE produced in October 1954 concluded that the Soviets had undertaken 'an extensive guided missile program, giving highest priority to air defense missiles.'[80] It was nevertheless believed that the Soviets would make a concerted effort to produce an ICBM for service production by 1963. The estimate also warned that if the Soviets developed an ICBM capability before the US had developed adequate countermeasures, 'it would acquire a military advantage that would constitute an extremely grave threat to US security.' By October 1955, the Americans believed that the Soviets had the capacity to produce missiles of 600–700 mile range, and would be likely to have an ICBM capability by 1963.[81] The Chief Scientific Adviser, Sir Frederick Brundrett, however, told the Minister of Defence that the Soviets would be unlikely to solve the problems involved in developing very long-range missiles to attack America before 1965, and 'will be unlikely to be able to mount any serious threat against North America until some years later, possibly even 1970.'[82] Of note was the fact that British estimates appear to have been based on the same intelligence as those of the Americans:

> The evidence on which the American views are based is known to us and is considered, in my opinion absolutely rightly, to be totally unacceptable. Our own views are based on an extremely able piece of scientific deduction by the scientific group in J.I.B.[83]

In May 1956, although the JIC believed that the Soviets would be able to mount 'a large scale surprise attack on North America from 1959 onwards', it was doubted whether this would increase the likelihood that the Soviets would choose to go to war 'because we do not believe that the Soviet leaders could be certain of being able to neutralize the western counter-offensive at the first blow.'[84]

On 3 August 1957 the USSR successfully test-launched its first ICBM. This was followed on 4 October by the launch of *Sputnik 1*, using the same missile as the booster, and thus demonstrating to the world that the Soviets could now strike at inter-continental ranges with weapons of mass destruction. The JIC and the JPS began systematic study of the consequences for Soviet policy when sufficient warheads and delivery systems existed to neutralize the targets it wished to destroy.[85] It was an issue that was to exercise western officials and leaders over the ensuing decades.

In the United States the system of producing agreed inter-service estimates of Soviet bomber and missile capabilities failed, both because of the paucity of sources, and as a result of mistaken assumptions in the estimating process. In part this reflected organisational weaknesses and inter-service rivalry within the US intelligence community. Details of British estimates are now emerging, which were significantly less pessimistic. For example, the Americans took the view that a Soviet missile threat existed 'as soon as flight trials were completed because the production for R and D tests could be diverted to build up a small operational capability'.[86] This definition was not shared by the British who believed that 'the threat would begin some 1-2 years later, the time estimated to allow for the production of a sufficient quantity of weapons to meet estimated operational requirements.'[87]

Methodological issues assumed a particular saliency within the US intelligence community over development of Soviet ICBMs in the 1950s/1960s where fierce disagreement emerged over when the Soviets would move from testing their ICBMs to deploying them.[88] The initial CIA estimate after Sputnik suggested that prototype Soviet ICBMs could be available by 1959;[89] the American intelligence community quickly agreed that a hundred or more would be deployed within three to five years.[90] The British were more sanguine. As Kenneth Strong explained to CAS in 1958: 'Not only do we think that the Soviet strategic missiles will enter service a year or more later than the American estimate, but we think that the operational and logistic limitations on their use... will delay the accumulation of "operational quantities"'.[91] Initial British estimates suggested that it would take the Soviets some three years after Sputnik before ICBMs were operational. The subsequent development of Soviet ICBMs and the American 'missile gap' demonstrated that British estimates were more accurate.

Within Whitehall, however, there were disagreements over Soviet capabilities, reflecting different assumptions and methodologies. The Air Ministry and the JIB, for example, held different views on when Soviet MRBMs would become operational, and how many ICBMs the Soviets would eventually deploy.[92] These disagreements surfaced over proposal for reform of the system for evaluating missile intelligence put forward by Field-Marshal Templer in 1961. The view of the Chief of the Air Staff, Sir Thomas Pike, was that:

Professional foresight and 'feel' are important factors in assessment if we are to see, as we must, into the future. Where hard intelligence is available there is normally no difficulty in agreement; it is in the area of opinion that differences are most likely to arise. I believe that in such cases the professional opinion of the responsible Service should be accepted as a working basis until such time as the advent of new intelligence can resolve the issue. [93]

Such thinking played an important and deleterious role in the saga of the American bomber and missile 'gaps'. Nonetheless the CAS made clear that such assessments should occur within the JIC machinery and that 'of course these final assessments are subject to approval by the JIC'.[94]

One important source for British and American estimates appears to have been monitoring of Soviet testing. Intelligence on operational characteristics and the whereabouts of the missiles in question was more difficult to obtain. Oleg Penkovsky, whose career as a western agent is noted above, was himself trained in ballistics, and supplied the west with considerable information on the operational characteristics of the SS-4 (NATO designation) missile, which it has been claimed was of decisive significance in the Cuban missile crisis.[95] In 1961 Penkovsky confirmed that the SS-4 (and also the 300 mile range SS-1 (NATO designation)) were in serial production while the SS-5 IRBM (NATO designation) was experiencing production problems.[96] He also identified the testing facilities on Novaya Zemlya in the Arctic as a launching site for SS-4 and SS-5 strikes on Western Europe, and other launch sites in the south able to target Iran and Pakistan.[97] Penkovsky's espionage coincided with the advent of the American photo-reconnaissance satellites, the Corona programme. Although his espionage is cited as the mean reason for the dispelling the myth of the missile gap it is clear that it was photo-reconnaissance satellites which were the principal source of intelligence on which American estimates were radically revised.[98]

SOVIET TACTICS AND STRATEGY

The development and operational employment of nuclear weapons posed considerable challenges to all military organisations, and inevitably generated debates about all aspects of tactics and strategy. Initial British expectations concerning the Soviet use of the atomic bomb believed that in order to occupy the European mainland, the Soviets would 'deal a "knock-out blow" to the United Kingdom' which for the next few years would be the 'No. 1 target on the Russian list.'[99] To achieve this objective, the Chiefs of Staff concluded that the Soviets would use atomic bombs against airfields and centres of population combined with ground burst thermonuclear weapons to produce the maximum amount of radioactive fall-out over the whole of the UK.[100]

The scale of the Soviet attack on Britain was a major concern. In 1958, the allocation of the Soviet nuclear stockpile for attacks on the United Kingdom was estimated at '15 bombs of 1-5 megaton yield and 200 bombs, or ballistic missile warheads of 10-100 kiloton yield.'[101] The JIC concluded that the main targets for these weapons would be American SAC and V-force airfields with the main cities and industrial areas of the UK secondary targets. By 1960, however, the Soviets would have sufficient megaton weapons to attack 'all the targets they would wish'.[102] The JIC estimated in 1962 that the Soviet initial launch capability to cover all NATO targets was 250 land-based missiles rising to 600-700 by 1966.[103] This was further strengthened by a fleet of 34 submarines capable of firing missiles to ranges of 300 nm. From this combined force, the JIC estimated that 250 missiles were allocated for attacks on the V-force airfields.

Penkovsky provided the West with particularly illuminating insights into debates conducted at the highest echelons of the Soviet General Staff. In particular he photographed copies of the Top Secret version of the journal *Military Thought* (Voyennaya Mysl), restricted to general officers in command and other senior posts.[104] Schecter and Deriabin argue that Penkovsky's material indicated that by 1961 the Soviets were moving toward a nuclear war fighting strategy, in the opposite direction to American thinking. Though such conclusions raise complex questions about the nature and goals of nuclear strategy in the respective countries, they illustrate the potential significance of Penkovsky's espionage. What is not clear is how this information was viewed by the British intelligence community nor its effect on intelligence assessment. British estimates were already much less alarmist than those of the American intelligence community. Whereas in the United States, in the period 1961–62, satellite photography (supplemented by electronic and human source intelligence) resulted in a radical reassessment of Soviet capabilities, British estimates exhibited greater consistency as well as greater prescience. Penkovsky's intelligence appears to have corroborated and reinforced British strategic assumptions, while providing very considerable and unprecedented information, most notably in documentary form. The 1962 JIC report on Soviet Bloc Capabilities and Intentions, for example, gave the following assessment of Soviet aims:

(a) to secure the Soviet Union and Communist bloc from external attack by the possession of a credible deterrent.

(b) To defend the Soviet Union and bloc and secure the most favourable outcome to hostilities if the deterrent fails.

Although the Russians are aiming to build up massive nuclear forces, there are no indications that they have attempted or are attempting to build up a strategic force powerful enough to destroy or neutralize the major part of the strategic strike force of the United States. There seems no reason to suppose that there will be any fundamental change in the above Soviet objectives between now and 1967.[105]

The report also contained an assessment of the Soviet nuclear capability that was placed at 1000 strikes in the megaton range with a restrike capability amounting to an additional 600 further strikes. It was also believed that the Soviets had developed a 100-megaton warhead and that 'a 1000 MT weapon could be technically possible although the development of a ballistic delivery system for it might take longer.'[106]

THE LIKELIHOOD OF WAR

Assessing Soviet objectives in war was one priority for western intelligence. So too was evaluating the likelihood of general war. Overall, the British took a more sanguine view of the threat of war, while the Americans were more sensitive to the dangers of surprise attack. By the early-1950s there was growing British concern that American actions could lead to nuclear war. Initial British planning assumed that war was possible by means of Soviet aggression or 'by a miscalculation of the extent to which she can pursue a policy of ideological and territorial expansion short of war with Democratic Powers'.[107] Post-war British strategy proceeded on the assumption that the Soviets would not want to start a war until they were in a position of strength, namely 1956/7. The explosion of the Soviet atomic bomb in the autumn of 1949 did not fundamentally change the basis of these assessments, though it was one factor in the review of British strategy in 1950. In the summer of 1950, a matter of weeks before the North Korean invasion of South Korea, the Chiefs of Staff made clear that they did 'not now regard a shooting war as inevitable or even likely', providing the western allies remained steadfast and resolute in using atomic weapons in response to Soviet aggression.[108]

The Korean War heightened international tension, and had major consequences for the western alliance and the American commitment to NATO. In the United States it led to adoption of a deeply pessimistic and controversial assessment of Soviet aims and the risk of war, NSC-68.[109] A particular concern to the British was the Pentagon's expectation of global war: a view not shared by their British counterparts. Describing the current atmosphere in Washington to his fellow Chiefs, CIGS Sir Bill Slim expressed his anxiety:

> The United States were convinced that war was inevitable, and that it was almost certain to take place within the next eighteen months; whereas we did not hold this view, and were still hopeful that war could be avoided. This attitude of the United States was dangerous because there was the possibility that they might think that since war was inevitable, the sooner we got it over the better, and we might as a result be dragged unnecessarily into World War III.[110]

British views were less alarmist, although the prospect of American adventurism was a concern. Ernest Bevin confided to the Indian Prime Minister, Pandit Nehru, that 'the United States is a young country and the Administration was too apt to take unreflecting plunges. We made it our business to restrain them.'[111] By the summer of 1951 the JIC considered that the Soviets would be 'unlikely deliberately to start a total war during the next four years'.[112] On the other hand, Allied 'counter-action and defensive preparations' meant that 'there is the chance that they may be provoked into so doing by western rearmament'.[113] The Chiefs of Staff nevertheless concluded that 'the moment of greatest danger during these years will probably be about the end of 1952'.[114] British assessments in early 1953 were similar to those of the CIA rather than the American military, though Whitehall endorsed the US Chiefs of Staff belief that 1954 would be a year of particular danger.[115]

The death of Stalin in March 1953 and the signing of the Korean armistice facilitated a period of consolidation in the Cold War. Each year the JIC prepared an assessment of the likelihood of war. The principal themes of these assessments appear to have remained constant during the 1950s: Soviet attack was unlikely providing the western allies remained resolute, and the Soviet leaders understood the likelihood of an atomic response, though the risk of war could not be discounted given the possibility of miscalculation or misperception. The Chiefs of Staff did voice concern that the Soviets might mistakenly construe defensive western actions as offensive. Fear of misperception and miscalculation rather than premeditated aggression was the guiding concern. The JIC's 1956 assessment was prepared before the British attacked Egypt and the Soviets invaded Hungary. The JIC concluded that the likelihood of global war over the next ten years was limited. Various events might increase the risk, of which the most probable was that points of international friction could escalate from localized to global war. Nonetheless the JIC remained reassuring:

> We have appreciated over the last few years that the Soviet leaders do not want war. We believe that their views will remain unchanged, certainly over the next few years and probably over the whole period of review, unless the political situation changes in some completely unexpected fashion (such as through the emergence of more aggressive Soviet leaders) and provided the West maintains its strength and cohesion and continues to act with restraint. [116]

This assessment, it should be noted, took some account of the increased Soviet capacity to attack the United States possibly with ICBMs. Although this capacity might increase the risk of global war, the JIC doubted 'whether their increased capability of itself would make them wish to go to war because we do not believe that the Soviet leaders could be certain of being able to neutralise the western counter-offensive at the first blow.'[117] This argument was central to British thinking and appeared in subsequent JIC assessments when Soviet ICBMs began to emerge.[118] Both the British and the Americans however, shared the view that Soviet ICBMs were potentially significant for the conduct of Soviet foreign policy and that 'once the Russians possess the capability of attacking America with a good prospect of success, their leaders may be more inclined to take risks'.[119] By the early-1960s (especially in the aftermath of the Cuban missile crisis) this view was to change, as is apparent from the following 1963 JIC assessment on the Likelihood of War:

> We believe that the Soviets will not deliberately initiate global war, since they would be unable in such circumstances to prevent catastrophic damage to the Soviet Union. We also believe that they are unlikely deliberately to initiate limited war because of the risks of escalation, which might quickly present them with the choice of global war or abandonment of their immediate objectives. Therefore, assuming that the Soviet leaders act rationally, we can only envisage war coming about as a result of a process of miscalculation, for instance if:
>
> (a) The Soviet Union or the West in some critical or tense situation were to make a false appreciation of what was considered by the other side as intolerable.

(b) The Soviet Union were to believe wrongly that NATO had weakened in its determination to use nuclear weapons.
(c) Either side were to fail accurately to foresee the consequences of the policies being pursued by a third party with which it was associated.[120]

The impact of Soviet ICBMs had significant political consequences both for domestic American politics and Soviet-American relations where Khrushchev sought to exploit Soviet advances. Khrushchev's foreign policy from 1958 to 1962 provoked confrontation with the West and led to the most dangerous moments of the Cold War. Yet the period also saw growing western nuclear strength, and was indeed a period when British nuclear capabilities were at their largest, both numerically, and in proportion to those of the United States and the Soviet Union.

WARNING

The threat of what Sir Ian Jacob described as 'the sword of Damocles of a Russian attack on the Pearl Harbour model'[121] became an ever-present and inevitable concern for British officials in the nuclear age, and was later understood and shared by American decision-makers, and indeed public opinion on both sides of the Atlantic. Warning of Soviet attack was inextricably linked to perceptions of, and assumptions about, Soviet strategy. Initially, the Chiefs of Staff recognised that one of the implications of 'new weapons' was that there were 'greater possibilities than before of surprise attack, since the preparations required to deliver decisive attacks with new weapons could be on a smaller scale than with conventional weapons'.[122] Nevertheless, although concerned with 'bolt from the blue' attacks, until the advent of the ballistic missile there was confidence that Soviet preparations could be detected. In the US, the body given responsibility for warning of attack was the Watch Committee of the United States Intelligence Board. Established in the early 1950s (and receiving intelligence from the CIA, the FBI, the AEC, the State Department, and the military services), the Watch Committee was directed to provide the NSC 'with the earliest possible intelligence warning of, and a continuing judgement on, Sino-Soviet Bloc intentions to engage in aggressive action by regular or irregular armed forces.'[123]

In Britain, responsibility for warning of attack was undertaken by the JIC. Each week the JIC held 'a comprehensive review of the situation around the Soviet and Satellite perimeter, with the specific object of ascertaining whether there are any indications of Soviet, or Soviet inspired, aggression.'[124] In 1956 the JIC explained that:

> We could be certain that a decision to attack had been made only if we succeeded in intercepting the decision. We have virtually no chance of doing this and we must, therefore, rely on interpreting the significance of military and other moves and preparations; in the event of surprise attack we may never obtain such information.
>
> We cannot expect to give the time of attack much in advance. At best we might get warning of the assembly or take off of enemy aircraft at or from their bases: but it is probable that the detection of those aircraft on Allied radar screens would be the only warning. At present, in the case of ballistic missiles, there would be no warning. [125]

Throughout the 1950s, the expectation of a Soviet surprise attack remained low. The Chiefs of Staff told the Prime Minister in 1952 that a Soviet surprise attack with atomic weapons was 'unlikely', and that some warning was probable of Soviet preparations, troop movements and naval deployments.[126] In September 1949 American and British officials had disagreed over the Soviet ability to launch a war 'without requiring any appreciable period of notice'.[127] The Americans believed that by 1950 the Soviets would be in a sufficiently advanced state of preparation to achieve this. The British (and Canadians)

> ... while agreeing that the possibility of armed conflict with practically no notice cannot be discounted entirely, hold the view that the Soviet leaders are unlikely to commit the Soviet Union to war until they are better prepared. It is the U.K. and Canadian view that steps to achieve this preparation will include the accumulation of at least three months supplies in the forward areas, the necessary redeployment of forces, the concentration of vehicles and the psychological preparation of their people for war. It is estimated that the period required for this preparation will be 3–4 months, during which some evidence of Soviet intentions should be received. [128]

The issue of strategic warning was thus inextricably involved with questions about Soviet strategy, and in particular whether the Soviets would launch simultaneous full-scale offensives against Western Europe and the United States. With the development of the Warsaw Pact after 1955, the extent of western knowledge of Soviet preparations for war depended on whether these preparations were made solely within the USSR or also in the 'satellites'.[129] Illustrative of the opportunity this afforded was the joint SIS-CIA operation in 1953–4 to intercept traffic on telephone landlines under East Berlin, including those of the Group of Soviet Forces Germany

(GSFG). According to one account, for the thirteen months of the operation, 'coverage of the GSFG telephone lines furnished a reasonable assurance of advance notice that GSFG was gearing up to attack'.[130]

One assumption in the early 1950s was that 'the Russians will be unlikely to launch an atomic attack without simultaneously attacking on the ground with the object of advancing rapidly into Western Europe; and therefore we are likely to get some warning of an attack'.[131] For planning purposes it was assumed that warning indicators would provide seven days' notice of attack. In the event of full Soviet redeployment and mobilization the JIC was confident that, 'we expect to be able to forecast, at least a month ahead, the date by which the USSR would achieve such a state of preparation.'[132] By 1956, however the advent of Soviet ballistic missiles had changed British thinking. The more likely scenario was now considered to be some form of surprise nuclear attack. In 1956 the JIC believed that such an attack was then possible against the UK, though the Soviets were not yet ready for an assault on the United States. Nevertheless 'a large-scale surprise attack on North America' would be possible from 1959 onwards.

Initially, it was also believed that any campaign against Western Europe would coincide with 'attacks with limited objectives against Canada and the United States, including Alaska and the Aleutians'.[133] One consequence of this was that a Soviet attack on the US mainland would not provide warning for the British. The JIC believed that 'the Soviet Union would plan the timing of the attack so that the Allied radars both in Europe and North America were penetrated simultaneously, whether the attack was by aircraft or missiles or by both.'[134]

Warning of imminent attack, or tactical warning, is explored in Chapter 8, which focuses on these radar systems. Monitoring of the deployment and launching of Soviet (and Warsaw Pact) aircraft by signals intelligence (including traffic analysis) does not appear to have proffered a sufficiently reliable indicator on which the British authorities could depend. One means of detecting preparations for an air offensive was by human intelligence sources, including 'base-watchers' (clandestine agents), who could provide real-time intelligence on Soviet deployments. An example of human intelligence is illustrated in the Suez crisis in 1956, when two British officials from the Moscow Embassy (Daphne Park, an SIS officer, and a military attaché) were dispatched on a clandestine mission to discover details of Soviet aircraft deployments.[135] When the Soviet leadership threatened Britain and France with nuclear weapons over their attack on

Egypt, the British government took a sanguine view, discounting Marshal Bulganin's words as rhetoric.[136] Whether HMG's assessment of Soviet rhetoric as bluff was informed primarily by its own intelligence sources, or based on material supplied by the CIA, is unclear.[137]

The development of Soviet ballistic missiles capable of striking the UK presented significant challenges to the intelligence community, and in particular raised fears of a nuclear first-strike. Implications for force structures and nuclear strategies were considerable, especially as the Soviets were able to deploy ballistic missiles before the provision of adequate ballistic missile early warning facilities. For the Chiefs of Staff this meant increased reliance on what they termed 'political warning'. Planning had been based on the assumption that a period of seven days warning would be provided. With the Soviet ballistic threat, this period was reduced to a period of 'a day or two'.[138]

To increase response time and counter the threat of ballistic missiles, the governments of Britain, America and Canada agreed to establish a Tripartite Alert Procedure, the details of which were discussed at the 1957 Bermuda conference.[139] The function of the procedure was described as follows:

> Arrangements have recently been agreed with the United States and Canadian Governments for the exchange of Intelligence information about Soviet intentions. As soon as the necessary communication facilities have been established evidence of any Soviet hostile intentions obtained by one Government will speedily be available to the other two. Information obtained through this Intelligence network will first be received in this country by the Joint Intelligence Committee.[140]

To facilitate these exchanges, common indicator lists and intelligence alerts were established in each country to provide a 'clearly understood basis for quick exchange of judgement should the envisaged possible need for taking joint decision [on nuclear retaliation] arise.'[141]

PENKOVSKY AND STRATEGIC WARNING

The need for warning of nuclear attack was a predominant concern for western officials, and with the advent of ballistic missiles the threat assumed considerable importance in defence planning and strategy. For the CIA and SIS, Penkovsky's espionage provided unprecedented insights into Soviet capabilities, and the prospect of both strategic and tactical warning and as well as warning of other Soviet surprises. Penkovsky was not directly involved in Soviet decision-making, and for example, was clearly unaware of the highly secret arrangements for the deployment of Soviet missiles in Cuba in 1962. He was nevertheless able to learn of secret high-level decisions, most notably Khrushchev's decision to close the frontier in Berlin in August 1961. Earlier in the summer Penkovsky warned that Khrushchev planned to sign a separate peace treaty with East Germany, which would have precipitated a crisis, and quite possibly military confrontation between East and West. The construction of the Berlin wall took western intelligence and western leaders by surprise, though Penkovsky had managed to learn of plans to build the wall four days before open construction began.[142] Various proposals had been canvassed by SIS and the CIA to provide secure methods of communication with Penkovsky,[143] but in August 1961 he was unable to forewarn his handlers because he could not contact them.

After this experience procedures were agreed to enable contact to be made with western intelligence in an emergency. In October 1961 Penkovsky was briefed on an emergency procedure, conceived by British intelligence, to enable him to provide emergency warning of a Soviet attack. According to Schecter and Deriabin:

> Penkovsky was given two phone numbers of American Embassy personnel, either of which he could ring. When a man answered the phone, Penkovsky was to blow into the mouthpiece three times. Then wait one minute and repeat the procedure. The Americans would then go to a telephone pole 35 on Kutuzovsky Prospekt and look for a freshly marked letter X on the pole. This signal meant that Penkovsky would leave a detailed message in the dead drop. If it was not possible for him to promptly service the dead drop, the phone signal would be sufficient for an immediate early warning.[144]

It was explained to Penkovsky that the signalling system, code-named DISTANT, was to be used, 'only if he had learned for a fact that the Soviet Union had decided to attack, or that the Soviets had decided to attack should the West take specific action, or that the Soviet Union had decided to attack should the West fail to undertake specific action.'[145] The British were to be informed of this warning through the CIA Station in London.[146] The warning was to be passed to the JIC whose discussion would be attended by the CIA Station Chief.

It was made clear to Penkovsky that the telephonic warning alone, whether or not the dead letter drop had been serviced, would be sufficient to 'result in prompt action at a high level in the United States and Great

Britain'.[147] Reliance on such procedure raised considerable difficulties. British officials in particular were concerned that such a system could lead to miscalculation and war. In Britain any such warning would be evaluated by the JIC, before military or political commands were informed. Maurice Oldfield, senior SIS liaison officer in Washington, explained to the head of the CIA's Soviet Division, Jack Maury, that 'a DISTANT report will not be treated by the U.K. as an indicator [of Soviet intent to attack] unless the JIC accept it as such'.[148] This approach differed to that of the US, where the CIA would pass the raw 'data' on to its 'consumers', including presumably the President, for their evaluation. Such an attitude reflected differences in the structure and function of the respective intelligence communities. The potential consequences of such procedures were considerable. This was illustrated when in November 1962 the DISTANT warning system was activated.

On 2 November two phone calls were made to the US embassy who sent a CIA officer to check the dead drop. By this time Penkovsky had been under arrest, probably since 22 October. The CIA officer was detained by the KGB. In Washington the Director of Central Intelligence, John McCone briefed the President on 3 November, and told him that Penkovsky had probably been compromised. It is not clear when the JIC was informed or what view it took of the warning, nor what Prime Minister Macmillan or his colleagues were told. Only a week earlier the United States and the Soviet Union had confronted each other over the deployment of Soviet missiles in Cuba in what was probably the most dangerous crisis of the Cold War. Although the DISTANT system was activated after Khrushchev had made clear he would withdraw the missiles, US (and British) nuclear forces were still at higher than normal states of alert, and SAC remained at the unprecedented state of Defense Condition (DEFCON) 2. The incident illustrates the grave difficulties in relying on human sources for strategic warning and the potential for dangerous miscalculation.[149]

SOVIET ESTIMATES OF WESTERN CAPABILITIES AND INTENTIONS

Soviet planning reflected in part appreciations of western intentions and capabilities. Soviet estimates were therefore important targets for western intelligence, and a factor in western appreciations. In 1949, for example, the British provided 'the most likely Soviet estimate of the US stockpile' in discussions with American planners.[150] The material from Oleg Penkovsky included details of Soviet assessments of western exercises and capabilities.[151] Aside from the intrinsic value of such intelligence, understanding how Soviet leaders were furnished with information was crucial in any operations to feed disinformation to the Soviet authorities. During the Second World War the British had excelled in strategic deception against the Germans. After 1945 the British faced great problems in running similar operations against the Soviets, not least because of Soviet espionage successes, which began to become apparent after 1949. Little evidence has emerged of British attempts at strategic deception against the USSR, though after a review by the Chiefs of Staff in 1950, the wartime deception organisation was reinvigorated and retitled as the Directorate of Forward Plans with responsibility for deception of the Soviet Union.[152]

Some evidence has emerged of thinking about deception within the Air Ministry. In 1954 the Air Defence Committee examined a proposal from a Lt.-Col S. E. Skey to develop a deception that the UK had 'under R & D some defensive weapon infallible against all forms of air attack'.[153] If the illusion of effective defence against atomic weapons could be maintained, Skey argued, the Soviets would be deterred indefinitely. As to what kind of weapons might be involved:

> The 'Eldorado' of scientific fiction has always been some form of 'Death Ray'. It is probably true that such a conception would never be scientifically possible, but nevertheless it is a popularly held belief. It is suggested that here is a weapon, for example, though perhaps an over-imaginative one, which might be built up as the keystone for our long-term deception. It would be necessary to enter wholeheartedly into research on whatever weapon should be chosen, whether with present scientific knowledge it was really imagined to be possible or not. Moreover, it would be highly desirable that those actually working on the weapon should genuinely believe in its possibility. This would make the deception more convincing, whilst the research carried out might just conceivably lead to a useful development. Such work would continue over the years. The fact that this research was going on would probably not elude the Soviet intelligence, but we could from time to time allow hints to leak.

Official response to such ideas is not clear, though the problems of deceiving the Soviets on such a scale over time presented formidable problems. Viewed in hindsight, however, Skey's suggestion makes for striking and intriguing comparisons with the Reagan administration's Strategic Defense Initiative of the 1980s.

CONCLUSION

Any analysis of British nuclear intelligence is as tentative as many of the estimates themselves at the time. Nevertheless several broad and distinct themes emerge. Perhaps the most significant is how estimates and appreciations were based on deductive and inductive reasoning rather than accurate, timely and reliable intelligence. In the period 1945-64 there was no equivalent of the *Ultra* intelligence that provided so much insight into Axis intentions and capabilities. The paucity of British (and American) intelligence sources was matched by the formidable (and in some ways unsolveable) problems of estimating intentions in the nuclear age. British appreciations of Soviet capabilities were less alarmist than their American counterparts, and notwithstanding some early underestimates of Soviet progress, more accurate. British policy-makers were better served by their intelligence community than their American counterparts. Appreciations of likely Soviet objectives in a nuclear war nevertheless suffered from fundamental problems, including the difficulties of estimating the effects of nuclear attack on the Soviet ability to wage war.[154] More problematic was that, as ministers were told, 'we cannot know what the Russians themselves think of the potentialities and effects of the allied strategic air offensive'.[155] Most problematic of all, of course, was that no one could ever know how decision-makers would respond in the circumstances of nuclear combat. As the Director of the JIB explained to the Chief of the Air Staff: '... there is scarcely any evidence as to how their leaders think or would act in given circumstances. For this reason, hypotheses are made which are repeated from year to year, like advertisements, take root. This is inevitable, but we should not forget the lack of evidence and should keep open minds'.[156]

1. For an important account of Soviet capabilities, see David Holloway, *Stalin and the Bomb: the Soviet Union and Atomic Energy, 1939–1956* (Yale University Press, 1994).
2. Sun Tzu (Ed. James Clavell), *The Art of War* (Hodder and Stoughton, 1981), p. 90.
3. DEFE 13/44, Annex to DC(55)46, 28 October 1955.
4. An interesting exception was made with the declassification of decrypts from the British–American VENONA operation, against Soviet communications, also declassified by the NSA.
5. AIR 2/15001, Manual of Strategic Bomber Operations, Strategic Reconnaissance Element, May 1958.
6. For details, see Aldrich, 'British' and Paul Lashmar, *Spy Flights of the Cold War* (Sutton Publishing Ltd, 1996).
7. Robert S. Hopkins III, 'An Expanded Understanding of Eisenhower, American Policy and Overflights', *Intelligence and National Security*, Vol.11, No.2 (April 1996).

8. In a minute to Prime Minister Eden in February 1956, the Foreign Secretary, Selwyn Lloyd, alluded to Operation Plato and the use of British crews and aircraft in penetration overflights. Lloyd to Eden, 24 February 1956, PM/56/36, AIR 19/826.
9. Curtis Peebles, *The Moby Dick Project: Reconnaisance Balloons Over Russia* (Smithsonian Institution Press, 1991), p. 120.
10. Lashmar, *Spy*, pp. 61–75.
11. Hopkins, 'Expanded', p. 341n.
12. Lasmar, *Spy*, pp. 147–57; Nick Cook, 'How the CIA and RAF teamed up to spy on the Soviet Union', *Jane's Defence Weekly*, 7 August 1993.
13. Peebles, *Moby*, p. 121; see also Donald Welzenbach, 'The Anglo–American Origins of Overflying the Soviet Union: The Case of the "Invisible Aircraft" ' in Miller, *Seeing*, p. 200 and Lashmar, *Spy*, pp. 76–83.
14. Interview with SAC Historical Office Personnel, cited in Wainstein, *Evolution*, p. 150.
15. AIR 2/15001, UK Strategic Reconnaisance Force, January 1958.
16. Ibid
17. Ibid. The existing and envisaged photo–reconnaissance aircraft were the Canberra PR 3, PR 7, and PR 9, the Valiant B/PR1 and the Victor 1 & 2. AIR 2/15001, The Strength and Composition of the Strategic Reconnaissance Force, 9 September 1960.
18. Lloyd to Eden, 24 February1956.
19. AIR 19/826, CAS to Secretary of State for Air, 12 December 1956.
20. PREM 11/1763, Macmillan to Eisenhower, 22 March 1957. Documents relating to Aquatone can be found in AIR 19/826. For Macmillan's view of the programme, see Horne, *Macmillan*, p. 226. The declassified version of the CIA's official history of the U-2 programme provides no details of British involvement, Gregory W. Pedlow and Donald E. Welzenbach, *The CIA and the U-2 program, 1954–1974* (Washington: Central Intelligence Agency, 1998).
21. AIR 20/11370, Draft VCAS to Sir Patrick Dean, undated, circa March 1962.
22. AIR 20/11370, Amery to Prime Minister, 12 April 1962.
23. RG 59, Memorandum for the President, Proposed Service to Service Agreement, 741.56311/10–2160. National Archives.
24. RG 59, Memorandum for the President, Agreed Minute, 741.56311/10–2160. National Archives.
25. AIR 20/11370, Roberts, PS/S of S, to PS/VCAS, 19 April 1962.
26. AIR 20/11370, Roberts to de Zulueta, 20 September 1962.
27. AIR 20/11370, Thorneycroft to Secretary of State for Air, 19 September 1962,
28. AIR 20/11370, Air Ministry Note: U–2 Operations From the United Kingdom, 13 September 1962.
29. AIR 20/11370, Roberts to de Zulueta, 20 September 1962. This mission was referred to the Prime Minister and the Foreign Secretary for specific approval.
30. Col. O.H.Rigley, Directorate of USAF Intelligence, (Secret) Exchange of ECM Information between US and UK 1948, National Security Archive, *The US Intelligence Community 1947–1989* (Washington: Chadwyck–Healey), Doc: 2–19622. We are grateful to Richard Aldrich for drawing our attention to this document.
31. AIR 8/1852, Brief by ACAS(P) for CAS, 2 November 1953.
32. RG 218, JIC 265/177,'Military Policy Regarding the Integration of British and Canadian Officers in U.S. Military Intellligence Activities and Attendance at Military Intelligence Schools', 8 February 1954, National Archives.
33. Ibid
34. Cooper, 'Direction', p. 16.
35. AIR 8/2201, COS(57)224, 16 October 1957.
36. See David Martin, *Wilderness of Mirrors* (New York: Harper & Row, 1980) and Tom Mangold, *Cold Warrior, James Jesus Angleton: The CIA's Master Spy Hunter* (Simon & Schuster, 1991).
37. Hinsley, *British Intelligence*, Vol.1, p. 199n.
38. Aldrich and Coleman, 'Cold War', p. 539.

39. Lawrence Freedman, *US Intelligence and the Soviet Strategic Threat* (Macmillan, 1986), p. 68; see also Operation Dragon Return – Brief for Chief, STIB/7003/8033, 4 December 1950, DEFE 41/91 in Aldrich, *Espionage*, pp. 73–5.
40. Freedman, ibid; Jones, *Reflections*, pp. 24–5.
41. CAB 161/14, Terms of Reference and Composition of the Sub–Committee on Defectors, authority JIC(54)20.
42. For details, see Jerrold Schecter and Peter Deriabin, *The Spy Who Saved the World* (Charles Scribner's Sons, 1992).
43. For discussion of British attitudes, see Margaret Gowing, *Independence*, Vol.I, pp. 67–8, 220–1; for analysis of US estimates, see Charles A. Ziegler, 'Intelligence Assessments of Soviet Atomic Capability, 1945–49: Myths, Monopolies and Maskirovka', *Intelligence and National Security*, Vol.12 No.4 (October 1997).
44. This was prepared by a committee chaired by the Cabinet Secretary, Sir Edward Bridges, for the Cabinet Committee GEN 75, Gowing, ibid., p. 72.
45. DO(47)44, May 1947, reproduced in Lewis, *Changing*, p. 375.
46. JIC(48)9(O), Russian Interests, Intentions and Capabilities, 23 July 1948, quoted in Aldrich and Coleman, 'Cold War'.
47. The Agreed American British Canadian Intelligence (ABCI) conference met in Washington, in September, ahead of American, British and Canadian planning staffs. The intelligence officials were tasked to provide agreed intelligence assessments of the USSR. Some of the papers for these meetings were released to the US National Archive.
48. RG 218, Appendix to Memo by Scientific Committee, Development of New Weapons, ABCI 9/1, 14 September 1949.
49. DEFE 32/1, Confidential Annex to COS(50)26th, 13 February 1950.
50. Gowing, *Independence*, Vol.I, p. 221. For discussion of the impact of Soviet espionage on the Soviet project see Holloway, *Stalin*, passim; see also David Holloway, 'Soviet Nuclear History, Sources for Stalin and the Bomb', *Cold War International History Project Bulletin*. (Washington: Woodrow Wilson International Center for Scholars, Fall 1994), Issue 4.
51. Clark and Wheeler, *British*, pp. 131–2, 136–7.
52. Peebles, *Moby*, p. 196.
53. Cathcart, *Test*, p. 108.
54. It appears that in contrast to the atomic test, the British were able to detect the Soviet hydrogen bomb independently of the United States. Jones, *Reflections*, p. 23.
55. For discussion of the MUSIC programme, and British unhappiness at US commitment to the enterprise, see Baylis, *Ambiguity*, pp. 163–4.
56. DEFE 13/60, Brundrett to Minister, Atomic Energy Intelligence Discussion with the US, 17 January 1955.
57. DEFE 13/60, Macmillan to Prime Minister, November 1954.
58. Ibid.
59. Jones, *Reflections*, pp. 17–18.
60. RG 340, Records of Special Interest No. 1 (England) 1943–1953 [hereafter RSI(E)], Report to the Commanding General Third Air Division, Strategic Air Command Forces in the United Kingdom, February 1951. National Archives.
61. DEFE 13/352, Strong to PS/MOD, 19 May 1952.
62. DEFE 13/352, Churchill to Alexander, 12 May 1952.
63. Strong to PS/MOD.
64. RG 218,CCS 373 (10–23–48), Section 8, JIC 526/42, Estimates of Soviet Stocks and Expenditure of Atomic Weapons and Guided Missiles in a War Beginning in mid–1954, 3 November 1952. National Archives.
65. DEFE 13/342, K.W.D.Strong, The Soviet Atomic Energy Programme, Note for MOD, 25 January 1961. In 1961 the CIA estimated cumulative Soviet plutonium production as 8.4 tons as against

the JIB's 8.5 tons up till end–1960, while U–235 production was put at 52 tons compared with the British estimate of 50.4 tons to end–1960.
66. Ibid.
67. The British calculated that, as of 1 January 1961 the Soviet stockpile could be: 600 warheads of half to 8 MT, with 3,400 of 1 to 100 KT or 1,000 warheads of half to 8 MT with 2,600 of 1 to 100 KT, or 1,800 warheads of half to 8 MT with 750 1 to 100 KT. The US estimate gave 500 'high yield' weapons with 2,800 'medium' and 'low yield' or 1,000 'high yield' weapons with 1,900 'medium' and 'low yield'. The principal significance of high–yield versus low–yield weapons, was that given the likely degree of accuracy high–yield ballistic missile warheads were necessary for targets in the United States, while low–yield warheads were sufficient for those in Europe, ibid.
68. Ibid.
69. AIR 20/11370, JIC(61)36(Final), 5 September 1961, referred to in ACAS(I) to VCAS, 17 April 1962.
70. Ibid.
71. See Special National Intelligence Estimate 13–4–64, 'The Chances of an Imminent Communist Chinese Nuclear Explosion', 26 August 1964, in Kevin C. Ruffner (Ed.), *CORONA: America's First Satellite Program* (Washington: CIA, 1995), pp. 237– 45 and PREM 11/5197, Record of a conversation between the Prime Minister and the head of the Central Intelligence Agency, Mr J.J. McCone, at 10 Downing Street, at 3–30pm on Monday September 21, 1964, in Aldrich, *Espionage,* pp. 107–8.
72. RG 218, ABCI 14/12, Strategic Air Operations, Appendix A to Memo by the Air Committee, ABCI 14/12, 26 September 1949. National Archives.
73. For discussion of estimates of Soviet capabilities see Lawrence Freedman, *US Intelligence and the Soviet Strategic Threat* (Macmillan, 1986) Chapter 4; Fred Kaplan, *The Wizards of Armageddon* (Stanford University Press, 1983) Chapters 10 and 19; John Prados, *The Soviet Estimate,* (Princeton University Press, 1986); Walter Laqueur, *The Use and Limits of Intelligence* (Transaction, 1993), Chapter 5; see also Scott Koch (Ed.), *CIA Cold War Records: Selected Estimates on the Soviet Union 1950–1959* (Washington: CIA Center for the Study of Intelligence, 1993), Donald P. Steury (Ed.), *Intentions and Capabilities: Estimates on Soviet Strategic Forces, 1950–1983* (Washington: CIA, 1996) and Ruffner, CORONA.
74. DEFE 4/103, discussion of JIC(57)120(Final), The Effect on Soviet Policy of the Attainment by the USSR of Nuclear Sufficiency.
75. JIC(49)9(Final), Scale and Nature of Initial Air Attack on the United Kingdom – 1949/50, 1 February 1949, PSI(E), National Archives.
76. AIR 20/10060, Annex to AC(57)35, 14 May 1957.
77. 'Warning time' was the time taken for the missiles to arrive in the UK from the position at which they had broken the radar screens, DEFE 13/342, Henderson to PS/MOD, JIC/1713/60, 21 October 1960. This assumed that human intelligence sources were unable to provide warning of imminent attack.
78. JIC 526/42, Estimates of Soviet Stocks.
79. DEFE 13/414, Brundrett to MOD, Annex to DC(55)46, 28 October 1955.
80. NIE 11–6–54, 5 October 1954, cited in Wainstein, *Evolution,* p. 256n.
81. Brundrett to MOD.
82. Ibid.
83. Ibid.
84. CAB 134/1315, Likelihood of Global War and Warning of Attack, JIC(56)21(Final), 1 May 1956, appendix B to Norman Brook, The Future of the United Kingdom in World Affairs, PR(56)3, 1 June 1956.
85. The Effect on Soviet Policy of the Attainment by the USSR of Nuclear Sufficiency.
86. DEFE 7/698, comments of a British official at Tripartite Conference on Defence Against Ballistic Missiles, 18–20 January 1956, DBM/M(56)1, 8 February 1956.

87. Ibid.
88. For discussion see Freedman, *US Intelligence*, pp. 74–7; Kaplan, *Wizards*, pp. 162–73; Schecter & Deriabin, *Spy*, pp. 273–82.
89. DEFE 13/342, CIA Memorandum, Comments on Various Military Factors Affecting Soviet Capabilities and Intentions over the Next Five Years, Annex to JIC/2291/57, 22 October 1957.
90. DEFE 13/342, Atkinson to Sir Patrick Dean, 31 October 1957.
91. DEFE 13/342, JIC(58)4(Final), Soviet Strategy in Global War up to the end of 1963, Note for Marshal of the RAF, Sir William Dickson, 6 February 1958.
92. AIR 8/1953, Some Major Differences in Estimates Between JIB and the Air Ministry, Appendix A to Note by the Chief of the Air Staff, Missile Intelligence: Air Ministry Comments on the Templer Report, (undated) 1961. We are grateful to Richard Aldrich for drawing our attention to this document.
93. Note by CAS, ibid. The CDS, Lord Mountbatten, supported the Templer committee's proposals. AIR 8/1953, Missile Intelligence: Memorandum by the Chief of the Defence Staff, 15 March 1961.
94. Note by CAS.
95. See views of Richard Helms in Schecter and Deriabin, *Spy*, pp. 334–5; for an assessment see Scott, *Macmillan*, pp. 120–30, 177.
96. Schecter and Deriabin, *Spy*, p. 239
97. Ibid., p. 232
98. For details of US estimates, see Ruffner, *Corona*; for discussion of Penkovsky see Scott, *Macmillan*, pp. 120–30.
99. DEFE 4/70, COS(54)53rd, discussion of JIC(54)47, 10 May 1954.
100. DEFE 4/75, COS(55)4th, discussion of JIC(55)12(Revise), 19 January 1955.
101. AIR 20/10060, Annex to AC(57)35, 14 May 1957.
102. JIC(57)7, ibid.
103. AIR 20/11448, V Bomber Dispersal, extract from JIC(62)4(Final), 11 September 1962.
104. Schecter and Deriabin, *Spy*, pp. 83, 190–1, 247, 377. The Top Secret version of the journal was then unknown.
105. DEFE 4/151, JP(62)110(Final), extract from JIC(62)81(Final), 17 January 1963.
106. Ibid, extract from JIC(MT)(62)5(Second Revised Draft).
107. DO(47)44, para. 8
108. DO(50)45, 7 June 1950, Defence Policy and Global Strategy 1950 [CAB 131/9] reproduced in H.J. Yasame and K.A.Hamilton, *Documents on British Policy Overseas*, Series II, Vol.IV, Korea, June 1950–April 1951 (HMSO, 1991), Appendix A, p. 417.
109. For differing views of NSC-68, see John Lewis Gaddis, 'NSC 68 and the Problem of Ends and Means', *International Security*, Vol.4, No.4, 1979–80 and Beatrice Heuser, 'NSC 68 and the Soviet Threat: a new perspective on western threat perception and policy making', *Review of International Studies*, Vol.17, No.1, January 1991.
110. DEFE 4/38, COS(50)206th, 14 December 1950.
111. Alex Danchev, *Oliver Franks: Founding Father* (OUP, 1993), p. 129.
112. DO(51)64, 7 June 1951, reproduced in Yasame & Hamilton, *Documents*, Appendix II, p. 433.
113. Ibid
114. Ibid
115. DEFE 13/352, Brief by N.C.D. Brownjohn (Cabinet Office) for MOD, Likelihood of General War with the Soviet Union up to the end of 1955, D(53)3, 10 February 1953.
116. CAB 134/1315, JIC(56)21, 1 May 1956.
117. Ibid.
118. See, for example, DEFE 7/970, The Likelihood of Attack on the British Isles in Each Year Between Now and 1965, extract from JIC(57)30. We are grateful to Richard Aldrich for drawing our attention to this document. For similar CIA views, see CIA Memorandum, Annex to JIC/2291/75.

119. Ibid
120. DEFE 4/151, Appendix A to Annex to JP(62)110(Final), Soviet Bloc Capabilities and Intentions, extract from JIC(62)77(Draft), 17 January 1963.
121. DEFE 32/2 Background note to minute COS 1137/19/6/52, arising from COS(52)90th. We are grateful to Richard Aldrich for drawing our attention to this document.
122. DO(47)44, para. 22.
123. RG 273, NSC 116, Channels for Transmission of Warning of Attack, 23 August 1951; NSAM No. 226, Directive Relating to Transmittal of Information to the Watch Committee of the United States Intelligence Board, Director of Central Intelligence Directive No 1/5, Terms of Reference, Watch Committee of USIB, 27 February 1963. National Archives.
124. DEFE 13/352, Alexander to Churchill, 1 August 1952, According to R.V. Jones the meetings, held on Thursday mornings, were known as the 'Perimeter Review'. Jones, *Reflections*, p. 26.
125. JIC(56)21.
126. DEFE 32/2 Confidential Annex to COS(S)(52)7th, 18 June 1952. According to the service chiefs 'the real tell–tale would be the movement of their naval forces'. We are grateful to Richard Aldrich for drawing our attention to this document.
127. RG 218, ABCI 7/4, Draft summary of Soviet Intentions and Capabilities – 1950, 23 September 1949. National Archives.
128. Ibid.
129. JIC(56)21.
130. Joseph C. Evans, 'Berlin Tunnel Intelligence: A Bumbling KGB', *International Journal of Intelligence and CounterIntelligence*, Vol.9 No1, (Spring 1996), p. 45.
131. DEFE 13/352, Brownjohn to MOD, Soviet strength in western Europe, 10 February 1954
132. JIC (56) 21.
133 RG 218, ABCI 7/4, 23 September 1949. National Archives.
134. Henderson to PS/MOD. See also Chapter 8.
135. Baroness Daphne Park, interview with Prof. Peter Hennessy, *What Has Become of Us?* (Wide Vision Production for Channel Four TV, 1994)
136. Navias, *Nuclear,* p. 190.
137. The Air Ministry 'was assured by military intelligence that Soviet Rockets could not reach Britain since the Soviets did not have launch sites in East Germany or Poland.' W. Scott Lucas, *Divided we Stand: Britain, the US and the Suez Crisis* (Hodder & Stoughton, 1991), p. 290. For reports of the US role, see Tom Bower, *The Perfect English Spy—Sir Dick White and the Secret War 1935–90* (Mandarin, 1996) p. 200.
138. DEFE 13/342, Record of Meeting between MOD and COS, 23 November 1960. Despite advances in Soviet rocketry, HMG still believed surprise attack unlikely. In assessing the procedures to launch nuclear retaliation, Lord Mountbattan was informed that 'we are not organised to cope with a 'bolt from the blue' attack. This is perhaps in accord with our belief that there will be no such thing'. DEFE 25/49, Nuclear Retaliation Procedures, 13 March 1961.
139. PREM 11/1763, Macmillan to Eisenhower, 22 March 1957.
140. RG 59, Launching of Nuclear Reprisal, Aide Memoire, 14 May 1958, Policy Planning Staff Records, 1957–61, Lot 67D548, Box 130, Great Britain, National Archives.
141. RG 59, Launching of Nuclear Retaliation, 2 June 1958, Policy Planning Staff Records, 1957–61, Lot 67D548, Box 130, Great Britain, National Archives.
142. Schecter and Deriabin, *Spy,* p. 226.
143. Ibid, pp. 192–3.
144. Ibid, p. 262.
145. Ibid, p. 263.
146. Ibid, p. 285.
147. Ibid, pp. 262–3.
148. Oldfield to Maury, 27 October 1961, quoted in ibid, p. 285.

149. For discussion of the incident and its escalation potential see Sagan, *Limits*, pp. 146–50; for details of the episode, see Schecter and Deriabin, *Spy*, pp. 337–49.
150. RG 218, Appendix to JIC531/7/D, 21 August 1950. National Archives.
151. See for example Col-Gen. S. Ivanov, 'Some Conclusions on the NATO Armed Forces—Exercise SIDE STEP', and Maj.-Gen. P.Vysotskiy, 'American Military Technical Means of Combat in Space'; CIA Popular Document Collection web–site at http://www.foia.ucia.gov/frame2.htm
152. Aldrich, *Espionage*, pp. 229–30.
153. DEFE 8/48, Lt-Col S.E. Skey, Defence by Deception, AD(WP2)(54)17, 13 July 1954, discussed at WP(2)(54)9th.
154. DEFE 13/352, Brownjohn to MOD, 26 June 1953.
155. Ibid. This ignored the potential role of human intelligence, though it seems clear there were no such sources within the Soviet state at this time
156. Strong to Dickson.

CHAPTER 8

Tactical Early Warning Intelligence 1945–64

'At this height they might harpoon us, but they wouldn't spot us on no radar screen' (Major King Kong, commander of B-52 *Leper Colony, en route* to attacking Soviet ICBM base at Laputa).

The credibility of nuclear deterrence depends on the ability to mount a retaliatory attack under all conditions. Assured retaliation can be provided by survivable systems, such as a submarine-based force. Otherwise, early warning of enemy attack is crucial to deterrence. In the absence of strategic intelligence indicators (discussed in Chapter 7) tactical early warning intelligence is the only method of confirming the nature and scale of attack. Tactical early warning also determines response time. The greater the range of the system, the greater the difficulty in successfully mounting a disarming first strike. Early warning is only one aspect of tactical intelligence: an additional element is provision of information on the post-attack environment. This chapter discusses both these requirements but focuses primarily on the development of British early warning and air defence systems.

Modern air defence systems comprise three elements: tactical early warning (radar), intelligence assessment (command centres), and active air defence (fighters and missile systems). The interaction between these is discussed with analysis centred on the development of radar and the assessment of intelligence. The chapter is organised into five sections. The first considers the wartime development of radar and its influence on air defence. The second examines the consequence of the atomic bomb and considers Britain's decision, taken in 1950, to begin construction of the Rotor early warning network. The development of the H-bomb and the problem of achieving a fully effective air defence system are also discussed with attention focused on the Air Ministry's '1958 Plan' and the Plan Ahead programme. The introduction of the ballistic missile is then examined: a development that resulted in a marked contraction of active air defence measures; the adoption of the Linesman/Mediator programme (a joint civil-military project for the control of British airspace); and Britain's participation in the NATO Air Defence Ground Environment (NADGE). Britain's involvement with the US is also examined, in particular, the Ballistic Missile Early Warning System (BMEWS) and the Missile Defence Alarm System (MIDAS).

AIR DEFENCE AND EARLY WARNING

The effectiveness of air defence relies primarily on the capability of long-range sensors. Without early warning, interception of attack is severely limited. Indeed, in the absence of early warning, the only alternative is to maintain a standing patrol, a procedure both unreliable and expensive. Efforts to increase the range of detection beyond the limit of human observation began at the start of World War I. The aim was to detect German Zeppelins approaching the British coast. Large concrete sound mirrors were constructed on cliff tops to focus and amplify the sound of a Zeppelin's engine.[1] Despite its short range and poor discrimination, the sound mirrors provided a crude form of early warning. In 1935, the potential of early warning was dramatically increased. Results from the government's Radio Research Station at Slough demonstrated that short wave radio pulses could be reflected from an aircraft and displayed on a cathode ray tube. Initially known as Radio Direction Finding (RDF), the discovery marked the birth of radar.[2]

The military application of radar was readily appreciated. In 1935, the government ordered the construction of twenty 'chain home' (CH) radar stations capable of detecting enemy aircraft at ranges of up to forty miles at heights above 3,000 ft.[3] The result was the creation of a defensive belt stretching from the River Tees to the Solent. Introduction of radar required central co-ordination and resulted in the creation of RAF Fighter Command in July 1936.[4] In addition to supplying early warning to the fighter squadrons, Fighter Command was also responsible for relaying air raid warnings to the civil authorities. In this role, Fighter Command was assisted by the Royal Observer Corps (ROC), a wholly civilian organisation administered by the Air Ministry through ROC Headquarters.[5] Details of enemy attack were passed by direct telephone line to three trunk exchanges at London, Liverpool and Glasgow. On receipt of positive radar warning, a preliminary 'yellow' caution notice (giving ten minutes warning) was issued, followed by a 'red' action notice, timed at least five minutes before the enemy's arrival. In response to the Munich crisis, resources were increased and by June 1939, the GPO reported that the network was complete and available for use.[6]

Original British assumptions regarding German strategy had concluded that the most probable scenario would be a 'knock out blow' aimed at densely populated areas and vital links in the country's system of supply and distribution. Events in Poland, however, did not support this view: initial German attacks would most likely be directed against the RAF and its associated airfields. This conclusion was reinforced by events in Norway and Holland. The Air Staff was nevertheless confident that the RAF would escape swift annihilation on the ground, as it was protected by 'an unrivalled early-warning system and a well planned system of dispersal'.[7] After the fall of France, the British Chiefs of Staff concluded that if Germany wished to mount a successful seaborne invasion of the UK she must first destroy Fighter Command.

The expected German attack to gain air superiority began in August 1940, with concentrated attacks on a wide range of airfields, aerodromes and radars. Moreover, as the radar system was centralized, damage caused to the sector stations threatened to disrupt the entire fighter control system. Provision of alternate operations rooms and the ability of the GPO War Group to repair and re-route damaged communication lines was sufficient to permit continued operation. Despite initial German successes, it was soon realized that air superiority of the level required to sustain an amphibious invasion could not be achieved and Operation Sealion was indefinitely postponed. Several reasons have been put forward to explain this outcome, foremost amongst them (and of relevance to later developments) was that the German Air Force had no operational experience of engaging an enemy equipped with a comprehensive early warning network and a centralized command and communications system.[8]

POST WAR DEVELOPMENTS AND THE ATOMIC BOMB

The wartime application of radar was a major success. After 1945, the Tizard Committee (tasked to report on scientific advances during the war) concluded that 'radio location has had more effect in this war than any other scientific development.'[9] The research and development required to improve the system, however, was expected to be a lengthy process. In the immediate post-war period, defence had to compete with social reconstruction and economic revival for scarce resources. Consequently, heavy reliance was placed on retention of existing wartime equipment.

At the beginning of 1946, Fighter Command was composed of three groups: 11 Group with headquarters at Uxbridge, 12 Group located at Watnall and 13 Group at Inverness. These groups were further subdivided into eleven sectors with each group and sector headquarters possessing an operations room for receipt of early warning and the control of fighter aircraft. The Fighter Command Operations Room at Bentley Priory was responsible for overall co-ordination of the system but exercised no direct control of interceptions.[10] The advent of the atomic bomb presented severe difficulties for the Air Defence of the United Kingdom (ADUK). The prevailing strategy based on attrition of enemy bombers was no longer valid. Penetration of Britain's air defences by only a few bombers armed with nuclear weapons would be catastrophic. In 1946, the JPS concluded that a limited number of atomic bombs accurately delivered would decisively affect Britain's war-making potential.[11] However, using existing techniques, it was impossible to guarantee the destruction of all enemy bombers.

Accordingly, the Chiefs of Staff approved an interim programme to provide air defence cover for those areas of the UK considered most vulnerable to aerial attack.[12] The improvement programme aimed to use wartime equipment for existing defence needs whilst developing a more advanced system capable of defending Britain against high performance bombers carrying the atomic bomb. To provide the necessary air cover, all resources were concentrated into a Main Defended Area covering the coastline between Portland Bill and Flamborough Head. The strategy required only 36 operational radars with a further 158 stations placed on a care and maintenance basis.[13]

Throughout the late-1940s, the priority given to air defence was minimal. The lack of emphasis was based on the belief that the present system 'would not be required to operate in a defence role during this time'.[14] Although the Soviet blockade of Berlin in July 1948 significantly increased the defence budget, no provision was made for improvements to the early warning system. This situation soon changed. In August 1949, the Soviets successfully conducted a nuclear test. In response, Fighter Command was issued with a new directive that stated unequivocally that the Command's primary objective was defence of the UK against aerial attack.[15]

In 1949, two major studies on air defence were presented to the Chiefs of Staff. The first, by the Sub-Committee for Air, Coast and Seaward Defences (ACSD), examined the forces that could be deployed by the UK in an emergency. The second, conducted by the Air Defence Committee, was concerned with Britain's longer-term requirements.[16] Both reports offered a gloomy assessment. The position was summarized by the ACSD:

> Present intelligence information indicates that it is reasonable to assume some prior warning of outbreak of war. If, however, air attacks commence without any warning our defences will be virtually impotent. We cannot over emphasise the seriousness of this eventuality... Even if we have a period of warning, the forces available for air defence of the United Kingdom will not be adequate either in quantity or quality, to provide an effective defence, nor shall we be able to sustain these forces.[17]

The Air Defence Committee reached similar conclusions, but suggested a different solution. Although it was recognised that a large increase in conventional forces in tandem with the development of guided weapons would enhance the effectiveness of air defence, 'neither of these measures will on present knowledge be adequate in the face of heavy and sustained atomic attack to prevent grave danger to this country, except at a cost which is outside our resources. It is for this reason that we lay primary importance on the offensive.' [18]

By 1950, Britain's air defences had deteriorated to such an extent that precautions against sudden air attack were directed solely towards protection of the USAF bombers stationed in the UK.[19] No forces were available for the protection of the Main Defended Area. To defend the USAF bases, the early warning system was continually manned from half-an-hour before dawn until half-an-hour after dusk. Fighters were also placed on fifteen minutes alert with orders to intercept any unidentified aircraft approaching the coast. To provide warning of attack, Soviet 'wireless frequencies' were constantly monitored.[20] It is now evident that British views on early warning were at variance with those of the USAF. A particular disagreement centred on expectation of a Soviet surprise attack:

> The RAF and USAF views on the subject of intelligence warning are quite different: While the USAF people in the UK hold that a Soviet attack is quite possible with very little warning, the Air Ministry believes that an advance intelligence warning of an impending Soviet attack will be obtained far enough in advance to enable the preparations of the British defenses to be completed.

The British further insist that it is unrealistic as well as impractical to set up and maintain an adequate defense against a surprise attack.[21]

The inadequacy of Britain's air defences was drawn to the attention of the Cabinet by Sir Henry Tizard, chairman of the Defence Research Policy Committee. Tizard argued that the strategic nuclear offensive should be left to the Americans. He further contended that the priority given to British atomic weapons was diverting resources from the vital needs of air defence.[22] This view was endorsed by the Minister of Defence who insisted that the paramount strategic objective was now the defence of Britain against atomic attack.[23]

THE ROTOR PROGRAMME

In response to these concerns, the Defence Committee agreed to modernize and extend Britain's early warning system. To emphasize the importance now placed on air defence, the programme was granted priority status over all other areas of defence work with the exception of atomic energy and guided missiles.[24] The programme (known as 'Operation Rotor') was divided into four development phases with overall completion scheduled for December 1953.[25] The demands placed on the Rotor programme were formidable. To improve the effectiveness of air defence a comprehensive re-evaluation of the entire system was required. Specific measures included: a substantial increase in the reliability of the radar equipment; an expansion in overall cover by duplication of stations; a reduction in vulnerability including construction of underground facilities; and an improvement in response time requiring provision of additional watches and trained personnel.[26]

A major feature of the Rotor programme was the division of the UK into six separate air defence sectors. Although overall control of air defence was still exercised by the Air Defence Commander (situated at Bentley Priory) operational control of the air battle within each sector was now delegated to the Sector Commander located within the Sector Operations Centre (SOC). The SOCs were constructed underground and located at Barton Quarry, Longley Lane, Shipton, Box, Bawburgh and Kelvedon Hatch.[27] In addition to the six SOCs, Rotor also required the integration of intelligence data from four distinct types of radar system. The four systems were:

Chain Home (CH): reporting stations utilizing wartime equipment.

Chain Home Extra Low (CHEL): designed to provide cover against low flying aircraft and surface vessels.

Centrimetric Early Warning (CEW): an improved version of CHEL designed to detect low and medium/high level aircraft and incorporating an auxiliary control function.

Ground Control Interception (GCI): the most technologically advanced system, consisting of a combination of different radars types to provided full control facilities as well as auxiliary reporting cover.

When completed, Rotor was designed to provide full-scale cover from Portland Bill to the Moray Firth. Air defence for the rest of the UK remained limited. In the West and South West of England cover was limited to medium and high altitudes, while in the north of Scotland only reporting cover was provided. In total, the Rotor programme comprised 28 modified CH stations, 38 new stations and 6 SOCs, with the majority of the new stations located underground.[28] Given the complexity of the system, reliable communications were vital. In the period 1950-52, almost the whole of the GPO's cabling work was devoted to the provision of landline communications for Rotor. Moreover, no additional trunk cables were laid which did not contribute to meeting the Rotor requirement. In addition, over 1,200 public circuits were temporarily withdrawn to meet the extra demand imposed by the Rotor programme. Security was also a concern, MI5 complaining that it was unable to vet all the personnel who had access to the network.[29]

THE HYDROGEN BOMB AND AIR DEFENCE

In January 1953 the Chiefs of Staff submitted a comprehensive review of Britain's air defences to the Defence Committee. This was based on two overriding criteria. First, global war appeared less imminent. Second, military preparations should be directed to ensure survival in the initial intense phase. Central to the analysis was the belief that the Soviets would possess 150 large atomic bombs by 1954.[30] In considering the implications, the Defence Committee concluded that the attrition theory of defence was no longer valid and that 'no known form of defence can prevent a really determined, suitably equipped enemy from dropping a proportion of his atomic bombs on this country.'[31] Two possible solutions were advanced: reliance on air defence or nuclear retaliation at source. Initially, the Chiefs of Staff sought to combine both approaches: the primary goal of British strategy would be to maintain and develop a nuclear strike force as a deterrent to attack with higher priority being given to the early warning system manned on a 24-hour basis. Specifically, the exigency of nuclear war mandated the creation of forces in being. This position was accepted by the Chiefs of Staff, who cautioned that, 'the danger of atomic attack necessitates a much higher state of readiness than in the past. It would be suicidal to follow our former practice of marshalling our defences as the attack develops.'[32]

The broad outline for the phased improvement of Britain's air defence system was established as follows:

Stage I: to be completed by 1954, incorporating the build-up of the Plan K fighter force to a maximum of 220 A.W. fighters and 644 S.R. fighters, the completion of Rotor I and the retention of 142 Anti-Aircraft regiments.

Stage IA: to be completed by 1958, incorporating the Plan K fighter force at its maximum strength of 264 A.W. fighters and 644 S.R. fighters, the introduction of air-to-air guided weapons, the development of the C&R system in line with Rotor II and III and the phased withdrawal of Anti-Aircraft units.

Stage II: to be completed after 1958, incorporating ground-to-air guided missiles and provision for a form of defence against ballistic missiles.[33]

Responsibility for the programme was given to the Air Defence Committee. Composed mainly of technical personnel, the committee foresaw the inherent difficulty of establishing a fully effective air defence system, later acknowledged in the 1957 Defence White Paper. A particular concern was the H-bomb and the realization that anything short of a fully effective air defence system meant complete annihilation. Moreover, based on present techniques, the development of an impregnable defensive barrier was impossible. To ensure against a nuclear attack required a complementary strategy: an unstoppable nuclear threat, ready for instant retaliation in conjunction with a defensive screen and guaranteed early warning.[34]

A major problem in developing an effective early warning system was the reduction of response time brought about by the speed of the modern jet bomber. The total time available from initial detection of an enemy bomber to its destruction 20–50 miles from the coast was estimated at seven minutes. To intercept such a target, re-organisation of the command structure was essential. Moreover, such reorganization 'would require a radical change of thought regarding the chain of control and responsibility.'[35] The task of examining the various alternatives was given to Sir Arnold Hall, the Director of the Royal Aeronautical Establishment. The Hall Report recommended the following:

(i) Effective early warning at all altitudes from sea level to 70,000 ft.
(ii) Interception of enemy bombers at a minimum distance of between 20–50 miles from the coast.
(iii) High resistance to ECM and a handling capacity to process information from an enemy force of 250 bombers.
(iv) A capability for expansion and improvement to counter any increase in the quality or quantity of threat.
(v) An ability to counter ballistic missiles.[36]

As shown above, the proposed development schedule for improvement of the air defence system was divided into three distinct phases (Stage I, IA and II). The Hall Report intended to improve Britain's air defences by proceeding directly to Stage II. The proposal had the advantage that scarce R&D resources would not be required for interim Stage IA projects. A disadvantage was that Stage II defence was not expected to be completed until 1965. A decision between these two alternatives was therefore heavily dependent on the strategic intentions of the Soviet Union.[37]

A major factor in the outcome was the Soviet development of thermo-nuclear weapons. In December 1954, assessing the consequences for air defence, the Chiefs of Staff concluded: first, the close defence of vulnerable points was no longer credible. Second, a future war would not last long enough for an enemy to reach the channel. Third, the aim of air defence must be to destroy the high-speed high-altitude bomber carrying the hydrogen bomb before it reached the British coast.[38] The Chiefs also recommended that the primary role of Fighter Command should be protection of Bomber Command from surprise attack—air defence was now perceived as an integrated component of the deterrent.

THE 1958 PLAN

Within this new framework, the Air Ministry was no longer required to guarantee the complete protection of the UK from air attack.[39] The resources allocated to ADUK were therefore reduced. The ROC was reorganized and the Rotor system considerably revised.[40] By early 1955, Britain's air defence system consisted of seven radar stations in the Eastern sector that were manned from half-an-hour before dawn to half-an-hour after sunset. In addition, four fighter aircraft were at fifteen minutes readiness with predelegated authority to open fire under certain conditions.[41] To improve this state of readiness, Fighter Command initiated a comprehensive review of Britain's air defence system. In April 1955, the review (known as the 1958 Plan) was submitted to the Air Ministry. Its major conclusion was that to counter the threat posed by Soviet high-performance bombers, a radical change in the overall design of the system was now essential. The report recommended a fully integrated early warning system—a radical departure from the previously accepted principles governing air defence.

Since the origins of radar, the division of responsibility between early warning and the interception of enemy forces had been vested in two separate and self-contained organisations. As a result of the Fighter Command proposals, this division was abolished. The new organisation was based solely on nine Type 80 radar stations that combined both warning and control functions linked directly to designated fighter stations. A major advantage of the reorganization was consolidation of the communication and information system that increased response time and allowed direct control of both fighters and missile defences.[42]

Despite the self-contained nature of the new radar stations, centralized control was still maintained through the Air Defence Operations Centre (ADOC) at Bentley Priory. The function of the ADOC was an essential element of Britain's nuclear deterrent: it formed the nexus between receipt of tactical intelligence and initiation of nuclear war. On receipt of enemy attack (i.e. positive radar evidence) the C-in-C Fighter Command, stationed at Bentley Priory, was to immediately inform both the Air Ministry Operations Centre and C-in-C Bomber Command.[43] For those concerned with implementation of Bomber Command's Alert and Readiness Plan, this procedure proved unsatisfactory. The position in late-1956 was described as follows:

> The present Early Warning System is organised to alert only Fighter Command. No link-up exists between the E.W. system and HQ Bomber Command and no detailed arrangements have been made to alert the Medium Bomber Force on the receipt of information showing the intention of a hostile act against the United Kingdom or any other NATO country. In order for the M.B.F to take

off for the counter-offensive before it is destroyed on the ground it is essential that information of any impending raid be passed as soon as possible to HQ Bomber Command so that the M.B.F. may be alerted.[44]

Increased emphasis was placed on direct defence of the V-bomber airfields. This became a priority when it was revealed that with the early warning system then available, only one third of the V-force would become airborne in the event of a Soviet surprise attack.[45] To improve response time, C-in-C Bomber Command sought authority for both High Wycombe and Bentley Priory to receive intelligence 'indicators' of Soviet attack directly from the originating source. The purpose of the request was threefold: to speed up transmission of information by removing the need to first 'filter' the intelligence; to guard against misinterpretation by providing a separate system of evaluation; and to provide operational Commanders with information on which to initiate alerts on their own authority.[46] Although the Air Ministry considered the proposal 'quite valid', the request was denied on the following grounds:

(a) Evaluation must take place at the Air Ministry or JIC as immediate consultation may be required between UK and US intelligence agencies.

(b) To triplicate intelligence evaluation staffs by giving Fighter Command and Bomber Commands the same facilities as the Air Ministry will neither safeguard against errors nor make for quick decisions.[47]

To protect the V-bomber airfields against surprise attack, the Air Ministry argued that a minimum of 450 fighters was essential. In contrast, Duncan Sandys, the Minister of Defence, viewed air defence as a continued drain on resources and demanded substantial reductions in Fighter Command's front line strength. The Air Ministry resisted these demands. They argued that the proposed reductions would so weaken the defensive screen that the Soviets 'could launch attacks on our deterrent bases with a good prospect of success'.[48] The claim was dismissed by Sandys who stressed the remaining force would be adequate for the defence of the V-bomber bases. This would be especially the case if the force was dispersed prior to the initial attack and provided adequate communications were available with the dispersal sites to issue the launch order.[49] Sandys' long-term objective was abolition of the manned fighter and its replacement with surface-to-air guided weapons—a view totally rejected by the RAF.[50]

The future direction of government policy was formally announced in the 1957 Defence White Paper:

> Since peace so largely depends upon the deterrent fear of nuclear retaliation, it is essential that a would-be aggressor should not be allowed to think he could readily knock out the bomber bases in Britain before their aircraft could take off from them. The defence of the bomber airfields is therefore an essential part of the deterrent and is a feasible task. A manned fighter force, smaller than at present but adequate for this limited purpose, will be maintained and will progressively be equipped with air-to-air guided missiles. Fighter aircraft will in due course be replaced by a ground-to-air guided missile system.[51]

Unfortunately for Sandys, introduction of a fully developed missile system was not expected until 1962. A defence gap would therefore exist between the run down of the manned fighter and the introduction of guided missiles. This was accepted by Sandys, as he believed that the Soviets would not contemplate war until they possessed a sufficient ICBM capability to attack the US mainland, which he did not expect until 1962.[52]

PLAN AHEAD

Although air defence was now directed to the defence of the deterrent, agreed policy was still based on the Air Ministry's 1958 Plan which relied on nine high powered Type 80 radar stations to provide air cover for the whole of the UK. Implementation of the 1958 Plan, however, was never realized. In late 1957, Soviet advances in ECM made the Type 80 radar stations susceptible to jamming. In response, the Air Ministry suspended the 1958 Plan and eventually concluded that implementation was untenable.[53] For many, it was becoming evident that whatever system was established for ADUK, the primary threat would soon come from ballistic missiles against which a fighter force would provide no defence. This view was championed by Sandys, who argued that fighters provided only marginal security for the deterrent and that real defence lay in dispersal and increased readiness. Behind the strategic logic lurked Sandys' real concern with economies:

> ... some major economy in defence expenditure is essential and the possibility of reducing the fighter defence of the deterrent bases may have to be re-examined. Whatever may be decided about fighter defence cannot affect the need for an efficient radar chain. This is a vital element of our nuclear deterrent and is essential to the safety of the bomber force.[54]

To provide ADUK with immunity to jamming required development of a completely new system. This entailed deployment of a new high-power multi-frequency Type 85 radar called Blue Yeomen and the incorporation of passive detection techniques.[55] The Air Ministry concluded that installation of five Blue Yeoman stations would provide complete coverage of the UK. The use of passive detection techniques, however, was heavily dependent on computers, which were too expensive to install at every location. A centralized control station was therefore essential. Although a single station was capable of controlling the entire ADUK, the initial proposal recommended two stations to guard against communications failure or possible destruction. In January 1959, the Air Council approved the proposal in principle, with development begun under the codename Plan Ahead.[56]

Despite Air Council approval for Plan Ahead, formal agreement was necessary from the Treasury. On close examination, it was discovered that full implementation of the programme would cost almost twice the initial Air Ministry estimate.[57] Due to escalating costs, the ADUK requirements were re-examined once again. The new Chief of the Air Staff, Sir Thomas Pike, was bluntly informed of the position now facing the Air Ministry:

> The problem is briefly this: how can you justify an expenditure on air defence of some £900M over the next five years when the end products in terms of Plan Ahead and SAGW defences does not begin to materialise until 1964 at the earliest; and when Intelligence estimate that the Russians will be capable of attacking all our offensive bases - above and underground—with an adequate number of missiles by 1962 (UK alone) and by 1964/65 (UK and US together).[58]

The increased threat posed by ballistic missiles proved difficult to counter. Intelligence estimates suggested that by 1965, the majority of bombers would be withdrawn from the Soviet order of battle. Consequently, as the need to realize savings in the defence budget was paramount (and the Air Ministry was unable to advance a convincing alternative) the early warning system was reduced to the minimum necessary to give advanced warning of enemy attack.

The revised system comprised three Type 85 radars located at Neatishead, Staxton Wold and Bramcote and a single Main Control Centre (MCC) at Bawburgh. To supplement the system, radar coverage to the North was provided by retention of two Type 80 stations at Saxa Vord and Buchan. Although overall control of ADUK was still exercised by the Air Defence

Commander operating from the ADOC at Bentley Priory, tactical control of the entire air defences was delegated to the Air Battle Commander situated at the MCC. Procedures were also implemented to enable the ADOC to exercise control via individual radar stations in the event of communications being disrupted.[59] In advocating the procedure, the Air Ministry recognised that 'the traditional system of delegation to Group Commanders of the operational control of their own forces will no longer apply.'[60]

In response, the Chiefs of Staff initiated a comprehensive review of future policy. The JPS produced a report, 'A Strategic Review of Air Defence' in May 1960. The conclusions were emphatic and governed air defence policy for the next decade: the role of ADUK was to guarantee deterrence and not provide an air defence system as part of a war fighting capability. The JPS concluded that, 'If the deterrent to global war failed, no air defence system could save the United Kingdom from devastation, certainly not by ballistic missiles. No expenditure can therefore be justified on the creation of air defences... simply for fighting a global war.'[61]

In September 1960, the revised proposals for ADUK were brought before the Defence Committee. In the ensuing debate, the Prime Minister, Harold Macmillan, voiced his concern over the cost of the project and doubted whether such a system would be required by the late-1960s. The new Minister of Defence, Harold Watkinson, defended the programme and emphasized the potential threat posed by Soviet jamming. He contended that if Plan Ahead was not fully developed, the only response to jamming would be to constantly order the bomber force into the air whenever an unidentified plane was observed approaching British air space. This would be essential, as in the event of Soviet jamming, HMG would be unable to determine whether an attack was underway or the level of forces involved. This view was supported by CAS who stressed that in the absence of adequate warning, the bomber force could be 'exhausted and caught on the ground by false alarms and feint attacks.' Implementation of Plan Ahead was regarded as essential. Without the system, Soviet aircraft would be able to jam the proposed BMEWS station at Fylingdales from a position 300 miles off the British coast.[62] At Macmillan's insistence, no immediate decision was taken. In further discussions with Watkinson, a reduction in the overall cost of the programme was agreed.[63]

To fully assess the future requirements for ADUK, Macmillan sought the advice of Sir Solly Zuckerman, Chief Scientific Adviser at MOD.

Zuckerman recommended that some form of control and reporting system was essential. Otherwise, Britain would be abdicating sovereignty over its air space and allowing reconnaissance aircraft to operate over the UK with complete immunity. He further suggested that substantial long-term savings would be achieved if the military and civil requirements for air control were combined into a single system.[64] In December 1960, a JPS study of a combined civil-military system was presented to the Defence Committee, which agreed that future policy for air defence should be limited to four requirements:

(a) Providing warning of attack to enable the government to decide upon the appropriate political or military reaction.
(b) Preventing unrestricted access to the air space of the UK.
(c) Countering the possible threat to BMEWS by hostile aircraft equipped with modern jamming devices.
(d) Contributing effectively to the air defence of NATO under the integrated air defence scheme approved by the Cabinet in 1958.[65]

As a result, Britain's air defences were reduced to twelve missile units deployed at six specified missile sites and twelve front-line fighter squadrons, four of which were to be deployed overseas. To assess the practicalities of adopting a dual system, the Defence Committee invited the Controller of the National Air Traffic Control Service, Sir Lawrence Sinclair, to examine the consequences of an integrated programme. To distinguish between the two elements of the project, the military system was given the name Linesman, whilst the civil programme was called Mediator.

THE LINESMAN/MEDIATOR PROGRAMME

In May 1961, the Sinclair Assessment Group completed its study on the development of a joint military-civil control system and presented their findings to the Air Ministry and Ministry of Aviation.[66] The report concluded that the proposed system was both practical and necessary; would yield significant technical and operational advantages; and result in substantial savings. The main features of the integrated system were:

(a) Three high power defence radars on the East coast to provide air traffic control on the upper air space and to supplement the civil radar cover at lower levels. Radar coverage to the North to be provided by the early warning radar at Saxa Vord in the Shetlands.

(b) Seven medium power civil radars primarily concerned with air traffic control but capable of providing additional radar cover in the lower airspace.

(c) Two additional high looking radars on the West coast to complete the high level cover over the whole of the United Kingdom.[67]

The report also recommended establishment of a single centralized control facility. A suitable location was West Drayton, near Heathrow. Significantly, the proposal envisaged construction of a single unprotected building housing both the civilian Air Traffic Control Centre and military Main Control Centre. As the building was both unprotected and did not allow the RAF undivided control of air defence, the idea was rejected. Agreement was only reached after the RAF was assured that two of the defence radars would be provided with autonomous control facilities in the event of failure in the centralized system.[68] In October 1962, the Defence Committee approved the development of a joint military-civil programme with the proviso that the projected cost of the programme remained under close scrutiny by the Treasury.[69]

Despite some initial success, however, the Linesman/Mediator programme proved only partially effective. Faced with rising costs, lack of protection and limited coverage, and the difficulty of integrating three generations of computer and data derived from a variety of different radars, the control part of the system was never fully implemented. In 1968, following NATO's adoption of Flexible Response (MC 14/3), Linesman was significantly decentralized and integrated into NADGE (the NATO Air Defence Ground Environment).[70]

NATO AIR DEFENCE GROUND ENVIRONMENT

The deployment of tactical nuclear weapons in Europe led to a reappraisal of both early warning and air defence requirements within the NATO area. The strategy of threatening immediate nuclear response was largely dependent on obtaining sufficient warning of enemy attack. The development of an efficient early warning system under control of SACEUR was therefore essential for the credibility of NATO strategy. In 1953, development of a NATO Early Warning Chain was proposed by SACEUR General Gruenther. To improve NATO's early warning capability, Gruenther further recommended creation of three separate air defence regions: a Northern Region comprising Norway and the Scandinavian approaches; a Southern

Region, including Turkey and Greece; and a Central Region, covering West Germany, Holland, Belgium and Eastern France. Although minor modifications were proposed for both the Northern and Southern Regions, the main substance of the programme was confined to the Central Region into which a new generation of radar station was introduced. All radars in the three regions were to be linked via the recently developed VHF troposcatter communications system.[71]

Despite the improvement of NATO's early warning system, responsibility for air defence remained under the control of each member government—a position that was soon to change. In April 1958, at the NATO Defence Ministers Meeting in Paris, SACEUR (General Norstad) proposed that under conditions of both peace and war, he should assume operational command of the air defence forces of all NATO countries in Europe.[72] After reconciling certain ambiguities, the British government agreed to support the plan in principle. Agreement was reached after HMG obtained assurances that Britain retained the right to decide the role of Fighter Command (including its size, composition and deployment) and the ability to redeploy air defence units assigned to NATO in defence of vital British interests overseas.

In August 1961, with specifications for NADGE now complete, Norstad sought full authorisation for implementation. The proposal was forwarded to the Military Committee, with subsequent approval granted by the NATO Council of Ministers in March 1962.[73] To provide early warning, the territory comprising ACE was divided into a series of early warning regions each reporting directly to a designated evaluation centre. The intelligence collated at the evaluation centres was then transmitted via a digital link to the SHAPE Operations Centre (SHOC). To increase the capability of ADUK, information from SHOC was also passed directly to ADOC. In addition, six continental radar sites were linked directly to the UK MCC at West Drayton.[74]

THE UK WARNING AND MONITORING ORGANISATION

To ensure a credible second-strike capability, the government required immediate confirmation that a nuclear weapon had exploded over British territory. To determine an appropriate response, information was also required on the probable Soviet target set and anticipated scale of destruction. Rapid receipt of positive confirmation was imperative: once the bomber force had been launched under positive control, transmission of the executive order was essential before the communications system was destroyed. The body responsible for supplying HMG with tactical intelligence of enemy attack was the United Kingdom Warning and Monitoring Organisation (UKWMO). Formed in the late-1950s, UKWMO was responsible for supplying information on impending attack and the location of nuclear detonations.[75]

To undertake this task, the ROC was reorganized and became an integrated but autonomous element within the UKWMO. In September 1960, the revised functions of the ROC were described in a new operational directive issued by the C-in-C Fighter Command, Sir Hector McGregor. The priorities were:

(a) Reporting of nuclear bursts.
(b) Low level aircraft recognition and reporting.
(c) Reporting of radioactive fall-out.[76]

To provide a nationwide reporting system, 29 protected group headquarters and over 1,500 field stations were located throughout the UK. The majority of these posts were constructed underground and designed to operate throughout the initial stages of nuclear attack. The primary purpose of the system was to provide HMG with a rapid and reliable means of obtaining positive evidence of nuclear attack. A nuclear explosion was considered to have occurred when atmospheric overpressure exceeded 0.3 lb./sq. inch. When positive confirmation was obtained, the ROC post issued a designated codeword and location directly to group headquarters. This information was then immediately relayed to the ADOC. Finally, using a conference facility, ADOC would simultaneously inform both BCOC and AMOC in Whitehall.[77] In optimum conditions, the time taken from detonation to receipt at ADOC was estimated at less than thirty seconds.

To ensure against possible disruption of communications, the landline network was supplemented by the addition of a radio relay system. This entailed installation of VHF equipment at all group headquarters and at one post in every ROC cluster known as the master post. In the mid-1960s, the communications system was further improved by introduction of teleprinter facilities in preference to the less reliable telephone lines.[78] However, as the UKWMO was largely a civilian organisation, doubts were expressed as to its reliability under conditions of nuclear attack. To strengthen the network, the Home Office agreed to automate the system by the introduction of bomb alarm monitors.

The proposal relied on bhangmeters, previously used in UK atomic tests and which were no longer required by the Ministry of Aviation.[79] The instruments were installed at all SOCs and sited to cover London and various other targets. Initial plans for the installation of the bhangmeters were based on the existing landline network. However, it soon became apparent that landlines could be disrupted before information was relayed to the ADOC. The Home Office therefore conceded that 'if the bhangmeter is to be used for deterrent purposes it would be essential to replace the line communications with wireless links'.[80] Before planning could proceed further, the system became entangled with the requirement for a NATO Bomb Alarm System (discussed in Chapter 6). In general, the reporting of nuclear blasts was considered to be of secondary importance to the primary concern of assuring retaliation. The requirement was placed in doubt by the introduction of ballistic missiles.

BALLISTIC MISSILE EARLY WARNING SYSTEM

Conceived in the mid-1950s, BMEWS was designed to provide the US authorities with fifteen minutes warning of a Soviet missile attack. The system comprised three long-range ground based radar stations located in Alaska (Clear), Greenland (Thule) and Britain (Fylingdales). The US viewed the development of BMEWS as both critical to the survival of the bomber force and to provide sufficient warning time for the NCA to formulate an appropriate response. BMEWS also enabled SAC to argue for retention of a large bomber force: tactical warning allowed bombers to be launched under positive control, conferring a flexibility not available in the case of land-based missiles.

In January 1958, the Pentagon formally approved the BMEWS programme. Through airforce channels, HMG was aware that the USAF was interested in locating a missile detection facility in north-east Scotland.[81] The government considered that joint participation in the project would serve British interests and approval was granted for the USAF to explore potential sites. For Britain, the benefits of the system were considerably enhanced if the station was located further south. The preferred location was Lincolnshire/East Anglia, to provide warning for the V-force and Thor missile squadrons.[82] The US agreed that a site in the south of England would be acceptable, provided a suitable location was provided. However, as the land required was estimated to cover an area of over two square miles, finding a site proved difficult. Fylingdales Moor in Yorkshire was eventually selected. Although a compromise, one advantage was that the land was a government-owned National Park and currently in use as a War Office training area. In November 1958, Britain received technical details of the BMEWS system and was formally invited to participate in the programme.[83]

In January 1959, Sandys informed the US Deputy Secretary of Defense, Donald Quarles, that subject to technical and financial considerations, Britain was willing in principle to participate in BMEWS. The Cabinet gave approval for British participation in November, though it was emphasized that, 'as the project was primarily in the interests of the United States', Britain's financial contribution should reflect this position.[84] Details of the project were later issued in a joint memorandum.[85]

Construction work began in early-1960 and consisted of three, high power, pencil beam search radars with an effective range of 3,000 nm. Two of the radars were used in a scanning role with the third acting as a tracking station to determine the impact area. The three radars were housed in separate radomes connected by a shielded passage. The information from Fylingdales was coupled to the North American Air Defense (NORAD) System by a digital data system. To improve reliability, the data was transmitted on GPO circuits via two separate transatlantic cables. The primary circuit was routed directly to the US with a secondary circuit passing through SHAPE HQ.[86]

In its national capacity, Fylingdales was linked directly to both ADOC and AMOC. To use the information supplied by BMEWS, a programme known as Legate was undertaken to develop equipment capable of handling data from US radars and computer systems. Initial plans for BMEWS envisaged sending information directly to both SAC and Bomber Command. This proposal however met resistance from USAF HQ who were anxious to establish a unified command and control system. Consequently, in the US alert procedures, warning information was only supplied to SAC via NORAD.[87] In the case of Britain, the procedure was modified. Due to the decrease in warning time, it was vital that no delay was encountered in alerting the bomber force:

> It is essential that information drawn from the BMEWS system be displayed in the Bomber Command Operations Centre in the same time scale as the Air Ministry Operations Centre or Air Defence Operations Centre. This informa-

tion must not be delayed in any way or filtered or 're-told' through other organisations.[88]

Prior to completion of the Fylingdales site, Britain relied on the Jodrell Bank radio telescope as an interim measure for detection of M/IRBMs. Preliminary investigations with the Director, Professor Bernard Lovell, revealed that within an hour, the telescope could be realigned to detect missiles at a maximum range of 1,000 nm. As a result of these investigations (and with the consent of Professor Lovell) it was agreed that 'in times of strategic alert the telescope would be pointed at an area of known IRBM launching sites.'[89] Due to the limitations of Jodrell Bank, however, there was no guarantee that the system could discriminate between missiles and atmospheric phenomena or identify an attack with absolute certainty. Consequently, the warning provided by the system was not to be acted on in isolation but would provide 'a valuable contribution to the general appreciation of the situation.'[90]

In January 1964, the Fylingdales BMEWS station was declared fully operational. The British Legate programme, however, which provided dedicated warning information to the British authorities was only completed in September. Initially it was anticipated that Fylingdales would provide some twelve minutes warning of a Soviet ballistic missile attack on the UK.[91] Subsequently, estimates of warning time ranged from a worst case analysis of four minutes to a maximum of twenty minutes. These differences represented the various launch scenarios put forward by the JIC. In the former case, this consisted of a Soviet missile attack (possibly using SLBMs) directed solely against the UK with the missiles penetrating the BMEWS screen at a low angle of trajectory. The latter scenario (and considered the most likely) consisted of a co-ordinated Soviet missile attack directed against both Britain and North America.[92]

When operational, Fylingdales generated three different alarm states: Alarm State 1 (three high confidence predictions of missile attack); Alarm State 2 (two highly probable predictions); and Alarm State 3 (one highly probable prediction). The reaction of Bomber Command to these various Alert States was planned as follows:

(a) On receipt of an Alarm Level 3 the Duty Controller at BCOC will bring the QRA forces to cockpit readiness. He will also inform the C-in-C and SASO, if they are available, and the Duty Group Captain operations who is available, throughout his tour of duty, at 15 minutes standby.

(b) Assuming that the C-in-C or SASO cannot be contacted or that they have not been able to reach the BCOC by the time that the Alarm Level changes to either 2 or 1, the Duty Group Captain will scramble the force under positive control.[93]

In adopting these procedures, worry was expressed by the Air Staff that in certain circumstances, such as a false alarm, instructions to scramble the force could be authorized by a Group Captain without reference to higher authority. A particular concern was that 'in an operational scramble on a false alarm, the QRA force would be carrying nuclear weapons [and] Ministers had not in fact authorised the carriage of nuclear weapons by Bomber Command over the UK in peacetime, though no public statement had been made to this effect.'[94] It was feared that if ministers became aware of this, 'they would almost certainly wish to restrict scramble to Alarm Level 1 except perhaps in time of acute political tension.' In the view of C-in-C Bomber Command, such a restriction would mean the effective end of QRA—a development that would be 'profoundly unfortunate'. To guard against this, it was decided that ministers should not be informed of these problems and that given suitable two-way radio equipment, arrangements could be made for an officer of at least Air Vice-Marshal rank to be available for immediate consultation at all times. Moreover, 'the Command Directive already authorised the C-in-C to scramble the force if he thought it under grave and imminent threat, and it did not debar him from delegating this authority.'

MISSILE DEFENSE ALARM SYSTEM

To supplement information supplied by BMEWS, the US was also developing a non-terrestrial Missile Defense Alarm System (MIDAS). The system consisted of eight satellites in polar orbit that continuously monitoring the USSR. Intelligence was supplied by infra-red receivers mounted on each satellite. MIDAS was designed to monitor the boost phase of ballistic missiles and provide tactical warning of attack. The first MIDAS satellite was successfully launched on 24 May 1960.[95] To receive signals from the satellites, two ground stations were required. The first station was already established in Alaska, with Britain the preferred location for the second. To establish a suitable location, informal discussions were initiated with the Air Staff. The provisional site was RAF Kirkbride near Carlisle. In return for the use of the site, together with a small contribution to running costs, the US was prepared to offer the intelligence supplied by MIDAS to the British authorities.[96]

In June 1961, the Defence Committee considered the relative merits of British participation. The Secretary of State for Air, Julian Amery, considered British involvement essential:

> It is in our own interest, as well as that of our allies, to have the best possible warning of missile attack. The additional warning which MIDAS is expected to provide of an attack by MRBMs will be of particular importance in enabling our own bomber force to fly clear of any pre-emptive strike on their bases. For a relatively modest investment we shall enjoy the fruits of an American investment of about £350M.[97]

The Defence Committee approved the scheme and a draft agreement specifying both financial and technical responsibilities was agreed.[98] Announcing the decision to Parliament, Amery argued that involvement in MIDAS would increase Britain's level of early warning by 'a considerable margin over and above that which we would get from Fylingdales alone.'[99] In May and July 1963, two successful tests of the MIDAS system were conducted. These were followed by three further launches in 1966, two of which produced successful results. Development contracts for MIDAS (now renamed Program 461) were eventually issued in the late-1960s and resulted in the deployment of the DSP satellite system, first launched in 1970.[100]

CONCLUSION

Within government, the decision to develop the atomic bomb and a modern bomber force rested on a secure and enduring consensus. The debate over air defence, however, was never fully resolved and characterized by ambivalence, indecision and delay. A significant reason for this uncertainty was a perception of air defence based largely on its role during the Second World War. As a result of this orthodoxy, air defence was viewed as a single entity. The three components (early warning, assessment and interception) were usually considered together and their relative priorities often reflected this position. By the late-1950s, the indivisible structure of air defence was brought into question. A dominant feature of the debate was the impact of the hydrogen bomb and the ballistic missile on home defence. As an effective ABM system was expected to cost billions and absolute invulnerability could not be guaranteed, development on a national basis was considered untenable. Britain therefore sought co-operation with America and became involved in both the BMEWS and MIDAS systems.

Despite realization that active air defence was no longer effective, the RAF was reluctant to disband Fighter Command. The resultant debate was often acrimonious and for the Air Ministry 'absorbed more time and effort than any other question'.[101] In contrast to the controversy surrounding the future of the manned fighter, the provision of early warning was still a major requirement. Without such a capability, Britain's strategic deterrent could be destroyed on the ground. To reconcile conflicting demands, the concept of air defence was redefined and replaced with the more attainable goal of an effective early warning system for the defence of the deterrent. This resulted in a system comprising only three main radar stations and a centralized command structure. In the course of the 1950s, air defence had been transformed. Its purpose was no longer to defend the civil population against aerial attack but to defend the deterrent and provide sufficient warning to enable HMG to launch a retaliatory nuclear strike. By the 1960s, the full implications of this policy became apparent and the active defence of the deterrent was effectively abandoned.

1. Robert Jackson, 'Air Defence against the Zeppelin, 1915–1917', in Sandy Hunter (Ed.), *Defending Northern Skies, 1915–1995* (RAF Historical Society, 1996).
2. Robert Watson-Watt, *The Pulse of Radar: The Autobiography of Sir Richard Watson-Watt* (New York: Dial Press, 1959). See also, Alexander Rose, 'Radar and Air Defence in the 1930s', Twentieth Century British History, vol. 9, no. 2, 1988, pp. 219–45.
3. Jack Gough, *Watching the Skies: A History of Ground Radar for the Defence of the United Kingdom by the Royal Air Force from 1946 to 1975* (MOD Air Historical Branch, HMSO, 1993), pp. 2–24.
4. Basil Collier, *The Defence of the United Kingdom* (HMSO, 1957), p. 33; Richard Overy, *The Air War 1939–1945* (Macmillan, 1988), p. 15.
5. For further details, see Henry Buckton, *Forewarned is Forearmed: An Official Tribute and History of the Royal Observer Corps* (Ashford, Buchan & Enright, 1993) and Wood, *Attack*.
6. T. H. O'Brien, *Civil Defence* (HMSO, 1955), p. 225.
7. Collier, *Defence*, pp. 73–9, 120. For analysis of British command and control during the Battle of Britain, see Stares, *Command*, pp. 32–8.
8. Overy, *Air*, p. 16.
9. CAB 80/94, COS(45)402(O), Future Development in Weapons and Methods of War, 16 June 1945. The report was compiled without access to information on the atomic energy programme.
10. Gough, *Watching*, p. 32.
11. CAB 84/85, JP(46)201(Final), 28 November 1946.

12. AIR 20/3420, COS(45)430(O), Air Defence of Great Britain During the Ten Years Following the Defeat of Germany, 7 July 1945.
13. CAB 131/7, DRP(48)168(Final), 15 December 1948.
14. AIR 2/7671, CAS to AOC-in-C Fighter Command, 18 September 1947.
15. Gough, *Watching*, p. 48.
16. The COS established the Air Defence Committee in 1948 as a combined scientific and military body to examine and make recommendations for the command, control and general organization of Britain's air defences. The committee absorbed many of the functions of the Air Defence of Great Britain Committee, a sub-committee of the War Cabinet, which was abolished in September 1948.
17. AIR 20/9118, COS(49)96, 21 March 1949.
18. AIR 20/9118, AD(49)19(Final), October 1949.
19. AIR 8/1465, ACAS(Ops) to S6, 4 December 1950.
20. Ibid.
21. RG 340, PSI(E), Report to the Commanding General Third Air Division, Strategic Air Command Forces in the United Kingdom, February 1951. National Archives.
22. For more details, see Gowing, *Independence*, Vol.I, pp. 232–4.
23. CAB 131/9, DO(50)52, 5 July 1950.
24. PREM 11/72, Memorandum to Minister of Defence, 10 December 1951.
25. In addition to ROTOR, a development programme known as VAST was undertaken to provide mobile radar equipment for overseas deployment.
26. AIR 2/5921, Operation Rotor, June 1950.
27. PREM 11/72, Control and Reporting System, Report by the Inter–Departmental Working Party, December 1951.
28. Ibid.
29. AIR 20/10070, ACAS(P) to CAS, 7 April 1953.
30. CAB 131/13, D(53)5, 29 January 1953.
31. Ibid.
32. AIR 20/9768, AD(54)2(Final), 23 January 1954.
33. DEFE 8/48, AD(WP2)(54)16, 14 July 1954.
34. For discussion of the H–bomb and air defence, see Clark and Wheeler, *British*, pp. 216–18; Baylis, *Ambiguity*, pp. 189, 418–22.
35. AD(WP2)(54)16.
36. DEFE 5/60, AD(55)12(Final), 4 August 1955.
37. The report recommended that if war was likely before 1965, research should not be solely aimed at attaining a Stage II defence and full deployment of presently conceived systems would be necessary. However, if the Soviets were unlikely to precipitate war until they had a fully developed MRBM and long–range bomber force (i.e. about 1965) then a Stage II air defence was preferable.
38. Gough, *Watching*, p. 152.
39. DEFE 8/51, AD(55)11, 29 July 1955.
40. The original Rotor programme had been completed in 1953 and upgraded in July 1954, when permanent links were established with continental early warning systems. Further improvements to the system were also envisaged. These included the addition of the Type 80 radar (known as Green Garlic) and extension of radar coverage to the west of the UK. Respectively, these two development schedules were known as the Rotor 2 and Rotor 3 improvement programmes.
41. Gough, *Watching*, p. 153.
42. AIR 6/99, AC(56)53, 15 April 1956.
43. These procedures are detailed in the Murphy–Dean Agreement. See Appendix 4.
44. AIR 20/10277, Medium Bomber Force, Readiness During a period of Tension, 28 September 1956.
45. DEFE 5/69, COS(56)262, 10 July 1956.

TACTICAL EARLY WARNING INTELLIGENCE 1945-64

46. AIR 20/10277, BC/TS80347, 19 November 1957.
47. AIR 20/10277, ACAS(I), to SASO, 12 December 1957.
48. DEFE 5/69, COS(56)262, 10 July 1956.
49. AIR 19/855, Melville to Chilver, 2 November 1956.
50. Navias, *Nuclear*, p. 175.
51. *Defence*, Cmnd 124, para. 17.
52. AIR 19/856, Sandys to Ward, 12 March 1957.
53. The development of the carcinetron valve in the mid–1950s dramatically improved the capability of airborne jamming. The carcinetron was a French invention that consisted of a large magnetron. Unlike previous magnetrons, however, it was not fixed to a single frequency but was able to transmit high–energy pulses (white noise) throughout the entire frequency spectrum. This enabled it to jam ground radars whatever their operational frequency. Whether the Soviets had such a device was unknown, but as the scientific principles were published in the *Proceedings of the Institute of Electrical Engineers*, it was assumed the Soviets were equally aware of its potential. For details, see Gough, *Watching*, pp. 156–61.
54. CAB 131/20, D(58)61, 14 November 1958.
55. Passive detection relied on two radar stations to triangulate the position of the jamming aircraft and enable fighters to intercept and destroy it.
56. AIR 6/120, AC(59)1, 8 January 1959.
57. The initial Air Ministry estimate significantly underestimated the cost of the data handling computers and did not include any provision for the work undertaken by the GPO.
58. VCAS to Sir Thomas Pike, 28 August 1959, cited in James, *Defence*, p. 146.
59. Air Ministry Signals Plan No. 59/59. Plan Ahead, cited in Gough, *Watching*, Appendix H.
60. AIR 16/1249, FC/TS.79/Plans, 9 March 1959.
61. DEFE 6/62, JP(60)31(Final), 10 May 1960.
62. CAB 131/24, D(60)42, 13 September 1960.
63. To reduce overall costs, work on Blue Joker was abandoned. This project was initiated in the mid–1950s and consisted of a balloon–supported radar system capable of detecting low flying bombers. For details, see Gough, *Watching*, pp. 165–7.
64. PREM 11/3703, D(60)56, 6 December 1960.
65. CAB 131/24, D(60)12th, 7 December 1960.
66. The Ministry of Aviation, created in October 1959, brought together under one Minister responsibility for civil aviation and the supply of civil and military aircraft. The Ministry was also given responsibility for the supply of guided weapons, ballistic missiles, radar equipment, defence electronics and nuclear weapons.
67. CAB 131/27, Integration of air defence and air traffic control radar plans for the United Kingdom, Note by the Ministry of Aviation and Air Ministry, October 1961.
68. Gough, *Watching*, p. 248.
69. CAB 131/27, D(62)45, 4 October 1962.
70. Derek Wood, 'UKADGE: Britain's stronger home defence', *Interavia*, Vol.10 (1981), p. 1020.
71. Gough, *Watching*, p. 231.
72. PREM 11/4160, Sandys to Macmillan, 3 April 1958. For further details of troposcatter communication systems within NATO, see Chapter 6.
73. DEFE 4/148, COS(62)21st, 2 April 1962.
74. In the NADGE plan, air defence sites were designated into two distinct categories; Reporting Points (RP), which possessed only radar; and Control and Reporting Centres (CRC), which exercised a control function. Originally, 37 sites were to be available by mid–1973. The location of the six CRCs linked to UKAD were Reitan (Norway), Maakeroy (Norway), Vedaek (Denmark), Nieuw Milligen (Holland), Glous (Belgium), and Doullens (France). For a diagram of the UK early warning network, see Appendix 8.

75. On 15 June 1955, the Home Secretary announced in Parliament that the ROC in conjunction with the Air Raid Warning Organisation would be responsible for monitoring fall out.
76. Wood, *Attack*, p. 229.
77. Ibid, p. 233.
78. Campbell, *War*, pp. 285–95.
79. The Bhangmeter was an electronic device that used a photocell light receiver to detect the high intensity flash produced by an atomic explosion immediately after detonation.
80. AIR 8/1956, Home Office to MOD, 2 January 1962.
81. AIR 8/2172, Cannon to ACAS(Ops), 19 December 1957.
82. AIR 8/2172, AMSO to CAS, undated.
83. Clark, *Nuclear*, pp. 148–52.
84. AIR 20/9983, Extract from CC(59)60th Conclusions, 26 November 1959.
85. *Ballistic Missile Early Warning Station in the United Kingdom*, Cmnd 946, February 1960.
86. AIR 20/9983, Appendix to DGO/365, 27 May 1960.
87. Wainstein, *Evolution*, p. 218.
88. AIR 24/2624, Supply of BMEWS Data to HQ Bomber Command, 28 December 1960.
89. AIR 20/9983, AMSO to Minister of Defence, 30 January 1961.
90. Ibid.
91. JIC(60)33Final(Revise) referred to in ibid.
92. DEFE 13/342, Warning and Timing of Soviet Attack on the West in Global War up to 1965, 15 November 1960. Although apparently unknown to western intelligence, early generation Soviet M/IRBMs (SS-3s, SS-4s, and SS-5s) were incapable of being launched at depressed trajectories, inteview with MOD official, April, 1999.
93. AIR 2/16433, BMEWS procedures, undated.
94. AIR 2/16433, Notes of Meeting with CAS, 15 January 1964.
95. Wainstein, *Evolution*, p. 219.
96. PREM 11/4158, Bligh to Macmillan, 27 June 1961.
97. CAB 131/26, D(61)38, 26 June 1961.
98. *Exchange of Notes... on the Missile Defence Alarm System*, Cmnd. 1444 (HMSO, July 1961).
99. *HC Deb.*, Vol.635, Col.1253, 19 July 1961.
100. Correspondence, Jeffrey T. Richelson, September 1997.
101. James, *Defence*, p. 140.

Chapter 9

Conclusion

'We don't want to start a nuclear war unless we really have to, do we?' (Group Captain Mandrake to General Ripper).

The principal aim of this book has been to provide an archival-based study of the development of British nuclear Command, Control Communications and Intelligence (C^3I) during the period when the UK emerged as a nuclear power. The story of this development is both complex and incomplete. The concept of C^3I itself provides *post facto* coherence to policies and procedures that developed incrementally and in often *ad hoc* fashion in response to various and competing factors: technological, strategic, political and financial. In the conclusion we provide a survey of this development and identify particular themes and issues that emerge from our study. We also make some brief remarks about the subsequent development of British C^3I, including arrangements for the submarine-based deterrent. In addition we attempt to relate our findings to recent theoretical approaches in the study of C^3I. Using Peter Feaver's analysis of US command and control we apply and refine his model. Third, we identify some of the areas where our work corroborates or clarifies recent British nuclear historiography. Finally we make some general if preliminary observations about the relevance of our study to recent debates about nuclear proliferation and in understanding the problems confronting, and the problem of, emerging nuclear states.

By the early 1960s, Britain's C^3I had been transformed from a largely autonomous collection of radar stations, operations rooms and nuclear storage sites to an integrated network linking early warning, command centres and nuclear forces. These developments were accompanied by procedural innovation with *ad hoc* and pragmatic safeguards replaced by a clearly defined chain of command and formalised release procedures covering nuclear operations. This transformation raises a number of salient questions. First, what accounts for this change? Second, what do these factors tell us about the operative goal of British C³I? Third, is there evidence to support the conjecture that Britain, as an emerging nuclear state with limited resources, was 'bound to cut corners' leaving both itself and the world vulnerable to inevitable failures.[1] In short, was British C³I an accident waiting to happen?

These questions raise significant methodological and analytical difficulties. Primarily, as important documentary evidence remains classified, detailed empirical analysis of British C³I is inevitably constrained. Significant difficulties are also presented at the analytical level. A specific issue is whether systemic or unit level factors offer a more compelling (and informative) explanation of nuclear operations. Rational deterrence theory, for example, favours a systemic approach and contends that the prime determinant in the development of C³I is external military threat.[2] Moreover, this threat will determine the function of a state's C³I system: a state facing a minor external threat will adopt a different command and control system to a state facing a major threat. This mono-causal explanation has been criticized by those who argue that in presenting a simple deterministic approach, rational deterrence theory fails to address the interplay of domestic politics, organisational interests and psychological motivations which operate within a C³I system.[3] In analyzing the evolution of British C³I, this study has focused primarily on unit level factors - a methodology that supports the contention that:

> there is scant reason to believe that the emerging nuclear states will exercise greater wisdom in their operational choices than their nuclear predecessors did. It would be a mistake to draw conclusions solely on the basis of rational deterrence theory or any systems level of analysis. The question demands, first and foremost, a careful examination of the actual evolving command and control systems of the proliferant states.[4]

In his own study on the dynamics of civil-military nuclear operations, Feaver outlines four key variables as primary factors in determining whether particular nuclear command and control arrangements adopted by a state will favour 'assertive' or 'delegative' control.[5] The variables identified by Feaver are: (1) the size and dispersal of the arsenal, (2) the perceived vulnerability of nuclear forces, (3) nuclear doctrine, and (4) presidential style. Whilst the first three can be readily applied to Britain, the latter is more problematic. While substituting Prime Minister for President might be considered sensible, the relative powers and constitutional position of the British Prime Minister and American President are markedly different. A more apt term would be governmental style. However, this description fails to take proper account of the permanent civil service - an important element in the development of British governmental policy. To address these concerns, we suggest the more suitable term is 'political culture'. In the proceeding analysis, these four variables are employed in an attempt to illuminate the development of British nuclear operational policy.

FAIL DEADLY—BRITISH C^{3}I AND ASSURED RETALIATION

In the early post-war years, British nuclear ambitions centred primarily on development of a viable nuclear weapon. Both political and military leaders regarded provision of delivery systems and methods of operational control as secondary to the primary political objective of establishing Britain as a nuclear power. The emphasis on weapons production diverted resources from other defence projects such as the V-force. Consequently, by 1955 Britain possessed a stockpile of atomic weapons but lacked either a modern bomber force or accurate navigational aids, to deliver the weapon effectively.[6] In short, throughout the early-1950s, operational control of British nuclear weapons was not an issue for civilian or military leaders. In contrast, UK control of US nuclear forces during the same period was a major concern of British diplomacy, with HMG seeking assurances on the use of American nuclear weapons from British bases (Truman-Attlee) and in NATO (Eden Agreement). These developments also support the view that a significant factor in command and control is perception of external threat: though in this case, the threat that Britain could be destroyed in a nuclear attack 'because of a US atomic strike from the UK over which British ministers had no control.'[7]

In the development of command and control arrangements for British nuclear forces, the perceived vulnerability of nuclear forces was crucial. The requirement for British nuclear forces to survive a Soviet nuclear attack was central to the credibility of the deterrent. To protect Britain from atomic attack, initial plans for the V-force, drawn up in the early-1950s, were based on counter-military targeting, with destruction of Soviet airbases the primary objective. Adoption of a counter-military strategy, however, placed a premium on the supply of timely intelligence. A further requirement was the need for post-strike reconnaissance to determine the success of the initial attack and the ability to mount subsequent operations. In short, a

CONCLUSION

counter-military strategy required a robust C^3I system capable of surviving a nuclear attack. Whether Britain actually adopted a counter-military strategy is open to question. Although planning documents existed, Britain's first nuclear weapons did not enter service use until 1953 and could not be used effectively until 1956, when the first Valiant squadron became fully operational. Moreover, by the time Britain possessed the capability to attack military targets, the strategy was no longer effective: Soviet airbases had increased from 15 to over 150 and M/IRBMs were soon expected to enter the Soviet inventory.

The development of the ballistic missile marked a watershed in the evolution of British C^3I. In 1949 Britain planned on a warning period of 3–4 months before going to war. By 1960, this had been reduced to fifteen minutes. To meet these new conditions, British deterrent policy was re-examined. The outcome was twofold: first, active air defence was effectively abandoned and increased emphasis placed on early warning and strategic intelligence. Second, in the event of a unilateral British nuclear response, Bomber Command was directed to attack Soviet cities. To implement this strategy and maintain the credibility of the deterrent further measures were introduced. These included a rapid reaction capability, centralization of operational control, an unambiguous chain of command, improved communications, and the introduction of positive control. The requirement was to satisfy two conflicting demands: to increase operational reaction time and retain political control.

Establishing the correct balance between these requirements proved problematic. The decision ultimately depended on political judgement. Indeed, there was an implicit trade-off between these two positions. Measures designed to increase the speed of military response reduced the degree of political control. To strike a balance was made more difficult as, 'political goals and trade-offs cannot be programmed like tactical operations or weapons procurement. The latter functions are clear, tangible, quantifiable, and verifiable, while the former are more inchoate, ambiguous, inconstant and uncertain.'[8] This dilemma is clearly evident in the decision to cancel Blue Streak. Avoiding destruction on the ground meant a policy of launch-on-warning. However, as the government was not prepared to delegate authority 'on an issue of such appalling magnitude' the project was abandoned.[9] The decision was taken, however, only after US assurances that Skybolt would be made available. Whether, in the absence of Skybolt, Britain would have continued with Blue Streak and adopted a launch-on-warning strategy is open to speculation. It should be noted that, denied US assistance, the French deployed silo-based S-3 ballistic missiles and launch control centres on the Plateau d'Albion.

A second factor that helps explain command arrangements is the size and dispersal of the nuclear arsenal. In the case of Britain, the size of the arsenal is difficult to determine, as stockpile numbers were never disclosed. However, there is strong evidence to suggest that in the early 1960s, the British nuclear stockpile comprised between 100–200 weapons.[10] From the available evidence, control of a relatively small number of weapons stored within the UK was not problematic. Deployment of weapons overseas, however, required a significant modification of command structures. The decision to disperse nuclear weapons in Cyprus, the Far East and within the fleet required the creation of the Nuclear Strike Coordinating Committee. Moreover, the need to control nuclear operations overseas highlighted deficiencies in Britain's C^{3}I system, raising doubts over the reliability of communications and the problem of maintaining close political control over nuclear operations whether at home or abroad.

Given the deficiencies in Britain's C^{3}I system, the ability to guarantee a retaliatory nuclear strike was placed in doubt. The two most intractable issues were continuity of command authority and retention of reliable communications. To address the former, Britain constructed the Turnstile complex to function as an alternate command centre to Whitehall and appointed a designated deputy to the Prime Minister with authority to order nuclear retaliation in the event of the Premier's death. Whether such a procedure was feasible in the event of a nuclear attack is a matter of conjecture. It nevertheless reinforced the principle of civilian control. Maintaining communications was more problematic. To protect communications from EMP required hardened facilities and the use of satellite technology. In the early 1960s, Britain did not possess the financial resources, technical capability or political will to undertake such an enterprise on a national basis. Increased reliance was therefore placed on the use of American facilities. Indeed, in 1961, Sir Robert Scott, Permanent Secretary at MOD, suggested that HMG should consider giving up the idea of independent control of the deterrent and 'negotiate the best terms possible with the Americans in return for handing control over to them.'[11]

British use of American facilities had advantages for both countries. For Britain, it saved money, provided access to the latest technology and was perceived (at least by the British) as a means 'to exert an influence on the

Americans which might otherwise be difficult to achieve.'[12] For America, the decision was based on relative advantage: the more Britain increased its reliance on US systems the greater the opportunity to limit Britain's freedom of independent action and secure more centralized command of western nuclear forces.[13] Against this, however, was the perception of continental Europeans (particularly France) that western nuclear policy was directed to securing 'Anglo-Saxon' strategic priorities. Moreover, to establish an integrated command structure, commonality of interest was fundamental—a position clearly recognized by Washington:

> McNamara did not consider it would be a sufficient safeguard to apply the existing British pattern to France. In the case of Britain, independent political control coupled with integrated targeting was tolerable to the United States because of basic identity of political outlook and aims and because we understood each other well. These could not be taken for granted by the United States in the case of France.[14]

A further possible factor why Washington supported the British but not the French nuclear programme, was, as Raymond Aron notes: 'in Britain the generals obey.'[15]

The potential consequences of undue reliance on US systems were certainly not lost on HMG. With Suez still fresh in mind, the prospect of granting American a *de facto* veto on British nuclear weapons by the denial of joint facilities was to be avoided. Indeed, the requirement to maintain the political and operational right to use strategic nuclear weapons independently of the United States remained a central and constant aspect of British nuclear policy. For Macmillan the position was clear: a primary purpose of the deterrent was to secure US co-operation in a situation where American interests were less immediately concerned, 'by threatening to use our independent nuclear power'.[16] The difficulty was achieving this objective within the limited resources available.

To remain an effective deterrent, Britain's strategic nuclear forces were required to fulfil three conditions:

a. They must be seen to be capable of inflicting more damage on the nuclear power envisaging such bombardment than it could accept as the price of nuclear attack on the United Kingdom.
b. They must be seen to be capable of inflicting this damage before, while, or after the United Kingdom was under nuclear bombardment.
c. They must be sovereign (independent) in the strictest military sense.[17]

As described in Chapter 3 the level of destruction required to constitute a minimum deterrent capability was ultimately dependent on political judgement. By the mid-1960s, assured destruction of five Soviet cities (including Moscow and Leningrad) was considered sufficient to deter the Soviets. The requirement to inflict this damage after nuclear attack was more problematic, especially if reliance was placed on the manned bomber. However, with the introduction of Polaris, assured retaliation was considered 'practical of solution.'[18] To rely on the Americans for the supply of Polaris missiles, however, brought into question the independence of Britain's deterrent:

> By 'sovereign' we mean that the final authority for the use of the strategic nuclear force must be retained by the United Kingdom Government. Its position need be no different from that of other nuclear or conventional forces which are committed to alliances but which remain in peacetime under United Kingdom control and are available for use if necessary in support of purely national operations. *In order that such authority could be exercised, however, every element of the weapons system should be British owned, manned, maintained and controlled.* It is not necessary, however, that the equipment should be British produced. British strategic nuclear strike forces are committed to NATO in the same way as are other forces, thereby demonstrating that we have no deliberate 'go it alone' policy. However, a 'go it alone' capability remains and must always be an important consideration in the mind of any potential enemy. There can be no question of lack of resolution preventing our strategic nuclear capability from working as a deterrent to attack on the United Kingdom, since there can be no doubt that it would be used in retaliation.[19]

The requirement that every element of the deterrent was 'British owned, manned, maintained and controlled' applied equally to C^3I and consequently ruled out dependence on American facilities.[20] The apparent belief that there would be 'no doubt' in Britain's determination to retaliate, however, raises salient issues concerning nuclear use, especially if civilian or military leaders believed retaliation served no political or morally justifiable purpose. Notwithstanding these concerns, to retain independent use of the deterrent only two solutions were available: development of a survivable C^3I system on a purely national basis or delegation of nuclear use authority to the military.

The choice between these two options is significantly influenced by Feaver's two other factors—nuclear doctrine and political culture. Within nuclear doctrine, the timing and targeting of a nuclear response are of primary concern. For counter-military attacks to succeed, for example,

CONCLUSION

considerable demands are placed on both timing and targeting - demands moreover, that require a robust and survivable C^3I system. In contrast, a nuclear doctrine based on countervalue attack, places less demands on C^3I. The location of cities is well known and rapid response is not essential. To satisfy a countervalue nuclear doctrine, certainty of retaliation rather than speed of response is paramount. Given Britain's limited resources, a countervalue nuclear strategy was seen as the only option available. Moreover, the less demanding requirements of a countervalue C^3I system were capable of being met on a wholly national basis. Despite adopting the simpler demands of countervalue strategy, a Soviet decapitation attack would still negate the operative goal of British C^3I. To ensure retaliation, the military was granted delegated authority to initiate nuclear retaliation. This decision was conveyed to C-in-C Bomber Command in September 1962.[21]

Although these delegated powers were only to come into operation after nuclear attack and in the absence of communications with the political leadership, the decision to delegate nuclear control to British military leaders was nevertheless a significant development. The decision, however, reflects a political culture in which military insubordination was not a major concern. Feaver argues that the more the military is institutionally strong and refrains from direct intervention within the political process, 'the more likely it will demand and enjoy the political clout to achieve more delegative command and control measures.'[22] In the US, there was genuine and understandable fear of SAC commanders (or in the context of Korea, General McArthur) starting a nuclear war. Moreover, as close civilian control was an overriding requirement of US C^3I during the Kennedy Administration, delegation of nuclear authority to the military was strongly resisted. For HMG, with less resources to devote to command and control, the alternatives were stark: 'trust in military professionalism or else the arsenal is truly useless.'[23] Moreover, if such worries were present, they were of secondary importance to the operative goal of British C^3I: to ensure retaliation by whatever means possible.

The need to ensure retaliation explains Britain's continued refusal to accept the US offer to install PALs on its nuclear weapons. For if the British NCA was unable to transmit the executive order to fire, it would also be unable to transmit the enabling codes to disable the PALs. Consequently, a communications blackout with PAL-fitted weapons would paralyze Britain's nuclear forces. This position was politically unacceptable to the British government, on the grounds that:

CONCLUSION

> The introduction of PALs into the command and control system for our Polaris submarines would seriously prejudice our ability to withdraw the submarines if we should wish to do so…This could not be ensured if their weapons were fitted with inhibiting devices which could not be unlocked except with the agreement of other members. Thus, while we had a juridical right to withdraw this would be frustrated in practical terms by the fitting of PALs… In these circumstances, the best course would appear to be to emphasise to our allies the technical difficulties of such a system and to seek to dissuade them from insisting on PALs, using the argument that this would cause the deterrent to lose its credibility.[24]

This position reflected earlier assurances given to Parliament by the Prime Minister, Harold Wilson, that: 'there will not be any system of locks which interferes with our right of communication with the submarine.'[25] In contrast, the absence of PALs removed any requirement to make contact with strategic forces: in any prolonged absence of communication, nuclear retaliation could be initiated at the discretion of the military commander in control of the force.[26] To ensure retaliation under all conditions, Britain adopted a delegative C^3I system, designed in the last resort to 'fail deadly'.

The adoption of a 'fail deadly' system had several consequences. First, the requirements imposed on the C^3I system were less demanding. The most significant aspect is that the system was not required to survive for a prolonged period after nuclear attack. In short, an unhardened C^3I system could only be used for a one-shot war. For Britain, delegation of nuclear use authority to the military ensured that in the event of a Soviet decapitation attack all civilian constraints on the use of nuclear weapons were removed. A Soviet attack on the British NCA would 'be an attack on the safety catch of the entire command structure, and the Soviets would be destroying the one mechanism holding back all-out retaliation.'[27] That the resulting nuclear response might be uncoordinated was not important, as the operative goal of British C^3I was to ensure retaliation by whatever means:

> The effectiveness of the UK nuclear strike forces and their credibility as a deterrent rests first and foremost on the certainty of their ability to retaliate, and not on the speed with which the retaliatory blow is delivered, provided that any delay does not affect the certainty that the blow will be delivered. It follows that, from this point of view, a quick reaction time is not an essential requirement for an effective deterrent weapon system.[28]

A further consequence of a 'fail deadly' system is that the risk of nuclear inadvertence or unauthorized use is subordinated to the primary objective of ensuring retaliation. The possible scenarios in which nuclear weapons might be used against the wishes of the civilian leadership are varied and difficult to quantify. Moreover, while it may be true that Armageddon would not unleashed solely on the basis of radio silence, the concern nevertheless remains that a decapitation attack on Britain may have left cities unharmed. Given these conditions, British retaliation against Soviet cities would invite a similar response and trigger escalation of the conflict. For Britain, 'with fewer resources to lavish on command and control' (and in the absence of any viable alternative) such a risk was considered politically acceptable.[29]

Delegation of nuclear use authority to the military has been described 'as an extremely powerful aspect of deterrence, and one that overcomes any technical or procedural weaknesses in the C³I system.'[30] The potential dangers of operating such a system, however, were equally apparent to allies as well as adversaries. Moreover, the use of British weapons in a countervalue strike would have negated the American strategy of limiting nuclear conflict at the lowest possible level. In short, Britain's C³I system was unable to fulfil the operational requirements imposed by Flexible Response. The system was vulnerable and unable to operate effectively in the post-attack environment. The consequences for Polaris were described as follows:

> This is an ultimate weapon. It is for deterrence and there is no question of using the submarine for any other purpose than an ultimate warning to any potential aggressor that we retain a second strike capability if he ever contemplates striking us first. It could only perform that function; it could not combine that function with any other.[31]

Consequently, to operate Polaris within the NATO command structure, Britain required use of American facilities. The result was a dual system operating two distinct strategies: the first (with American assistance) to control British nuclear forces under flexible response; the second (under national control) 'infinitely simpler' and designed specifically for a countervalue strike.[32] In adopting this dual strategy, Britain sought to establish a second centre of decision to insure against 'any weakening of the United States nuclear guarantee'.[33] The policy also reaffirmed Britain's historical tradition of favouring deterrence by punishment rather than denial. How these two strategies operated in tandem in less than clear. It can be assumed however, that in the improbable event of independent

British action, a retaliatory strike at Soviet cities was the only strategy available. By contrast, in the more likely event of co-ordinated action with America, reliance on US facilities would have permitted a more flexible strategy. Britain's reliance on external facilities, introduces a further variable not mentioned in Feaver's model—namely, the C³I system adopted by an emerging nuclear state is influenced by the degree of 'linkage' or technical assistance offered by an established nuclear state. In the case of the UK, two examples are apparent: the nuclear relationship with America and the deployment of British forces within NATO.

THE BRITISH-AMERICAN RELATIONSHIP

As shown above, the objective of the British government to establish control over US nuclear forces based in the UK and gain access to American nuclear know-how was a constant feature of post-war British planning. The period under review includes two particular phases. The first, which covered the period up to the mid-1950s, was concerned primarily with establishing control over American nuclear forces stationed in Britain. The second, which began in the late-1950s, reflected Britain's emergence as an operational nuclear power and centred on proposals to co-ordinate the nuclear strike plans of Bomber Command and SAC. A common theme underpinning both objectives was the desire to use American influence for British ends and act as a constraint on possible American adventurism. In short, as Macmillan apparently told McNamara, British nuclear strength was 'to prevent foolish decisions being made to our detriment... [and] to mesh the United States in totally... to the defence of Britain.'[34]

In the initial post-war years, the British-American nuclear relationship was characterized by growing inequality, with Britain's status reduced to that of a junior partner. This disparity was reflected in loss of the British veto over the use of American nuclear weapons and Britain's increased reliance on the US strategic air offensive for the defence of Europe. To consolidate the US nuclear commitment to European defence, Britain agreed to establish American nuclear bases in the UK. The use of these bases in an emergency, however, has remained ambiguous. Moreover, Britain's right of consent over operational control has never been formally accepted. In short, despite the procedures outlined in the Murphy-Dean agreement and Eisenhower's personal assurance that it would be 'treasonous' to use nuclear weapons without British consent, HMG did not re-establish a veto.[35] Indeed, the formula agreed between Truman and Attlee in 1951

CONCLUSION

has governed the use of American nuclear forces stationed in Britain to the present day. Whilst the formula has been criticized as a totem of Britain's subservience, its ambiguity has also been commended. To serve both countries needs, 'its apparent weakness conceals its real strength: it is open to interpretation.'[36]

The stationing of US nuclear bombers in the UK strengthened the relationship between the two airforces. It is also evident that RAF-USAF exchanges were far more significant than previously assumed. Details of the Offtackle/Galloper plan drawn up in 1950, for example, were negotiated by the RAF on its own initiative.[37] Involving the supply of intelligence and atomic information, these exchanges offered the RAF the invaluable opportunity of gaining privileged access to American nuclear capability and strategic intentions. Indeed, only a handful of individuals outside the Air Ministry were aware of the arrangements and officially no plan existed. Disclosure of these informal channels, together with discussions of 'covert' command structures, gives further credence to Hathaway's contention that 'contrary to the desires of their superiors, a small group of officers took it upon themselves to enter into arrangements with the British which had the effect of tying the two countries together far closer than all but a few imagined.'[38] To what degree this small cadre of officers influenced British control arrangements or the implementation of joint war plans is as yet unclear. However, the existence of these informal linkages raises the question of whether 'the delicate diplomacy of policy makers' could have been 'imperiled, overridden and wrecked' by the autonomous action of military leaders.[39] Moreover, to maintain their autonomy, military organisations are often reluctant to provide civilian policymakers with details of doctrine and operational tactics—a tendency that increases civilian unfamiliarity with military operations and heightens the danger of inadvertent military confrontation.[40] Indeed, in June 1962, the Prime Minister's Private Secretary, Philip de Zulueta, informed Macmillan 'that an independent British plan [for unilateral nuclear retaliation] does not in fact exist.'[41] Although later corrected by an official in the Ministry of Defence, the episode is nevertheless indicative of civilian ignorance concerning nuclear operations.

Although the informal exchanges proved useful to the RAF, they provided only limited assistance in HMG's primary objective—access to the US nuclear stockpile. This was eventually achieved in the mid-1950s and represented acceptance that Britain could not expect 'to have a say in the formulation of the critically important allied strategic air plan unless we ourselves have a worthwhile contribution to offer.'[42] In effect the agreement was a rational division of resources: Britain had more bombers than bombs while American had more bombs than bombers.[43] Stored on RAF bases under US supervision, use of the weapons in war was determined by the co-ordinated nuclear strike plan that came into operation in 1958. Further nuclear collaboration proceeded under the terms of the 1958 US Atomic Energy Act. Details of these exchanges remain classified. Britain asked for design information on the following weapons: a lightweight pre-initiation proof IRBM warhead, a low-yield warhead for air defence, a lightweight high-yield pre-initiation proof thermonuclear bomb for delivery by the V-force, a lightweight high-yield warhead for a long-range air-to-surface missile, and a low-yield warhead for a short-range surface-to-surface missile.[44] Whether the US agreed to exchange this information is unclear. However, discussing the arrangements in 1960, MOD indicated that it possessed 'a catalogue of US weapons which included the yield of each one and... access to design information on most if not all of these weapons.'[45]

In agreeing to supply the UK with nuclear weapons, Washington had to resolve two basic policy objectives: the desire to constrain nuclear proliferation and the requirement to place all Western strategic nuclear forces under centralized US command. On one hand, to assist Britain in its nuclear programme would have maximized American influence (and increased British dependency) but would have been seen to encourage proliferation. On the other, refusal to supply nuclear technology would not have stopped the British nuclear programme and would have resulted in divided control of the West's strategic nuclear forces. As noted above, to reconcile these objectives, agreement was reached that Britain would receive US nuclear technology on the understanding that the strategic nuclear force would be assigned to NATO and only used independently of US strategic objectives if Britain's supreme national interests were at stake. 'Ever thereafter the British government, whatever its political hue, was able to play the NATO or the independent card according to the mood of the time and the audience they were addressing.'[46]

NUCLEAR CONTROL IN NATO

Britain's ambivalence to placing its nuclear forces under alliance control has been a constant theme of Britain's relationship with NATO. Indeed, the primary objective of successive British governments has been based on maintaining strategic nuclear weapons outside NATO's command structure, thus retaining control within British-American hands. In the context of Massive Retaliation this presented few difficulties: in the event of Soviet attack, strategic nuclear forces would be used from the outset, thus rendering the control of tactical nuclear forces largely irrelevant to the final outcome. The implications were described as follows:

> The launching of strategic nuclear forces is the start of all-out nuclear war and the outcome would be determined by those forces. The role of the NATO shield forces at this stage would be of quite secondary importance... Any fighting in Europe after the strategic nuclear exchange could be continued only by units and groups of individuals without coherent direction from any central political authority. In the absence of a home base, there could be no sustained operations. There is no need to make specific provision of [tactical] nuclear weapons for use at this stage.[47]

Consequently, for as long as Massive Retaliation remained NATO's declared strategy (and NATO possessed no strategic nuclear forces under its command), the control of the strategic offensive would remain a British-American responsibility. In short, the control of tactical nuclear weapons was secondary to the primary objective of maintaining control over the decision to initiate global nuclear war. However, the trip-wire strategy was only effective as long as the West possessed a meaningful advantage in nuclear forces. By the early-1960s, the Soviets began to acquire a secure second-strike capability targeted at the US homeland, and the strategy of Massive Retaliation was increasingly recognized as both inflexible and suicidal. In response, Britain and America pursued different strategies. For Britain, the solution lay in selective use of tactical nuclear forces. This position required the use of only a handful of weapons for the specific purpose of signalling NATO's intent to escalate if aggression continued. In short, Britain advocated intra-war deterrence in which the use of tactical nuclear weapons would deter the Soviet Union from further aggression by threatening a strategic nuclear exchange. In advocating this strategy HMG sought to increase the credibility of deterrence whilst maintaining strategic nuclear forces under British-American control. The concept placed considerable emphasis on command and control. Specifically, to reduce the risk of escalation, the C^3I system was required to function both during and after a nuclear exchange. In practice, Britain did not possess the necessary infrastructure to implement the strategy effectively.

In contrast, America was reluctant to commit its strategic nuclear forces until absolutely necessary and sought to contain any conflict in Europe at the lowest possible level. To achieve this meant increases in conventional forces and the ability to control military operations through a series of levels from non-nuclear through tactical to strategic nuclear war. The concept of escalation control, however, required even more rigorous command and control and a single focus of authority. To be accepted by the European members of the alliance, the strategy was also required to address the paradox of extended deterrence. On one hand, increasing control over tactical nuclear forces in Europe was perceived to decouple US strategic nuclear forces and raised fears of limited war in Europe. Conversely, decreasing control over tactical weapons reduced the credibility of the US strategic commitment. To resolve this dilemma, America pursued a variety of hardware and procedural solutions resulting in proposals to establish the MLF and the Athens guidelines. The aim was to provide European NATO members with a greater degree of participation in both formulation and implementation of nuclear strategy. Washington's aim was to satisfy its European partners that a flexible nuclear response was both credible and capable of collective political control. The consequences of such a policy, however, began to concern the British who cautioned that, 'the creation of a NATO nuclear force would focus attention on who orders "fire". Whereas today it is, let us face it, primarily a US/UK decision.'[48]

The difficulties presented by collective control were not confined to Britain. Indeed, as described in Chapter 5, despite introduction of political arrangements to control nuclear forces in NATO, America maintained the operational capability to initiate nuclear war in Europe solely through the US chain of command. Furthermore, this was used to implement a strategy of limited nuclear use without revision of existing NATO strategy. Given the various demands, the C^3I system adopted in NATO attempted to reconcile various national priorities. Moreover, 'since NATO did not go to war, while states did, national policies generally took preference.'[49] Within NATO, command and control was perceived primarily as fulfilling political objectives. The result was a series of parallel C^3I systems with little or no overall co-ordination and no centralized process for designing and acquiring a coherent and efficient theatre architecture.[50]

NUCLEAR HISTORIOGRAPHY

Most recent studies of British nuclear history discuss aspects of command and control, most importantly where C^3I has been crucial to strategy and diplomacy. The development and cancellation of Blue Streak, the deployment of Thor, the attempt to acquire Skybolt, and the purchase of Polaris are only the most prominent of a host of crucial decisions reflecting the significance of operational aspects. At various stages command and control assumed a critical importance in British procurement decisions and in dealings with the US. The various nuclear history studies chronicle and interpret these decisions in differing contexts (e.g. strategy, alliance diplomacy, procurement). In any model of nuclear policy, in which strategy, technology and finance were seen as variables, C^3I would be added an independent variable (assuming the disparate aspects of C^3I can be treated as a coherent whole). As with these other variables the exact significance on policy outcomes varies. Strategic, diplomatic, economic and bureaucratic factors influence, on occasions decisively, command and control arrangements and policies. Our principal contribution to British nuclear historiography is to provide a systematic and detailed analysis of British C^3I, and illuminate the role, as well as the limitations, of C^3I in policy-making. In addition various themes in the nuclear history literature are developed, of which three are noted below.

First, a principal conclusion of the study is that there was a distinctive British approach to C^3I, echoing Clark and Wheeler's argument that there was a distinctive British view of nuclear strategy in the period 1945–55. This interpretation reflects various aspects of the British experience, including the vicissitudes of strategy, diplomacy and financial constraint. One particular and crucial theme is also civil-military relations. 'Fail deadly' reflected the imperatives of technological and financial constraint. Yet it also reflected a perception of British military professionalism, and the effectiveness of procedural safeguards for the operation of nuclear forces. Such perceptions were at variance with the American experience.

Second, the study explores (and amplifies) the twin themes of national independence and British-American interdependence, which permeate British nuclear historiography. C^3I is a focus for conflict and co-operation in the relationship with the US, and at key points, as in acquisition of Polaris, was at the heart of British-American diplomacy. John Baylis has characterized the development of British nuclear strategy and British policy toward Washington in terms of ambiguity. One source of ambiguity was that a rationale for an independent deterrent was to act as a lever to influence American decision-making concerning the use of nuclear weapons, while another was to provide a national capability should there be doubt about American involvement. British command and control objectives aimed to secure a British finger on the trigger as well as another on the safety catch. These aims entailed very different C^3I implications and infrastructures. By the early-1960s, a multi-tiered system of safeguards and release procedures had developed that allowed Britain control over its national, alliance and bilateral forces. At the heart of the system, however, were delegated nuclear release procedures to enable nuclear retaliation under all conditions. Moreover, the dual strategy of holding a finger on the trigger as well as the safety catch reflected British fears about scenarios of American action or inaction. The idea that Britain might exercise influence (including possible restraint) on American actions in war, remained an article of faith among many military and civilian officials. Indeed, in the absence of ironclad guarantees concerning nuclear use, faith was a cornerstone of alliance defence:

> The practical situation is that NATO Governments recognize that there is at present no alternative but for them to put their faith in SACUER and in the US and UK Governments to use nuclear weapons without delay when they should be used and not to use them when they should not be used, consulting the Council before the event if time permits and otherwise as soon as possible after.[51]

A third element illuminated by the study is the relationship between operational factors, diplomacy and strategy. A good illustration of this is Thor. Although, as Ian Clark observes, the main significance of Thor was in terms of what it symbolized rather than its intrinsic military importance, its operational history is of note. As Clark has demonstrated it was military and operational objections that were crucial to the cancellation of Blue Streak. Yet the operational history of Thor suggests that the first generation, liquid-fuelled, IRBMs were not as vulnerable as many believed, and that they were not simply 'fire first' weapons. The experience of the deployment, and of their role during the Cuban missile crisis, clearly convinced not only the head of Bomber Command, but the Air Ministry, that the missiles had a military (and political) utility. The British rationale for Thor was different than that of Blue Streak, because the former was conceived as a contribution to the Western deterrent, while the latter would constitute the national deterrent. Nonetheless, the fact that the missiles could be held commensurate with NATO's Quick Reaction Alert and that a proportion of the Thor force could be held at higher states, including T-2, raises questions about the potential strategic value of such weapons systems.

CONCLUSION

Certainly, it seems inappropriate to describe the 'slow reaction time' of the missiles. Nonetheless, even at such higher states of readiness, the credibility of the Thors as a retaliatory force depended on a combination of adequate tactical warning and a willingness to launch on warning. The problems associated with such a posture, identified by the British Nuclear Deterrent Study Group, meant delegating authority to launch on warning.

A further aspect of the Thor deployment concerns the operation of dual control. Thor was an experiment and precedent for bilateral/multilateral control of nuclear forces, at a time when such concepts held attraction for those, mainly in Washington, who saw their potential for constraining the proliferation of nuclear weapons. Notwithstanding the protracted and difficult negotiations between London and Washington, it was only once the missile had been deployed that the decision was taken to mate the warheads to the missiles under normal peacetime conditions. Taken together with previous decisions that the missiles were to be jointly manned by the RAF and USAF personnel, British independent control of the weapon was very limited. The British could re-target and fire the missiles, with the warheads fitted, though not armed. As the Cuban missile crisis demonstrated changes in the alert posture of the Thors could be taken by the British alone. Comparison between the operation of the Thors and the NATO-assigned Jupiter IRBMs in Turkey and Italy is noteworthy. During the missile crisis the American government took precautions against unauthorized host county use. In Britain, aside the prospect of American servicemen somehow sabotaging the launch of the missiles, all that stood between an 'unauthorized' host country launch was the USAF authentication officer.

Finally, one area of omission in our study should be emphasized. Although in various contexts we note the importance of Soviet perceptions, we do not discuss how Soviet military and political leaders understood the development of British C^3I. This indeed reflects a significant gap in Western nuclear history, and encompasses a range of questions of great importance to British-American relations, NATO strategy and the debate about the British deterrent. No studies have yet emerged to explain how the Soviets interpreted and understood the development of British nuclear forces. In the evaluation of British C^3I this is potentially crucial. While issues of command and control are primarily concerned with how nuclear weapons are used, the perception of how they might be used (and indeed whether they would be capable of being used) are central to notions of deterrence.

Did, for example, the Soviets operate on the assumption of British (or American) military pre-delegated authority? How did they view the vulnerabilities of the British National Command Authority? Did Soviet perceptions of British (and US/NATO) C³I enhance or imperil deterrence? The difficulties of studying Soviet attitudes to British C³I are very formidable indeed. Yet they remain crucial to assessing the role of nuclear weapons and the risk of nuclear war in the latter part of the twentieth century. One area where this is particularly apparent is the Soviet perception of British (and American) nuclear forces during Cold War crises.

CRISIS CONTROL AND NUCLEAR INADVERTENCE

The ability to control nuclear forces in time of crisis is a major requirement of C³I. The dynamics of crisis management, however, present considerable problems for command and control. To ensure that nuclear forces are not destroyed in a pre-emptive attack, the alert state of these forces is raised. By alerting nuclear forces, however, procedural and technical safeguards are removed, which increase the probability of inadvertent nuclear use. Unauthorized use of a nuclear weapon at the height of an international crisis would further increase alert levels and lead to a 'nuclear Sarajevo' in which nuclear conflict occurs 'because of a chain reaction of alerts and counter-alerts... resulting in a ratchet effect ineluctably leading to war as the interacting mobilizations of European militaries in 1914 thrust Europe into war.'[52] Moreover, military rules of engagement and delegation of authority must be pre-planned. Consequently, they can run counter to the specific diplomatic and strategic needs of a particular crisis. The problem can be compounded where implementation is largely automatic (determined by the level of alert) and procedures are poorly understood by the political leadership. Political leaders may be largely ignorant of the extent to which alert authority rests in the hands of individual military commanders - a position which (in the absence of specific orders to the contrary) allows military commanders to place their forces on a higher state of alert.[53]

In the period under review, the possible use of British nuclear forces arose in at least three distinct crises. The first was the invasion of Egypt in 1956 in which the Chief of the Imperial General Staff, General Templer, recommended that to force Egyptian compliance Nasser should be told that Britain would attack with 'all possible weapons'.[54] Whether British nuclear forces were alerted during the Suez crisis is as yet unknown. However, as described in Chapter 7, actions were taken to increase British warning intelligence concerning Soviet nuclear forces and US nuclear forces stationed in Britain were placed on higher alert. The second crisis in which the possible use of British nuclear forces was contemplated occurred during the Berlin crisis in late-1961. The Cabinet Secretary, Sir Norman Brook described the situation, in the following terms:

> We must be prepared for a lengthy period of fluctuating political tension with the possibility that, either suddenly or in the course of negotiations if they begin, a critical, politico-military situation may develop. If such a situation arises, urgent consideration will have to be given to the possibility of action - diplomatic, economic or military. We must therefore be ready, when the situation becomes sufficiently critical, to introduce without delay a system of working for the central government machine, agreed and prescribed in advance, which will allow vital decisions to be taken in an orderly and speedy way.[55]

The government organisation envisaged by Brook consisted of a Ministerial Committee on Berlin and the formation of a 'Berlin Room' in the Cabinet Office to act as focus for all intelligence and military assessment. Despite the possible threat of military action, however, it was nevertheless agreed that 'we shall not go underground or have executive decisions taken by "map rooms".'[56] So far, no evidence has emerged that HMG adopted a heightened alert and readiness posture during the crisis. Discussing the situation with Sir Norman Brook, Macmillan was firmly against undue provocations 'since any real war *must* escalate into nuclear war.'[57]

While the risk of nuclear war in 1956 or 1961 was perhaps low, the third crisis involving British nuclear forces in October 1962 is generally regarded as the most dangerous between the two superpowers in the nuclear age. Despite its nuclear status, Britain's role (in particular its military role) in the Cuban missile crisis has only begun to emerge in recent years.[58] This omission is potentially significant for several reasons. First, Britain was the third nuclear power in 1962 and capable of targeting as many nuclear weapons on the USSR as the Soviets could target on the USA. Second, on 25 September 1962, Air Marshal Cross, the Commander-in-Chief of Bomber Command, was given pre-delegated authority to launch British nuclear forces should a Soviet nuclear attack on the UK result in a total breakdown in communications. Third, US nuclear forces were stationed in Britain with a significant element (60 Thor IRBMs) under dual control. Fourth, the operation of Britain's nuclear command and control procedures during the crisis provides an opportunity to examine the interaction of national, bilateral and alliance control measures and the possible consequences of a delegative C^3I system during a nuclear crisis. Finally, the crisis demonstrates the differing perspectives of America and her NATO allies, as well as the inability of the Europeans to control events. As the US Council on Foreign Relations observed:

> From a European standpoint, the Cuban crisis presented exactly the kind of situation that made existing arrangements regarding the control of nuclear weapons so unsatisfactory. American insistence on the removal of Soviet missiles from Cuba had admittedly involved a danger of nuclear war; and while there might be some doubt about the USSR's ability to wipe out the United States with its existing stocks of intercontinental missiles, there was no doubt whatever that it had at its disposal sufficient intermediate-range missiles to destroy Western Europe. Yet no one, apparently, had thought to inquire of the Europeans whether they wished to be destroyed or not.[59]

As described in Chapter 4, the Cuban missile crisis resulted in both British and American nuclear forces stationed in Britain adopting a higher state of alert. It now seems apparent that both Macmillan and Kennedy were not fully aware of (or did not fully understand) the various UK military preparations during the crisis. In his meeting with the Chief of the Air Staff, for example, Macmillan stressed his desire to avoid overt preparations for mobilization and was adamant that Bomber Command should not be alerted. Exactly what Macmillan meant by the term 'alerted' is not clear. In the context of his conversation with CAS, it can be assumed that Macmillan did not want the V-force dispersed (Alert Condition 2) rather than adopting a vulnerable deployment (Alert Condition 5) which a literal interpretation of Macmillan's statement would imply. In contrast to the apparent imprecision displayed by the Prime Minister, for Bomber Command the various alert states adopted by the V-force had a clear and specific meaning. At the height of the crisis and on his own initiative, Sir Kenneth Cross, the C-in-C Bomber Command placed the V-force and Thor missile squadrons at Alert Condition 3. While Cross' actions were not *ultra vires*, falling within the scope of his authority, the decision might be construed to be at variance with Macmillan's wishes.

Macmillan's apparent uncertainty over the control of British nuclear operations is not an isolated incident. In June 1960, for example, he wrote to the Minister of Defence to ask whether there were 'any plans with the Americans for the sharing of bombs... should the situation deteriorate.'[60] Given that a co-ordinated nuclear strike plan had been agreed between SAC and Bomber Command in late-1957 with US nuclear weapons stored at British bases since October 1958, the inquiry seems quite extraordinary. Similarly bemusing was the apparent ignorance of the Prime Minister (and his advisors) concerning the command and control arrangements for the NATO-assigned Jupiter IRBMs. At the height of the Cuban missile crisis, Macmillan's private office contacted the White House to ask whether the Turkish Jupiters were operational, whether they were manned by the Turks or Americans, and whether the missiles were 'regarded as part of the NATO forces or are they, like the Thors in the UK, part of a separate Turko-American arrangement.'[61] Given that major policy decisions on nuclear issues seem to have escaped the Prime Minister's attention, it is perhaps less than surprising that operational details were overlooked. Whether lack of civilian oversight of nuclear operations increased the possibility of nuclear inadvertence is a matter for speculation. The deployment of Blue Steel missiles, however, is illustrative of the dangers. Scheduled for service introduction in late 1961, full approval for operational deployment was not obtained until April 1964.[62] However, in common with the deployment of Britain's first thermonuclear weapon (Violet Club), the capability of using the missile in a national emergency was retained. The decision was given to the Air Ministry in September 1962:

> we have issued the present clearance on the understanding that, should a national crisis occur which warrants the carriage of the operational Blue Steel with its warhead, limitations as to its use could be overridden... by cutting certain corners and taking certain risks, we could if necessary use Blue Steel in an emergency.[63]

As a consequence of this decision, the Air Ministry was granted authority to deploy Blue Steel during the Cuban missile crisis. Moreover, as highlighted in Chapter 3, Britain—in common with some emerging nuclear states—placed availability of weapons before considerations of safety, with the result that safeguards were 'bound to be cruder and weaker.'[64] To guard against inadvertent or unauthorized use of Blue Steel, the primary hardware solution relied on removal of the missile's battery! To buttress retaliation, HMG seemed prepared to compromise safety conceivably risking an accidental nuclear explosion that in the context of the Cuban crisis could have resulted in unforeseen and uncontrollable consequences.

The Cuban missile crisis demonstrates the differing perceptions of civilian and military leaders and the demarcation between political and operational control. For Macmillan, the events of October 1962 demonstrated the benefits of the British-American relationship and 'did not reach a point, as far as we know, at which the early use of nuclear weapons might have been contemplated or the President required to fulfil his undertakings to consult HMG on their use.'[65] For the military the situation was not so clear cut - a position succinctly expressed by Air Marshal Cross who later remarked that 'during the crisis, from him downwards, everything worked perfectly; from him upwards, he perceived nothing worked at all.'[66] The lack of clarity between Britain's nuclear policy and operational objectives was expressed by the Chief of the Defence Staff, Earl Mountbatten. Meeting on 28 October with the Chiefs of Staff and Minister of Defence, news was received that the Soviets had accepted the American terms: 'Dickie broke the silence. "Well, what would we have done if the Russians had not pulled back? Do we know? We've got to work this out." No-one knew, but he was the only one to put the question.'[67] As was shown in Chapter 3, this realization led to a post-Cuba review of Britain's command and control procedures, with power becoming more centralized in the office of the Prime Minister. Given such uncertainty, perhaps, as Macmillan once famously remarked, 'events' would in the end determine the response.

Whether events could have been controlled, however, is again a matter for speculation. In discussing the dangers of nuclear proliferation with President Kennedy in January 1962, Macmillan's doubts and concerns over the future stability and control of nuclear weapons are all too apparent:

> If all this capacity for destruction is spread about the world in the hands of all kinds of different characters - dictators, reactionaries, revolutionaries, madmen - then sooner or later, and certainly I think by the end of this century, either by error or folly or insanity, the great crime will be committed... It may be that there is no way out. It may be that we are condemned, like the heroes of the old Greek tragedies, to an ineluctable fate from which there is no escape; and like those doomed figures we must endure it.[68]

Kennedy took a somewhat different view. In private he told his friend, the British ambassador in Washington, David Ormsby-Gore, 'that the existence of nuclear weapons made a secure and rational world impossible. We must somehow find a means to get rid of nuclear weapons'.[69] Neither Kennedy's vision nor Macmillan's fears have yet come to fruition. As humankind confronts the challenges posed by nuclear weapons in the twenty-first century, issues of command and control may well be crucial in whichever future unfolds.

CONCLUSION

1. Blair, *Logic*, p. 254.
2. For detailed analysis, see Kenneth Waltz, *Theory of International Politics* (Reading: Mass: Addison-Wesley, 1979), Chapters 8-9; Thayer, 'Risk', pp. 466-8.
3. For discussion, see Scott Sagan and Kenneth Waltz, *The Spread of Nuclear Weapons: A Debate* (New York: Norton, 1995); see also essays on the Waltz-Sagan debate in *Security Studies*, Vol.4, No.4 (Summer 1995).
4. Bruce Blair, 'Nuclear Inadvertence: Theory and Evidence', *Security Studies*, Vol.3, No.3 (Spring 1994), p. 500.
5. See Chapter 1.
6. CAB 131/15, D(55)4, The Supply of Aircraft and Guided Missiles, 10 January 1955.
7. Gowing, *Independence*, Vol.1, p. 316.
8. Richard Betts, *Soldiers, Statesmen and Cold War Crises* (Harvard University Press, 1977), p. 157.
9. See Chapter 3. Underground silos for Blue Streak would cost £600 million. In 1960, total expenditure on public education was £895 million. Morton, p. 446n.
10. See Simpson, *Independent*, Appendix 4.
11. Baylis, *Ambiguity*, p. 278.
12. AIR 19/999, BND(SG)(62)1, 22 January 1962.
13. This was raised by McNamara at the Nassau Conference, where it was agreed that US communications facilities should be used jointly, both when UK submarines were under NATO as well as under national command. 'The Americans certainly did not want the British to spend money on these facilities and so impair their ability to meet other non-nuclear goals.' PREM 11/4429, Record of Meeting, 19 December 1962.
14. AIR 19/999, Notes on talks during the Minister of Defence's visit to the United States, September 1962, Nuclear Problems in Europe, 19 September 1962.
15. Beatrice Heuser, *Nuclear Mentalities? Strategies and Beliefs in Britain, France and the FRG* (Macmillan, 1998) p. 89.
16. AIR 8/2400, DB(58)10, 29 October 1958.
17. DEFE 6/92, DP113/64(Final), The British Strategic Nuclear Capability, 9 October 1964.
18. Ibid.
19. Ibid., emphasis added.
20. Ibid.
21. See Appendix 2.
22. Feaver, 'Command', p. 176.
23. Feaver, *Guarding*, p. 252.
24. FO 371/184412, The Mechanism of Command and Control: Permissive Action Links, June 1965.
25. *HC Deb*. Vol.704, Col.694, 17 December 1964.
26. While it may be overly simplistic to assume that a communications blackout would provoke immediate retaliation, the submarine crew can execute the firing procedure with complete autonomy. The more likely scenario is that retaliation would be postponed while efforts were made to determine the situation on the British mainland. For further details, see Gregory, *Nuclear*, pp. 118–19.
27. Bracken, *Command*, p. 202.
28. DEFE 25/13, COS(JGW)(59)12, The Time Factor and the Deterrent, Report by the Joint Global War Study Group, 12 October 1959.
29. For discussion of the problems faced by emerging nuclear powers, see Blair, *Logic*, p. 9.
30. Daniel Shuchman, 'Nuclear Strategy and the Problem of Command and Control', *Survival*, Vol.29, No.4 (July/August 1987), p. 340.
31. House of Commons, *First Special Report from the Defence Committee on Strategic Nuclear Weapons Policy* (HMSO, 1982), p. 17. How this policy relates to Trident's sub-strategic capability is less than clear.
32. *First Special Report*, p. 5.

33. 1974 memorandum from the Ministry of Defence, cited in Freedman, *Britain*, p. 129.
34. Undated transcript of interview with Sir Philip de Zulueta, cited in Katherine Pyne, 'Art or Article? The Need for and Nature of the British Hydrogen Bomb, 1954-58', *Contemporary Record*, Vol.9, No.3 (Winter 1995), p. 566.
35. CAB 131/23, D(60)21, 20 May, 1960. The closest Britain has come to re-establishing a veto was the assurance given to Alex Douglas Home in 1963 by President Johnson that 'no US nuclear weapons will be used from British territory without your consent and that we should consult if possible before either of us uses them anywhere.' *FRUS*, 1961–1963, Vol.XIII, p. 1139.
36. Danchev, *Oliver*, p. 134.
37. For further details, see Simon Ball, 'The Royal Air Force and British Nuclear Strategy 1945-59', (PhD, Cambridge University, 1991), pp. 105-7. In the event of war, the plan entailed redeployment of six nuclear-capable USAF heavy bomber groups to Britain. Discussing the implications with Leon Johnson, Slessor stated that he was uneasy about agreeing to a paper plan without political approval and if details were to leak, it would have embarrassing repercussions. Ibid.
38. Hathaway, *Ambiguous*, p. 264
39. Blair, *Logic*, p. 31.
40. Jack Levy, 'Organisational Routines and the Causes of War' *International Studies Quarterly* Vol.30 (1986); Barry Posen, *The Sources of Military Doctrine: France, Britain and Germany Between the Wars* (New York: Cornell University Press, 1984); Samuel Huntington, *The Soldier and the State* (New York: Vintage, 1957).
41. PREM 11/3712, de Zulueta to Macmillan, 24 June 1962.
42. AIR 8/1998, DP(O)13, 21 February 1953.
43. In December 1958, SAC had 380 B-52s and 1,367 B-47s compared to Bomber Command's front-line strength of 45 Valiants, 18 Vulcans and 10 Victors.
44. RG 218, CCS 350.05(3-16-48) Section 12, JCS 2220/140, Memorandum for the Secretary of Defense, Further Cooperation with the United Kingdom and Canada in Military Applications of Atomic Energy, 6 June 1958. National Archives.
45. AIR 20/10056, Note on Target Coordination, 27 July 1960.
46. Carver, *Tightrope*, p. 61.
47. CAB 131/25, D(61)23, UK Views on NATO Strategy and Nuclear Weapons, 1 May 1961.
48. FO 371/152114, Cole to Ramsbottom, 7 March 1960.
49. Gregory, *Nuclear*, p. 195.
50. Lt. Gen. John Cushman, 'Command and Control of Theater Force' (Program on Information Resources Policy, Harvard University, April 1983), p. 96.
51. RG 59, Kohler to Murphy, Letter from Prime Minister to President Proposing US-UK Talks on Procedural Arrangements Leading to Decision to Launch Nuclear Retaliation, 8 May 1958, Policy Planning Staff Records, 1957–61, Lot 67D548, Box 130, Great Britain, National Archives. We are grateful to William Burr for drawing our attention to this document.
52. Thayer, 'Risk', p. 441.
53. Alexander George, 'Crisis Management: The Interaction of Political and Military Considerations' *Survival* Vol.26, No.5 (September/October 1984), pp. 227–8.
54. Lucas, p. 281. Britain was not the only nuclear state where the use of nuclear weapons was raised. Bulganin hinted at the possible deployment of Soviet rockets, while Eisenhower privately hinted at the use of nuclear weapons to keep the Soviets out of Egypt: 'if those fellows start something, we may have to hit them, and if necessary, with *everything* in the bucket.' Ibid.
55. PREM 11/3815, Organisation of Government to deal with a crisis on Berlin, memorandum by the Secretary to the Cabinet, September 1961.
56. Ibid.
57. PREM 11/3815, Macmillan to Brook, PM's Personal Minute, M243/61, Berlin, 29 July 1961. Emphasis in original.
58. For details of the British response to the crisis, see Stephen Twigge, 'Anglo-American Air Force

Collaboration and the Cuban Missile Crisis: A British Perspective', in Miller, *Seeing,* pp. 209-21; Scott, *Macmillan,* Chapter 8.
59. Council on Foreign Relations, *The United States in World Affairs, 1962* (New York: Harpers & Row, 1963).
60. Wynn, *RAF,* p. 259n.
61. PREM 11/3691, de Zulueta to Bundy, 28 October 1962.
62. For details, see Chapter 3.
63. Wynn, *RAF*, p. 213.
64. Blair, *Logic,* p. 9.
65. Shuckburgh, 'Cuba'.
66. Madelin, 'Additional', p. 225.
67. Zuckerman, *Monkeys,* p. 303.
68. PREM 11/3718, Macmillan to Kennedy, PM's Personal Tel. T5/62, 5 January 1962.
69. PREM 11/3689, Ormsby-Gore to Macmillan, Tel. 2650, PM's Pers. Tel. T.505/62, 23 October 1962.

Appendix 1: Key Terms

Alternate Command Centre (ACC): a secret and secure seat of government located away from main population centres and intended to house the National Command Authority in the event of the capital's destruction.
Assured Destruction: the capability to inflict unacceptable damage upon an adversary in all circumstances.
Backbone: communications system linking London, Manchester, Birmingham and Leeds.
Counterforce Strike: nuclear attack directed against military targets (including command centres and lines of communication).
Countervalue Strike: nuclear attack directed against population centres.
Decapitation Attack: nuclear strike targeted at command centres and political leadership rather than delivery systems.
Electromagnetic Pulse (EMP): strong burst of ionising radiation released by a nuclear explosion that disrupts communications systems.
Escalation Control: concept related to limited nuclear operations in which use of force is applied incrementally in a controlled and deliberate manner.
Extended Deterrence: the application of deterrence to protect third parties.
First-Strike: initial offensive targeted at opponent's means of retaliation.
Inadvertent Nuclear Use: the accidental or unauthorized release of nuclear weapons.
Intra-war Deterrence: strategy using nuclear weapons but designed to terminate hostilities at the lowest level by threatening escalation to strategic nuclear exchange.
Launch-on-Warning: strategy in which missiles and bombers are launched on radar warning alone.
Minimum Deterrence: a force structure composed of the minimum requirement to inflict assured destruction.
National Command Authority (NCA): body possessing the constitutional authority to direct nuclear operations.
Negative Control: procedures designed to prevent unauthorised or inadvertent use of nuclear weapons.
Nuclear Warhead: a weapon employing the release of nuclear energy for its destructive power. Two types exist: atomic weapons (fission) which

APPENDIX

use uranium or plutonium, producing yields between 20–200 KT; and thermonuclear weapons (fusion) which employ a fission primary to ignite the thermonuclear fuel (usually tritium or lithium 6 deuteride) and capable of yields ranging from 1–50 MG. The British arsenal employed both types of weapon, including:

Blue Danube (5–30 KT), Britain's first atomic weapon, which entered service with the RAF in 1953;
Green Grass, thermonuclear warhead for *Violet Club* and *Yellow Sun I* based on a modified *Orange Herald* design;
Orange Herald, a boosted fission warhead for the Blue Streak IRBM;
Red Beard (2–15 KT), tactical nuclear weapon deployed by the RAF and navy in the late-1950s;
Red Snow, thermonuclear warhead for *Yellow Sun II* and Blue Steel;
Violet Club, interim megaton weapon (1958–60) employing *Green Grass* warhead in *Blue Danube* casing;
Yellow Sun I, megaton weapon using *Green Grass* warhead, housed in new ballistic casing which entered service in 1960.
Yellow Sun II, megaton weapon using *Red Snow* warhead deployed with RAF in 1961.

Permissive Action Links (PALs): electronic device, blocking detonation of nuclear weapon. Activation required input of authenticated codes.
Pickwick: encrypted telephone system used in Whitehall.
Positive Control: a procedure that required the transmission of a fully authenticated strike order before nuclear weapons are released.
Pre-emptive Attack: a first-strike launched in anticipation of an enemy attack.
Quick Reaction Alert (QRA): condition in which forces are kept in a high state of readiness ready for immediate action.
R-Hour: specified time at which NATO nuclear strikes would be directed at the enemy.
Second-Strike: a retaliatory nuclear attack.
Single Integrated Operational Plan (SIOP): US nuclear war plan designed to co-ordinate nuclear strikes undertaken by different commands.
Turnstile: codename given to UK ACC.
Twilight: communication system linking Prime Minister to US President.
Watch Committee: US body responsible for providing warning of Soviet attack.

Appendix 2

TOP SECRET
SPECIALLY RESTRICTED CIRCULATION

SUPPLEMENTARY DIRECTIVE TO
AIR MARSHAL SIR KENNETH CROSS
K.C.B., C.B.E., D.S.O, D.F.C.

This supplementary Directive gives you certain delegated powers in addition to those set out in your Command Directive dated 21st May, 1962, and specifies the circumstances in which they may be exercised.

2. When either:-
   (a) From all sources of information available to you, you judge that your force in this country is about to be attacked with nuclear weapons and there has been no preceding period of strategic warning that a nuclear attack is imminent.

   or

   (b) Nuclear bombs from an enemy attack have burst on this country before you have been authorised to retaliate, you are authorised:-
      (i) To order all bomber aircraft within your command to be airborne under positive control in accordance with the agreed plans covering this procedure.
      (ii) To seek contact by any means of communication open to you with the Prime Minister or his Deputy in London or at the alternate Government Headquarters (Burlington) and act in accordance with his instructions.
      (iii) To ascertain, if possible, what instructions the Commander, 7th Air Division, has received and, if action under sub-paragraph (b) (ii) above proves abortive and enemy nuclear bombs have burst in this country, co-ordinate with the Commander, 7th Air Division, instructions to release nuclear weapons under joint control.

APPENDIX

3. If enemy nuclear bombs have burst in this country, and action under 2 (b) (ii) and (iii) above has proved abortive, you are authorised in the last resort to order on your own responsibility nuclear retaliation by all means at your disposal.

T.G. PIKE
Marshal of the Royal Air Force,
<u>Chief of the Air Staff</u>

<u>25th September, 1962</u>

Source: AIR 8/2530.

Appendix 3

TOP SECRET

ANNEX 'A'

TERMS OF REFERENCE FOR MEASURES TO FURNISH
THE ROYAL AIR FORCE WITH UNITED STATES
ATOMIC WEAPONS IN EVENT OF GENERAL
WAR AND TO CO-ORDINATE THE
ATOMIC STRIKE PLANS OF
UNITED STATES AIR FORCES
WITH THE ROYAL AIR FORCE

1. <u>Concept for Co-ordination of the Atomic Strike Effort of United States and United Kingdom Air Forces.</u> Co-ordination of the atomic strike plans of that portion of the Royal Air Force which has been committed to NATO shall be the responsibility of USCINCEUR/SACEUR. Co-ordination of the atomic strike plans of United States air forces with the atomic strike plans of that portion of the Royal Air Force which is not committed to NATO shall be the responsibility of the United States Air Force and the Royal Air Force.

2. <u>Concept for Logistic Support Operations</u>. The United States Air Force will provide personnel and associated equipment for maintaining custody and operational readiness of United States atomic weapons on operational Royal Air Force bases. Physical facilities and normal base support will be provided by Royal Air Force units. Operational delivery and loading capability, to include all necessary ancillary equipment, will also be a responsibility of the Royal Air Force. The United States Air Force unit involved will be charged with the custody, storage, maintenance, modification, operational readiness and internal security of United States atomic weapons to the extent required by existing United States law. The United States atomic weapon must be married to the Royal Air Force delivery aircraft by having both physically located on the same base.

APPENDIX

3. <u>Method of Co-ordination of Operational Plans and Determination of Responsibility for Target Selection, Related Problems, and Security of United States Plans</u>. Operational plans for the employment of all Royal Air Force atomic capable forces will be co-ordinated in accordance with a modus operandi as agreed to by the United States unified and specified commanders and approved by the Joint Chiefs of Staff. The co-ordination of plans will be accomplished in three phases:
   (a) USCINCEUR/SACEUR will co-ordinate the efforts of the Royal Air Force atomic capable units committed to him.
   (b) The atomic strike plans of USCINCEUR/SACEUR will be co-ordinated with the plans of all other United States unified and specified commanders in accordance with existing procedures.
   (c) The atomic strike plans of Royal Air Force atomic capable units not committed to NATO will be co-ordinated by the Chief of Staff, United States Air Force, either directly or by delegation of authority to CINCSAC, who in turn will be responsible that such plans are co-ordinated with plans of all other United States unified and specified commanders in accordance with existing procedures.

4. <u>Method of Allocation</u>.

(a) Weapons allocated by the Joint Chiefs of Staff for delivery by that portion of the Royal Air Force under the operational control of a NATO commander will be included in the Joint Chiefs of Staff bulk allocations to appropriate United States unified and specified commands.

(b) Weapons allocated by the Joint Chiefs of Staff for delivery by that portion of the Royal Air Force not under the operational control of a NATO commander will be earmarked by the Joint Chiefs of Staff, included in the bulk allocation to an appropriate United States commander and retained under the custodial responsibility of a designated United States commander.

5. <u>Basis for Allocation</u>. Weapons for delivery by the Royal Air Force will be allocated on the basis of:

(a) Delivery capability.

(b) Missions and tasks and their importance relative to the defeat of Communist air power.
(c) Availability of weapons.
(d) Other considerations

6. <u>Procedures to Release Weapons in Event of Emergency, Usage Authorization, Responsibility for Preparing and Executing Procedures</u>. Atomic weapons will be released to the Royal Air Force in accordance with the present procedures for obtaining Department of Defense custody of all finished atomic weapons in event of a Defense emergency by the appropriate unified or specified commander, or in the event that CINCONAD declares a condition of Air Defense Readiness, Air Defense Alert, Warning Yellow or Warning Red, the United States commander having custody of atomic weapons allocated for delivery by the Royal Air Force will prepare for the immediate release of these weapons to the Royal Air Force. Actual release will not, however, be accomplished until the United States commander concerned has been instructed to release the weapons for delivery or stand-by for delivery.

7. <u>Method of Co-ordinating Combat Operations</u>. The co-ordination of actual combat operations of the Royal Air Force atomic capable forces committed to NATO will be a responsibility of USCINCEUR/SACEUR. The atomic strike intents of these forces will be transmitted to the Joint Co-ordination Center, Europe, and the Joint War Room Annex in accordance with existing procedures. The actual combat operations of Royal Air Force forces not committed to NATO will be co-ordinated through the Joint Co-ordination Center, Europe, and the atomic strike intents of these forces will be transmitted to the Joint War Room Annex through the Joint Co-ordination Center, Europe, in accordance with existing procedures. The Royal Air Force will provide personnel and resources to establish and maintain a Royal Air Force section of the Joint Co-ordination Center, Europe. Strike and reconnaissance information will be provided by the Royal Air Force and transmitted to the Joint Co-ordination Center, Europe, in accordance with existing procedures employed by United States forces for transmitting this information.

Source: AIR 20/11338, COS (56) 451, 31 December 1956, Annex A.

Appendix 4

THE MURPHY-DEAN AGREEMENT

REPORT TO THE PRESIDENT AND THE PRIME MINISTER

Subject: Procedures for the Committing to the Attack of Nuclear Retaliatory Forces in the United Kingdom

1. Pursuant to the suggestion made by the Prime Minister to the President on April 24, 1958, representatives of the United States and United Kingdom Governments, led respectively by Mr. Robert Murphy and Sir Patrick Dean, have met in Washington. They studied how procedures of the two Governments might be concerted for reaching a decision to respond to a Soviet attack by committing nuclear retaliatory forces to the attack from the United Kingdom. The present report summarizes the results of these talks.

2. The basic understanding between the United Kingdom and United States Governments, regarding the use of bases in the United Kingdom by United States forces, provides that such use in an emergency shall be a matter for joint decision by the two Governments in the light of the circumstances at the time. A similar provision is incorporated in the Agreement of February 22, 1958, pursuant to which certain intermediate range ballistic missiles are to be provided to the United Kingdom Government by the United States Government. Decision by both parties would also be required in order to commit to the attack aircraft of the Royal Air Force Medium Bomber Force carrying nuclear weapons [of United States origin].

3. If Western retaliation is to be successful, there must be mutually understood procedures for ordering the retaliatory forces referred to in paragraph 2 above into action with the minimum of delay.

4. An outline of United Kingdom procedures is attached at Annex A, and an outline of United States procedures at Annex B. Representatives of

the two Governments are satisfied that these procedures, which are designed to be put into effect with the minimum delay, are mutually understood and mutually consistent. It will be seen that the "joint decision" required by the basic understanding between the two Governments would be taken by the President and the Prime Minister, who would speak personally with each other.

5. It should be noted that the attached procedures relate only to the committing to the attack of retaliatory forces referred to in sub-paragraphs (a), (b) and (c) of paragraph 6 below. They do not deal with the employment of United States retaliatory forces located outside the United Kingdom or with the employment of United Kingdom retaliatory forces other than those specified in sub-paragraphs (a) and (b) of paragraph 6. The United States Government, of course, retains the right in accordance with normal procedures to withdraw from their United Kingdom bases United States Air Force units deployed in the United Kingdom, and to redeploy such units elsewhere.

6. The categories of retaliatory forces to which the attached procedures apply are as follows:
    (a) Aircraft of the Royal Air Force Medium Bomber Force which would carry nuclear weapons [of United States origin pursuant to the Memorandum of Understanding of August 8, 1957];
    (b) Royal Air Force IRBM force to be created pursuant to the Agreement of February 22, 1958;
    (c) Units of the United States Strategic Air Command located in the United Kingdom.

In addition, there are also located in the United Kingdom certain United Kingdom and United States tactical bomber units committed to SACEUR and having a nuclear retaliatory capability. The use of the bases in the United Kingdom on which United States tactical bomber units are located falls under the basic understanding referred to in paragraph 2 above. Some adaptation of the attached procedures may be required to make them applicable to the NATO-committed tactical bomber units referred to earlier in this paragraph. Accordingly, the two Governments have agreed that they will respectively review as soon as possible their procedures

APPENDIX

covering such units. After consultation with SACEUR, they will make any additions and/or modifications to the attached procedures that may prove necessary in order to make such procedures applicable to all categories of retaliatory forces, including tactical bomber units, located in the United Kingdom.

    Robert Murphy   Patrick Dean

Washington, June 7, 1958.

Amended Annex A

UNITED KINGDOM PROCEDURES PRIOR TO ACTION BY NUCLEAR RETALIATORY FORCES BASED IN THE UNITED KINGDOM

1. In setting out courses of action to precede the despatch of nuclear retaliatory forces based in the United Kingdom two conditions of alert or warning periods are envisaged:-

    (a) <u>Strategic warning</u>. This implies the receipt of early information by the Joint Intelligence Committee concerning enemy intention to attack. Under these conditions the maximum number of bomber aircraft would be deployed at readiness as quickly as possible.

    (b) <u>Tactical warning</u>. This implies short warning of imminent attack derived from positive radar or other means. Under these conditions that portion of the medium bomber force held at readiness would be available for instant retaliatory action whilst the remainder of the force would come to readiness and be despatched in accordance with existing plans.

STRATEGIC WARNING

2. Following the receipt of intelligence information that enemy attack may be expected in the near future the following are to be informed:-
    (a) The Prime Minister and certain designated Ministers;
    (b) The U.K. Chiefs of Staff;
    (c) The U.S. intelligence authorities;
    (d) SACEUR.

3. The Chief of the Air Staff will take all necessary action to bring the Royal Air Force to a high state of operational readiness and the Commander, 7th Air Division, SAC will be notified of action taken to increase the readiness of the medium bomber force.

   SACEUR will be notified of action to increase the readiness of the tactical bomber force.

APPENDIX

4. The Prime Minister and the President of the United States will consult together regarding a joint decision to commit to the attack retaliatory forces based in the United Kingdom.

TACTICAL WARNING

5. When the Commander-in-Chief, Fighter Command, receives positive radar or other warning of impending enemy attack he will immediately inform:-

(a) Air Ministry;
(b) C-in-C Bomber Command;
(c) Commander, 7th Air Division, SAC;
(d) Commander, Third Air Force;
(e) SACEUR.

6. The Chief of the Air Staff will inform the Prime Minister, certain other designated Ministers, and the Chiefs of Staff. The Prime Minister will speak personally with the President of the United States regarding a joint decision to commit to the attack nuclear retaliatory forces based in the United Kingdom.

7. (a) On receipt of tactical warning the Chief of the Air Staff will order the medium bomber force to immediate readiness for take-off. At his discretion he may order the force into the air under "positive control" procedure, if he deems such action necessary to avoid loss on the ground by enemy action. In this sense "positive control" means the aircraft will fly on pre-arranged routes towards targets, but will not pass beyond a specified line pending the receipt of further definite instructions. The time at which aircraft are scheduled to reach this specified line will be made known to the Prime Minister and the United Kingdom Chiefs of Staff. The Commander of SAC units in the United Kingdom and SACEUR will be informed of this action.

(b) On receipt of tactical warning the Chief of the Air Staff will order the RAF Tactical Bomber Force assigned to SACEUR to immediate readiness. At his discretion SACEUR may order the Force into the air under "positive control" procedure, if he deems such action necessary to avoid loss on the ground by enemy action. In this sense "positive control" means the aircraft will fly on pre-arranged routes towards targets, but will not pass beyond a specified line pending the receipt of further definite instructions. Instructions to pass beyond the specified line would not be given until the joint decision referred to in paragraph 6 has been taken. The time at which aircraft are scheduled to reach this specified line will be made known to the United Kingdom Chiefs of Staff.

WARHEADS OF AMERICAN ORIGIN

8. Under both conditions described above, namely strategic and tactical warning, when the Prime Minister and the President of the United States consult together regarding the launching of nuclear retaliatory forces, it will be necessary for them to agree on the use of nuclear warheads of American origin, if they are deemed to be required. The United Kingdom retaliatory forces affected by this decision are:-

(a) The Medium Bomber Force;
(b) The Royal Air Force IRBM force to be created pursuant to the agreement of February 22, 1958.
(c) The Tactical Bomber Force.

9. Following agreement on the use of American warheads the Prime Minister will authorise the Chairman COS Committee to implement war plans requiring their use.

APPENDIX

Amended Annex B

PROCEDURES PRECEDING ATTACK BY UNITED STATES RETALIATORY FORCES FROM THE UNITED KINGDOM

1. These procedures apply under two conditions, that of strategic warning and that of tactical warning, defined as follows:-

    a. Strategic warning – warning, based on all available information, concerning possible enemy intent to initiate hostilities. Strategic warning is considered to be a time sufficient to permit United States forces in being to be deployed and in a state of maximum readiness.
    b. Tactical warning – warning based on information which positively indicates that an enemy attack is under way, or has occurred. Tactical warning will allow little or no deployment of forces.

2. On receipt by the National Indications Center of Intelligence information which indicates that an enemy is likely to launch an attack, the United States Intelligence authorities will be informed and they will immediately notify the Joint Chiefs of Staff and the members of the National Security Council.

3. In the case of strategic warning (1a above) received by the United States, the intelligence information and the evaluation thereof will have been passed to the Joint Intelligence Committee (London) and the Joint Intelligence Committee (Ottawa) pursuant to the Tripartite Alert procedure agreed to among the Governments of the United Kingdom, Canada and the United States.

4. (a) Upon receiving tactical warning (1b above), the Commander-in-Chief, Strategic Air Command may launch his Alert Force under "Positive Control" procedure, which proceeds on prearranged routes towards targets, but will not pass beyond a specified line without further definite instructions.

(b) Upon receiving tactical warning (1b above), SACEUR may launch his supporting strike forces under "Positive Control" procedure, but such forces will not pass beyond a specified line without further definite instructions.

5. The following actions will be taken, depending upon the type of warning received:-

   a. The Secretary of Defense will advise the President of the situation.
   b. The Department of Defense will notify appropriate Government agencies of the situation.
   c. The Joint Chiefs of Staff will simultaneously dispatch prepared alert messages to all field commanders including CINCEUR and CINCSAC; the Members of the NATO Standing Group; major NATO commanders; and the Chairman Chiefs of Staff Committees, United Kingdom and Canada.

6. The President will speak personally with the Prime Minister of the United Kingdom regarding joint decision to commit forces located in the United Kingdom.

7. Upon the President's authorization, the Joint Chiefs of Staff will direct the implementation of appropriate war plans, stating that the use of atomic weapons is authorized.

Source: DDEL, Ann Whitman File, Admin. Series, Box 5, AEC 1958 (2), 7 June 1958; AIR 8/2201, 22 January 1959. The sections in square brackets are sanitized in the US released version but which can be determined from related British documents.

Appendix 5

TOP SECRET

FROM WASHINGTON TO FOREIGN OFFICE

POLARIS

"With reference to the launching of missiles from United States Polaris submarines outside United Kingdom territorial waters, the United States re-affirms the assurance given by President Eisenhower to Foreign Minister Eden on March 9, 1953, that in the event of emergency such as increased tension or the threat of war, the United States will take every possible step to consult with Britain and other Allies."

Source: PREM 11/2941, 28 August 1960.

Appendix 6

SECRET

MEMORANDUM BY THE PRIME MINISTER

Recalling his long-standing arrangements first with President Eisenhower and then with President Kennedy by which neither the United States nor the United Kingdom will use their nuclear force without consultation with the other, the Prime Minister stated in a response to a request from the President that in the same spirit he would give as much notice as possible to the President of the United States of any British intention temporarily to withdraw POLARIS submarines from their assigned role for other purposes. He also expressed his confidence that his successors would act similarly.

(Signed) HAROLD MACMILLAN

December 20th, 1962

Source: PREM 11/4229.

Appendix 7

TOP SECRET

C.O.S. (62) 262　　　　　　　　SPECIALLY RESTRICTED
21ST JUNE, 1962　　　　　　　　CIRCULATION

CHIEFS OF STAFF COMMITTEE

CONTROL OF NUCLEAR WEAPONS IN ACE—RELEASE PROCEDURES
Note by the Secretary

At their meeting# on 19th June, 1962, the Chiefs of Staff approved the report, at Annex, which examined the SHAPE Documents dealing with R-HOUR and S-HOUR release procedures for the control of nuclear weapons in ACE. In approving the report the Chiefs of Staff:-

(a) Instructed the Secretary to forward it to the Ministry of Defence as an expression of their views.

(b) Invited the Government Departments concerned to take the appropriate War Book action.

(Signed) J.K. WATKINS

MINISTRY OF DEFENCE, S.W.1.
21ST JUNE, 1962.

COS (62) 41st Meeting, Minute 19.

TOP SECRET

ANNEX TO COS (62) 262
CONTROL OF NUCLEAR WEAPONS IN
ACE—RELEASE PROCEDURES

<u>INTRODUCTION</u>

1. Two new documents, the SACEUR/USCINCEUR R-Hour[@] and S-Hour[£] Release Procedures, have been issued by SHAPE to augment the instructions contained in SACEUR's revised Emergency Defence Plan[%] for the control of nuclear weapons in ACE. The former is concerned with the release of nuclear weapons in General War, and the latter with their selective use under conditions of aggression less than General War: both relate only to the provision and use of nuclear weapons from American sources. We understand that the former is to become effective on 16th June, 1962, and that no date has yet been stated for implementation of the latter. These documents are not subject to national approval, but we consider it necessary to examine them in view of our previous comments[&] on the arrangements for the control of nuclear weapons in ACE, and in particular for their discriminate use.

2. As distribution of these two documents in the United Kingdom has been limited to one copy each to the Ministry of Defence, Bomber Command, and Fighter Command we outline the procedures below.

<u>AIM</u>

3. To examine the SACEUR/USCINCEUR R-Hour and S-Hour Release Procedures for the control of nuclear weapons in ACE.

[@] SHAPE 10/62
[£] SHAPE 11/62
[%] SHAPE 144/61
[&] COS (61) 191

APPENDIX

THE R-HOUR RELEASE PROCEDURES

<u>R-Hour Messages</u>

4. R-Hour Release Procedures deal with the format and implementation of R-Hour messages, and with the use of authentication codewords. There are two R-Hour messages. The first (RH-1) is prepositioned at appropriate ACE and United States commands and units but does not become effective until a second message, the implementation one, is received. The RH-1 message contains instructions for the General War use of nuclear weapons in implementation of SACEUR's Scheduled Programme, SACEUR approved Regional Programmes and ACE Air Defence Employment Directives.

5. The second message (RH-1A) will contain the authentication codewords (one for the US custodian and one for the appropriate NATO authorities) and other instructions necessary to complete the prepositioned message and to authorise the recipient to implement R-Hour at a specified time. Because all the classified details are already contained in the prepositioned message, the information can be sent unclassified in a simple letter code by the fastest means available.

6. With these procedures SACEUR can:-

   (a) Cancel nuclear strike operations against the USSR or any or all Satellite countries.
   (b) Direct whether Contingency Plan 1 or 2 should be put into effect in Regional Priority Programmes.*
   (c) Direct whether JUPITER missiles are to be used against primary or alternate targets.*
   (d) Delete one or more target categories from strikes against specific satellite countries.*
   (e) Pass the execution time for external national strike forces (E-Hour) should this vary by more than five minutes from R-Hour.

---

* Explanations of Contingency Plans, Jupiter primary or alternate targets, or target categories in satellite countries are not given in this document.

(f) Co-ordinate his scheduled programme strikes with the external forces, by passing the latter's force generation rates (the rates at which forces become ready for or committed to operations after the alert or order to go). Depending on the degree of warning the numbers of immediately available delivery units will change, thus affecting rate of effort and timing co-ordination.

7. Although normally passed by separate messages the RH-1A message can also indicate:-

   (a) The ACE force generation rate effective at R-Hour.
   (b) SACEUR's sanction for the use of nuclear weapons larger than 10kt in friendly and neutral countries, the use of which, except for air defence weapons, requires SACEUR's specific approval.%

8. <u>Authentication Codewords</u>. SACEUR/USCINCEUR codewords are prepositioned at appropriate ACE and United States commands and units (e.g. in Northern Army Group/ 2 ATAF at the Joint Headquarters, all corps headquarters, the TOC (Tactical Operations Centre), SOCs (Sector Operations Centres), nuclear strike wings and related custodial units). The RH-1A message, by conveying the authentication codewords, verifies the authorization for custodial units to release weapons and for ACE delivery units to employ them in accordance with NSP. Alternate codewords are held in case current ones are compromised.

<u>Our Comments</u>

9. We consider the R-Hour release procedures give a desirable degree of flexibility to SACEUR in the implementation of nuclear strikes at R-Hour.

10. The placing of SACEUR's authentication codewords at nuclear strike wings will enable them to act immediately on the RH-1A implementing message. Northern Army Group/ 2 ATAF will use their own codewords to pass R-Hour to lower headquarters and units which do not hold SACEUR's authentication codeword.

APPENDIX

11. The effectiveness of the system depends upon the adequacy of available communications, and in proposing a Basic Military Requirement for a Command and Control Communications System for ACE Retaliatory Forces, which we have approved, SACEUR recognized that existing telephone, teletype, and operations room procedures do not fully meet the requirement for speed and accuracy. We are advised that the FAST CAT system which has been offered[$] by the United States meets the NBMR, and that these procedures could be implemented if it were adopted.

12. The authentication codeword system appears to provide a sound safeguard against R-Hour being acted upon except by SACEUR's declaration.

THE S-HOUR RELEASE PROCEDURES

General

13. The S-Hour Release Procedures provide the means for SACEUR/USCINCEUR to authorize the transfer of single or limited numbers of nuclear weapons by United States Custodians to designated ACE Executing Commanders and to authorize those commanders to deliver the weapons against the enemy when specifically directed by the SACEUR approved Releasing Commander. The document repeats the circumstances, set out in SACEUR's revised Emergency Defence Plan[%], in which the selective use of nuclear weapons may be authorized, which we accept in our examination[&] of the EDP. The document also adds that in requesting the selective release of nuclear weapons commanders will be guided by the following:-

(a) The objective to be achieved will be to confine or eliminate the threat when conventional means are inadequate.
(b) The weapon(s) and delivery system selected will be those which are the most consistent with the military task to be accomplished.
(c) The authority to release nuclear weapons will never be delegated to a level where localized operational emergencies might result in a hasty premature decision to direct the employment of nuclear weapons.

APPENDIX

(d) The releasing authority will be retained at the highest possible level and in no case will be delegated below the level of Corps Commander, ATAF Commander or Naval Task Force Commander.

14. The document also includes instructions and format for requesting and approving messages, and directions for the use of authentication codewords.

S-Hour Messages

15. The message requesting SACEUR's authority for the selective release of nuclear weapons (SU-1) for strikes against surface targets, and for air defence and ASW, must in all cases state plan name or area and justification for the strike(s). Only in the case of strikes against surface targets, however, do details have to be given of the target(s), number/ type of weapons, height of burst, time over target, and delivery units. Requests may be initiated only by NATO commanders not lower than Army Group/ ATAF or Navy Task Force level, but the applicable Custodian, Releasing, and Executing Commanders will be information addresses.

16. SACEUR's reply (SU-1A) will go direct to the originator of the request, and applicable Custodian, Releasing and Executing Commanders. The same message format enables SACEUR to initiate selective use when no request has been received (see paragraph 19 below).

17. By establishing the format of both messages in advance the procedure makes it possible to reduce the length of the transmissions to a minimum. However, unlike the R-Hour implementation message, these have to classified COSMIC TOP SECRET.

Authentication Codewords

18. Five alternative USCINCEUR codewords are to be prepositioned in separate sealed envelopes with United States custodial detachments only, and will not be opened until receipt of the SACEUR/ USCINCEUR SU-1A message, which will specify the envelope number

APPENDIX

and give the codeword. These alternative codewords are provided in case there is more than one S-Hour or in case one of the codewords is compromised.

Our Comments

19. We agree with the additional guidance now given to subordinate commanders (sub-paragraph 13 (a) to (d) above) on the selective use of nuclear weapons, and in particular with the level of the releasing authority. We note that the format of the SU-1A message would allow SACEUR to authorize the explosion of a nuclear weapon on a military target for political purposes should this be required in the concept of forcing a pause. We also note that the SU-1A message is sent direct for action to custodial units and executing commanders at the same time as to the releasing authority. We accept this procedure despite the risk that an executing commander could conceivably give the order to fire before authorization from a releasing authority had been received.

20. We accept the detail required in the request for strikes against land targets. We agree that similar detail would not be practicable in requests for nuclear weapons to be used for air defence or ASW purposes in view of the need for more rapid tactical decisions in these circumstances.

21. The authentication codewords system appears to provide an adequate safeguard against nuclear weapons for selective use being released by the United States Custodians except on the authority of USCINCEUR. Should nuclear weapons in ACE occur in other than United States custody, the procedures would have to be expanded to cover this.

22. We consider that delays may occur in SACEUR's communications with releasing authorities because of the inadequacy of current on-line cypher equipments and the problem of handling information between field headquarters and higher headquarters especially when different languages are being used. We are advised that these difficulties will be obviated where the equipment is applicable if the FAST CAT system is accepted by NATO to meet SACEUR's NBMR.

GENERAL

23. We emphasize that nothing in these procedures is designed to expedite or alter inter-governmental arrangements for authorizing SACEUR to declare R-Hour or S-Hour.

CONCLUSIONS

24. We conclude that:-

    (a) The new R-Hour and S-Hour Release Procedures for ACE are acceptable.
    (b) For both procedures the system of authentication codewords appears to provide adequate safeguard against the release of nuclear weapons except on the authority of SACEUR/USCINCEUR.
    (c) Communications for implementing R- and S-Hour require improvements as set out in SACEUR's Basic Military Requirement on this subject, and we are advised that the FAST CAT system will be able to meet this need.

Source: AIR 20/10056, COS (62) 262, 21 June, 1962.

APPENDIX

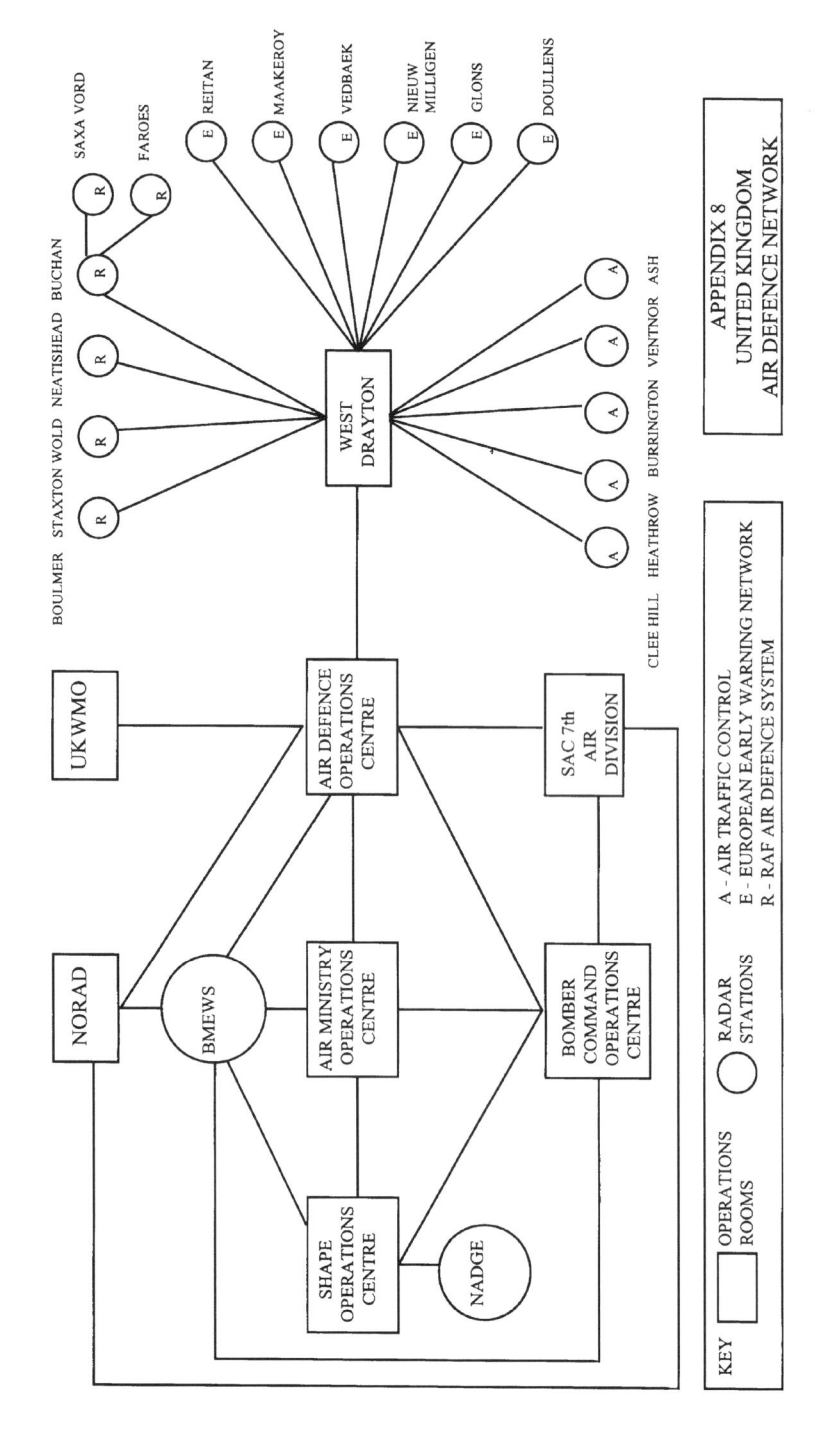

APPENDIX 8
UNITED KINGDOM
AIR DEFENCE NETWORK

KEY: OPERATIONS ROOMS ☐ RADAR STATIONS ◯

A - AIR TRAFFIC CONTROL
E - EUROPEAN EARLY WARNING NETWORK
R - RAF AIR DEFENCE SYSTEM

344   PLANNING ARMAGEDDON

APPENDIX

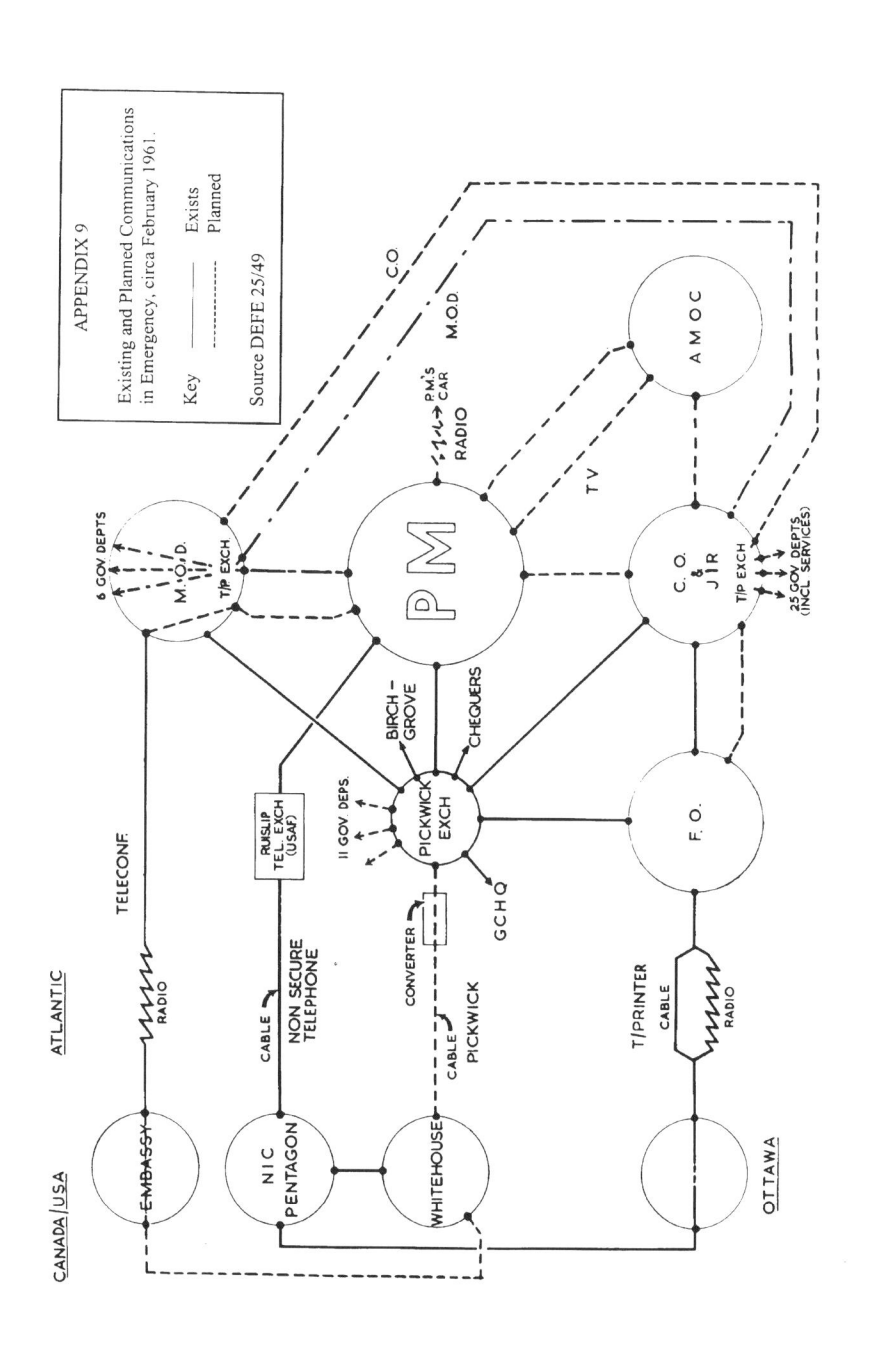

APPENDIX 9

Existing and Planned Communications in Emergency, circa February 1961.

Key ——— Exists
 ------- Planned

Source DEFE 25/49

PLANNING ARMAGEDDON 345

Select Bibliography

PRIMARY SOURCES

Archival Collections

Central Intelligence Agency web-site.
Dwight D. Eisenhower Library, Abilene, Kansas.
Harry S. Truman Library, Independence, Missouri.
John F. Kennedy Library, Boston, Massachusetts.
Library of Congress, Manuscript Collection, Washington DC.
Lyndon B. Johnson Library, Austin, Texas.
National Archives and Record Administration, Maryland.
National Museum of Labour History, Manchester.
Public Record Office, Kew.

Chadwyck-Healey Microfiche Collections

Cuban Missile Crisis, 1962.
Nuclear Non-Proliferation 1945–90.
US Intelligence Community 1947–89.

Official Publications

Command Papers (HMSO).
Congressional Budget Office, *Strategic Command, Control and Communications: Alternative Approaches for Modernisation* (Washington: USGPO, 1981).
Congressional Research Service, US Congress, House, *Authority to Order the Use of Nuclear Weapons (United States, United Kingdom, France, Soviet Union, People's Republic of China)*, Report prepared for the Subcommittee on International Security and Scientific Affairs of the Committee on International Relations by the Congressional Research Service, Library of Congress, 94th Cong., 1st Sess., 1 December 1975 (Washington: USGPO, 1975).
Department of State, *Bulletin* (Washington: USGPO).
First Special Report from the Defence Committee, Session 1981–82, *Strategic Nuclear Weapons Policy*, HC 266 (HMSO, 1982).

Foreign Relations of the United States (Washington: USGPO).
Fourth Report from the Defence Committee, *Strategic Nuclear Weapons Policy*, Session 1980–1, HC 36 (HMSO, 1981).
Hansard, *House of Commons Debates* (HMSO).
Pedlow, G. and Welzenbach, D. *The CIA and the U-2 Program, 1954–1974* (Washington: Central Intelligence Agency, 1998).
Public Papers of the Presidents of the United States: John F. Kennedy, 1961 (Washington: USGPO, 1962).
Ruffner, K. (Ed.) *CORONA: America's First Satellite Program* (Washington: CIA, 1995).
Steury, D. (Ed.) *Intentions and Capabilities: Estimates on Soviet Strategic Forces, 1950–1983* (Washington: CIA, 1996).

SECONDARY SOURCES

Books

Aldrich, R. (Ed.) *British Intelligence, Strategy and the Cold War, 1945–51* (Routledge, 1992).
Allison, G. Carnesale, A. and Nye, N. (Eds.) *Hawks, Doves and Owls: An Agenda for Avoiding Nuclear War* (New York: Norton, 1985).
Andrew, C. *For the President's Eyes Only: Secret Intelligence and the American Presidency From Washington to Bush* (Harper Collins, 1995).
Armacost, M. *The Politics of Weapons Innovation: The Thor-Jupiter Controversy* (New York: Columbia University Press, 1969).
Ball, D. *Can Nuclear War be Controlled?* Adelphi Paper No. 169 (IISS, 1981).
——— and Richelson, J. (Eds.), *Strategic Nuclear Targeting* (Ithaca, NY: Cornell University Press, 1986).
Baylis, J. *Anglo-American Defence Relations, 1939-1980: The Special Relationship* (Macmillan, 1984).
——— *Ambiguity and Deterrence: British Nuclear Strategy 1945–1964* (OUP, 1995).
Betts, R. *Soldiers, Statesmen and Cold War Crises*, (Cambridge, Mass.: Harvard University Press, 1977).
Blair, B. *Strategic Command and Control* (Washington: Brookings, 1985).
——— *The Logic of Accidental Nuclear War* (Washington: Brookings, 1993).
Bluth, C. *Britain, Germany and Western Nuclear Strategy* (OUP, 1995).

Bobbitt, P., Freedman, F., and Treverton, T. (Eds.), *US Nuclear Strategy: A Reader,* (Macmillan, 1989).

Botti, T. *The Long Wait: The Forging of the Anglo–American Nuclear Alliance 1945–1958* (New York: Greenwood Press, 1987).

Bowie, R. *The North Atlantic Nations Tasks for the 1960s: A Report to the Secretary of State, August 1960* (CISSM, University of Maryland: NHP, Occasional Paper 7, 1991).

Bracken, P. *The Command and Control of Nuclear Forces* (New Haven: Yale University Press, 1983).

Buckton, H. *Forewarned is Forearmed: An Official Tribute and History of the Royal Observer Corps* (Ashford, Buchan & Enright, 1993).

Bundy, M. *Danger and Survival: Choices about the Bomb in the First Fifty Years* (Random House, 1988).

Campbell, D. *War Plan UK: The Truth about Civil Defence in Britain* (Paladin Books, 1982).

Carnovale, M. *The Control of NATO Nuclear Forces in Europe* (Oxford: Westview Press, 1993).

Carter, A., Steinbruner J. and Zracket, C. (Eds.) *Managing Nuclear Operations* (Washington: Brookings, 1987).

Carver, M. *Tightrope Walking: British Defence Policy Since 1945* (Hutchinson, 1992).

Cathcart, B. *Test of Greatness: Britain's Struggle for the Atom Bomb* (John Murray, 1994).

Clark, I, *Nuclear Diplomacy and the Special Relationship: Britain's Deterrent and America, 1957–1962* (OUP, 1994).

—— and Wheeler, N. *The British Origins of Nuclear Strategy 1945–1955* (OUP, 1989).

Collier, B. *The Defence of the United Kingdom* (HMSO, 1957).

Duffield, J. *Power rules : the evolution of NATO's conventional force posture* (Stanford: Stanford University Press, 1995).

Duke, S. *US Defence Bases in the United Kingdom: A Matter for Joint Decision?* (Macmillan, 1987).

Dunn, L. *Containing Nuclear Proliferation,* Adelphi Paper No. 263 (IISS, 1991).

Esposito L. and Schear, J. *The Command and Control of Nuclear Weapons* (Workshop Report, Aspen Institute for Humanistic Studies, 1985).

Feaver, P. *Guarding the Guardians: Civilian Control of Nuclear Weapons in the United States* (Ithaca, NY: Cornell University Press, 1992).

BIBLIOGRAPHY

Ford, D. *The Button* (Simon & Schuster, 1985).
Freedman, L. *Britain and Nuclear Weapons* (Macmillan, 1980).
────── *US Intelligence and the Soviet Strategic Threat* (Macmillan, 1986).
────── *The Evolution of Nuclear Strategy* (Macmillan, 1989).
────── Martin Navias and Nicholas Wheeler, *Independence in Concert: The British Rationale for Possessing Strategic Nuclear Weapons* (CISSM, University of Maryland: NHP Occasional Paper 5, 1989).
Gottfried, K. and Blair, B. (Eds.) *Crisis Stability and Nuclear War* (OUP, 1988).
Gough, J. *Watching the Skies: A History of Ground Radar for the Defence of the United Kingdom by the Royal Air Force from 1946 to 1975* (MOD, Air Historical Branch, HMSO, 1993).
Gowing, M. *Britain and Atomic Energy, 1939–1945* (Macmillan, 1965).
────── *Independence and Deterrence: Britain and Atomic Energy 1945–1952*, 2 vols. (Macmillan, 1974).
Gregory, S. *The Command and Control of British Nuclear Weapons* (University of Bradford School of Peace Studies, Peace Research Report No. 13, December 1986).
────── *Nuclear Command and Control in NATO: Nuclear Weapons Operations and the Strategy of Flexible Response* (Macmillan, 1996).
Groom, A. *British Thinking about Nuclear Weapons* (Frances Pinter, 1974).
Grove, E. *Vanguard to Trident: British Naval Policy since World War II* (Bodley Head, 1987).
Hathaway, R. *Ambiguous Partnership: Britain and America, 1944–1947* (New York: Columbia University Press, 1981).
Healey, D. *The Time of My Life* (Michael Joseph, 1989).
Hennessy, P. *Never Again: Britain 1945–1951* (Jonathan Cape, 1992).
────── *The Hidden Wiring: Unearthing the British Constitution* (Victor Gollancz, 1995).
Herman, M. *Intelligence Power in Peace and War* (CUP/RIIA, 1996).
Hinsley F. *et al, British Intelligence in the Second World War*, Vols. 1–4 (HMSO, 1979–1990).
Holloway, D. *Stalin and the Bomb: the Soviet Union and Atomic Energy, 1939–1956* (New Haven, Conn.: Yale University Press, 1994).
Horne, A. *Macmillan 1957–1986, Volume II of the Official Biography* (Macmillan, 1989).
Howard, M. *British Intelligence in the Second World War*, Vol. 5 (HMSO, 1990).

Hunter, S. (Ed.) *Defending Northern Skies, 1915–1995* (The Royal Air Force Historical Society, 1996).
Hyde, H. *British Air Policy Between the Wars, 1918–1939* (Heinemann, 1976).
Jackson, R. *Strike Force: The USAF in Britain since 1948* (Robson Books, 1986).
Jervis, R. *Perceptions and Misperceptions in International Politics* (Princeton NJ: Princeton University Press, 1976).
Jones, R. *Reflections on Intelligence*, (Heinemann, 1989).
——— *Most Secret War, British Scientific Intelligence 1939–1945* (Coronet, 1990).
Kaplan, F. *The Wizards of Armageddon* (New York: Simon & Schuster, 1983).
Karber, P. et al. *Trends in the Deployment of Nuclear Weapons in Central Europe: 1948–1988*, Nuclear History Program Data Base Series (Washington: Nuclear History Program, July 1989).
Kennan, G. *Memoirs 1950–1963* (Hutchinson, 1973)
Lashmar, P. *Spy Flights of the Cold War* (Sutton Publishing Ltd, 1996).
Lewis, J. *Changing Directions: British Military Planning for Post–war Strategic Defence 1942–47* (Sherwood Press, 1988).
McCamley, N. *Secret Underground Cities* (Leo Cooper, 1999).
McDonald, I. *Anglo–American Relations Since the Second World War* (David & Charles, 1974).
McLean, S. *How Nuclear Weapons Decisions Are Made* (Macmillan, 1986).
Macmillan, H. *Riding the Storm, 1956–1959* (Macmillan, 1971).
——— *At the End of the Day 1961–3* (Macmillan, 1973)
Melissen, J. *The Struggle for Nuclear Partnership: Britain, the United States and the Making of an Ambiguous Alliance 1952–1959* (Groningen: Styx, 1993).
Miall, H. *Nuclear Weapons: Who's in Charge?* (Macmillan, 1987).
Menaul, S. *Countdown: Britain's Strategic Nuclear Forces* (Robert Hale, 1980).
Miller, R. (Ed.) *Seeing off the Bear: Anglo–American Air Power Cooperation during the Cold War* (Washington: United States Air Force, 1995).
Morton, P. *Fire across the Desert: Woomera and the Anglo–Australian Joint Project 1946–1980* (Canberra: Australian Government Publishing Service, 1989).
Navias, M. *Nuclear Weapons and British Strategic Planning, 1955–1958* (OUP, 1991).

Neustadt, R. *Alliance Politics* (New York: Columbia University Press, 1970).
Nitze, P. *From Hiroshima to Glasnost: At the Center of Decision* (Weidenfield, 1990).
Norris, R., Burrows, A. and Fieldhouse, R. *Nuclear Weapons Databook, Volume V: British, French and Chinese Weapons* (Westview, 1994).
O'Brien, T. *Civil Defence* (HMSO, 1955).
Overlord – 1944: A Symposium on the Normandy Landings (RAF Historical Society, 1995).
Overy, R. *The Air War 1939–1945* (Macmillan, 1988).
Pierre, A. *Nuclear Politics: The British Experience with an Independent Nuclear Force, 1939–1970* (OUP, 1972).
Prados, J. *The Soviet Estimate*, (Princeton, NJ: Princeton University Press, 1986).
Reaping the Whirlwind, A Symposium on the Strategic Bomber Offensive 1939–45 (RAF Historical Society, 1993).
Rhodes, R. *The Making of the Atomic Bomb* (New York: Simon & Schuster, 1986).
——— *Dark Sun: The Making of the Hydrogen Bomb* (New York: Simon & Schuster, 1995).
Richelson, J. and Ball, D. *The Ties That Bind, Intelligence Cooperation between the UKUSA Countries — the United Kingdom, the United States of America, Canada, Australia and New Zealand* (Unwin Hyman, 1990).
Ruston, R. *A Say in the End of the World: Morals and British Nuclear Weapons Policy 1941–1987* (OUP, 1989).
Sagan, S. *Moving Targets: Nuclear Strategy and National Security* (Princeton, NJ: Princeton University Press, 1989).
——— *The Limits of Safety: Organisations, Accidents and Nuclear Weapons* (Princeton, NJ: Princeton University Press, 1993).
——— and Waltz, K. *The Spread of Nuclear Weapons: A Debate* (New York: Norton, 1995).
Schwartz, D. *NATO's Nuclear Dilemmas* (Washington: Brookings, 1983).
Schecter, J. and Deriabin, P. *The Spy Who Saved the World* (Charles Scribner's Sons, 1992).
Scott, L. *Macmillan, Kennedy and the Cuban Missile Crisis: Political, Military and Intelligence Aspects* (Macmillan, 1999).
Simpson, J. *The Independent Nuclear State: The United States, Britain and the Military Atom* (Macmillan, 1986).

Slessor, J. 'Command and Control of Allied Nuclear Forces: A British View', *Adelphi Paper,* No. 22, August 1965.
Smith, M. *British Air Strategy Between the Wars* (OUP, 1984).
Spaven, M. *Royal Navy Nuclear Capable Ships,* (ADIU, University of Sussex, 1985).
Stares, P. *Command Performance: The Neglected Dimension of European Secuirty* (Washington: Brookings, 1991).
Stein, P. and Feaver, P. *Assuring Control of Nuclear Weapons: The Evolution of Permissive Action Links* (Center for Science and International Affairs, Harvard University, Occasional Paper 2, 1987).
Steinbruner, J. *The Cybernetic Theory of Decision: New Dimensions of Political Analysis* (Princeton, NJ: Princeton University Press, 1974).
Stromseth, J. *The Origins of Flexible Response* (Macmillan, 1988).
Taylor, R. *Against the Bomb: The British Peace Movement 1958–1965* (OUP, 1988).
Tuschhoff, C. *Causes and Consequences of Germany's Deployment of Nuclear Capable Delivery Systems 1957–1963* (CISSM, University of Maryland: NHP Occasional Paper 9, 1994).
Twigge, S. *The Early Development of Guided Weapons in the United Kingdom 1940–1960* (Harwood Academic Press, 1993).
Vaisse, M. (Ed.) *L'Europe et la Crise de Cuba* (Paris: Armand Colin, 1993).
Wampler, R. *NATO Strategic Planning and Nuclear Weapons 1950–1957* (CISSM, University of Maryland: NHP Occasional Paper 6, 1990).
Watson, R. *The History of the Joint Chiefs of Staff: The Joint Chiefs of Staff and National Policy, Volume V, 1953–54* (Washington: GPO, 1987).
Webster C. and Frankland, N. *The Strategic Air Offensive Against Germany* (HMSO, 1961).
Wood, D. *Attack Warning Red: The Royal Observer Corps and the Defence of Britain 1925 to 1975* (Macdonald and Jane's, 1976).
Wynn, H. *RAF Strategic Nuclear Deterrent Forces: their origins, roles and deployment 1946–1969* (HMSO, 1994).
Ziegler, P. *Mountbatten* (Collins, 1985).
Zuckerman, S. *Monkeys, Men and Missiles 1946–88: An Autobiography* (Collins, 1985).

Articles

Aldrich, R. 'British Intelligence and the Anglo–American "Special Relationship" during the Cold War', *Review of International Studies,* Vol.24, No.3 (July 1988).

―――― and Michael Coleman, 'The Cold War, the JIC and British Signals Intelligence', *Intelligence and National Security* Vol.4, No.3 (July 1989).

Baylis, J. 'American Bases in Britain: "the Truman–Attlee Understandings"', *The World Today* (August/September 1986).

Blair, B. 'Nuclear Inadvertence: Theory and Evidence', *Security Studies*, Vol.4, No.4 (Summer, 1995).

Blight, J. and Welch, D. 'Risking "The Destruction of Nations": Lessons of the Cuban Missile Crisis for New and Aspiring Nuclear States', *Security Studies*, Vol.4, No.4 (Summer 1995).

Bracken, P. 'The Political Command and Control of Nuclear Forces', *Defense Analysis*, Vol.2, No.1 (January 1986).

Buchan, A. 'The Multilateral Force: A Study in Alliance Politics', *International Affairs*, Vol.40, No.4, (October 1964).

Caldwell, D. 'Permissive Action Links: A Description and Proposal' *Survival*, Vol.29, No.3 (May/June 1987).

Carter, A. 'The Command and Control of Nuclear War', *Scientific American*, Vol.252, No.1 (January 1985).

Clark, I. and Angell, D. 'Britain, the United States and the Control of Nuclear Weapons: The Diplomacy of the Thor Deployment 1956–58', *Diplomacy and Statecraft*, Vol.2, No.3, November 1991.

Cooper, F. 'The Direction of Air Force policy in the 1950s and 1960s', the Royal Air Force Historical Society, *Proceedings*, No. 11, 1993.

Cross, K. 'Bomber Command's Thor Missile Force', *Journal of the Royal United Services Institute* (May, 1963).

Culligan, A. 'An Overview of EMP Effects and their Control', *Journal of the Society of Environmental Engineers*, (September 1985).

Davis, R. 'Royal Air Force/United States Air Force Co-operation: Higher Command Structure and Relationships', Royal Air Force Historical Society, *Proceedings*, No. 9, October 1990.

Dulles, J. 'Challenge and Response in United States Policy', *Foreign Affairs*, Vol. 36, (October 1957).

Elliot, D. 'Project Vista and Nuclear Weapons in Europe', *International Security*, Vol.11, No.1 (Summer 1986).

Feaver, P. 'Command and Control in Emerging Nuclear Nations', *International Security*, Vol.17, No.3 (Winter 1992/93).

―――― 'The Politics of Inadvertence', *Security Studies*, Vol 3, No. 3 (Spring, 1994).

Flank, S. 'Exploding the Black Box: The Historical Sociology of Nuclear Proliferation', *Security Studies*, Vol.3, No.2 (Winter 1994).
Ford, P. 'The Defence Communications Network', *Journal of the Royal Signals Institute* (Summer, 1989).
Foster, G. 'Contemporary Command and Control Theory and Research: The Failed Quest for a Philosophy of Command', *Defense Analysis*, Vol.4, No.3 (September 1988).
Lawrence Freedman, 'British Nuclear Targeting', *Defense Analysis*, Vol.1, No.2 (1985).
Gates, D. 'American Strategic Bases in Britain: The Agreements Governing Their Use', *Comparative Strategy*, Vol. 8 (1989).
Heisbourg, F. 'The British and French Nuclear Forces', *Survival*, Vol.31, No.4, (July/August 1989).
Heuser, B. 'The Development of NATO's Nuclear Strategy', *Contemporary European History*, Vol.4, No.1 (1994).
Hopkins, R. 'An Expanded Understanding of Eisenhower, American Policy and Overflights', *Intelligence and National Security*, Vol.11, No.2 (April 1996).
King, M. and Flemming, P. 'An Overview of the Effects of Nuclear Weapons on Communications Capabilities', *Signal* (January 1980).
Melissen, J. 'Prelude to Interdependence: The Anglo–American Relationship and the Limits of Great Britain's Nuclear Policy, 1952–1957', *Arms Control*, Vol.11, No.3 (1990).
——— 'The Thor Saga: Anglo–American Nuclear Relations, US IRBM Development and Deployment in Britain, 1955–1959', *Journal of Strategic Studies*, Vol.15, No.2, (June 1992).
——— 'The Restoration of the Nuclear Alliance: Great Britain and Atomic Negotiations with the United States, 1957–58', *Contemporary Record*, Vol.6, No.1 (Summer 1992).
——— 'Nuclearizing NATO, 1957–1959: the 'Anglo–Saxons', nuclear sharing and the fourth country problem', *Review of International Studies*, Vol.20, No.3 (July 1994).
——— 'Pre–Summit Diplomacy: Britain, the United States and the Nassau Conference, December 1962', *Diplomacy and Statecraft*, Vol.7, No.3 (November 1996).
Pyne, K. 'Art or Article? The Need for and Nature of the British Hydrogen Bomb, 1954–58', *Contemporary Record*, Vol.9, No.3 (Winter, 1995).

Roman, P. 'Curtis LeMay and the Origins of NATO Atomic Targeting, *Journal of Strategic Studies*, Vol.16, No.1 (March 1993).

Rosenberg, D. 'The Origins of Overkill: Nuclear Weapons and American Strategy, 1945–60,' *International Security*, Vol.7, No.4 (Spring 1983).

Sagan, S. 'SIOP–62: The Nuclear War Plan Briefing to President Kennedy', *International Security*, Vol.12, No.1 (Summer 1987).

Shuchman, D. 'Nuclear Strategy and the Problem of Command and Control', *Survival*, Vol.29, No, 3 (July/August 1987).

Steinbruner, J. 'Nuclear Decapitation' *Foreign Policy*, No. 45 (Winter 1981–82).

——— 'Launch Under Attack', *Scientific American,* Vol.250, No.1 (January 1984).

Suit, W. 'Anglo–American Amity: Transferring B–29s to the Royal Air Force', *Air Power History* (Winter, 1994).

Thayer, T. 'The Risk of Nuclear Inadvertence: A Review Essay', *Security Studies,* Vol.3, No.3 (Spring 1994).

Tucker, J. 'Strategic Command–and–Control Vulnerabilities: Dangers and Remedies', *Orbis*, Vol.26, No.4 (Winter 1983).

Twigge, S. and Macmillan, A, 'Britain, the United States and the Development of NATO Strategy, 1950–1964', *Journal of Strategic Studies*, Vol.19, No.2 (June 1996).

Wohlstetter, A. 'The Delicate Balance of Terror', *Foreign Affairs,* Vol.37, No.2 (January 1959).

Yaffe, Y. 'A Higher Priority than the Korean War! The Crash Programs to Modify the Bombers for the Bomb', *Diplomacy and Statecraft,* Vol.5, No.2 (June 1994)

Yost, D. 'The History of NATO Theatre Nuclear Force Policy: Key Findings from the Sandia Conference', *Journal of Strategic Studies*, Vol. 15, No. 2 (June 1992).

Young, J. 'Churchill, the Russians and the Western Alliance: the three–power conference at Bermuda, December 1953', *The English Historical Review*, Vol.101, No.3 (October 1986).

Zraket, C. 'Strategic Command, Control, Communications and Intelligence', *Science,* Vol.224 (June, 1984).

Unpublished Material

Ball, S. *The Royal Air Force and British Nuclear Strategy, 1945–59,* (PhD, Cambridge, 1991).

Bird, M. *Political Firepower: Nuclear Weapons and the US Army 1945–1973*, (PhD, University of Wales, Aberystwyth, 1998).

Ehrman, J. *The Atomic Bomb: An Account of British Policy in the Second World War* (Cabinet Office, 1953).

James, T. *Defence Policy and the Royal Air Force 1956–1963* (Ministry of Defence, Air Historical Branch, 1987).

Klotz, F. *The US President and the Control of Strategic Nuclear Weapons*, (DPhil, Oxford University, 1980).

Wainstein, L., Cremeans, C., Moriarty, J. and Ponturo, J. *The Evolution of US Strategic Command and Control and Warning, 1945–1972*, Study S–467 (Arlington, VA: Institute for Defense Analysis, June 1975).

Wampler, R. *Ambiguous Legacy: The United States, Great Britain and the Foundations of NATO Strategy, 1948–1957*, (PhD, Harvard University, 1991).

Index

ABM (Anti–Ballistic Missile), 287
ACE (Allied Command Europe), 162, 220, 222, 225, 281, 336
Acheson, Dean, 36, 172, 173, 184
Accidental nuclear war (see also inadvertent nuclear use) 4, 10, 17, 87
Adenauer, Konrad, 190
Admiralty, 27
Admiralty House, 205
Adriatic, 130
Aegean Sea, 130
Aircraft:
    B29, 23, 30, 31–3 Washington 31–2
    B52, 9, 171, 265
    Buccaneer (NA 39), 62
    Canberra, 62, 101, 102, 104, 107, 108, 191, 144n, 233, 235, 259n
    F100, 114
    F104, 191
    F111, 191
    Halifax, 240
    Javelin, 101
    KC135, 236
    Lancaster, 31
    Lincoln, 31
    RB47H, 235
    RB45, 233
    TSR2, 191
    Tu 4, 23, 242
    U2, 233–6
    V–Bombers (see also V–Force):
        Valiant, 47, 92, 107, 125–7, 144n, 259n, 220, 223, 296,
        Victor, 107, 130, 259n
        Vulcan, 130
    Zeppelin, 266
Aircraft Carriers, 62–3, 108
    HMS Hermes, 62
Air Council, 52, 59, 115, 277
Air Defence of the United Kingdom (ADUK), 268, 273, 277–8, 281
Air Defence Committee, 269, 272, 289
Air Defence and Nuclear Weapons, 267–81
Air Defence Operations Centre (ADOC), Bentley Priory, 123, 201, 203, 211, 216–18, 274–8, 281, 282, 284, 268, 275
Air Ministry, 27, 38, 40, 63, 66, 70, 72, 86, 91, 102, 112, 151, 218, 236, 245, 257, 275, 276, 279, 288 309

INDEX

Air Ministry Operations Centre (AMOC), 83, 201, 205, 209, 211, 282, 284
Air Staff, 23–4, 32, 68, 86, 151, 267, 287
Alaska, 253
Alert, airborne, 2–3, 142n, 171
Alert states, 4–10,
  BMEWS Alarm States, 285–6, 288
  Bomber Command Alert and Readiness Plan, 86, 274, 309, 337
  Bomber Command Alert Conditions, 54, 123–5, 313
  NATO Alert Plan, 8, 154
  Tripartite Alert Procedure, 254, 332
  (see also DEFCON, Quick Reaction Alert)
Aleutians, 253
Algeria, 160
Algerian Crisis, 159
Alternate Command Centre, 12, 83–5, 88, 202, 210–12, 321
Alternate National Military Command Centre, Fort Ritchie, 84, 96n
Alternate Government Headquarters, see Alternate Command Centre
Amery, Julian, 287
Anderson, Sir John, 18–19
Anti–Aircraft Guns, 272
Army, 6
Army Council, 65
Aron, Raymond, 298
Athens, 180, 186, 193
Atlantic Nuclear Force (ANF), 191, 192
Atomic Bomb,
  British development of, 37–41 (see also independent British deterrent)
  Soviet development of, 23, 239, 242
  use of against Japan 18–22,
  Nazi atomic bomb project, 18
Atomic Energy Commission (AEC), 39, 251
Atomic Energy Intelligence Committee, 26
Atomic Weapons Research Establishment, Aldermaston, 60–1
Attlee, Clement, 7, 20, 21–4, 25, 35, 303
Australia, 28, 64, 208
Automobile Association (AA), 81, 205

Ball, Desmond, 29
Ball, George, 132
Ballistic Missile Early Warning System (BMEWS), 266, 278–9, 283–6, 288
Baylis, John, 308
Belgium, 281
Bellamy, Chris, 11
Bennett, John, 20
Berlin Air Lift, 31, 36, 268
Berlin Crisis (1961), 312
Berlin (East), 114, 252, 282
Bermuda Conference (1957), 40, 105, 235
  (1962) see Nassau Conference
Bevin, Ernest, 31, 249
Bhangmeters, 283, 291n
Biological weapons, 239
Birmingham, 203
Blackett, Professor PMS, 25

Blair, Bruce, 2
Blake, George, 237
Blanchard, General, 106, 138
Bletchley Park, 28
Blue Steel, 56, 314
Blue Streak, 77–9, 90, 113, 115, 187, 296, 308–9
Blue Water, 65, 94n, 183
Bomber Command, 7, 24, 26, 31–4, 41, 53, 57, 69, 70–4, 86, 87, 105, 109, 113, 125, 138, 139, 150, 151, 165, 178, 180, 205, 211–214, 216, 221, 224, 227, 273, 275, 296, 303, 314
  Bomber Command Armament School, 47
  Bomber Command Operations Centre, High Wycombe, 55, 73, 89, 110, 118, 124, 202, 203, 211, 215, 217, 219, 275, 282, 285, 300,
  Operational Readiness Platforms, 55
  (see also Alert States, Aircraft: V–Bombers, Thor, V–Force)
Bowie Report, 165
Bowie, Robert, 165–8, 199
Boyle, Sir Dermot, 104
Bracken, Paul, 11
British Broadcasting Corporation (BBC), 215–16
British Joint Services Mission, 32
British Joint Communications Electronics Board (BJC–EB), 203–7
British Nuclear Deterrent Study Group (BNDSG), 49, 56, 71, 72, 77–8, 310
British Railways, 205

Brook Report, 48–9
Brook, Sir Norman, 48, 74, 81, 87, 204, 312
Brook, Henry, 90
Brundrett, Sir Frederick, 26, 232, 244
Bulganin, Marshal, 254
Bundestag, 192
Bundy, McGeorge, 132, 138
Burgess, Guy, 30
Burlington, see Alternate Command Centre
Burma, 108
Butler, Rab, 82, 116

Cabinet Office, 83, 202
Cabinet War Room, 202
Caccia, Sir Harold, 120
Cable & Wireless Company, 207, 228
Camp David, 83, 119, 129, 138, 188
Canada, 28, 36, 64, 188, 242, 252, 254, 333
Carcinetron valve, 290n
Cavendish–Bentinck, Victor, 25
Central Intelligence Agency (CIA), 25, 27, 28, 29, 76, 233, 242, 245, 249, 251, 252, 254
Central Reconnaisance Establishment (CRE), 234
Chadwick, Sir James, 18
Cherwell, Lord, 29
Cheshire, Group Captain Leonard, 21
Chequers, 191
Chiefs of Staff, (UK), 19, 22–4, 25, 27, 32, 68, 76, 151, 160, 164, 173, 189, 204, 208, 225, 243, 247–9, 251, 252, 258, 267, 269, 273, 278, 315
Chilver, Richard, 168

INDEX

China, Peoples Republic of, 107–8,
   141n, 164, 236, 242
Churchill, Winston S, 18–20, 21, 29,
   37, 45, 100–1, 118, 150, 238, 241
Clark, Ian, 308–9
Cochrane, Air Marshal Sir Ralph,
   7, 38
Combined Chiefs of Staff Committee,
   19, 29, 103
Combined Policy Committee, 19
Command Control Communications
   and Intelligence (C3I)
   alliance control of nuclear weapons,
      12–13, 147–229,
   Assertive Control, 4, 294,
   civilian control of nuclear
      weapons, 12
   bilateral control of nuclear weapons,
      12–13, 98–146,
   Command Authority 5–8,
   Delegative Control, 4, 85, 97,
      294
   "Fail Deadly", 295, 301–3,
   Higher Command Authority,
      73–76
   National Command Authority
      (NCA), 3–5, 9, 10, 201, 283,
      300–1 (see also decapitation)
   national control of nuclear
      weapons, 12, 47–97
   Positive Control/ "Fail Safe", 3, 77,
      88, 301–3, 333
   Two Person Rule, 83, 86
   U.S. Procedures, 5
   see also NATO C3I, PALs
C3I Procedures (UK)
   Act of Indemnity, 75
   Cabinet Order of Precedence, 96n

Cabinet Ruling on Nuclear
   Custody (1953), 60
Constitutional Implications, 5–8
Defence Transition Committee, 74,
   85, 215
Defence Regulations Bill, 75
deputy Prime Minister, role of,
   7–8, 82
Emergency Powers, 74–5, 89
Orders in Council, 75
Prime Minister, role of, 5, 6, 7–8,
   16n, 79–90, 92
Transition to War Committee, 80
   (see also Royal Prerogative, War
   Book)
Commonwealth Relations Office,
   205
Communications
   airborne command posts, 95, 220
   Anchor Telephone Exchange, 202
   Director for Communications
      Electronics Joint Staff, 108
   full pipeline philosophy, 213
   Guardian Telephone Exchange, 202
   Kingsway Telephone Exchange, 202
   Silk Purse Airborne Command
      Post, 221, 224, 225, 226
   Tropospheric Scatter, 223
Communications Agencies and
   Committees
   Communications Research
      Establishment, Brampton, 234
   Defence Communications Agency,
      108, 210, 226, 228
   Defence Signals Staff, 209
   Defence Traffic Centre, 209
   Land Communications Electronics
      Security Board, 203

Official Committee on Communications, 203
U.S. Defence Communications Agency, 207
(see also British Broadcasting Corporation, British Joint Electronic Communications Board, Cable & Wireless Company)
Communications Systems:
  Ace High, 222
  Backbone, 203
  BBC Radio Four, 216
  Commonwealth Telephone Cable System, 208
  Emergency Manual Switching System, 203
  Federal, 203
  GLOBECOM/STRATCOM, 221
  HFSSB, 221, 224
  KY9, 206
  MILTAT, 205
  PICKWICK, 205–6, 228
  Sorcerer, 206
  Telephone Preference Scheme, 203
  Twilight, 206
  See also UHF, VHF
Connectivity, 9–10
Conscription, 48
Cooper, Sir Frank, 14, 41, 237
Corona Satellite, 245–6
Corporal, 94n, 156, 157, 196n
Cross, Air Marshal Sir Kenneth, 73, 88, 106, 110, 124–6, 138, 312–13, 315, 321
Cuban Missile Crisis, 7, 9, 13, 89, 99, 112, 122–3, 142n, 145, 199n, 206, 246, 250, 255–6, 310, 312–15
Cyprus, 62, 297

Davy Crockett nuclear bazooka, 196
Dean Committee, 49
Dean, Sir Maurice, 115
Dean, Sir Patrick, 49, 117
Decapitation, 5, 86n, 89, 300
Deception, 256–7
DEFCON states, 128, 145n, 256
Defence Committee, 23, 31, 40, 51, 63, 71, 72, 74, 115, 119, 183, 278, 280, 287
De Gaulle, Charles, 159
Delegation of nuclear authority, see pre–delegation of nuclear authority
Denmark, 188
Department of Defense, 187, 325
(see also Pentagon)
Deriabin, Peter, 247, 255
Dewer, Thomas, 201
De Zulueta, Philip, 304
Dickson, Sir William, 69, 102
Directorate of Forward Plans, 257
Dortmund, 157
Douglas Aircraft Corporation, 112
Douglas, Lewis, 31
Downing Street, 83, 205, 209, 212
Draper Committee, 163
DSP Satellite, 287
Dulles, John Foster, 116, 117, 151, 153, 157, 159

Early Warning, 265–92
  Bomb Alarm System, 223
  DISTANT, 255–6
  duel phenomenology, 9

Legate, 284–5
National Indications Centre, Washington, 205, 332
strategic warning, 10, 254–6
tactical warning, 10, 13, 265–91
United Kingdom Warning and Monitoring Organisation (UKWMO), 282
Watch Committee of the United States Intelligence Board, 251
(see also alert states, intelligence, Royal Observer Corps)

East of Suez (withdrawal from), 50, 68
Eden, Sir Anthony, 47–9, 82, 119, 149, 234, 235, 334
Egypt, 87
Eisenhower, Dwight D, 2, 26, 33–4, 100, 102, 105, 116, 119, 120, 122, 138, 149, 153, 168, 171, 234, 235, 334–5
Electro Magnetic Pulse (EMP), 10, 216, 241
Electronic Countermeasures (ECM), 273, 276
Elizabeth II, 7
Emergency War Plan, 71
Ethics of nuclear use, 6, 7, 11
Evacuation, 75
Evill, Sir Douglas, 25
Evill Report, 27

Falklands War, 16n
Fallex 62, 84, 142
Far East Planning Team, 66
Feaver, Peter, 2, 11–12, 293–4, 299

Federal Bureau of Investigations (FBI), 251
Fighter Command, 266–8, 273, 337
Finletter, Thomas, 177, 186
Foreign Office, 20, 25, 28, 188, 205, 208, 236
Fort Halstead, 38
France, 148, 159, 164, 172, 175, 180, 182, 185, 188, 190, 192, 193, 253, 281, 297, 298
Franks, Sir Oliver, 36
Frisch, Otto, 18
Fuchs, Klaus, 30, 240
Future Policy Committee, 49
Fylingdales, 278, 283–5
(see also BMEWS)

GEN 75 Committee, 22
GEN 163 Committee, 42
GEN 743 Committee, 79, 82, 204, 211
General Post Office (GPO), 203, 207, 210, 267, 271, 284, 290n
General Post Office War Group, 267
George VI, 82
German air force, 266–7, 280
German Democratic Republic, 56, 164, 263n
German rocket scientists, 238, 243
Germany, Federal Republic, 50, 62, 102, 148, 164, 165, 175, 182, 185, 188, 189, 190, 191, 193, 280
Government Communications Headquarters, (GCHQ), 28, 211, 232, 241
Greece, 281
Group of Soviet Forces Germany (GSFG), 252–3

INDEX

Groves, General Leslie, 18, 42
GRU (Chief Intelligence Directorate of the Soviet General Staff), 238
Gruenther, General, 280
Grundy, Air Marshal Sir John, 72
Gulf War, 16n

Hall Report, 273
Hall, Sir Arnold, 273
Hainan, 108
Halifax, Lord, 19, 20
Harris, Air Chief Marshal Sir Arthur, 26
Hathaway, Robert, 304
Healey, Denis, 191, 192
Heisbourg, Francois, 1
Hennessy, Peter, 90
Herod Committee, 38–9, 45
Herter, Christian, 110, 163, 168
Hiroshima, 12, 21, 22
Holland, 189, 281
Holy Loch, 13, 99, 119–22, 128–9, 143
Home, Sir Alec Douglas, 119n, 190
Home Office, 202, 283
Honest John, 157
Hound Dog, 131, 134
Huddleston, Sir Edmund, 216
Hungarian Uprising (1956), 147, 250
Hyde Park Aide Memoire, 21

ICBM (Intercontinental Ballistic Missile), 117, 148, 169, 239, 243–5, 250–1, 276
Independent British nuclear deterrent, 22, 133–9, 298–9 (see also Atomic Bomb, Blue Streak, Nuclear Weapons, V–Force)

India, 242
In–Flight Loading System, 57
Intelligence,
  Aquatone, 235
  Canadian Intelligence, 28
  HUMINT, 233, 238–9, 246–7, 254, 255, (see also Penkovsky)
  overflights, 233–7 (see also aircraft, U2)
  satellite photography, 242 (see also satellites)
  Soviet Intelligence, 30
  Soviet saboteurs, 87
  strategic intelligence, 8, 13
  Ultra, 24, 258
  UK intelligence organisation, 24–8
  (see also CIA, Early Warning, GRU, KGB, NSA, OSS)
UK Intelligence Agencies and Committees:
  Defence Intelligence Staff, 27, 139
  Directorate of Scientific Intelligence, 233
  Government Code and Cipher School, 238
  Joint Air Reconnaissance Intelligence Board (JARIB), 233
  Joint Air Reconnaissance Intelligence Committee (JARIC), 233
  (see also JIB, JIC. MI5, SIS, SOE)
Inter–Allied Nuclear Force, (IANF), 188
International law, 6
Iran, 246
IRBM, 117, 217, 285, 296 (see also Blue Streak, Jupiter, S3, SS5, Thor)

INDEX

Ismay, Lord, 150
Italy, 159, 175, 189, 190, 310

Jacob, Sir Ian, 251
JIB (Joint Intelligence Bureau), 25–8, 29, 30, 71, 233, 241, 242, 244, 245, 255, 258, 260
JIC (Joint Intelligence Committee), 23, 24–6, 72–3, 76, 87,110, 204–5, 238, 239, 244, 246, 247, 249–53, 256–75, 285
Jodrell Bank, 123, 285
Johnson, General Leon, 31, 35, 192
Johnson, Lyndon, 119n
Joint Chiefs of Staff (US), (JCS), 33, 36, 108, 145, 236, 249, 243, 332–3
Joint Co–ordinating Centre (Ruislip), 34, 105
Joint Planning Staff (JPS), 70, 103, 139, 168, 182, 244, 268, 278, 279
Joint Strategic Targets Planning Staff, 108
Joint Technical Warfare Committee, 22
Jones, Professor RV, 24, 44, 241
Jupiter missile, 112, 114, 310, 314, 338

Kaputsin Yar, 233
Kennan, George, 196n
Kennedy, John F, 9, 13, 99, 100, 112–113, 122–3, 125, 127, 129, 132–5, 137, 168, 171–2, 177, 180, 183–84, 186, 188, 190, 194, 199, 206, 300, 315, 335
KGB (Soviet Committee for State Security), 238
Killian Committee, 2–3

Kokura, 21
Kong, Major King, 265
Korean War, 16n, 41, 117, 248, 249, 300
Khrushchev, Nikita, 125, 238, 239, 251
Kutuzovsky Prospekt, 255
Kyle, Air Vice–Marshal Wallace, 238

Labour Party, 50, 115–16, 137, 191
Landa, Ronald, 129
Landon, General Truman, 127–8
Laputa, 265
Lee, Admiral John, 186
Leeds, 203
Lees, Dr DJH, 241
Le May, General Curtis, 30, 34, 154
Lemnitzer, General Lyman, 172, 199n
Leningrad, 71, 95n, 299
Likelihood of war, 248–51, 315
Lisbon Conference, 149, 158
Lloyd, Air Marshal Sir Hugh, 33
Lloyd, Selwyn, 120–1
London, 203
Los Alamos, 18, 240
Lovell, Professor Bernard, 285

MacArthur, General Douglas, 41, 300
Maclean, Donald 30
Macmillan, Harold, 7, 13, 47, 49, 51, 70, 81–2, 88, 99, 105, 107, 116–20, 124, 129, 131–3, 135–8, 170, 183–4, 188, 190, 206–7, 227, 235–6, 240, 256, 278, 298, 303, 313–15
Mandrake, Group Captain Lionel, 99, 293
Manhattan Project, 18, 240

INDEX

Marshall, General George, 19, 31, 42
Maud Committee, 18
Maud Report, 22
Maury, Jack, 256
Madelin, Group Captain Ian, 124
McCone, John, 256
McElroy, Neil, 156
McGregor, Sir Hector, 282
McNamara, Robert, 130–1, 134, 168, 173, 182, 184–7, 227, 298, 303, 316n,
  Ann Arbor Speech, 134, 186
Medhurst, Air Chief Marshal Sir Charles, 32
Merchant, Livingston, 188
Menaul, Air Vice-Marshal Stewart, 124
MI5 (Security Service), 271
Missile Defence Alarm System (MIDAS), 266, 286–8
Mills, Air Marshal Sir George, 53, 69–70, 151
Military attitudes to nuclear weapons, 1, 7, 8, 11, 88–9, 300
Military Thought Journal, (Voyennaya Mysl), 247
Ministry of Aviation, 290n
Ministry of Defence, 25, 26, 87, 124, 189, 205, 244, 278, 304, 305, 337
Ministry of Economic Warfare, 26
Ministry of Supply, 38, 39, 41, 60
MLF (Multilateral Force), 13, 132–4, 137, 148, 184–6, 188–90, 192–3, 307
Monarch, 75, 81 see also Elizabeth II, George VI, Royal Prerogative
Montague (Nuclear Bunker), 202

Monte Bello, 48
Morrison, Herbert, 36
Moscow, 72, 95n, 233, 299
Mottershead Report, 174
Mountbatten, Lord Louis, 6, 78, 204, 243, 263n, 315
MRBM (Medium Range Ballistic Missile), 122, 217, 245, 285, 287, 289n, 296 (see also MLF, NATO MRBM force, SS–3, SS–4)
Muffley, Merkin, 17, 147, 201
Murphy, Robert, 117
Murphy–Dean Agreement, 13, 79, 99, 115, 117–19, 138, 143n, 205, 303, 326–32

Nagasaki, 12, 21, 37
Nassau Agreement (1962), 13, 72, 99, 114, 132, 137–8, 187–8, 227, 316
Nasser, Colonel Abdul, 311
National Air Traffic Control Service, 279
National Intelligence Estimates (NIEs), 231, 244.
National Security Council, 36
NATO (North Atlantic Treaty Organisation), 12, 13–14, 32–4, 49, 52, 64–5, 67, 72, 84, 107, 114, 118–19, 126–7, 134–8, 142, 147, 149, 150, 152, 157–8, 161, 164, 165, 168–70, 173–5, 178–9, 181–2, 184–9, 191, 201, 222, 226, 279–81, 299, 302, 305–7, 309–10, 313, 323, 325, 327, 333,
NATO Council of Ministers, 281
  Military Committee, 161, 163, 176, 186, 281

NATO MRBM force, 114, 129, 131, 158, 162–5, 169, 173
NATO Secretary–General, 179, 180,
North Atlantic Council, (NAC), 148, 153, 155, 167, 174–8, 186, 188, 198n
see also ACE, SACEUR, SACLANT, SHAPE, Strategy
NATO C3I,
  Athens Guidelines, 13, 148, 174, 179, 199, 307
  NATO Command and Control System, 223
  NATO Emergency Defence Plan (EDP), 155, 180–1,
  NDP 62/2, 177
  Nuclear Planning Group, (NPG), 13, 190, 193
  R–Hour, 155, 161, 162, 165, 175, 198n, 225–6, 336
  S–Hour, 337–43
Naval Research Laboratory (US), 240
Nehru, Pandit, 249
New Zealand, 28, 64
Niigata, 21
Norstad, General Lauris, 34, 104, 124, 128, 145, 154, 157, 160, 166, 174, 181, 186, 199, 222, 281
North American Air Defence Headquarters (NORAD), 9, 284
Norway, 188, 267, 280
Novaya Zemlya, 246
NSA (National Security Agency), 29
Nuclear Artillery:
  203mm Howitzer, 157
  280mm Atomic Cannon, 149
Nuclear Weapons:

United Kingdom
  Blue Danube, 37–8, 47, 58, 103
  Green Grass, 59, 61, 94
  Orange Herald, 59
  Red Beard, 61, 63, 94n, 196n
  Red Snow, 61
  Ro 106, 65
  Violet Club, 59–61, 92, 94n, 314
  Violet Vision, 196n
  Yellow Sun, 61, 94n, 123
United States
  B 28, 61, 107
  C 31, 64
  Mk 3, 37
  Mk 5, 104, 105, 126
  Mk 7, 104
Nuclear Control Commission, 189
Nuclear Planning Group, 143, 148, 190
Nuclear Strike Co–ordinating Committee, see targeting
Nunn May, Alan, 30
Nuremberg War Trials, 6

Oldfield, Maurice, 256
Open Skies, 234
Operation Sealion, 267
Ormsby–Gore, Sir David, 123, 130–2, 138, 315
OSS (Office of Strategic Services), 29
Ottawa Statement, 184, 185, 188, 205
Owen, Henry, 199

PALs (Permissive Action Links), 112, 123, 184, 300, 301
Pakistan, 246
Paris, 281

INDEX

Park, Daphne, 253
Parliament, 65–6, 67, 75, 79, 116, 301
Pearl Harbor, 2, 251
Peierls, Rudolf, 18
Penkovsky, Oleg, 233, 238–9, 246–7, 254–6
Pentagon, 121–2, 184, 283, (see also Department of Defense)
Penney, William, 18, 21, 38
Pershing missile, 191
Philby, Kim, 30, 236
Pike, Air Marshal Sir Thomas, 107, 124, 245, 277, 322
Plan Ahead, 277–8
Plateau d'Albion, 297
Plutonium, 242
Poland, 263n, 267
Polaris, 13, 73, 99, 113, 119, 120–2, 125, 129, 131–8, 143, 146, 167, 188, 189, 192, 209, 299, 302, 308, 334, 335 (see also Holy Loch, MLF, Nassau Agreement).
Police, 205
Portugal, 188
Potsdam Conference, 20, 42
Powell, Sir Richard, 49
Power, General Thomas, 97, 116, 142
Pre–delegated authority, 4, 12, 13, 21
  NATO, 151, 160–1, 176
Preventive war, see strategy
Project E, 46, 100–1, 138, 144, 323–5

Quarles, Donald, 284
Quebec Agreement, 18–19, 35, 45
Quick Reaction Alert (QRA), 55, 123, 125, 126–7, 309

Radar Systems:
  Blue Joker, 290n
  Blue Yeoman (Type 85), 277
  Centimetric Early Warning (CEW), 271
  Chain Home (CH), 266, 270–1
  Chain Home Extra Low (CHEL), 271
  Green Garlic (Type 80), 274, 276, 277, 289
  Ground Controlled Interception (GCI), 271
  Linesman/Mediator, 266, 279, 280
  NATO Air Defence Ground Environment (NADGE), 280, 290
  Rotor, 265, 270, 274, 289n
  (see also Ballistic Missile Early Warning System)
Radford, Admiral Arthur, 29
Radio Research Station, Slough, 266
Rocket Assisted Take Off (RATO), 91
Redmayne, Martin, 136
Richelson, Jeffery, 29
Ridgway, General Matthew, 149
Ridgway Report, 149, 153
Ripper, General Jack D, 1, 99, 293
Roosevelt, Franklin D, 18, 238
Royal Aircraft Establishment Farnborough, 38
Royal Air Force, 6, 30, 32, 38, 39, 41, 116
  Far East Air Force (FEAF), 207
  Near East Air Force (NEAF), 62
  see also Air Staff, Bomber Command, Fighter Command

INDEX

Royal Air Force Stations:
  Acklington, 215
  Akrotiri, 62, 94n
  Barnham, 56
  Barton Quarry, 270
  Bawburgh, 270, 277
  Bawtry, 73, 89, 215, 219
  Beaconsfield, 85
  Box, 270
  Bramcote, 277
  Brize Norton, 236
  Buchan, 219, 277
  Butterworth, 107
  Chenies, 219
  Dishforth, 215
  Driffield, 113, 115
  Faldingworth, 56, 123
  Feltwell, 109
  Helmswell, 109
  Honnington, 56, 107
  Kelvdon Hatch, 270
  Kinloss, 215
  Kirkbride, 287
  Lakenheath, 35, 109
  Leuchars, 215
  Longley Lane, 270
  Marham, 35, 56, 107, 127
  Mildenhall, 73, 215, 219
  Muharraq, 62
  Neatishead, 219, 277
  North Luffenham, 109
  Saxa Vord, 219, 277
  Sculthorpe, 35, 102
  Sharjah, 62
  Shipton, 270
  Stanmore, 215
  Staxton Wold, 277
  Syerston, 215
  Tengah, 107
  Upper Heyford, 236
  Waddington, 56, 107, 123
  Western Zoyland, 215
  Wittering, 41, 47, 56, 60, 92
Royal Air Force units:
  51 Squadron, 235
  76 Squadron, 235
  1321 Flight, 92
Royal Navy, 6
Royal Navy Headquarters, Portsmouth, 203
Royal Observer Corps, (ROC), 203, 266, 273, 282, 290n
Royal Prerogative, 15, 75, 79, 90
Rusk, Dean, 187, 191

S–3, 297
Sagan, Scott, 2, 124, 126
Sandys, Duncan, 49, 101, 104, 140, 275–6, 284
SACLANT (Supreme Allied Commander Atlantic), 162, 170, 179, 226
SACEUR (Supreme Allied Commander Europe), 13, 33–4, 72, 104, 107, 114, 118, 127, 138, 149, 150–8, 160–3, 165–7, 169, 170, 174, 175, 179, 180, 181, 186, 194, 218, 220, 222–5, 280, 323, 325, 327, 329, 330, 333, 337
Schecter, Jerrold, 247, 255
Schlieffen Plan, 171
Scott, Sir Robert, 297
SEATO (South East Asia Treaty Organisation), 107, 108, 141
Secretary of State for Air, 102
SHAPE (Supreme Headquarters

Allied Powers Europe), 33, 138, 150, 158, 163, 181, 186, 221, 222, 224–6, 336, 337–43
SHAPE Operations Centre (SHOC), 281, 284
SIS (Secret Intelligence Service), 232, 237, 283, 284–6
Shinwell, Emmanuel, 26, 27
Sinclair Assessment Group, 279
Sinclair, Sir Lawrence, 279
Singapore, 63, 109, 208
Skaggerak, 130
Skey, Lt Col S E, 257
Skybolt, 56, 72–3, 96n, 119, 120, 129–31, 133–4, 187, 296, 308
SLBM (Submarine Launched Ballistic Missile), 119, 169, 285 (see also Polaris)
Slessor, Marshal of the Royal Air Force Sir John, 35, 36, 44, 45
Slim, Field Marshal Sir William, 249
Smith, Gerard, 187
Smith/Lee briefings 1961, 188
Snyder, Glen, 1
SOE (Special Operations Executive), 28
Soviet Union,
   military capability 13, 23, 26, 50–1, 56, 68–70, 79, 100, 117, 69, 204, 214–15, 235, 239, 241–4, 247–9, 276
   threat assessment, 256–58,
   see also Atomic Bomb, Stalin
Spaak, Paul Henri, 159
Spaatz, General, 21, 30, 32
Sputnik, 148, 157, 244, 245
SS1, 246
SS3, 291n

SS4, 246, 291n
SS5, 246, 291n
Stalin, Josef, 249
State Department, 121, 160, 165, 184, 185, 236, 251
Stewart, Brigadier Sir Findlater, 25
Stikker, Dirk, 177
Stimson, Henry J, 19, 21
Stockwell, see Alternate Command Centre
Strachey, John, 115
Strategic Air Command (SAC), 2, 32–4, 48, 53, 68, 70, 76, 105, 126, 138–9, 142, 147, 165,171, 178, 203, 213, 220, 221, 224, 247, 256, 283, 284, 300, 313, 324, 332
   Third Air Division, 31, 33
   Seventh Air Division, 33, 88, 100, 106, 109, 126, 203, 218, 321, 329, 330
   (see also United States Air Force)
Strategic Defense Initiative, 257
Strategy,
   British atomic strategy, 22–4
   (see also independent British deterrent)
   Flexible Response, 181, 280, 302
   first–strike, 78–9
   launch on warning, 76–9
   Massive Retaliation, 168, 169, 171, 175–180, 182, 306
   preventive war, 31, 69
   second strike, 2–3, 8,
   surprise attack, 2–3
UK Strategy Documents
   1947 Review of Global Strategy, 23

1952 Global Strategy Paper, 51, 67, 74, 148
1957 Defence White Paper, 47, 272, 276
1958 Defence White Paper, 53
1960 Strategic Review of Air Defence, 278
1962 Defence White Paper, 50, 183
US Strategy Documents
  NSAM 40, 145
  NSAM 147, 185, 186
  NSAM 218, 188
  NSC 68, 249
  NSC 151/2, 149, 150
  NSC 162/2, 149
NATO Strategy Documents
  MC14/2, 148, 152–3, 157, 181, 194
  MC14/3, 280
  MC 48, 148, 152
  MC 70, 165
  MC 95, 176, 179
Strauss, Franz Joseph, 192
Strong, Major General Sir Kenneth, 26–7, 242, 245
Sub–Committee for Air, Coast and Seaward Defences (ACSD), 269
Suez Crisis, 6, 7, 47, 49, 102, 250, 254, 298, 311
Sun Tzu, 232

Tactical Nuclear Weapons, U.S., 68
Targeting, 11, 12, 22–4, 112–14, 171–2
  Bomber Command Emergency War Plan, 71
  counterforce targeting, 68–70
  countervalue targeting, 70–3
  National Retaliatory War Plan, 66
  NATO Atomic Strike Plan, 198
  Nuclear Strike Co–ordinating Committee, 66, 67, 297
  Single Integrated Operational Plan (SIOP), 66, 171
  target policy, 68
  Targets Working Party, 66
  (see also Nuclear Planning Group, strategy)
Technical Research Unit, (MOD), 26
Tedder, Air Marshal Sir Arthur, 30, 32
Templer, Field Marshall Lord, 245, 311
The Times, 22
Thor Missile, 13, 99, 109, 110, 111–15, 125–6, 138, 141–2n, 188, 216, 283, 309, 310, 312, 326–8
Thorneycroft, Peter, 131, 190, 236
Tinian Island, 21
Tizard Committee, 267
Tizard, Sir Henry, 240, 270
Trade Union Congress (TUC), 116
Treasury, 59
Truman, Harry S, 20, 24, 36, 117, 153, 239
Tube Alloys, 18–20
Turgidson, General Buck, 47, 201, 231
Turnstile, see Alternate Command Centre
Turkey, 159, 281, 310, 314
Twining, General Nathan, 103

UHF, 219, 221
United Nations General Assembly, 160

United States Congress, 5
United States Navy, 34, 119
  USS Abraham Lincoln, 128
  USS Proteus, 128
United States/United Kingdom Relations:
  shooting US Custodians, 206–7
  possible British espionage against USA, 44
  US–UK Co–operation, 28–30, 41
  US forces in Britain, 30–7, 41
  US–UK Intelligence Operations, 28 (see also Penkovsky)
Treaties and Agreements
  Agreement for Co–operation on Uses of Atomic Energy for Mutual Defence Purposes (1958), 105
  Bermuda Agreement (1957), 160
  Eden–Eisenhower Agreement, 143, 295, 334
  Holy Loch Memorandum of Understanding, 122
  Truman–Attlee Agreement, 37, 295, 303
  Truman–Churchill Communiqué, 117
  UKUSA Agreement (1947), 29 (see also Hyde Park Aide Memoir, Murphy–Dean Agreement, Nassau Agreement, Quebec Agreement)
Military Collaboration:
  Music, 233, 240
  Offtackle/Galloper, 304
  Project Lamarchus, 143n
  (see also Holy Loch, Project E, Thor)

US Legislation:
  Atomic Energy Act (1954), 101, 117
  McMahon Act (1946), 30, 100, 150
USAF (United States Air Force), 12–13, 30–7, 31, 34, 116, 233, 235
  Collaboration with RAF, 13, 30–7
  Officer Exchange Program, 99
  Third Air Force, 33, 100, 203, 218, 330
University of Birmingham, 18
Uranium 235, 242
USSR Planning Team, 66
Uxbridge, 268

Vandenberg, General Hoyt, 35
VENONA decrypts, 258n
V–Force, 3, 51–3, 56, 74, 91, 101–2, 114, 187, 191–2, 221, 247, 274, 283, 295, 313, 326–8, 331 (vulnerability of), 51–6
Voice of America, 215
VHF, 130, 282

War Cabinet, 80
Ward, Sir George, 106
War Book, 79–80, 87, 90, 205, 336
War Office, 27
Warsaw Treaty Organisation, 147, 252
Watkins, J K, 336
Watkinson, Harold, 65, 78, 79, 107, 119–21, 129, 278
West Drayton, 280, 281
Wheeler, Nicholas, 308
White, General Thomas, 106, 107
Wilson, Charles, 104

INDEX

Wilson, Harold, 7, 137, 191, 301
Wilson, Field Marshal Sir Henry
    Maitland, 18–19
Wilton Park, 85, 97
Wohlstetter, Albert, 1

Yugoslavia, 16n

Zuckerman, Sir Solly, 124, 278–9